THE RECORD OF SINGING

To my father and mother

Quelle est la vraie raison d'être du phonographe? Quel est son rôle? En quoi résident sa beauté, son mystère, sa grandeur, sa noblesse? Voilà les questions qui viennent à l'esprit on songe à quoi on l'emploie trop et surtout à quoi on ne l'emploie pas assez. La véritable fonction du phonographe, consiste non seulement à enregistrer mais encore—et surtout—à conserver (pour ne parler aujourd'hui que de chant) la voix et l'art des grands chanteurs qui, ainsi, grâce à cet instrument magique, ne périraient pas tout entiers.

Reynaldo Hahn

THE RECORD OF SINGING
To 1914

Michael Scott

CHARLES SCRIBNER'S SONS
NEW YORK

Copyright © 1977 by Michael Scott

Copyright under the Berne Convention

All rights reserved. No part of this book
may be reproduced in any form without the
permission of Charles Scribner's Sons.

1 3 5 7 9 11 13 15 17 19 I/C 20 18 16 14 12 10 8 6 4 2

Printed in Great Britain
Library of Congress Catalog Card Number 77-85293

ISBN 0-684-15528-1

Contents

PART IV Wagner and the German Style

PART V Singers of Imperial Russia

Illustrations

Preface

This is the first of a three-volume illustrated survey of the art of singing as it survives on gramophone recordings. This volume covers the period up to 1914. There are two short essays by way of Introduction: the first, 'The Record', deals with the immediate impact of the invention of the gramophone on singers and singing and the significance of old recordings to us today; the second, 'The Singing', attempts a brief outline of developments in the art of singing in the centuries for which we have no direct evidence. From the arrival of the gramophone, when the main part of the book begins, I have let the records—so to speak—sing for themselves and been content to act as guide to features of technique, style and interpretation. There is no subtle thesis embodied in the text. I have preferred the analytical approach; except to demonstrate a particular point, I have avoided making direct comparisons between singers past and present. No criticism can be wholly objective—it would not be valuable if it were—but there are undoubtedly degrees of subjectivity. In the interpretative arts generally it is possible to establish certain aspects of technique as matters of fact rather than taste. I have been especially concerned with these, taking my cue from the standards of contemporary critics, many of whom were students of singing and regarded it as the raison d'être of opera rather than, as their counterparts do today, as just one facet in a total art-form. If modern scholarship has taught us the value of correct style in performance, it applies equally to criticism: we shall understand little of the art of singers of previous generations if we persist in clinging to post-Freudian terminology and the kind of picturesque prose which though sometimes suggestive explains nothing.

The book is organised into five parts, each of which deals with a different national style. The titles are, I hope, self-explanatory; perhaps only the first, 'The Old School', calls for some comment. Here I have linked the English ballad and oratorio tradition to the classical Italian style, whose influence on singing in the Anglo-Saxon world was profound. This was partly the direct result of the ever-present example throughout the nineteenth century in Great Britain (and later in the United States) of the leading Italian singers of the old school, from Catalani, Malibran, Grisi and Mario to Nicolini and Patti, and partly the effect of the teachings of Garcia, Lamperti and Marchesi, whose best pupils were none of them Italians, but mostly from English-speaking countries. This influence worked in the reverse direction too: Jenny Lind, Garcia's greatest pupil, settled in England after she retired from the stage and became the leading 'English' oratorio singer, while Patti, the greatest soprano of pre-verismo Italian opera, was, according to Bernard Shaw, also the greatest interpreter of the English ballad. The classical virtues of the old Italian school—a pure tone and limpid legato poised on the breath, and mastery of portamento and messa di voce and all the other traditional graces and refinements—are better exemplified in the recordings of Patti, Santley, Lloyd, Beddoe, Melba, Evan Williams etc. than in those of all but a handful of the French and Italian singers.

Each national school embraces not only native-born singers (and here I have bracketed the Austrians with the Germans, the Belgians with the French and so on), but those foreigners who identified themselves with its repertory and whose style and technique were conditioned by it. Thus the de Reszké brothers and Mary Garden appear among the French; Elena Teodorini, Ada Adini, Teresa Arkel and Salomea Krusceniski come among the Italians, as do all Spanish and Portuguese singers at a time when Spain, Portugal and South America were in effect outposts of the Italian operatic empire. Conversely Olimpia Boronat and Medea Mei, though the latter created roles in the operas of Tchaikovsky and Napravnik and both spent many years in Russia, remained in style and technique Italian singers. No scheme, however, is perfect and the Poles have not always been easy to accommodate. Until the Treaty of Brest-Litovsk in 1918, Poland was only a province of Russia, but Polish culture has always had a separate identity. As the events of 1830 and 1863 demonstrated to the world, the Poles resisted Russian domination. Polish singers tended to identify either with the French, like Jean and Edouard de Reszké, or with the Italians, like Didur and Krusceniski. However, the baritone Waclaw Brzezinski and the sopranos Janina Korolewicz-Wayda and Felicie Kaschowska, whom I have included with the Russians, Italians and Germans respectively, since they were principally associated with those repertories, had a character which ideally should put them in a class of their own.

Under the main headings are grouped accounts of the careers, as well as some appraisal of the art, as it survives in recordings, of the most important operatic and concert artists active in the period up to the outbreak of the First World War; in general space is apportioned according to importance. In a few rare instances I have reluctantly omitted a singer who ought by right to have been included—one such, the French soprano Rose Caron, because her records are wholly inadequate technically. Certain artists whom the reader may be surprised not to find—Peter Dawson, Hermann Jadlowker and John McCormack for example—have been held over for a later volume when they were at the height of their careers. Others whose careers are here considered only in part, such as Giuseppe de Luca and Feodor Chaliapin, will make re-appearances in later volumes.

Biographical information—vital statistics, lists of appearances, roles and so forth—and contemporary reviews, criticism and opinions, which I have quoted wherever it seemed appropriate, have been selected in order to give perspective to the singer's art. Quite deliberately I have made no attempt at completeness. At the risk of echoing one of those disclaimers at the beginning of a British Railways timetable, I must apologise in advance for errors in detail that are bound to have slipped in, in spite of what I should like to think was proper care and vigilance, and in spite of the many friends who have been so generous with their time in checking through the manuscript. The trouble is—Robert Rushmore has put it so well—singers lie, not only about their ages but about other details, in order to put the best gloss on their achievements or otherwise (indeed, if we are to believe them, it is really quite amazing how many have been obliged to give up their careers through failing sight, faulty hear-

ing, lameness etc.—almost never from vocal problems). A full bibliography is given at the end of the book. The sources of most direct quotations and some indirect ones will also be found at the end of the book, the principal exception to this rule being the occasional story or anecdote, which I have included when they seemed plausible—*se non è vero è ben trovato*.

No subject—unless it be economics—is more burdened than singing with technical terms, with that kind of pseudo-scientific jargon which may originally have been intended as a language of communication but has long since ended up as the language of concealment. Any writer wishing to avoid getting bogged down in it has two alternatives open to him: he may eschew it entirely, which unfortunately will almost inevitably force him into just that excessive recourse to metaphors, with their oblique analogies, of which I have already complained, or he may do as I have tried to do, and use it as sparingly as possible, explaining the terms in the narrative as they arise and listing them in a glossary (see page 228) so that the reader will be in no doubt as to what they mean. I have also tried to keep foreign terms to a minimum, translating them into English wherever possible. Although Italian is the accepted language for most musical terms, it is useful to discriminate between those which are supported by precedent and which may be considered valuable and meaningful, and the whimsies of some modern Italian writers which are too often bandied about—'soprano sfogato', 'coloratura mezzo-contralto', 'soprano drammatico d'agilità' and the rest, which are not only unhistoric, but tell us less about the singer than about the writer's mentality. In the seventeenth and eighteenth centuries there were only four types of voices generally recognised: soprano, alto, tenor, and bass. During the next hundred years these were extended to include the mezzo-soprano and baritone (even this rudimentary classification was resisted by many of the greatest singers, from Senesino and Pacchierotti to Malibran and Viardot). By 1900 and the invention of the gramophone there was a growing tendency to sub-divide these categories, but the process was by no means complete: Lillian Nordica sang Philine as well as Brünnhilde; Marianne Brandt sang Donna Elvira, Fidès and Fidelio; Francesco Tamagno sang Edgardo and Otello. These achievements demand to be considered individually; they defy glib categorisation, or lengthy labelling more suitable for bottles.

The spelling of proper names in a book of this sort

presents certain problems. With the singers I have followed the English custom of common practice (it is, after all, the basis of our spelling), wherever possible preserving the character of opera-house cast lists, old programmes and gramophone record catalogues. Difficulties have arisen over the Poles and Czechs, when sometimes their names appear in the original spellings and sometimes in German or French versions, and with the Russians when rendering the Cyrillic into Roman. In such cases logical systems too often lead to absurdities; for example, the kind which abound in the current edition of Grove's Dictionary—Shaliapin, Rakhmaninov, indeed! Wherever possible I have copied the singers themselves—it is surely every man and woman's inalienable right to spell their own name as they please. Apart from anything else it seems to me appropriate that Krusceniski, for example, who spent the major part of her career in Italy, and Vignas, who made his reputation there, should have used Italianised versions of their names, and that Chaliapin (with or without the final 'e') preferred the French version; Paris was his home from the time he left Russia until his death. When spelling the names of operas, for the sake of brevity I have followed the usual practice and generally dropped the articles in German and Italian, but never in French. In the matter of capital letters, I have here taken the style from the score or libretto, preferring e.g. *Il Barbiere di Siviglia* to the modern way—*Il barbiere di Siviglia*—where Seville appears to be more important than the Barber. When operas have been given in translation, so as to avoid having to repeat constantly that a particular Italian singer sang a German opera in Italian, I have translated the titles, thus: *Maestri Cantori, Franco Cacciatore, Crepuscolo degli Dei* and so on. Of course, this does not work for *Lohengrin* or *Tannhäuser*. In the same way, *Pagliacci* in German is *Bajazzo*; *Trovatore, Troubadour*; and *Guillaume Tell, Wilhelm Tell*, though *Traviata* is *Traviata* in any language. I have not gone on from there to render the names of the characters as well, as this would certainly have led to absurdities—*Mi chiamano Mimi, ma il mio nome è Mime!* I have been only as consistent as good sense will allow, in the end reserving the right of every author occasionally to indulge his own fancy.

There are occasions, to paraphrase Oscar Wilde, when it is not just a duty to speak one's mind, it becomes a positive pleasure. Without the kind offices of so many friends it would have been impossible for me to write this book. In a sense it has been in my mind almost since I first fell in love with the singing voice nearly a quarter of a century ago, but it might well have remained there gestating—or fermenting—for another twenty-five years, had it not been for one particular friend who gave me the opportunity to translate it into print and obliged me actually to get down and write it. It would be impossible for me to thank Vivian Liff sufficiently. From the beginning he has given me unceasing encouragement, and the benefit of his encyclopaedic knowledge and his friendly and always constructive criticism. He has been equally generous with his possessions. He and George Stuart have put at my disposal the entire resources of the Stuart-Liff collection, permitted me to play and copy for my own use countless of their unique historical recordings, and opened their comprehensive library of books and pictures—from which I have drawn more than two hundred illustrations used in this book (many of them reproduced here for the first time). Their stimulating companionship and gracious hospitality—and the cuisine of their house-keeper Mrs Charlotte White—have made each of my many visits to Tunbridge Wells as delightful as it has been informative.

It is a pleasure, too, to have this opportunity to thank Richard Bebb, not only for his and Gwen's innumerable kindnesses to me, but for the way he has so often—I rather think deliberately—provoked me with his challenging but always informed opinions, which many times have caused me to reconsider my judgments. I thank him also for his assistance with various pieces of research and for information relating to one of the pioneers of recording, Edison's agent Colonel Gouraud. To John Freestone go my thanks for the loan of many books and records, for his courtesy in explaining (also demonstrating) various aspects of vocal technique and for fascinating anecdotes relating to his teacher Blanche Marchesi. For direct recollections of Emma Eames, Marcella Sembrich and Pasquale Amato I am indebted to the writer and critic Max de Schauensee, who has entertained me warmly on several of my visits to Philadelphia. Over the years I have been entertained by many record collectors: I shall always be grateful to Harold Burros who first played me the records of Melba, which I still love; to Philip Sacaloff of Manchester who transformed so many dull Saturday evenings during my undergraduate days when he introduced me to the voices of Battistini, Chaliapin, Martinelli and many other great singers; and to Bennet Fynn from whose own skill and knowledge of vocal technique I have learned much. Lack of space forbids me mentioning everyone here but I thank them all the same.

For the photographs of Teresa Arkel and Angelica Pandolfini I am indebted to Laurence Witten and the Sound Archives of Yale University, and for information relating to a number of Russian artists to Michael Wyler of West Moors, Dorset. I have many reasons for being grateful to Patric Schmid and Don White; in particular they have given me the benefit of their vast knowledge of operatic music of the early nineteenth century and have allowed me to consult freely scores and other books in the Opera Rara collection. I should like to acknowledge the encouragement and generosity of Bryan Crimp of EMI records, Jack Henderson of the Camden Festival, Ralph Mace of RCA records, Robert Roberts of Opera Rara and Robert Slotover of Allied Artists. To Michael Hartnall, Heather Edwards and Randolph Mickelson go my thanks for

what seems like an unending discussion (certainly we resume it every time we meet) on many aspects of the art of singing, from which I have learned a great deal. I must not forget those who by their example have indirectly contributed to this book; I refer to the great singers of our own day with whom I have had the good fortune and pleasure of working, among them Carlo Bergonzi, Montserrat Caballé, Piero Cappuccilli, Boris Christoff, Marilyn Horne, Sherrill Milnes, Ruggiero Raimondi and Joan Sutherland.

Finally to Michael Aspinall, whose knowledge of the art of singing is unrivalled (as he wittily demonstrates in his brilliant satires), my thanks for advice and assistance at every stage in the production of this book.

I must, however, absolve all these kind friends from any responsibility for the interpretation that I have put on the information they have so unstintingly given.

Rome, 1977   Michael Scott

Introduction

The Record

It would be difficult to exaggerate the value of the gramophone in an appraisal of the art of the great singers of the past. Of all the aids science provided the arts in the nineteenth century, not even the invention of photography was more important. The Dutch and Venetian masters during the seventeenth and eighteenth centuries approximated reality to such a degree in their topographical accuracy that a camera's records could hardly have been more exact. Among the aural arts there was no equivalent to painting, no medium through which it was possible to reproduce the sound of a man's voice as accurately as portraiture can represent his appearance. No musical instrument has been devised, however wide its range or great its power, as eloquent as the human voice—threading words onto sound. Each man's voice is as peculiar to him as his finger prints; no Stradivarius or Steinway has the variety of nuance or individuality of timbre. Before the gramophone, the only records were literary ones—descriptions that would have been beggared by quite primitive recordings. Even the fine prose and vivid word-pictures of writers like Dr Burney, Stendhal and Hanslick only convey in the most generalised subjective fashion the impression that voices made.

Although Edison took out his first patents for a recording apparatus in December 1877, a quarter of a century was to elapse before the gramophone came of age—on that April day in 1902 when Enrico Caruso took the lift to the third floor of the Grand Hotel in Milan, to a private drawing-room which had been rigged out as a recording studio, and there, in the space of two hours, left records of ten operatic arias. In hindsight they seem twenty-five wasted years, a history of lost opportunities. Only think: had Edison resisted the blandishments of the electric light companies, and devoted himself instead to the refinement of his invention, today we might have had recordings of Wagner, Liszt and Tchaikovsky playing their own compositions. Apart from their musical importance, they could tell us more about performance practice in the later Romantic age than any amount of library research is likely to divine. Yet it would be absurd, and ungrateful too, to blame Edison. He was an inventive genius, not a missionary. The invention of the gramophone was not in response to any musical prompting; unlike Edison's other inventions—the light bulb and the electric chair—it was not conceived to fulfil a specific function. It is not surprising that initially it was taken for just an ingenious toy, a diverting novelty—who is there who doesn't like to hear the sound of his own voice? And then, like all novelties, in spite of Edison's various attempts to promote it in the United States and Europe, it was quickly put aside. Nor is it surprising that he should have turned his attention to other more practical and profitable experiments, in particular, the challenge of providing electric light for New York City. Edison was deaf; and deaf men, *pace* Beethoven, are not generally interested in music.

Those early years, however, were not entirely fallow; some interesting relics have survived. One of Edison's agents, a certain Colonel Gouraud, took a machine to London and there recorded the voices of Gladstone, Henry Irving, Robert Browning, Alfred Lord Tennyson, Henry Stanley and Prince Napoleon, a nephew of the great Emperor. Once he even ventured as far as the Crystal Palace, scene of Victorian England's greatest musical jamborees, and from a remote vantage, captured a few brief and noisy fragments out of a performance of Handel's *Israel in Egypt*. For the benefit of Emperor Menelik of Ethiopia Queen Victoria was persuaded to say a few words into Edison's contraption; when he got the message, it was destroyed. In Germany, another agent had been busy coaxing Brahms into playing a snatch of one of his own pieces; the Herr Doktor's spoken introduction is clearly audible and the piece unmistakable—the Fifth Hungarian Dance.

Rumours of a Jenny Lind cylinder have never been substantiated, and its existence seems unlikely as she died in 1887, the year before Gouraud's experiments. The Colonel was by no means the only important pioneer, there were at least two others: Lieutenant Bettini, another military gentleman, and Lionel Mapleson, nephew of one of the greatest operatic showmen of those days. Bettini, an Italian with good looks and an engaging social manner who had married into American money (a traditional recipe), went to New York and there with the money and the wife played host to many of the Metropolitan's leading opera stars. At some point he acquired a recording machine and after attempting to modify its worst defects (he fancied himself an inventor too), set to work to try and persuade his celebrated guests, Calvé, Sembrich, Melba, Nordica, Tamagno and the de Reszkés, to leave behind vocal autographs as souvenirs of their visits. A few years later he started up in business, but his catalogue (1899), though it quotes examples of the art of Rosalia Chalia, Eugenia Mantelli and Emilio de Gorgorza, makes no reference to the really stellar names. It is unlikely that we shall ever know just how far Bettini's charm went in allaying the not unreasonable fears of the great, that this new-fangled gadget might too easily compromise their reputations.†

Lionel Mapleson was only related to the military, his uncle being the irrepressible Colonel J. H. Mapleson, sometime lessee of Her Majesty's, Covent Garden and Drury Lane theatres, who several times soldiered right across the United States with his own opera company, with Patti in the vanguard and the bailiffs never far behind. On one of these eventful progresses young Lionel went along to carry the music, and after it was all over, when the Colonel and the diva laden with the spoils had re-embarked, he stayed on, eventually becoming Librarian at the Metropolitan. There he installed a cylinder machine in the prompt box and when the prompt complained of its noisy company took it up to the paint bridge, from which giddy height he made the first-ever live opera recordings: three- and four-minute fragments out of a variety of operas, with glimpses of many of the greatest singers (Mapleson too was chiefly interested in stars) in full flight. In the end it was full flight, indeed at least for Johanna Gadski: during a performance of Mancinelli's *Ero e Leandro*, she only just managed to

get out of the way when the machine plunged from its precarious perch, hit the stage and smashed into smithereens, putting an abrupt stop to an experiment which was not to be repeated for another quarter of a century. Thirty years later some of the surviving Mapleson cylinders were gathered together on to 78 rpm records by W. H. Seltsam, for the International Record Collectors' Club. In the 1950s these were collected on to LPs, the covers engagingly over-printed 'This is not a Hi-Fidelity record'—a masterly understatement. To play one of the tracks is to open Pandora's box. It is as if Ford's assembly line and Niagara had somehow got inside the Metropolitan Opera House. But when the ears have grown accustomed to the racket, it is possible, with score in hand as guide, to make out echoes of the voices of Melba, Sembrich, Eames, Calvé, Nordica and Scotti caught literally in the act, and, more important—for they never made commercial recordings—Lucienne Bréval, Milka Ternina, Jean de Reszké and Emilio de Marchi, in scraps of *Les Huguenots, Aida, Tosca, L'Africaine, Tristan und Isolde, Cavalleria Rusticana* and others. For all their primitive sound quality, these cylinders preserve the only record of the great singers of seventy years ago away from the cramped and inhibiting conditions of the early recording studio—in real life, as it were. They suggest not only the fine vocalists that gramophone records led us to expect, but artists equally certain in their ability to communicate the drama. One example will suffice: the fragments out of Act 2 of *Tosca*, given within a couple of years of its first performance, with Emma Eames, Emilio de Marchi and Antonio Scotti under Mancinelli. How menacing is Scotti's Scarpia—yet still smoothly vocalised (including, interestingly enough, unwritten appoggiaturas). As for Eames, can this be the 'cold' singer who, when Amherst Webber tried to get her to be more demonstrative in the first act duet from *Walküre*, replied with a genteel smile, 'But *so* unlike *me*, Mr Webber'? There can have been few Toscas since so passionately eloquent and yet, at the same time, containing her emotion within the bounds of good taste. Mancinelli's conducting—intense and vivid, but yet not overwhelming his singers—makes us question whether Toscanini was the only Italian conductor of genius in those days. Mapleson's originals have now passed into the collection of the New York Public Library where, for want of the right equipment and expertise, they are never played: a great pity, as in recent years immense strides have been made in re-recording techniques and a qualified engineer

---

† Recently, however, Bettini cylinders have been discovered of Sembrich, Saléza, Saville, del Puma and Campanini.

should be allowed to reproduce all that was really left on them.

Of this trio Mapleson was the most important from our point of view; the other two soon tired of the new toy and went off to fresh pastures—literally, in Gouraud's case, as we last glimpse him hastening along the front at Brighton, swathed in a Bedouin's flowing robes, pursued by a crowd of jeering urchins. It was the fancy-dress part of a hair-brained scheme to raise funds to water the Sahara. By 1908, Bettini too had deserted the gramophone, thereafter devoting himself with inconsiderable success to cinema cameras, journalism, a 'golf practice device' (whatever that was) and an automatic cigarette-lighter, which Cartier's manufactured for a time. He died in 1938, having outlived his wife and her money.

Exit the gentlemen, enter the players: Emil Berliner and Fred Gaisberg. The biggest obstacle in the way of the speedy development of the gramophone was the difficulty of copying cylinders in commercial quantities. One solution was the flat disc, patented by Berliner in 1895. From a positive master, via a negative stamper, any number of records could be manufactured easily and cheaply; the way was now open. One of the Berliner company's earliest recruits was a 21-year-old American, Fred Gaisberg. Even at this tender age he was something of a gramophone veteran. His name first crops up as a teenage piano player, accompanying a musical whistler in warblings of 'Home, Sweet Home', 'Marching through Georgia' and 'Pretty Mocking Bird'. Berliner employed him as a talent scout. He soon showed signs of the enterprise which was to make him the gramophone's leading impresario for almost half a century. For Berliner he made the first important operatic recordings: of the Italian tenor, Ferruccio Giannini. Though Giannini was only a provincial artist, his records sold well, and Gaisberg was ready to assault bigger citadels. In 1898, he moved to London, where he joined the new Gramophone and Typewriter Company. It flourished: within a couple of years the catalogue had been built up to more than 5,000 titles with recordings of artists like Corradetti, Adami and Noté, all by this time established and admired names, if scarcely stars. Demand for the introduction of a new, more exclusive, label had been growing for some while. In particular, this had come from Russia; in a country where all the greatest singers from Pasta, Viardot and Grisi to Patti, Battistini and Tamagno had been lavishly feted (and paid) it was perhaps not so remarkable that the

gramophone should have made such a hit. The first Red Label records were made in Russia with Russian artists. Among the first titles was a group by a young bass, Feodor Chaliapin. Though these sold well, as did others by the great tenor Nicolai Figner, they were a local event. Chaliapin had not yet sung abroad, his triumphs in Paris and London with the Diaghilev company were still nearly a decade away and Figner, as the records all too obviously reveal, was well past his best, the voice sadly frayed, the singing uncertain. Nevertheless, the Russian experiment persuaded the company in London that the time was now ripe for a major programme of international expansion. To that end, in the spring of 1902, Gaisberg set out for Milan. There he first heard Caruso, as Federico in a performance of Franchetti's *Germania* at La Scala. On the spot he determined to get him into the recording studio, and in spite of the tenor's demand for £100 for ten 'songs', and in defiance of head office, which was in no mind to shell out that kind of money on a singer who had not yet sung in London or New York, Gaisberg went ahead.

In the career of many of the greatest singers there comes a particular performance, as often as not given in adverse—or at any rate relatively unpublicised—circumstances, which acts as a kind of catalyst, throwing the artist and public into an embrace: Tetrazzini's sensational debut, as Violetta, at Covent Garden in 1907, Flagstad's first Metropolitan Sieglinde in 1935, and more recently Montserrat Caballé's Lucrezia Borgia at Carnegie Hall. In the case of Caruso this event did not take place in the opera house or concert hall but at the Grand Hotel, Milan, with a pianist deputising for an orchestra and a primitive recording trumpet the only audience. These ten records were not just the first steps in a recording career which eventually netted Caruso a half a million pounds during his life time, and his estate as much again since his death: they were also the deciding factor in persuading Conried, the Met's director, to put him on the 1903/4 roster of artists. According to Conried's biographer the Director had never heard Caruso when he went into a Paris store and asked to hear one of his records.[1] The gramophone's role did not end there. From the moment the Victor company issued the records in the United States, their fame spread, to quote Gaisberg, 'like prairie fire'. When he eventually made his Met debut on 23 November 1903, Caruso's name was already a box-office draw. Victor was not slow to follow this up with nation-wide advertising and sales promotion. The records made Caruso, and

Caruso made the company, and himself, by no means a small fortune.

It was an example not lost on others. No longer was much persuasion needed to get artists of the repute of Victor Maurel, Nellie Melba and Adelina Patti into the studio. Some were dignified by special coloured labels. It flattered them as well as helping to keep accounts straight. So there was lilac for Melba, orange for Battistini and green for Tamagno. The last-named, Verdi's original Otello, was lured from retirement like the great Adelina Patti, and like her he too demanded to be recorded at his own villa. He also demanded a royalty on each record sold with a cash advance of £2,000. To accommodate his rapacity, the company was obliged to price the records at what was then a staggering amount, £1 apiece, for only three minutes or less of music. Yet they must have sold: over forty years later most of them were still in the catalogue. These singers, and practically every other of any consequence at that time, who only five years previously had looked askance at the gramophone, were only too anxious to join in this new and rewarding avenue for the exploitation of their talents. From 1905, the record of singing is virtually complete.

In fact it is surprising just how extensive were the activities of the recording companies during those early years. Roberto Bauer's catalogue, *Historical Records*, which tells only part of the story and stops in 1909, runs to nearly five hundred pages of closely set type, detailing examples of the art of many hundreds of different singers. By no means all of these were famous or even important. But except for a few at the end of their careers, practically all the famous and important are included. Quite apart from any intrinsic beauty of the singing, these early records are of considerable historical importance. They provide indelible proof of the great changes that have taken place since then in vocal art—both in style and technique, and in taste and interpretation. Robert Donington, in his *Performer's Guide to Baroque Music*, is almost the first musicologist prepared to treat the gramophone as a significant repository of information.[2] If the gramophone is relevant to the interpretation of Baroque music, how much more relevant is it to the works of the Romantic age. It is not only the records of those who were associated with, or created particular roles in, the operas of Puccini, Strauss, Mascagni, Massenet, Saint-Saëns and the later Verdi and Wagner, that are of special significance. Many of the earliest recordings are of singers who were part of a performing tradition which extends back at least to the middle of the last century, to the early Verdi, Donizetti, Bellini, Rossini; and from the oldest of them, Patti for example, it is not too imaginative to claim that we hear something even of the vocal style of Mozart's day.

Today it is a generally accepted fact that a full and stylish realisation of the music of the baroque and classical periods is not possible simply by playing, however accurately, just what is written in the score. It is less generally realised that even in the nineteenth century, in the early Romantic period especially, the singer's prerogative was still far greater than it has been at any time since. It is surprising just how much was still expected of the performer—much more than merely providing an occasional cadenza or some decorations for the second verses of cabalettas. If it were possible by some acoustic miracle to conjure out of the aether the voice of one of the great singers of that age, Maria Malibran for example, we should be astounded by the freedom of her interpretative style. In the first edition of *L'Art du chant* (1847), Garcia compares, in parallel notation, Sara's aria from Cimarosa's *Sacrifizio d'Abramo*, as it appears in the score and as his sister sang it. The differences are vast. It is not simply a matter of changes in the rhythm, ornamentation and embellishments: it could almost be two different pieces. It is certainly impossible, probably undesirable, that any attempt should be made to sing like that today. Yet even so, when interpreting the music of the late eighteenth century and much of the nineteenth century, which still provides the bulk of most opera houses' repertory, it is as well to remember that the music was not composed for the theatres, singers, orchestra players and public of today. Our interpretations, however fine in their own way, can never be as stylish as those that were given by the composers' contemporaries. Changes in vocal method and technique, in the instruments of the orchestra, in the design of the theatres, and even, in a way, in the ears of the audience, have seen to that. When comparing recordings made seventy or so years ago with those made today, we should be cautious before condemning the older singers— before throwing the score at them because of any changes they make. Very often these changes are part of a performing tradition as old as the music itself and provide an insight into the interpretative manners of an age far removed from our own. We are, of course, entitled to dislike them, but before ascribing them to carelessness or wanton caprice, we should be able to recognise them when we hear them. Such manners—the appoggiatura, for example—are very often a part of the music. It is not disrespectful to make changes that the composer would himself have expected.

What the gramophone has preserved is unfortunately but a very small part of a great tradition, one that extends back at least to the very beginning of the seventeenth century and, in a rudimentary form, to the very beginning of time. To get the record straight, it needs to be put into historical context.

The Singing

In all probability man has been singing since the caves: it seems likely that song is even older than speech. Whereas speech is an artificial means of communication, intellectual in conception, singing is an extension of the cry of man the animal, affecting in itself. How primitive man found the way to produce this sound self-consciously, and then modulate it into song, we can only guess. Those first songs were doubtless crude in manner and execution but still effective enough to give their singer an ascendancy over his fellow man, even over nature itself. History, through the poetry of mythology, has ascribed artistic and spiritual motives to the genesis of song, though we may prefer more prosaic explanations. While accepting that the Thracian legend of Orpheus subduing the wild beasts to the accompaniment of a lute is based in fact, we may wonder whether the stimulus was getting Eurydice from hell or fear of getting hell from her if he came home without anything to eat. Almost certainly self-interestedness played a part in it. Just as an infant quickly learns how affecting its cry is on all but the most resolute parent, so early man learned how to simulate its effect for gainful ends. The functional application of song, though it has long ceased to be vital, has never entirely disappeared. For centuries it played an important part in the advertisement of wares through the street vendors and their cries, and to this day it persists in television jingles.

Man having once learned to imitate himself, it was but a short step to the imitation of nature, the classical basis of all art. Like so much else in western civilisation it is in ancient Greece that the history of singing really begins. There music was quite as important as the literary, graphic and plastic arts, though few traces of it have survived; in all we have only a dozen or so fragments of music in Greek notation. But in spite of this paucity of direct evidence we know that Greek singers had already learned to release the affecting element of song in the chorus of the Aeschylean tragedy. It was of the nature of this simplest and most ancient form of drama that when feeling and excitement were at fever pitch they turned into song; only thus was it possible to communicate the most intense, most extreme, emotions. Through what modes of expression these early singers represented the psychological effect of Aeschylean drama we are not ever likely to know; perhaps some of them might not have been so alien to our ears. We do know that later, in ancient Rome, there flourished a great school of virtuosi. Here the song was no longer, as it had been in Greece, an integral part of the drama, but an interpolated solo, usually written by the soloist to show off his skill—a skill acquired by the same rigorous adherence to scale exercises that has been the foundation of the art of great singing ever since. From Quintilian we know too that these singers wrought effects on their audiences similar to those of their confrères in the eighteenth and nineteenth centuries. They were feted in society and lionised by impressionable matrons, and their influence spread even to the highest places. The Emperor Nero fancied himself a virtuoso. It is said that the last words he uttered as he lay dying were 'Qualis artifex pereo'—'What an artist is lost in me!' Alas, that there is no record of the melody with which he supposedly serenaded the conflagration of Rome ('Keep the home fires burning', in Latin perhaps) nor of the embellishments of his fiddle obbligato.

With the triumph of Christianity the history of singing becomes the history of choral music—of the chant. In the early Eastern church it was monodic in character (as indeed it has remained ever since, in those areas unaffected by Western influence), its traditions inherited partly from ancient Greece, partly from the Orient; its melodies free in rhythm and movement, at first simple and concise, and later, under renewed influence from Islam, becoming increasingly florid, decorated with long and elaborate vocalises. In the Western church too, diminutions, or divisions, existed in an elementary form from the beginning. Again, oriental influence was significant; for example, in the highly ornate Alleluias introduced into the liturgy at the beginning of the fifth century. St. Augustine offers a classical explanation for them: 'They expressed things that could not be expressed by words or letters.' The single most potent factor in the development of the art of singing in the West was the establishment in Rome of the Schola Cantorum, which provided the example in vocal technique and style for the rest of Christendom to copy. It was the principal agency through which Pope Gregory the Great, at the end of the sixth century, carried out his sweeping reforms. Improvisation was repressed and the soloist eliminated; the choir sang the psalmody 'as if it were with one voice; none of the singers faster or louder than the others'.[1] In Gregory's own lifetime the other St. Augustine took these reforms to the British Isles, and two hundred years later, through the direct agency of the Emperor Charlemagne, they were introduced into the Frankish dominions. For centuries the Gregorian music was the only kind officially known, taught and practised. But by the twelfth century, as its authority was spread to the farthest corners of Western Europe, it gradually lost the certitude of its proper execution. This process of decadence was accelerated by the invention of tonic sol-fa (that is, a set of symbols to denote the individual tones of the scale). Through this device the example of the Schola Cantorum was further weakened: it was now possible for every monastery to have its own copy of the antiphonal. The writings of its inventor, the Italian monk Guido d'Arezzo, confirm the growing importance of vocal study in the Medieval church, of a series of priorities we may believe to have been the basis of vocal art since classical times, and which remain so to this day:

> Voices should melt together . . . so that one tone begun seems limpidly to flow into another and not be completed . . .[2]

In a word, legato. Then as now, a sure legato was impossible without an understanding of the fundamental importance of breath control, so that at all times the voice is properly supported from the diaphragm; only thus is the singer able to ensure an uninterrupted flow of tone, smoothness of emission and surety of intonation.

Upon the basis of this fluent and undulating legato was reared the elegant floridity of the chant—graceful, suave, and decorated throughout with affecting modes of expression. Although the ornaments used in the chant were not delivered in the brilliant style of the eighteenth century, many of the actual devices employed were similar. The same were subsequently echoed in instrumental music, and survived into the early Romantic period, in the operas of Rossini, Bellini, Donizetti and Meyerbeer. Traces of them linger, albeit in a degenerate form, in the works of Wagner and Puccini. More recently still, they have made a spontaneous reappearance in a quite alien idiom, Afro-American popular music: mordents, staccati, gruppetti, even ad libitum cadenzas, now styled 'scat'. It is difficult to resist the conclusion that these effects are not mere singer's vanity, as critics from Sutherland Edwards to Ernest Newman were for ever complaining, but part of a basic vocal grammar—as old as, perhaps older than, music itself.

Though profane music was only of secondary importance in the Middle Ages, the courtly songs of the troubadours and the popular strains of the minstrels were eventually absorbed into the prevailing sacred style—a contributory factor in the rise of polyphony. Where the plain chant had been monophonic, i.e. in a single vocal line, polyphony introduced a vertical as well as a horizontal disposition. Through this new perspective, the indigenous music of the people was married to the Gregorian melodies. In such fashion the church militant joined what it was finding increasingly difficult to beat. Polyphonic music made new, more exacting, demands on the singers. The need to balance the sound, to blend different voices, encouraged a study of the physiology of the voice and lead to the recognition of its different registers:

> Different kinds of voices ought not to be mingled in the chant, whether it be chest with head, or throat with head. Generally low voices, basses, are of the chest, light voices, of the head, those of the throat intermediate. They should not be mixed in chant, but chest voices should remain as such, just as the voices of the throat and the head. (Jerome of Moravia—13th century)[3]

In the mature male voice it is not difficult to recognise the existence of two registers. The separation is obvious. The chest register, which develops dramatically at puberty, characteristically dark-coloured, predominates; what is left of the infantile voice, called the falsetto or head register, remains by comparison thin and strident. In the female voice there exists a similar duality, but as there is no sudden downward shift in the pitch during adolescence, the basic range of the voice, though enhanced by maturity, does not alter. The chest register is significant but forms a much smaller part than in the male voice, being least in the high soprano, most of all in the contralto. Whereas it is natural for a man to sing predominantly in the chest register, many female singers can, and indeed do, sing virtually without recourse to it at all. Instead, they use what singing teachers call the 'middle register'. Unlike the chest and head registers, which involve different mechanical operations, as Professor Morel Mackenzie observed in the last century, the middle register cannot be so substantiated. For all that, it is real enough. For reality in singing is in the ear of the listener—the singer's own and his audience's. It is easy to detect the changes in quality in a fully developed and correctly trained female voice, as the singer moves up, at about F or F sharp above middle C, from the chest into the middle register, and then an octave above that into the head register—changes in quality the singer herself is just as aware of.

The history of singing, of music, in the later Middle Ages and the Renaissance mirrors the general conflict between the established Roman Church and the various Protestant separatist movements, between on the one hand the hierarchial tidiness of the Feudal state and on the other the increasing demands of the emergent mercantile class. In music, religious and secular forms become more evenly balanced, the spontaneous, popular song modifying traditional 'art' music; all of it, however, still contained under the general umbrella of polyphony. It was in the final synthesis of this style, in sixteenth-century Italy, during the Counter-reformation (in the motets of de Monte, the Madrigals of di Lasso, the Masses of Palestrina), that there first appeared a new type of singer, whose peculiar genius was to transcend anything heard hitherto.

The first of the castrati entered the papal choir in 1562, and others soon followed. Although the practice of castration is as old as civilisation, in the West at any rate it was not until the sixteenth century that the operation was carried out solely for musical purposes, as a substitute for the woman's voice banished by Pauline dictum from participation in church music. It was a voice that could cope with the increasingly complex, brilliant and wide-ranging music of the late Renaissance. Until then the function had been performed by boy sopranos or falsetto singers. Neither compromise was a success. The treble voice broke before it was possible to complete a thorough vocal and musical training. The male falsettist, comparable to the cathedral alto or counter tenor of our own day, though more reliable, lacked the upper fifth of a real soprano and for all the skill of some vocalists, the Spanish school developing a considerable degree of virtuosity, the sound quality itself was not—indeed is not—aesthetically pleasing. Mutilation was a

drastic but brilliant solution. The castrato retained the range and quality of a boy's voice enhanced and developed by maturity, to which was added the powerful lungs and diaphragm of a grown man. It was an irresistable combination, one that nature had deliberately eschewed—the child's naturally affecting cry delivered with the strength and surety of a man. Contemporary references confirm the remarkable effect of the castrato voice; 'Their timbre,' wrote de Brosses, 'is as clear and piercing as choirboys, and much more powerful':[4] 'Voices that give the idea of sentiment transmuted into sound', (Panzacchi):[5] 'The peculiar affecting quality of their voices' (Rossini).[6] Even those writers from Britain and France who initially were so moved and affected by the sight of the 'poor mutilated fellows', when they heard them, were soon even more moved and affected by their art. It was in this basic natural sound itself that the strange paradox of the castrato voice lay; though it was manufactured—artificial—its effect was more 'natural' than any natural voice. It is not surprising to find male sopranos referred to as 'soprani naturali' (Pietro della Valle),[7] in contrast to the artificial sopranos, the falsettists.

Though the castrati were conspicuously brilliant interpreters of the madrigals of the late Renaissance, of Luca Marenzio and Orlando di Lasso, it was in that quintessentially baroque art-form, opera, that they were to play the dominating role. The first opera that has survived, Peri's *Eurydice*, was staged in Florence, in 1600. It was the outcome of the deliberate rejection of polyphony. A group of Florentine literati were determined to upset the traditional relationship between the words and music—'prima la musica e poi le parole'—by abandoning the stultifying laws of counterpoint, in their place substituting a free-flowing recitative, in which the words would govern the musical rhythm, even the place of the cadences. In this they had some notion of resurrecting the classical drama, though at the time the only piece of ancient Greek music known was indecipherable. Solo singing in itself was nothing new, as it formed a significant part of the eastern chant. During the Renaissance the solo with the lute or viol accompaniment was a well-established practice, but it remained polyphonic in conception, lacking a melody capable of harmonic development or an affecting setting of words. The recitative style of the new opera introduced a hitherto unknown realistic pathos in which the singer resorted to acting, to the imitation of the inflections of speech, even gasping and crying. It was a style ideally suited to the theatre, where its affecting accents could be projected across to large audiences, who quickly became infatuated with it.

In less than a century the popularity of opera reached epidemic proportions, spreading the length and breadth of Italy: from the North, where it had begun, down to Rome and Naples and across to Venice, where by 1700, in a city of 150,000 people sixteen theatres provided nightly entertainment during the season. In Rome, in the year 1678, a diarist has recorded that there were more than 130 works given in private houses alone. In the beginning, opera was a courtly entertainment; there was no box-office, and admission was by invitation only. Its rapid popularity, however, encouraged the establishment of commercial companies, some of them itinerant, others permanently based. After the original self-conscious intellectual stimulus had spent itself, the emphasis shifted from the drama to the spectacle. And what spectacles they were! Nothing so splendid had been seen before, nor would be again, except possibly for the Diaghilev company in its heyday. The greatest painters and architects of the day went to the opera house, where they could give free rein to the baroque imagination at its most high-flown. On impermanent canvas they composed palaces of impossible splendour, vistas of pillars receding into infinity, and amid all the *trompe l'oeil* decked out in fabulous costumes, bedizened with plumes and jewellery, the heroes of myth and legend, impersonated by *monstres sacrés* (the real men were left to play elders, villains and impotent priests), dazzled too, with the glory of their virtuosity. It was a feast for ear as well as eye; for by the middle baroque period musicians had once again gained the ascendancy. The new idiom was an essentially vocal one, characterised by the penetrating quality and sustaining power of the castrato voice. In the early period exuberant embellishments had been inspired by the affecting power of particular words, but now they were subordinated to the smooth flow of the melody. It was in this period that the foundations were laid for what has since come to be styled 'bel canto'. From this time, too, dates the supremacy of Italian opera and Italian singers. In spite of the growth of indigenous forms in Germany, England and France, it was only in France that the local form was strong enough to resist the prevailing Italian mode. Travelling companies with Italian singers took Italian opera to London, Hamburg and Vienna. The fact that few people in those cities understood what was being sung was of small account; the eloquence

of the castrati transcended language barriers, their virtuosity translated opera into an international entertainment, the first ever, and they themselves became the first international stars.

It was in the middle baroque period that the art of singing was brought to a peak of perfection, the innate expressivity of the voice more completely developed than ever before. The singer's art was founded in mastery of the breath, of its control and application; in the words of Maria Celloni 'Chi sa respirare, sa cantare'.[8] This crucial conception was what writers like Giustiniani, Mancini, Agricola, Tosi and Burney called 'portamento'. Not, as the term is used today, in a narrow instrumental sense, as the linking of two or more intervals together to create a special effect. Then the word meant what it means literally, viz. 'carrying'—the carrying of the voice.

> By portamento, I mean the passing and blending of the voice from one tone to another, with perfect proportion and union, in ascending as well as descending.

Legato and support suggest something of it, but not enough; neither conveys a sense of momentum, of 'the passing and blending of the voice', interrupted but not stopped, continuing by implication through passages of non-legato, staccati, rests, hard consonants, even while the singer takes a breath. In his *Code de Musique Pratique* (Paris, 1760), Jean-Philippe Rameau has this to say:

> All the perfections of singing, all of its difficulties, depend solely on the breath which comes out of the lungs. The larynx, the windpipe, and the glottis are not at our disposal, we cannot see their different positions, transformations, to each sound we wish to give; but we do know at least that they must not be constricted in these differences, that they must be left at liberty to follow their natural movement, that we are only masters of the breath, and in consequence it is for us to govern it so well, that nothing can disturb the effect.[10]

It was breath control that the old Italian masters continually told their pupils to learn, how to 'filar il suono' (spin the tone), that is emit just enough breath to make a whisper and then convert it into tone; it was this which created the underlying tension that gave the singing of the castrati its unequalled eloquence, allowing the voice to follow its 'natural movement' without constriction, the tones pure and limpid, free to execute the most elaborate ornamentations with ease, accuracy and brilliance.

Second only to their mastery of the breath was the castrati's command of the registers of the voice, the different colours of which are as much a part of its eloquence as the registers in the baroque organ or harpsichord; indeed we may believe these to have been inspired by the vocal example. Their unification is only possible by a full exploitation of each of them; equalisation is achieved not by minimising their different characteristics, but by developing each to the full. To an extent this supremacy was a consequence of the castrati's peculiar physiology; though mutilation checked the downward shift in pitch that takes place in the voice of the un-castrated male at puberty, it did not arrest the development of the voice in any other way, which continued to grow much as a girl's voice does at the same age, except that, since the castrati grew to the same size as normal men, the development was greater, the fully-grown male soprano larynx being that much bigger and stronger than the female. In particular, this affected the size and power of the chest register, which was altogether greater than in any but the most remarkably endowed female voice. Some of the greatest castrati were described as contraltos. Senesino, perhaps the most famous of them all, and even the sopranos, Farinelli, Caffarelli, Carestini and Crescentini, were all able to sing with telling effect in what we today should call the contralto range. Pacchierotti indeed, according to Dr Burney, could go down as low as B flat on the second line in the bass. With such a range he could and did sing tenor music; yet for all that he was always called a soprano and does not seem to have suffered any corresponding diminution in the range or power of the head register—rather the contrary. This remarkable natural endowment enabled the castrati to sing divisions in the chest register with a brilliance and fluency for which we have abundant testimony. According to Quantz:

> Carestini showed great fire in passage work and like Farinelli, according to the good school of Bernacchi, produced these with the chest ... In an allegro, Gaetano Orsini, articulated, especially the triplets, very well from the chest.[11]

and Dr Burney tells how:

> Senesino sang rapid *allegros* with great fire, and marked rapid divisions, from the chest. . . .[12]

We should not be too surprised at all this prodigious skill, since, from the early years of childhood until they were mature artists, these singers were subjected to the most complete and rigorous musical education. Once purely mechanical matters of attack, tone formation etc. had been mastered, they concentrated on refinements. Of these, none was more emphasised than the messa di voce:

> The art in which the singer gives to any sustained note its gradation, starting it with almost a thread of voice, then reinforcing it proportionately to the greatest power in which it can be developed, then taking it back with the same gradation that has been used in going from soft to loud.[13]

Thereby they gave to the portamento its vitality—undulating, as it were, the flow of tone. These studies were by no means solely pre-occupied with vocal production; theory and composition were quite as fundamental. Many ornaments were not written down, but had to be provided by the singer, according to particular rules, which it was essential to know. These enriched the harmony by providing extra dissonances. The singing and the music, as we read in Mancini, were inextricable:

> The appoggiatura, trill and mordent in reality, are nothing but embellishments of the melody. They are so necessary that without them singing would be monotonous and imperfect, while with these embellishments singing acquires its greatest splendour.[14]

Through the singers' virtuosity, music itself was extended; it was impossible to separate the music from the singing, interpretation from technique. There was not then the absolute divorce between interpretation and composition that we are accustomed to today. No doubt some of the castrati were the empty-headed peacocks that various—in particular non-musical—writers have suggested: what else had they but *amour propre*? But the finest of them were much more than mere extravagant technicians. Their legendary ability to improvise all manner of vocal figurations and inform them with true musical feeling would have been impossible without a complete musical background. The greatest singing is a matter of mental control not muscular technique. Nothing could give a more inadequate account of the breadth of their culture than the oft-repeated anecdote about Porpora confining Caffarelli to one page of exercises for five or six years, and then dismissing him with the words: 'Go, my son, I have nothing more to teach you. You are the greatest singer in the world.' In fact, there was no branch of their art of which study had not made them complete masters. The trouble with a superlative is that there can be no going forward. Since then the art of singing has been in continuous decline.

To begin with the decadence was in style rather than technique. Although from about the second quarter of the eighteenth century, it was the instrumental idiom that prevailed, paradoxically this brought forth a new flowering of virtuosity, surpassing anything hitherto. Enough of the music survives of the greatest singers of this age, complete with their ornaments and embellishments, to leave no doubt that theirs was an incomparable art that has not been remotely approached in modern times.[14] In particular, some examples of Farinelli's cadenzas look as if they had been bodily lifted out of a violin concerto. The prowess of Farinelli (1705–1782) not only equalled and exceeded that of any other singer, but in purity of tone, celerity of technique, dynamic control, flexibility and exactitude of intonation, as Dr Burney confirms, he beat the instrumentalists at their own game:

There was a struggle every night between him and a famous player on the trumpet, in a song accompanied by that instrument; this at first seemed amicable and merely sportive, till the audience began to interest themselves in the contest, and to take different sides: after severely swelling a note, in which each manifested the power of his lungs, and tried to rival the other in brilliancy and force, they both had a swell and a shake together, by thirds, which was continued so long, while the audience eagerly awaited the event, that both seemed exhausted; and, in fact, the trumpeter wholly spent gave it up, thinking, however, his antagonist as much tired as himself, and that it would be a drawn battle; when Farinelli, with a smile on his countenance, showing he had only been sporting with him all the time, broke out all at once in the same breath, with fresh vigour, and not only swelled and shook the note, but ran the most rapid and difficult divisions, and was at last silenced only by the acclamations of the audience. From this period may be dated that superiority which he ever maintained over all his contemporaries.[15]

Yet for all Farinelli's coruscating brilliance, and that of the finest of his contemporaries, this was decadence. These cadenzas, like the fast divisions and strictly measured scale passages, disregarded the proper affections. As Tosi complained, ironically, 'the grand mode demands that the singer be quick and ready to burst himself in his lamentations and weep with liveliness'.[16] Later on in Farinelli's career, after the Emperor Charles VI advised him to give up trying to astonish his hearers and instead engage their emotions, he became equally successful in the cantabile and pathetic style. But music does not stand still. Though the greatest singers may still have been able to excel the instrumental virtuosi, the decline in the art of singing continued during the next century and a half, until the voice became no more than another instrument in the service of music.

For records of those legendary singers of the eighteenth century we must rely, *faute de mieux*, on prosaic accounts, but the sound of the castrato voice itself has been preserved by the gramophone. ALESSANDRO MORESCHI (1858–1922), described as a soprano of the Sistine Chapel, made a number of recordings, in Rome, in 1902/3. A word of caution is needed, however. Nearly two hundred years had passed by since the halcyon days of Senesino and Farinelli, and a hundred since the last operatic castrati, Crescentini and Velluti, were active in the theatre, and we shall not find on these recordings any of their virtuosity. But the voice itself is there, quite unlike any other, the tone pure and brilliant, with 'that peculiar affecting quality' Rossini spoke of, intense and passionate—the same we had been led to expect from the eighteenth-century descriptions. Paradoxically, it was not at all emasculated-sounding, unlike the voce bianca—so erroneously thought of as being authentic in Renaissance and baroque music—or the counter-tenor falsettists, or even the female soprano. The sound is unambiguously masculine. One can accept that there would have been nothing inherently absurd in a soprano Julius Caesar, Hercules or Aeneas—given that these mighty warriors burst into song in the first place.

As a singer and an artist, Moreschi seems not to have been very distinguished: certainly not in his taste in music—the sacred pieces he chose to record are written precisely in that saccharine style that Pius X's *Motu Proprio* was designed to suppress. In his selection of the Bach-Gounod 'Ave Maria' and Tosti's 'Ideale', there is more of the Salotto Umbertino than an echo of Velluti, let alone of Farinelli. It is a pity he recorded nothing florid; perhaps because his voice shows signs of incipient collapse, he felt it wiser to play safe. We do know, however, that in former days he was not so coy:

. . . that particular evening was unusually brilliant, for the monsignores and cardinals were super-abundant . . . The famous Morescha [sic], who sings at the Laterano, is a full-faced soprano of forty winters [in fact, at that time he was only twenty-five]. He has a tear in each note and a sigh in each breath. He sang the Jewel Song from *Faust*, which seemed horribly out of place. Especially when he asks, in the hand glass, if he really is Marguerita, one feels tempted to answer for him, Macchè![17]

Though his voice was failing by the time he came to make records, Moreschi's technique is not without interest: in particular, his way of approaching a head note with an upward acciaccatura, sometimes of more than an octave. Perhaps this is a degenerate form of an ornament used in the chant, about which Marchettus of Padua wrote in the early fourteenth century that it was in effect a yodel.[18] Caccini, writing in 1602 in his *Nuove Musiche*, refers to a similar device common at the time among male sopranos, of deliberately attacking a high note from a third or more below.[19] Herman Klein mentions it again in discussing the singing of the great Hungarian soprano Teresa Tietjens (1831–1877): 'the curious leap (not scoop) over an upward interval from the medium into the head voice, making it sound something like an acciaccatura.'[20] Although this was a deliberate effect, not to be confused with that unintentional sliding up to high notes which is such a disagreeable feature of a faulty technique, it was, like much else in the grammar of vocal ornamentation, technical in its origin. In this case a way of 'finding' the head voice. We can hear something similar even today, for example at the end of the cadenza in the *Lucia* Mad Scene, where many sopranos, in order to launch the high E flat securely, kick up to it by fleetingly repeating the B flat before it: the ornament Garcia calls 'la petite note inférieure'.[21]

By mastering the head voice as completely as the chest, the castrati were able to extend their ranges up to, and in some cases even beyond, three octaves. Though Moreschi, at least by the time he came to make records, does not seem to be able to manage anything above high B, one of his predecessors at the Sistine Chapel, the castrato Domenico Mustafà (1829–1912), had a command of the falsetto that must have been remarkable. At any rate it profoundly impressed one famous prima donna:

Strange, sexless tones, superhuman, uncanny! I was so much impressed that I decided to take some lessons from him. The first question I asked was how I might learn to sing those heavenly tones.

'It's quite easy,' he answered. 'You have only to practice with your mouth tight shut for two hours a day. At the end of ten years, you may possibly be able to do something with them.'

That was hardly encouraging. Nevertheless I set to work. My first efforts were pitiful. At the end of two years, however, I began to make use of my newly acquired skill; but it was not until the third year of study that I obtained a complete mastery of the difficult art.[22]

So wrote Emma Calvé in her autobiography *My Life*. Mustafà, unfortunately, did not make any recordings; but Calvé, the greatest Carmen of her day, and a passionate Santuzza, who was equally at home as Gounod's Marguerite, and even as Thomas's Ophélie, has left us a good number of records testifying to her claim. In none, perhaps, is her manipulation of the head voice more remarkable than in the traditional French song 'Ma Lisette', though we may believe that had she followed Mustafà's advice to the letter and spent ten rather than three years perfecting it, the separation of the different registers might not have been so drastic.

Altogether the reign of the castrati was barely two centuries, but in that time they brought the art of singing to a pitch that has not been equalled. It was their accomplishments, which Tosi and Mancini codified in various treatises, that are implicit in the writings of Garcia, de la Madeleine, Faure and Marchesi, and of virtually every vocal pedagogue since. It was the example, too, to which, in their own day, the female singers aspired. At the beginning of the seventeenth century there had been several of note, among them Vittoria Archilei, who created the title-role in Peri's *Eurydice*, and Leonora Barioni (Milton heard her during his stay in Rome and was greatly affected by her art); but the female singers of that time were essentially singers da camera. It was not for another hundred years or so that they began to play an important role in the theatre. Two of the greatest virtuosi in the early part of the eighteenth century were both sopranos: Faustina Bordoni and Francesca Cuzzoni. Faustina was preferred for her brilliance in execution of passage work, polished trill, and security of intonation, the result of a breath control that rivalled the castrati themselves. Cuzzoni, on the other hand, was mistress of the pathetic style and was much approved of by Tosi for her powers of extemporisation and for the innate sweetness of her voice. It was not only in matters of vocal art that these ladies took the castrati as their example; they were as quick to copy the less engaging aspects of the castrati's behaviour off-stage. The great public rivalry between Faustina and Cuzzoni provided John Gay with excellent material for parody in the prison scene from *The Beggar's Opera*. Faustina married the composer Johann Hasse; Cuzzoni seems to have been less successful in her marital adventures. In the *Daily News* of 7 September 1741, there appeared an item that she had been arrested, charged with poisoning her husband. Whether the accusation was not proven, or whether an acquittal was secured on the grounds of justifiable homicide, is not clear. When a few years afterwards she reappeared in London, wags observed that it was probably not the first time a prima donna had got away with murder.

The other great female sopranos of the eighteenth century, Mingotti (1722–1802), Mara (1749–1833), Banti (1756–1806), Billington (1768–1818) and Catalani (1780–1849), were all still in the thrall of the castrati. Of these, Angelica Catalani was, perhaps, the greatest virtuosa who ever lived. In her day she was famous for her combination of talent, tastelessness and rapacity. Her style was the reductio ad absurdum of the instrumental mode so deplored by Tosi. She had a passion for variations, even possessing herself of those composed for the violin by Rode, which she would introduce into whatever opera she happened to be singing with a superb disregard for their dramatic relevance. She represents to us today, with our notions of respect for the composer and his score, everything that seems most objectionable. Yet even the German composer Ludwig Spohr, who was scandalised by much of her liberty-taking, could not help being impressed by her skill:

> There was much sheer pleasure in the purity of her intonation, in the perfection of every kind of figuration and embellishment and the individuality of her interpretive style ... Her trill is especially beautiful whether in whole or half tones. Much admired was a run through the half tones, actually an enharmonic scale, since each tone occured twice ... Very beautiful was the way she accomplished another, and not uncommon, type of ornamentation, a descending scale of coupled eighths and sixteenths, pausing for breath after each sixteenth and giving to the whole passage a most melancholy expression. Among the variations was one in syncopation, which had a strikingly individual character, and another in triplets which she managed with the utmost perfection.[23]

In an age when we are grateful if a singer can trill at all—properly establish each note and clearly sustain it—we can only marvel at one whose art was such that she was able, at will, to execute a trill in either whole or half tones.

In spite of the reformations of Gluck and Mozart and the changes in musical style that took place in the later part of the eighteenth century, the priorities in vocal art remained what they had been. It was not till after 1800 that two new influences emerged to hasten the decline in the art of singing: the first, the growing size and power of the symphony orchestra; the second, the emphatic accents called for by the Romantic melodrama. In order to accommodate these, the technique of the old Italian school, a consummate vocal art with its own grammar of expression, affecting in itself, was compromised, and singers began to resort 'to that violent attack, forcing of tone, clarion delivery of high notes that came to be popularly demanded' (W. J. Henderson).[24] The history of singing ever since is an account of the inevitable failure to reconcile, on the one hand, the refined (though not effete) traditions of the castrati and the increasing demand for naturalism in the theatre, on the other. It was but one manifestation of what Nietzsche called 'the gradual erosion of contours', of that conflict between art and realism which was such a preoccupation of the nineteenth century and in which art was inevitably the loser.

One of the earliest and finest artists of the new age, Isabella Colbran, was also the wife of Rossini, a fact not without significance. Although her interpretation of the leading roles in his operas brought her to the pinnacle of her eminence, the demands these parts made were almost certainly an important factor in bringing her career to an untimely end. To our ears, the Rossini orchestra seems very small beer indeed, but it did not seem so to his contemporaries, who were for ever bewailing the din he had unleashed. Rossini met Colbran in 1815, when he was appointed Director of Music at the San Carlo, Naples, where at that time she was the reigning prima donna and already an artist of considerable renown. During the ensuing eight years he composed for her a whole gallery of queens and tragic heroines. From the scores of these works we can get a good idea of her prodigious skill, and also chart with some degree of accuracy her failing vocal powers. A comparison between *Armida* (1817) and *Semiramide* (1823) is instructive. In *Armida*, where the music is altogether more dramatic, the range of the part extends frequently to high C; in *Semiramide*, except for an occasional A and B flat in ensembles, there are no sustained notes above the stave. What had happened to them? Undoubtedly her own dramatic ambitions played some part in it. Spohr tells us that, even in 1816, she was by no means a perfect vocalist, 'with her strenuous high notes',[25] not to be compared with Catalani (who was five years her senior). It seems a reasonable conclusion to draw that her technique (she was a pupil of the castrato Crescentini) could not cope with the vehement accents required by Rossini's music, particularly in the new recitatives with their continuous orchestral accompaniment. Nor was Colbran an exception. Neither Giuditta Pasta, nor Maria Malibran, for all their unquestied genius, were the vocal paragons we might have imagined from latter-day commentators. It was not their singing, per se, that inspired the panegyrics of those great Romantics Alfred de Musset and Stendhal, but the manner in which, through their art, they embodied the passions of an age. Even so, we should not forget that these were flawed vocalists at a time when standards were altogether higher than at any time since. The role of Norma, for example, which the composer Bellini (who had himself studied singing with Crescentini) tailored especially to suit the voice of Pasta, remains still, after a century and a half, the *ne plus ultra* for every aspiring diva.

It was not just the female voice that was affected by the demands of the new Romantic style; it led to equally profound changes in the technique of the male singers, in particular of the tenor. It was this, the highest natural male voice, which, from the third quarter of the eighteenth century, had gradually begun to displace the castrato. But, for all their unquestioned skill, the eighteenth-century tenors, like Raaf, who created the title role in Mozart's *Idomeneo*, or Legros, for whom Gluck altered his *Orphée*, were still accomplished after the fashion of their predecessors. It was not until the representation of the sexual passions in opera of the first quarter of the nineteenth century that the tenor voice developed its own characteristics. Nor was this achieved at once. In Naples, at the time of Rossini's engagement, there were three very remarkable virtuosi active: Giovanni David, Andrea Nozzari and Manuel Garcia. It was for their very exceptional talents that he composed in each of the operas, *Elisabetta, Regina d'Inghilterra, Otello, La Donna del Lago* and *Zelmira*, two principal tenor roles (in *Armida* there were no less than five—five good reasons why this opera is rarely revived). Although in the elaborate brilliance of the writing Rossini was still composing in the old style, the remarkable vocal range of the roles, extending frequently to high C, sometimes C sharp, even D, was a new departure, an example that was soon to be copied by most of his contemporaries. This upper range was produced in falsetto, not the coarse open tone the term may suggest to us today, but an artful blending of registers in which the head voice predominated; only that way was it possible still to execute the brilliant fioritura with the required fluency and grace. A change took place in Rossini's style after he left Italy. Although the range of the tenor parts he composed in Paris is quite as extensive, the ornamentation in them was simplified. This had to do with the French taste. Here we may detect, almost for the first time, a foreign influence come to prevail over the traditional Italian style; one of the first signs of the emergence, in the Age of Nationalism, of a national vocal style. In the course of the nineteenth century most of the principal countries of Europe would develop their own different styles. It was not particularly remarkable that the Italian hegemony should have broken down in France; the French had never really cared for the florid style. France was the one country which had resisted Italian opera and laughed at the pretensions of the castrati. We may believe the example of the French theatre, the heroes of Corneille, Racine and Voltaire, with their more vigorous assertion of masculinity, was not lost on the opera or its singers. Whereas, in those pieces he had written for Naples, Rossini in his tenor-writing was still echoing the manner of the castrati, in his French operas the simplified but more dramatic line made it possible for the singer to concentrate on 'the clarion delivery of high notes', enabled him, with one stroke of the glottis, as it were, to satisfy the taste of his audience by dealing manfully with the challenge put up by the elaborate and louder French orchestras.

Appropriately enough, two of the most outstanding early nineteenth-century tenors were Frenchmen: Adolphe Nourrit and Gilbert-Louis Duprez. The former, who created several principal roles in Rossini's French operas, including Arnold in *Guillaume Tell*, was famous not only for his skill and security in high-lying tessitura but also for his histrionic talent. It was said of him that: 'he had been instructed by Garcia, but inspired by Talma'. It was Duprez, however, who made the more stunning effect; by singing high C from the chest. It may not have appealed to the judicious; Rossini, when Duprez came to call, asked him to leave it on the hat stand. Yet it was an achievement that was profoundly to effect the future of vocal art. Every aspiring tenor sought to emulate it. For want of it, so it was said, Nourrit committed suicide. Even so, it is doubtful whether the note was entirely from the chest if it sounded at all like the kind of high C we are accustomed to in this post-Puccini age. It should not be forgotten that Duprez created Edgardo in Lucia and sang, with notable success, Elvino in Bellini's *Sonnambula*, and that among his many and distinguished pupils was that personification of vocal elegance and suavity, Pol Plançon. Perhaps, were we to marry, in the mind's ear, to Plançon's style and easy alacrity of execution, something of the virile quality of another French artist from the end of the last century, the tenor Léon Escalaïs, we should get an idea of how Duprez sounded.

The new generation of Italian tenors was soon just as preoccupied with the sure and telling delivery of high notes as the French. At the time Bellini was looking for a tenor to create Pollione in *Norma*, Domenico Donzelli wrote to him:

> The extension of my voice is almost two octaves, that is from the bass D up to the high C. Chest tones up to the G [he was being modest; his chest A was by all accounts a thrillingly secure note]; it is within this range that I can declaim with strength and sustain the force of the declamation. From thence to high C, I avail myself of falsetto which used with artistry and strength is a resource for ornamentation.[26]

More spectacular was the singing of Giam-Battista Rubini. The tale of his mis-reading high F for D flat, accidentally, during a run through of *I Puritani*, and of Bellini's decision to mark it in the score, much to the embarrassment of every Arturo since, has become a legend. For certain, the F would have been completely in falsetto; physiologically it could not have been otherwise. No doubt, Rubini's complete mastery of every shade and graduation between the registers would, to some extent, have masked this. But it was not only by vaunting flights of virtuosity that he so deeply affected his contemporaries. He is generally held responsible for the popularisation of the vibrato, an effect with which he charmed a whole generation but which in the course of time, when deployed by lesser artists, degenerated into a bad habit, greatly deplored by critics and singing teachers.

Few terms create more confusion in their application to the art of singing than vibrato and tremolo. Certain modern writers, for the sake of convenience, have preferred to use the former for the natural movement that occurs in any healthy voice,

reserving the latter to describe something involuntary, the consequence of some obvious technical failing. But this arbitrary discrimination is not historical, for it was not so made nor implied by any of the great masters of the eighteenth century in their writings. Indeed, it was not a matter that greatly preoccupied them. Since the vocal cords must vibrate to produce any sound at all, all voices must have some vibrato, and to that extent they recognised its existence. But that a part of the basic mechanism of voice production should have obtruded noticeably, would to them have seemed intolerable. Mozart, in a letter to his father wrote:

> Meissner, as you know, has a bad habit in that he intentionally vibrates his voice . . . and that I cannot tolerate in him. It is indeed truly detestable, it is singing entirely contrary to nature. The human voice already vibrates of itself, but in such a degree that it is beautiful, that is the nature of the voice.[27]

The only significant references to vibrato before the nineteenth century refer to its deliberate use as an affecting device, an ornament to be used very occasionally to create a special effect. It is not until Rubini's day that we find it mentioned as a general characteristic of singing. In half voice, delicately deployed, it can be attractive, but at full throttle it quickly degenerates into the kind of bleat that Shaw deplored in the singing of the elderly Mario and which we can hear so abundantly in the recordings of a whole generation of Italian singers active around the turn of the century. In these days, when one form of vibrato or another has become such a conspicuous feature of singing, it is only the irregular slow wobble, the long-term consequence of muscular fatigue, and the vibrato which has worked itself loose over the years that critics comment upon adversely. At a time when instrumentalists, wind players in particular, concentrate so much on a pure and steady tone, cleanly focussed, when the throbbing violin has become a joke, it is surprising that the spread tone of even well-known singers, sometimes vibrating across a quarter of a tone or more, passes by unremarked. The public has been persuaded that a prominent vibrato is a natural feature of the human voice, whereas in fact it is the result of faulty breathing or deliberate exaggeration. It is not just aesthetically disagreeable; the biggest objection to any obvious vibrato or tremolo is that it inevitably involves oscillation in pitch as well as pulsation of intensity, and it is therefore unmusical.

Rubini's vibrato, like his affecting execution in

falsetto, was a response to the increasingly dramatic style of so much of the tenor music composed from Bellini and Donizetti onwards. Unable to beat Donzelli and Duprez, he went where they with their more intractable instruments could not follow. In so doing, he created a definite separation between the lighter and heavier type of tenor voice, part of that process of classification which is such a particular feature of the history of singing in the nineteenth century. It is the relics of his style and Mario's that survive in the recordings of three elegant but rather tremulous tenors of the early years of the gramophone: Fernando de Lucia, Alessandro Bonci and Giuseppe Anselmi. Perhaps, too, we can get some idea of the effect of Donzelli and Tamberlik's singing by listening to the heroic and yet smoother voice production of Tamagno.

At the same time, a new and more precisely defined classification was taking place among female voices. In the eighteenth century, as we have noted above, the castrati based much of their eloquence, in particular their command of bravura, on the full exploitation of the chest register. It was their example which was still implicit in the style and method of the three foremost prima donnas at the beginning of the nineteenth century. Isabella Colbran, Giuditta Pasta and Maria Malibran all had low voices, and their high notes were by consensus of opinion the products of art rather than nature, which is why they soon proved unequal to the demands made on them. Such notes were suitable purely for ornamentation; since they were not the characteristic part of the voice, they were neither brilliant nor powerful enough for bravura and declamation. From the second quarter of the century, there gradually came into prominence a new, high type of female voice, which, though scarcely capable of imbuing the roles of Semiramide and Norma with the dramatic accents that singers like Colbran and Pasta had given such parts, none the less had the great advantage of being able to soar easily and effectively over a full orchestra. Being at the same time an unambiguously feminine sound, psychologically, it suited that quintessentially Romantic conceit, the fey and hapless heroine: for example, Bellini's Amina and Elvira and Donizetti's Lucia. Unequivocally sopranos were: Henrietta Sontag, Fanny Persiani, Jenny Lind and Adelina Patti. Long before the end of the nineteenth century theirs had become, in the persons of Nilsson, Gerster, Sembrich and Melba, the prevailing type of prima donna voice. Low voices did not disappear, at least not at once, but as time passed they were gradually reduced to secondary parts. The great contralto Marietta Alboni, a favourite singer of Rossini, who in her youth had sung Anna Bolena, Semiramide, Norma, Amina and Marie in *La Fille du régiment* with the aid of liberal transpositions, was eventually obliged by changing taste to confine herself to the lay figures nowadays associated with the contralto voice.

Gradually we can trace the emergence of the vocal categories familiar today. Previously there had been only four: soprano, alto, tenor and bass. Even that classification was far from exact. Among the castrati—not unnaturally—there was a great variety of different ranges of voice; yet the terminology used by contemporary writers—Quantz, for example, who described Senesino as a low soprano when his highest note was only F at the top of the stave—is hardly suggestive. The fact is, more rigorous classification did not recommend itself. In the days of the opera seria a great virtuoso made whatever adjustments were necessary to fit a part to his voice, transposing it up or down if he felt more comfortable, possessing himself of anyone else's music if it took his fancy, and jettisoning anything that did not suit him. This was the age of the transposition, a device invented for singers. Today, when it is resorted to only rarely, even covertly, it may seem hard to believe that it was once as much the rule as the exception, that Handel, Hasse, Gluck, Mozart and Rossini were content if their music was well sung, and the singer would not be straight-jacketed into an uncongenial key.

As the high soprano emerged to prima donna status and possessed herself of the brilliant repertory, the influence of the French taste which had produced the dramatic tenor now introduced his counterpart in a dramatic soprano, a voice higher than that of Colbran, Pasta and Malibran, with the emphasis shifted from the chest to the medium and head registers, thus able to satisfy the demand for powerful, as well as brilliant, high notes. This singer found full expression for her talent in the works of the Grand Opéra, in particular those of Halévy and Meyerbeer. One of the earliest of the type was Rosine Stolz, who was the original Odette in Halévy's *Charles VI* and also created Zaïde in Donizetti's Grand Opéra *Dom Sébastien*. A comparison between the vocal writing here with that of his Italian operas, *Lucrezia Borgia*, *Roberto Devereux* or *Anna Bolena*, shows how the line had been simplified, how much greater was the proportion of concerted music; the singer had particular need of a commanding as well as a brilliant voice. More famous even than Stolz was Cornélie-Marie Falcon, whose name came to be identified with a type of repertory only a few parts of which she created or sang. Of these the most significant was Valentine in Meyerbeer's *Les Huguenots,* a dominating role in the opera and a challenge for every dramatic soprano for the next three-quarters of a century. In it, for the first time, the characteristics of the new dramatic soprano voice were most completely exemplified, most fully developed. A simple, unflorid line, though written predominately in the middle register, sweeps right through the entire voice, with frequent flights above the stave, including a number of high Cs, one of these sustained for four measures. Transposition is virtually impossible, since the part is almost entirely concerted music; unlike the other two, much smaller, soprano roles in *Les Huguenots*, the Queen and the Page Urbain, Valentine has no famous aria. In a note which appears at the end of certain early editions of the score, Meyerbeer gives some guidance in the matter of casting the roles, in order to contrast the colours of the different types of soprano voice effectively. It was an example that hastened further vocal classification, regularising, in particular, the position of that poor relative the lyric soprano—she who had not the voice for dramatic roles, nor the agility for the 'coloratura' repertory. It was not, however, until Gounod's Marguerite that she was finally legitimised.

The dramatic soprano was not solely a French phenomenon; one of the first and greatest was a German. In the eighteenth century there had been several outstanding German virtuosi, notably Regina Mingotti and Mme Mara, but these were both, as their *nomi di teatro* suggest, wholly Italian in style; it was not until after the beginning of the nineteenth century that there appeared a German singer whose style and method was totally the product of the demands of German music. It has been said that Wilhelmine Schroeder-Devrient was more actress than singer—a German Mrs Siddons. It is hardly surprising that the influence of the dramas of Goethe, Lessing and Schiller should have been an inspiration for any artist. It was their lyrics which were the direct stimulus of the song literature of Beethoven, Schubert and Schumann; works which later in her career Schroeder-Devrient was to declaim to great effect. Initially her operatic repertory included Beethoven's Fidelio, Weber's Agathe and Euryanthe and the heroines of Spontini (court composer to Frederick William IV of Prussia), with usually less than successful forays into the

Italian repertory. In due course, however, as she herself had been fired by the works of her contemporaries, so, in turn, she became the inspiration for Germany's greatest operatic genius, Richard Wagner. For her he wrote Adriano in *Rienzi*, Senta and Venus. By all accounts her vocalism in these left something to be desired. Even so, she charted a territory for a succession of great singers who were to follow on, the greatest of them being Teresa Tietjens and Lilli Lehmann. The former was a consummate vocalist, who sang with equal success in the German repertory from Mozart's Pamina to Wagner's Ortrud, and was also a notable Norma, Lucrezia Borgia and Semiramide—so much so that Patti, in spite of the natural ascendancy of her voice, refrained from adding the last-named part to her repertory until after Tietjens's untimely death. Though we may question whether Lilli Lehmann's voice was ever as fine a natural instrument as Tietjens's, the range and variety of her repertory was certainly astonishing: 128 roles, including the Queen of the Night, all three Brünnhildes, Norma, Violetta and even Carmen.

The Italian dramatic soprano was a much later arrival than the French or German, and was not completely typified until the later part of the nineteenth century and the verismo school. The modern mezzo soprano was also an Italian development, a twentieth-century solution to a nineteenth-century problem: how to make an effect in roles like Donizetti's Leonora, Ponchielli's Laura and especially Verdi's Eboli and Amneris, equivocal parts that in early years were quite often sung by sopranos and sometimes so marked in scores, and yet should still provide the necessary contrast in timbre and character with other higher soprano roles. It was not a problem that contraltos, like Alboni, Scalchi and Ravogli, could easily cope with; they had neither the power nor the stamina in the upper part of their voices for such passages as the Judgment scene from *Aida*, Eboli's 'O don fatale', or the love duet from Act 2 of *La Gioconda*. The solution was a voice which, though naturally darker than a soprano, was able to ride the full strength of an orchestra by taking up the middle register where a contralto would not dare. Here again, the chest register, which had produced the old-fashioned contralto voice (of which the two greatest examples on record are Ernestine Schumann-Heink and Clara Butt), was neglected in favour of the development of the middle and head registers, mostly the former, to satisfy that demand for 'the clarion delivery of high notes'. The virtual disappearance of the contralto voice is not, as is sometimes suggested, the result of a mutation in nature, but of a change in taste and the disappearance of a repertory.

From the middle of the nineteenth century, the production of brilliant and strenuous high notes, particularly in the Italian repertory, was a pre-occupation of the lower male voices as well, especially of the baritone. In the days of Handel, and even of Mozart, this classification, as such, did not exist, although many roles loosely designated as first bass parts, such as Figaro and Don Giovanni, we should today describe as falling within the baritone range, i.e. between approximately the A at the bottom of the bass clef, to the first G, sometimes A flat, above middle C. Figaro in Rossini's *Barbiere* is generally considered the first real baritone role. In spite of some uncharacteristic high notes in 'Largo al factotum' (for which it has been conjectured there were anomalous reasons),† during the first generation of its existence the bulk of the singer's work lay in the middle of the voice, following the classical example of Handel and Mozart. It was not until the time of Donizetti that there began a gradual upward shift in the emphasis of the writing. This was continued by Verdi, whose partiality for the top fifth of the voice is nowhere more apparent than in his baritone parts. For a time there was an attempt to resist it; at first Tamburini and Ronconi declined to sing Carlo Quinto in *Ernani*, on the grounds that it lay uncomfortably high in their voices, but as soon as it became obvious how effectively Verdi wrote, they capitulated. The effect on the art of singing of staking everything on the production of the high notes, in great part the responsibility of Verdi, was commented upon by Bernard Shaw, in typical vein:

> The whole secret of healthy vocal writing lies in keeping the normal plane of the music, and therefore the bulk of the singer's work, in the middle of the voice. Unfortunately the middle of the voice is not the prettiest part of it; and in immature or badly and insufficiently trained voices it is often the weakest part. There is, therefore, a constant temptation to composers to use the upper fifth of the voice almost exclusively and this is exactly what Verdi did without remorse. He practically treated the upper fifth as the whole voice, and pitched his melodies in the middle of it instead of in the middle of the entire compass, the result being a frightful strain on the singer.[28]

All of which assisted in the production of what Shaw noted elsewhere, a generation of baritones

† These are discussed fully by Henry Pleasants in his article 'How high the Gs in *Figaro*,' *Music and Musicians*, December 1969.

who seemed to be unable to do anything but bluster and rant and whose voices quickly degenerated into tremulous wrecks. In order to accommodate the high tessitura, the finest heroic baritones contrived to blend into their high notes some of the quality of the head register. We shall find this skill exemplified to perfection in the recordings of Mattia Battistini. Though Battistini's career commenced in the 1870s, he was still able almost half a century later to astound audiences with his mastery of every graduation of the messa di voce. In the upper part of his voice, he could take the thinnest thread of falsetto, and reinforce it with chest resonance, until by contrast it seemed of heroic proportions, the sound so virile that it was difficult to believe that its origins were based in the head rather than the chest register.

It is typical of Verdi that he should have passed over Battistini, as creator of the role of Iago, in favour of Victor Maurel. Though Battistini was the finer singer, in 1887 he was probably not yet a fully mature artist, able to rival so skilful and effective a stage personality as Victor Maurel. Though in earlier years Verdi had greatly admired Jenny Lind and Adelina Patti, he had always put a premium on dramatic effect (witness his much-quoted letter on the subject of a singer to create the role of Lady Macbeth), and in later years he specially admired Gemma Bellincioni in her interpretation of Violetta. Hers was a remarkable personality, one which covered a multitude of vocal sins and compensated to a considerable extent for the lack of a first-class voice or technique.

Paradoxically, Verdi's great contemporary, Wagner, who was so often blamed for the decline in the art, was more preoccupied with beautiful singing. In his directives to singers he was always holding up the Italian style as the example he wanted copying in his own operas. In 1881, while in Rome, he heard Battistini sing Wolfram in *Tannhäuser* at the Teatro Argentina, and though the opera was sung in Italian and Battistini transposed some of the music up, Wagner afterwards declared it the most beautiful interpretation of Wolfram he had ever heard—sung as he had only dreamed it could be. Great men generally suffer from the activities of their disciples, and none more so than Wagner. Much of the blame attached to him directly may, in fact, be traced to the baneful influence of Julius Kniese, principal repetiteur at Bayreuth after Wagner's death and close confidant of Cosima. The deliberate rejection of the traditional legato style in favour of 'Sprechgesang' was Kniese's decision, 'in order', as he put it, 'to convey the illusion of a dialogue in the declamatory voice parts'. It is worth noting Wagner's own words on this subject, in a letter to Liszt, dated 8 September 1850; there is no reason to believe that he ever changed his mind:

> I have been so intent upon weighing and indicating the verbal emphasis of speech, that the singers need only sing the notes, exactly according to their value in the given tempo, in order to get precisely by that means the declamatory expression.[29]

Apart from being unlovely to listen to, the 'Sprechgesang' style is also unvocal. Kniese has been accused, probably with justification, of being responsible for the premature loss of voice of the tenors Erik Schmedes and Ernst van Dyck, and of the baritone Anton van Rooy. Even so, Wagner himself cannot be entirely absolved from responsibility. The fact is that though he did not, as Shaw pointed out, write like Verdi at the edge of the voice, but like Handel in the middle of it, unlike Handel he gave his singers little relief; sometimes they are required to sing for half an hour without a break, all the while having to contend with the largest and most elaborate symphony orchestra that until then had been introduced into the opera house. For supermen and superwomen—Leider, Melchior and Flagstad, for example—this has been no problem: they have been able to manage a shapely cantilena and declaim authoritatively without regard to the noise the orchestra was making. Outside their ranks, however, and in general, the standard of singing in the operas of Wagner has been lower than in those of other composers. On the less well-endowed, the large orchestras and the Sprechgesang style have had a cumulatively disagreeable effect, encouraging a crude attack and forceful declamation, producing voices alternatively hoarse and racked with tremolo, which eventually were unable to sing in any other way or sing the music of any other composer even tolerably.

There does survive, however, a small but interesting legacy of recordings that suggests, after all, that it need not be impossible to reconcile the physical demands of Wagner's music with the old Italian legato style he admired. In the early years of this century, when the process of popularising Wagner's operas was still in full swing and it was the custom as often as not to give his works in the vernacular, a number of well-known Italian artists recorded excerpts from *Lohengrin, I Maestri Cantori, Valchiria* and *Sigfrido*. It has been the fashion to treat these slightingly, or at best smile on them indulgently. And certainly some do contain aberrations of style; yet they also preserve things of real beauty. For all the extravagant rubato, it is doubtful if there is any other version of the great love duet from *Lohengrin* more lovingly sung than that by Fernando de Lucia and Josefina Huguet. And surely Wagner himself would have approved of Giuseppe Borgatti's clear but never crude delivery of the Canto di Primavera from *Valchiria,* with the implicit legato underpinning the whole of it—an interpretation which demonstrates that a mere mortal may be expressive in this music without wrenching every muscle in his throat. Still, for this example to be followed today, for the lyrical style to be re-introduced into Wagner's operas, a cover would have to be put over the orchestra as it is at Bayreuth, and there does not seem any great likelihood of that.

It is not surprising that the wider pre-occupations of society at large should have been so closely mirrored in the various developments of an art form as social as opera. At no time was this more so than in the nineteenth century, when the dominating pre-occupation of European politics, the various struggles for national independence, was reflected in the gradual emergence of a gamut of different operatic, and hence vocal, styles—in particular in France, Germany and Russia. Previously, until Mozart's day, except in France (and, as Dr Burney noted, French singers were something of a bad joke), the hegemony of the Italian style was complete. By 1900, though there were still a few practitioners left, it was in eclipse, its example compromised by every composer and every different national style; finally even, from Verdi's day, by the Italians themselves. Which is not to say that the music then being composed for the voice was aggressively anti-vocal; in fact virtually none of it was (that was to be a characteristically twentieth-century development), but much of it was unvocal in conception, as in the operas of Spontini, Beethoven, Weber and Berlioz, where the essentially instrumental melodies are far more effective when played in the orchestra: to take one example, the lovely melody from Weber's *Oberon,* first heard in the Overture on the clarinet and then taken up by the strings to such enchanting effect. How different when it reappears in Huon's First Act aria 'From boyhood trained in tented field'. Reintroduced by the cello, it sounds as well as before. But when the singer takes it up, on the words 'A milder light, a milder beam' the effect is quite spoilt: the voice is strangled by the altitudinous tessitura and the wide instrumental intervals. It was not just in musical matters that the various national styles obtruded into the vocal art. The languages themselves modified it. Into it were assimilated such less than pleasing characteristics as the French nasal tone, the German hard consonants and the Spanish aspirate. By the later nineteenth century, the classical style, where it survived, as in the singing of Adelina Patti, came to be called 'bel canto', a term invented at that time to distinguish it from much of what was then being passed off as beautiful singing. By the time the gramophone began to keep records, there were relatively few singers left 'capable', in the words of Hanslick, 'of offering an utterly individual pleasure almost independent of the composition at hand'.[30] If the great tradition was breaking down, it did not disappear at once and the precepts which had formed the basis of fine singing since Tosi's day, and even earlier, were at any rate still being actively promoted, in particular through the writings and teaching of the younger Manuel Garcia and his pupils.

No record of singing would be complete without an account, albeit a cursory one, of the principal members of the Garcia family. It was their influence throughout the nineteenth century, first in exemplifying, later in teaching the finest traditions of their art in the face of rapidly developing and diverse vocal styles, that we can still hear in recordings made either by their pupils, or by their pupils' pupils. The founder of the family was Manuel Garcia, the virtuoso who created several of Rossini's tenor roles, notably Almaviva in *Barbiere*, was especially admired as Otello, and even with suitable transpositions sang Mozart's Don Giovanni. He appeared with equal success from Naples to Paris and London and even farther afield; he gave New York its first-ever taste of Italian opera in 1825, performing several of his own works, singing the principal roles himself, opposite his greatest pupil, his elder daughter, Maria Malibran. Of all the Garcias', Malibran's career was the most sensational. She studied not only with her father, but also with Velluti, the composer Zingarelli, and, her brother tells us, anyone else her father thought clever enough to teach her something! By all accounts the instrument itself was as much the product of unceasing labour as any effusion of nature; it was a low voice with an artfully acquired extension of head notes. According to her brother she could sing anything. She was certainly artistically ambitious, appearing with equal success in the

role of the youthful Rosina in *Barbiere* and the old maid Fidalma in *Matrimonio Segreto,* and she was not only a comedienne; it was in the tragic roles so beloved of the Romantics, such as Tancredi, Norma and particularly Desdemona in Rossini's *Otello* that she made the greatest impression. Of this last role, she herself wrote: 'In the final scene I often feel as if I too were about to be murdered, and act accordingly.'[31] It was the sort of heady talk that the Romantic Age loved, and when she perished at the early age of 28, following a riding accident, she became another of its legendary victims and like Chatterton, Shelley and Byron was apotheosised in her turn. Whether, had she lived, her voice could have survived such a surfeit of temperament is questionable. Increasing instances of voicelessness in the last years of her life, as at the Scala premiere of *Maria Stuarda*, suggest otherwise.

The career of Garcia's younger daughter, Pauline Viardot, was also cut short, not however by an early death—she lived into her ninetieth year—but by the failure of her voice to sustain the exacting demands she made of it in a repertory that embraced Amina in *Sonnambula*, Fidès in *Le Prophète*, Rosina in *Barbiere*, Gluck's Orphée and Verdi's Lady Macbeth. She created the part of Fidès, and it seems likely that a composer as concerned with effect as Meyerbeer preserved some of the essential characteristics of her voice in the writing of the part. Like her sister's, it was basically a low instrument, as Chorley tells us, extending from the G below middle C to high C, and above that by fabrication to the F in alt. This is confirmed by the music of Fidès, lying predominantly in the contralto range, the upper extension, in head voice, being kept solely for ornamental purposes, as in the cabaletta from Act 5, 'Comme l'éclair'. Further confirmation is provided in a letter Viardot wrote to the conductor Arditi, advising him of the transpositions she proposed to make in the music of Lady Macbeth: 'Vieni t'affretta' down a minor third, the Sleepwalking Scene down a tone. Though she was not ambitious in the head-strong Romantic fashion of her sister, she closely identified herself with the leading musical figures of her day. As well as Fidès, she created the title-role in Gounod's *Sapho*—in fact was largely responsible for encouraging Gounod to try his hand at opera in the first place. She also took part in Berlioz's famous revivals of Gluck's *Orphée* and *Alceste*, and had it not been for the endless procrastination of the authorities, who had no wish to mount the piece, she would almost certainly have created Dido in *Les Troyens*. After her retirement from opera,

Brahms wrote the *Alto Rhapsody* for her, and Saint-Saëns tells us it was her voice he had in mind when composing the role of Dalila. In her own home she once sang through the Love Duet from *Tristan* with Liszt at the piano and Wagner himself as Tristan; there too she organised the first performances of Bach's cantatas heard in Paris. Perhaps *Orphée* was her supreme achievement. Chorley tells us that her rendering of the aria 'Amour viens rendre à mon âme' was the very last example to be heard of one of the great glories of the old Italian school, the canto di bravura, which Viardot's brother Manuel Garcia the younger describes as a distinguishing feature of the singing of Catalani, Malibran and Grisi.[35] How much direct tuition Viardot received is not certain; it would seem that, like Patti, she imbibed much of her art at her mother's knee. It was probably her brother rather than her father who later put some order into her studies. Following the loss of her voice and her French husband's dismissal as Director of the Baden-Baden opera, on the outbreak of the Franco-Prussian war she began another career as a teacher of singing, first in London, and then, when hostilities had finally ceased, in Paris. Her influence as a teacher can be traced in a large number of recordings made by various pupils.

Unlike his father and sisters, the younger Garcia was not a successful performer. As a boy he had taken lessons from his father, Zingarelli and Panseron; later he studied with Fétis. After a brief career as a singer followed by a period in the French army, he commenced his real vocation—one that was to last more than fifty years—as the outstanding singing teacher of the century. Throughout his long life (he lived to be a hundred and one) he attempted to establish, in the words of his pupil, Salvatore Marchesi, 'a rational physiological system for the production and development of the human voice'.[36] He tried to do this by applying that typically nineteenth-century solution to all problems, science: by inventing the laryngoscope (essentially a dentist's mirror with a long handle). With it, for the first time, it was possible to watch the vocal cords in action, to hold the mirror up to nature. Unfortunately, he never did realise his expectations. In spite of the careful methodology of his famous treatise *L'Art du chant*, it encouraged the student to think of singing independently of the body, as the consequence of a mechanical operation rather than simply as a physical reflex to a mental conception. In particular, his use of the term coup de glotte caused no end of controversy. A correct attack is only possible with the smooth and even exhalation of the breath, and it is not contrived in the throat by some perceptible action of the glottis: a fact that Garcia was at pains to convey directly to more than two generations of his students. Unfortunately, his scientific description of the reflex action of the glottis when the attack is correct, which is what he called the coup de glotte, was confusing. It led to generations of students and teachers consciously trying to produce in the throat the image the term suggested and producing instead a crude—and worse, an injurious—attack. By focusing attention on the larynx, the transformations of which, as Rameau put it, are not at our disposal, Garcia unwittingly made singers too aware of what was useless to them—like the long-distance runner who, when the elaborate musculature of the legs was explained to him, could hardly manage a step thereafter without falling over. The fact is, that to be expressive singing must be, or at any rate sound to be, spontaneous. The danger of the scientific approach, of the laryngoscope, was that it held up the mirror not only to nature but to artifice as well.

It would be wrong, however, to think that Garcia's method was faulty. The exercises that form the main part of Volume One of *L'Art du chant* are as valid today as they ever were, providing a complete plan of study for the correct production and development of the voice. Volume Two, which deals with the words and music, is still, after more than a century and a quarter, the only comprehensive and reliable guide in matters of style and execution that survives from the early nineteenth century, an invaluable aid to musicologists, critics and musicians interested in a full stylistically correct realisation of the music rather than a literal reading of the score. In it, Garcia deals with such essential matters as phrasing, diction, where to breathe effectively and grammatically, how to use rubato and portamento, how to discriminate between staccato, marcato and martellato, the correct execution of trills, appoggiaturas, mordents and other ornaments. In dealing with embellishments, he gives examples of the art of his father, Malibran, Velluti, Galli, David, Pasta and many other famous singers. Regrettably this part of the treatise has long been out of print. Yet it ought to be readily available to every singer, teacher and conductor.

PART I

The Old School

1. Patti, Albani and Sembrich

While Garcia was teaching the method and style of the old school to increasingly indifferent generations of students, its finest exponent, some would say its last, was not actually a pupil of his. From her adult debut, at the age of 16, at New York's old Academy of Music in 1859, ADELINA PATTI (1843–1919) was the Queen of Song, and during fifty years her name was a by-word for her art; indeed the term 'bel canto' was first generally used in connexion with her singing. Patti's reign rivalled Victoria's in breadth as well as length. From San Francisco to St Petersburg audiences flocked to hear her, and see her; at the party in the first act of *Traviata*, she flaunted a Queen's ransom in diamonds, protected by a posse of detectives trying to pass themselves off as Violetta's guests—did they sing, too? Her rendering of 'Home, Sweet Home', as Shaw put it, brought tears to the eyes of club-loving cynics: her own home 'be it ever so humble' was a French-style chateau set down in the hills of South Wales, one of the spoils of a career that had earned the diva a fortune probably not equalled by any opera singer since. In his memoirs, the impresario Col. Mapleson gives a frank, but engaging, account of his dealings with Patti; her business acumen seems to have been not one whit less remarkable than her singing. On tour in the United States in the 1880s she was getting up to $5,000 a performance. When a journalist chided her for earning more in one night than the President did in a whole year, she made the obvious rejoinder, 'Well, let him sing!'

Like Malibran before her, Patti was born into a family of singers, but her achievement was more the product of a bountiful nature than of hours of solfeggio and artful fabrication. She learned to sing as she had learned to walk and talk, by imitating what was going on around her, which is why even as an old lady, her art, and even parts of her voice, remained fresh and spontaneous; it was to the manner born.

Nature had not only given her a lovely voice . . . She could surmount without labour difficulties that took others hours and hours of study and hard striving. By the time Maurice Strakosch took her in hand, at the age of seven, her mastery of vocal technique was well on the way to completion. Correct breathing, scales, trills, ornaments, fioriture of every kind, all came naturally to her and required only the finishing touches. She had just to be shown the various roulades and cadenzas to put them into her voice.'[1]

Which is not to suggest that she put no effort into her art; she must have applied herself with great diligence to be able to sing with effect principal roles in sixteen different operas in her debut season, including *Lucia, Trovatore, Don Pasquale, Ernani, Elisir d'amore, Traviata* and *Don Giovanni*. If she was not ambitious in the way of Malibran or Viardot, she was not, as has been suggested since, only interested in display vehicles. As well as the *Trovatore* Leonora and Elvira in *Ernani*, she attempted other dramatic parts: Valentine in *Les Huguenots*, the title-role in Verdi's *Giovanna d'Arco*, Aida, and even Carmen. Such enterprise was praiseworthy if misguided; the child of nature does not make an effective tragedienne. Her lightweight instrument, which in youthful days extended with ease to F in alt, was best suited to the lyrical and brilliant repertory: Zerlina in *Don Giovanni*, Rosina in *Barbiere*, Amina in *Sonnambula* and Gounod's Marguerite.

If Patti's range was not all-embracing, it was, within its limits, as near a perfect thing as nature and art could create. Verdi described her in a letter to Giulio Ricordi, as . . .

. . . perfectly organised (with) perfect equilibrium between singer and actress, a born artist in every sense of the word. . . . I was struck dumb not only by her marvellous technique but by certain dramatic traits in which she revealed herself as a great actress. I remember the chaste and modest demeanour with

1 Adelina Patti as Amina in *Sonnambula*

2 Patti as Rosina

which, in *La Sonnambula*, she lay on the soldier's bed, and how, in *Don Giovanni*, she left the libertine's room corrupted. I remember a certain reaction of hers during Don Bartolo's aria in *Il Barbiere* and, above all, in the recitative preceding the quartet in *Rigoletto*, when her father points out her lover in the tavern and says 'And you still love him?', and she replies 'I love him'. I cannot describe the sublime effect of those words as she sang them.[2]

Her variety of expression was the result of infinitely refined vocal colouring, the vitality of her interpretations produced by a voice alive to every rhythmic subtlety. Unfortunately much of the brilliance, the command of ornamentation which Klein refers to, was a thing of the past by the time she came to make recordings. Still her singing remains more affecting in itself than anyone else's on records. In her recordings, we can hear so many of the ancient graces of singing; here are the real

portamento style, the elegant turns and mordents, the trill free of any suggestion of mechanical contrivance. Behind the singing we can almost see the face, even if, by 1905, it was that of an old lady and heavily enamelled.

The story has been told many times of how, finally, she was coaxed into leaving an indelible impression of what had made nearly three generations of opera goers rise to their feet shouting bravas. When she declined to go down to City Road, then the headquarters of the G & T company, the mountain went to Craig-y-nos; and there, in a spare bedroom of her Welsh castle, she was able, as she felt inclined, to inscribe some of her favourite songs and arias, tactfully assisted at the piano by the ever-obliging Landon Ronald, ready to translate, for example, the Jewel Song, into whatever key the great lady and nature could agree upon. When the little trumpet gave forth the tones of her voice, Patti

3 Patti as Zerlina

4 Patti as Leonora in *Trovatore*

went into transports of joy. 'Ah, mon Dieu', she cried, 'maintenant je comprends pourquoi je suis Patti. Ah, oui. Quelle voix! Quelle artiste! Enfin, je comprends tout!'[3]

Though the records preserve, as Klein delicately put it, only the *beaux restes* of Patti's voice, the interpretations remain stylistically of the utmost importance. Her recording of 'Casta Diva' is a link in a chain leading back directly to Bellini. She studied this aria, by all accounts the first piece of music she ever sang, with Maurice Strakosch, accompanist to Guiditta Pasta, creator of Norma, and the embellishments in the second verse are Pasta's. From Strakosch too, she learned 'Batti, batti'. It is a point of some significance that Pasta sang the role of Zerlina in London, only twenty-five years after the death of Mozart. It is more than probable therefore that Patti's choice of a fast tempo in the concluding 6/8 section is a traditional one that goes back to

Mozart's day, and not merely an elderly diva's caprice, which in any case would seem unlikely when she can hardly manage it at that speed.

Patti's operatic recordings, notwithstanding the all-too-obvious depradations of age, contain many wonderful things; the trill and flourish at the beginning of the Jewel Song has never been executed by any other singer with such elegance and finesse. How perfectly she captures the mood in Thomas's beautiful setting of Mignon's song. Perhaps best of all is the subtle variety of graces and rubato in that most exquisite interpretation of Amina's sleepwalking aria. In the songs we have a recollection of all that was eloquent in the music of the salon; the abiding charm of her accents in Tosti's 'Serenata', 'Robin Adair', 'On the banks of Allen Water', 'Kathleen Mavourneen'—here is Garcia's canto di grazia exemplified to perfection; and in 'La Calasera' and 'Il Bacio', more than an echo of the *élan vital* which sustained her art through half a century. That witty and shrewd observer of the musical scene, the American violinist Albert Spalding, has left us a vivid glimpse of the incomparable old lady in action, at just about the time she made her recordings:

> Her performance was something I shall never forget, it was the masterly campaign of a general whose depleted army, ragged in equipment, lacking munitions, has to be supplemented by the genius of cunning and strategy. Lee in the battles before Appomatox, Napoleon at Waterloo, must have whispered some of their secrets in her ear—or perhaps she could have taught them a lesson or two! She was reckless enough to include an old war-horse, Arditi's 'Il Bacio'. There were high notes that simply could not be reached, scales and roulades that creaked at the hinges. It promised to be lamentable. But we reckoned without Patti. When she got to a passage, where she sensed difficulty, even disaster, she employed her fan with telling effect. She would start the scale or arpeggio with great aplomb, the fan outstretched in her hand slowly unfolding. This she would continue until the point beyond which lay danger. Then, with a sudden gesture up would fly her arm, the fan snapping shut with a click, the audience bursting into tumultuous applause drowning out voice and orchestra, thus did triumph a fioritura or high note that never was.[4]

Throughout her long career, Patti's supremacy was successively, though not successfully, challenged by many outstanding singers; among them Ilma di Murska, Christine Nilsson, Etelka Gerster, and later Emma Albani, Marcella Sembrich and Nellie Melba. The last three left recordings giving us some idea of the strength of their challenge. The eldest, EMMA ALBANI (1847–1930), was only four years Patti's junior. One of the first of the important American divas, she was born near Montreal. In 1867, she came to Europe, studying first with the great tenor Duprez in Paris; and then, at the suggestion of the composer Prince Poniatowski, she went to Milan to work with the elder Lamperti. Francesco Lamperti was the doyen of singing teachers in Italy—to Milan what Garcia was to London. In his youth he had worked with Pasta at her academy at Como and heard most of the great singers of that era. From 1850, he was Professor of Singing at the Milan Conservatory. Like Garcia too, he wrote a treatise on the art of singing. His most outstanding pupils included the tenor Italo Campanini, Albani, Marcella Sembrich and William Shakespeare, who later became one of the leading teachers in London and author of a number of books

on singing. Albani enjoyed a special place in Lamperti's affections; by his own acknowledgement, she was one of the finest exponents of his method, and to her he dedicated his essay on the trill.

She made a highly successful debut at Messina, Sicily, in 1870, thereafter touring Italy earning golden opinions wherever she went. Stories of a new diva were not slow to filter through to London, reaching, in particular, ears that were never far off the ground, those of the redoubtable Colonel Mapleson. Mapleson invited her to London. Unfortunately, at least for him, when she arrived at Victoria and ordered the cab to take her to the Italian Opera, instead of going to Her Majesty's the driver took her to Covent Garden and straight into the arms of its director, Frederick Gye. Gye lost no time in getting Albani's signature down on a five-year contract.

For her debut she chose *Sonnambula*. The evening was a great success, as the *Illustrated London News* has recorded:

> To a very prepossessing personal appearance, Mlle. Albani adds the possession of a voice of exquisite quality, the pure melodious charm of which is allied to sufficient power for the effective execution of the most brilliant and florid bravura passages ... The delivery of the first few bars of recitative at once showed off the beauty and sympathetic tone of voice and the accuracy of intonation. The applause which followed these initiatory phrases was significant of the recognition of an artist of exceptionally high class. The compass commanded by Mlle. Albani is upwards of two octaves to E flat in alt. The singer's success was great and complete.[5]

During the ensuing seasons, she confirmed this initial impression with appearances in Paris, New York, St Petersburg and Moscow, at first in the lyric repertory, but by degrees relinquishing Amina, Lucia, Martha, Linda, Elvira and Gilda for Elsa, Elisabeth, Eva, Senta, and eventually even Isolde. In part, this desertion of the repertory which most naturally suited her had to do with the death of Teresa Tietjens. Albani wanted to take Tietjens's place as the leading oratorio and dramatic singer of this country, but another more weighty factor was her failure to supplant Patti in the public's affections, in spite of her marriage, in 1879, to Frederick Gye's son Ernest and her inevitably privileged position at Covent Garden as 'padroncina'. Unable to beat Patti at her own game, she determined to go where she knew that lady either could not or would not follow. It does not seem to have been an entirely successful move. The strength of Albani's voice was in the head register, as Klein tells us:

> Neither then nor subsequently was there much power in the chest or lower medium notes . . . those registers had been sacrificed for the sake of adding resonance to the more acute section of the voice.[6]

It was not long before the effects of too much strenuous music began to show up in her singing. At La Scala, in 1880, as Lucia, she did not repeat her earlier Italian successes. Whether the hissing was on her account or because of the inadequacy of the

5 Emma Albani

tenor Aramburo is not established, but certainly in Brussels the following year, in the same role, the reception was unquestionably hostile. When Hanslick came to London in 1886, he commended her as the best singer to be heard at Covent Garden in the absence of Patti and praised her accomplishments: in particular a 'splendidly schooled' voice, 'genuine musical sensibility' and 'true artistry'; but he noted that she '[was] past her prime, and circumspect in her employment of an upper register now susceptible to fatigue'.[7] From that time, she began increasingly to confine her activities to the sphere of influence dominated by her husband's interests. Though she remained a popular idol in England and America, even in those countries not every theatre regarded her presence on the roster of artists as a prerequisite for success. At the time of the opening of the Metropolitan, in 1883, there was some question of the younger Gye becoming its first Director, but when he insisted on a place for his wife the board demurred, for they wanted at least Nilsson, and preferably Patti, to open the new house. As a result Gye did not go to New York and Albani did not go to the Met until 1891, by which time, as David Bispham noted, 'she was no longer at home as Isolde'.[8] Five years later she seems to have realised as much herself. Without any fuss she bade farewell to opera, to a career that had lasted twenty-six years, thenceforth confining herself to oratorio and concert work.

In her best years Albani's art had been characterised by deep sincerity, spontaneity and freshness, but as time went on she became a prey to mannerisms, in particular in the production of high notes, which she would slide up to and then back down from in the same fashion. Shaw heard her, in 1890, in a performance of Mendelssohn's *St Paul*:

> Mme. Albani pulled the music around in her accustomed fashion by hanging on to every note that showed off her voice, and her intonation compared with that of her colleagues was fallible, but she was equal to the occasion.[9]

As might be imagined, by the time she came to make her few recordings, more than a dozen years later, her singing could give little real pleasure. Unlike Patti she had no compensating charm of manner to offer, though occasionally there is some trace of the purity of tone that had once made her interpretations of Amina, Gilda, Desdemona, and Elsa so appropriate. Occasionally too, in a delicately executed figure such as the repeated upward arpeggio in the opening phrases of Chaminade's little song to summer, and in the same piece towards the end, where she just manages to turn a couple of trills neatly, we have evidence of the remains of a highly polished technique. But we shall listen in vain for any exceptional artistry, anything that could make endurable the incessant scoopings and slitherings, the uncertain intonation. These are nowhere more prominently displayed than in the recording of her favourite, 'Angels ever bright and fair' from Handel's *Theodora*. It was this piece that she brought out on all occasions—all, that is, save one: her Farewell concert in 1911, when Patti condescended to appear. Patti took no fee, instead she took Albani's 'Angels'. No doubt poor Albani was content to pocket her resentment with the takings, for the fact is, by then she *was* poor. Unwise speculation in the market had lost her two fortunes and she was eventually reduced to eking out a miserable existence. By 1925, she was in such straits she went on to the music hall circuit. What must she have felt like? At 78 years of age what could have been left of her voice, as she tried to recall an echo of glories long passed away? When word of her predicament reached Melba, herself by then 64, Melba organised a special benefit, and by its ameliorating effects Albani was enabled to live out her last days in dignified retirement.

On 12 June 1880, the Polish soprano MARCELLA SEMBRICH (1858–1935) made her Covent Garden debut as Lucia. The next day the *Illustrated London News* noted that 'a third soprano of rare gifts and powers has been added to the establishment already in possession of Mesdames Patti and Albani'. Herman Klein describes her voice at that time:

> It was singularly entrancing. I was immensely struck with the vibrant quality and bell-like purity of her tone, her impeccable intonation, and the faultless accuracy of her scales. She had a perfect shake, and the masterful ease and facility of her execution was displayed over a compass extending to the F in alt.[10]

Sembrich had been a pupil of Francesco Lamperti's son Giovanni Battista, but in spite of very real successes during her first three seasons at Covent Garden, in the summer of 1883 she went again to Milan, this time to study with his father. In the same year she made her New York debut, also as Lucia, on the second night of the Met's inaugural season. There too she was warmly received, the *Tribune* critic, Krehbiel writing: 'A lovely singer with nearly all the graces of beautiful singing in the

6 Marcella Sembrich

Italian sense.'[11] She reserved the real sensation of the season for the benefit of the Met's manager, Henry Abbey, appearing for the occasion in the triple role of singer, violinist and pianist. Nearly fifty years later, W. J. Henderson, in his recollections of the evening, confirms that this was no mere feat of versatility:

> It had been announced that the brilliant Marcella Sembrich would play a violin solo. When she walked on stage with her instrument there were indulgent smiles and kindly applause. With the orchestra in the pit and Vianesi in the conductor's chair, Mme. Sembrich, with their support, played the Adagio and Finale of de Beriot's 7th concerto. It did not take any of us long to realise that she was an accomplished violinist. After being recalled eight or ten times, she sat down at the piano and played a Chopin mazurka, proving she was an equally fine pianist. After a dozen or more recalls, she walked to the footlights, Vianesi raised his baton, and she sang with unsurpassable beauty, 'Ah non giunge'. None of us who were there have ever forgotten the impressions of that evening.[12]

Nothing of her violin playing has survived on records, but she can be heard accompanying herself at the piano, in Pauline Viardot's vocal arrangement of Chopin's D major Mazurka, Op. 33 No. 2 (which she sings in A), and in 'The Maiden's Wish'.

Like Patti and Albani, Sembrich's reputation was as great on either side of the Atlantic. Unlike those ladies, however, she was of a more approachable and accommodating disposition, which in part explains why when Patti did eventually relinquish her sovereignty, it was not Sembrich who succeeded, but Melba; Sembrich was too amiable. In one aspect of her art she surpassed both of them: as a singer of songs. Her first New York recital at the Carnegie Hall, in March 1900, was a big success; and thereafter, and until her final retirement in 1917, her annual recital was one of the season's most popular events. On these occasions she was not content with the highways of song literature, but sought out matter which was unfamiliar, forgotten or new, acquiring much of the necessary variety of styles from her linguistic skill; she sang in, and spoke, Italian, German, French, Russian and English, as well as her native language. This skill enabled her to contrast and complement, so as to hold the attention of an audience for up to two hours of singing. She was one of the first great singers to popularise the song recital without that inevitable group of supporting artists which till then had provided relief, as much for the audience as for the protagonist.

Patti and Melba may have been the darlings of the gods, at any rate those at the opera house, but it was Sembrich who was the critics' favourite. While the former ladies' carryings-on were constantly being held up to ridicule, it is difficult to find anything but unqualified praise for Sembrich. Which is hardly surprising. In the age of Nevin, Rasbach and Stephen Foster, here was an artist daring not just Schubert, Schumann and Brahms, but also Wolf, Pfitzner and Strauss. Even when, as at the Met she did revert to type and got them to revive Donizetti's *La Fille du régiment* and *Elisir d'Amore*, such aberrations were overlooked in view of her services to Mozart. One of her earliest recordings is of a snippet out of the Queen of the Night's second aria, caught by Lionel Mapleson from aloft during a performance of the *Flauto Magico* at the Met in 1902. It was among his most successful efforts; we can hear Sembrich's brilliant staccati, ascending with ease to the D in alt, and also note an alternative popular at the time—the high D at the end. She was never able to create the same effect in the studio.

In her youth Sembrich's singing was frequently likened to Patti's, but on records the resemblance seems slight, and mostly a matter of range and repertory, and perhaps of temperament. The voice itself is more brilliant, and drier too, the tone less warm. The method has more in common with Albani, and this we may assume, at least in part, to be the result of the teaching of Lamperti. As with another Lamperti pupil, the American baritone David Bispham, there is a narrow and rapid vibrato, which she seems to have been able, to some extent at any rate, to intensify at will. A less engaging feature is the forceful attack, which we may presume to have been a contributory factor in the vocal crisis which she went through in 1891 and which, according to James Agate, was the result of singing too dramatically. By the time she came to make records, her voice had lost much of its early elasticity. The coloratura has become approximate flurries of notes; the once brilliant staccati seem on the verge of collapse; she has difficulty sustaining tones; and from about 1907 a crack has begun to open up in the middle register. In spite of the exemplary musical line and phrasing there is not in her recordings so much real portamento as we are accustomed to from the best singers of this period— less than in Melba's, much less than in Patti's. Too much should not be made of these failings. Away from those pieces that require the virtuosity of youth, there is still, in her singing, much of great interest and real beauty.

A less stunning but more affecting example of Sembrich's Mozart singing than the *Flauto Magico* fragment can be heard in a recording of the letter duet from *Figaro*, which she made with her partner of so many Met performances, Emma Eames. It is a wonderful demonstration of the lost art of duet singing, the result not just of a vocal and musical compatibility but, as Eames recalled years later in a radio interview, achieved only after endless rehearsals: 'I was afraid my bigger voice would drown her more delicate tones.'[13] In the theatre, their performance of this duet always made a great effect, Finck writes: 'It was almost impossible with eyes closed, to tell which of the two happened to be singing, so amazingly alike in timbre and golden purity were their voices.'[14] Sembrich used to make sense of the 'inescapable' encore by showing the audience that a blot of ink on the page made it necessary to re-write the letter!

Of her other operatic recordings the most important, if not the most attractive, is 'Una voce poco fa'; for here are preserved some of the changes Rossini made for Patti. Apparently Sembrich took these down while Patti was in full flight, much to that lady's surprise and, perhaps, not unalloyed pleasure. Sembrich recorded a cross-section of her recital repertory, from Arditi's 'Parla' (done with great charm and splendid gusto) to songs by Schubert, Schumann, Chopin, Brahms, Loewe and Strauss. In the opinion of her accompanist, Frank la Forge (a pupil of Leschetizky) the finest of these is an unpublished coupling of Reynaldo Hahn's setting of Victor Hugo's lines, 'Si mes vers', in which she makes a great effect by a chaste and simple delivery, singing in perfect French, the tone sweet but never cloying, followed by the second song from Schubert's *Die Schöne Müllerin*, 'Wohin?' Those accustomed to the modern way of doing it may be disturbed by the variety of rubato, by certain alterations in note-values. But they need not be: these are stylistically correct in music of that period. If they needed any defence, the interpretation itself would be justification enough—it is the most purely vocal on records, utterly spontaneous in delivery, its bejewelled brilliance rippling along like Müller's brook in the sunlight (and do not brooks have impediments and rapids?). How well her interpretation suits Richard Capell's analysis of the song:

> 'Wohin?' represents a free holiday between the young journeyman's two jobs; and there is unmistakeably in the music a different poetry from the cheerful opening song—a sense of sheer nature sweet and wild—it has escaped from man and rambles at its own sweet will.[15]

2. Melba and the Marchesi Pupils

After her retirement, Sembrich took up another career, as a teacher of singing at the Curtis Institute, Philadelphia, with a salary of $40,000 a year. Her most outstanding pupil was the Romanian soprano, Alma Gluck. Max de Schauensee, then a student at Curtis, recalls Sembrich in those days: 'a little old lady in a wig, with elaborate combs, a lorgnette—she had always been very short-sighted, and a kindly smile.' At just about the same time in Australia, another superannuated prima donna had started teaching; at the Albert Street Conservatorium in Melbourne. If NELLIE MELBA (1861–1931) ever wore a kindly smile, no one there seems to have remembered it; the fact is she had other more unforgettable characteristics. Three years younger than Sembrich, she made her debut

ten years after her, in 1887, also as Lucia, and yet nearly forty years later she was still singing, if not as she had once done, certainly with extraordinary vocal freshness. Next to Patti's, Melba's career was the most outstanding, her voice the most remarkable.

She had, she afterwards declared, realised as much even when she was a girl in Australia. Early on she had taken singing lessons. As to their value biographers disagree, but they did no lasting harm. At twenty-one, she got married to a certain Charles Armstrong, the penniless youngest son of an Irish baronet, a good-looking man—Melba always took a shine to a handsome face. He mistakenly supposed that she had put away her vocal ambitions and was prepared to spend her life with him, under corrugated iron, having babies (there was a son of the marriage), darning his socks and doing the usual things that pioneers' wives did in the Australia of the 1880s. He was soon to learn better.

Melba made her father take her to London. There she wholly failed to create an impression. Sir Arthur Sullivan heard her sing and did not even offer her a place in the G & S chorus; worse, Carl Rosa, the opera manager, entirely forgot the audition. Wise young woman that she was, Mrs Armstrong took the hint, and with her remaining funds she went to Paris, to the rue Jouffroy, where presided Mme Marchesi, the Directrice of the Ecole Marchesi and one of the foremost singing teachers of the day. The story has become a part of operatic legend: how Nellie sang through 'Ah! fors' è lui', how Mme Marchesi jumped up (it doesn't sound like her), ran upstairs (she was 65 at the time) calling out to her husband, 'Viens, viens, Salvatore, j'ai trouvé une étoile'—or something of the sort. The fact is, however garnished the details of that initial encounter, the substance of it is true. The ladies hit it off at once; they were two of a kind. Sparks no doubt flew—it was diamond cut diamond—but Marchesi could see that here was a young woman not only with the requisite voice, but with the brains to understand and the character to profit from the best advice. Any discussion of Melba's career, or those of Eames, Adams, Arnoldson, Calvé, Kurz, Licette and Scotney, all of whom at one time or another studied in the rue Jouffroy, would be incomplete without some account of Mme Marchesi and of her renowned method. Marchesi made an unforgettable impression on all her students. Eames, who later on, perhaps unwisely, came to reject much of her teaching, has left us a picture of her, which, though uncharitable, has about it the ring of truth:

> She was the ideal Prussian drill master, a woman of much character and one to gain a great ascendancy over her pupils. A thorough musician, she was an indefatigable worker. Her school was an example of discipline, order and organisation. She herself at her piano by nine in the morning every week day, was always perfectly and rather richly dressed and with never a hair out of place . . . She had intelligence and the real German efficiency, but no intuition. She had a head for business which, with her excellent musicianship gave her the position she occupied for so many years—that of owner, manager and teacher of the greatest school of her day.[1]

Eames goes on to describe the method of payment, how on a certain day in each month a special vase was put on the piano, into which the students were required to slip their fees—surreptitiously, as Madame affected a complete disinterest in such matters, except when, as Eames noted, any student omitted to do so.

Mathilde Marchesi *née* Graumann, from Frankfurt, was, like her husband, a Garcia pupil, and her various writings are unstinting in praise and acknowledgement of the master. For all that, the Marchesi method differed in one salient respect from Garcia's. It was preoccupied with 'placement', a concept quite alien to the old Italian method, that is 'putting' the voice as high on the breath as possible so as to project the tones with the utmost brilliance; Marchesi only taught women and most successfully voices in the Sontag-Lind-Patti mould. It was, in brief, a showy technique. Also it was dangerous, working well when the voice was fresh and young, the energy of youth making up for real breath support. For this reason quite a few of the Marchesi students, after some initial successes, developed problems with the top of the voice: Eames, Adams, Abbot and Scotney, for example. For Melba it was the perfect method, enhancing what was already an extraordinarily natural and responsive instrument. With Marchesi's training she was able to make the greatest possible effect, above all with the high tones. This can be heard nowhere better than in another of Mapleson's experiments, in the closing measures of the Queen's aria from *Les Huguenots*, where her voice, freed from the restraints of the recording studio, in the words of Desmond Shawe-Taylor 'flashes out with amazing brilliance and strength. There is a high C sharp, attacked in full voice, which seems to echo round the huge auditorium; there are cascades of florid singing thrown off in a manner which might almost be called reckless.'[2]

Fraülein Graumann became Mme Marchesi by marriage, whereas Mrs Armstrong's transformation into Melba was achieved on her own. Within a couple of years of her debut, she was a star. Vocal prowess had been an important, but not the only, ingredient in the recipe for success. When she failed to set the Thames on fire at her Covent Garden debut, the management invited her to return, but only as Oscar in *Ballo in Maschera*. Melba was having none of it. With typical Aussie shrewdness she set about ingratiating herself where it really counted: not with the Director, Augustus Harris, for she had no mind to be at the beck and call of the management, but with those who paid the piper. No singer, not even Patti, used her social connections more ruthlessly. She persuaded the most influential patron of the opera, Lady de Grey, a friend of the Prince of Wales, to sue on her behalf for better things. Next season she returned as Juliette, and swept all before her, the management in particular. Thereafter, and for the best part of forty years, it was they who did her bidding.

Like Patti, during the first decade of her career Melba quickly followed up her initial successes, extending the frontiers of her domain, and also her repertory, and like Patti, when she discovered dramatic roles did not suit her voice, soon relinquished them. It was with Lucia, Ophélie, Juliette, Marguerite, Gilda, Violetta and Rosina that she made her reputation, with Nedda, Desdemona and Mimi that she consolidated it. W. J. Henderson, one of the leading New York critics of his day, has left us the best description of her voice in those early years:

> It extended from B flat below the clef to the high F. The scale was beautifully equalised throughout and there was not the smallest change in quality from bottom to top. All the tones were forward; there was never even a hint of throatiness. The full, flowing and facile emission of the tones have never been surpassed, if matched by any other singer of our time. The intonation was pre-eminent in its correctness; the singer was rarely in the smallest measure off pitch.[3]

With Melba we come, for the first time, to a singer who recorded while still in the plentitude of her powers, but with one qualification. Her first visit to the studio was in 1904, she was forty-three, her coloratura no longer quite able to dazzle as of yore, the uppermost tones produced more effortfully than once upon a time. Still, she was in a class of her

7 Melba as Lakmé

own, as the records amply demonstrate. Her account of the *Hamlet* Mad Scene, complete save for the part where Ophelia passes the flowers round, is a thing of real beauty. Melba's art was not of the modern school which tries, successively, to mirror each of the moods in the progress of Ophelia's dementia. She attempts no Freudian subtleties of interpretation. Instead, she sings the music with the utmost simplicity, the perfect finish of her art, in itself something quite exquisite and deeply affecting. Her voice is different from Patti's. Although as beautiful in its own way, the singing is more studied, and the portamento, trill and other graces, though done with rare accomplishment, do not come so naturally out of the vocal line. By the time she came to make records in 1904 the *Hamlet* Mad Scene was kept for concerts, but she was still singing Lucia in the theatre. It is unfortunate that her recording of the Mad Scene from this opera should have been reduced to little more than the cadenza (mostly Marchesi's). However, there does survive at the end of it an echo, within the confines of the recording studio, of an effect with which she electrified the New York audience on the night of her Met debut: a prodigiously long crescendo trill which was not merely astonishing but also beautiful. In quite different vein she unfolds the chaste, but exacting, vocal line of Mozart's 'Porgi amor' with lovely tone and perfect vocal poise, scrupulously observing all the appoggiaturas. (Sir Landon Ronald's 'saloon bar' accompaniment is regrettable.)

In the course of the ensuing twenty-two years Melba made a large number of recordings, earning herself in the process upwards of £400,000 in royalties. Though there was a freshness of voice in the earliest of them not always recaptured thereafter—sometimes the fault was hers, sometimes the machinery's—the best of them give a good idea of the beauty of her singing. Since she studied many of her roles with the composers—Gounod, Thomas, Delibes, Saint-Saëns, Massenet and Verdi, for example—her interpretations of them are of great significance stylistically. In particular, in 'Ah! fors' è lui' she makes a nice discrimination between the various non-legato markings, staccato and marcato (bracketed staccato), and the semi-quaver rests in the opening bars, which she treats like Lilli Lehmann, Tetrazzini and Bellincioni (a favourite Violetta of Verdi's) not literally but as rhetorical devices, a directive to enunciate the text with special clarity or particular emphasis and yet without disturbing the tension of

the musical line with aspirates or ugly snatched breaths.

Though Melba was not a singer of songs like Sembrich, and her interpretations are scarcely profound in the modern fashion, her singing made its own effect. With the possible exception of Battistini, she most nearly approaches Patti on records in spontaneity of utterance, in the pleasure the singing itself gives the listener. We can hear this especially well in the simplest and most unpretentious songs, 'Come back to Erin', 'The old folks at home' (how beautifully she modulates her voice when the trio enters), 'John Anderson, my jo', 'Auld lang syne' (the ravishing soft entry in the refrain), 'Songs my mother taught me', with its hauntingly lovely portamenti; or in Herman Bemberg's two little ditties 'Les anges pleurent' and 'Chant Vénétien', with even a touch of bravura at the end of them. Bemberg, a rich dilettante, was one of Melba's camp-followers who enjoyed playing the role of *cavalier servente*, composing for her a full-length opera, *Elaine*, and a number of *mélodies*. Melba's French may have owed more to Botany Bay than the Faubourg St. Honoré, but we should not make too much of that; Gounod, Thomas, Saint-Saëns and Massenet did not. She excelled in their music, and not only in the exacting coloratura of Gounod and Thomas, but where we might not have expected her to, in Chimène's lament from Massenet's *Le Cid*; here she quite explodes the myth that her singing could never be passionate. It is an outstanding example of the sostenuto marcato style; at the climax 'Ah! pleurez toutes vos larmes!', the lachrymose effect is produced by exactly following Massenet's directions to stress (sob) each note individually and yet sustain them within the phrase markings: that is, without breaking the line—easier said than sung.

The climax of Melba's recording career was the climax of her eminence, her 'Farewell' at Covent Garden—she gave others thereafter but those were subject to the laws of marginal diminishing returns. It was a great occasion, and not just socially, though it was certainly that ('In the gracious presence of Their Majesties'). As the *Daily Telegraph* critic wrote the next day, it was also a 'glorious exhibition of the noble art of singing as singing should be'.[4] Today we are able to appreciate that almost as well as those who were present on the night, since recordings of the scenes from *Otello* and *Bohème* have finally, fifty years after the event, been published in full for the first time. Of course, in 1926 she was not still, at the age of sixty-five, the Melba of 1893 with 'the tones glowing with a star-like brilliance',[5] but there remains much of what for so long had made her the Queen of Song, the last of the line.

When in 1888 Melba had declined to sing Oscar, Covent Garden engaged her contemporary, the Swedish soprano SIGRID ARNOLDSON (1861–1943). Arnoldson was born into a musical family, her father being a principal at the Stockholm opera. As a young woman she went to Paris to study with Maurice Strakosch. Strakosch, part singing teacher, part manager, had an ear for a good voice and an eye for the main chance. As well as playing a leading role in the early life of his sister-in-law Adelina Patti, he would have taken charge of Melba (he signed her up for a five-year contract shortly before her Brussels debut) had not death intervened. From Strakosch Arnoldson went to Marchesi, and later still, in Berlin, she took some lessons from Desirée Artôt de Padilla, a pupil of Pauline Viardot-Garcia.

Arnoldson's career, like Melba's, began in a small theatre; in her case, Prague. Subsequently she sang in Moscow, before coming to London in the summer of 1887 to take part in Augustus Harris's season of Italian opera at Drury Lane. Her first appearance was as Rosina. Opposite her, also making his debut, was the Neapolitan tenor Fernando de Lucia, but it was Arnoldson who walked off with the notices. Next year she was at Covent Garden, but this time she did not make such a favourable impression. As Zerlina, the critics found her voice tired-sounding, 'though her charming looks and personality were evidently to the liking of the audience'.[6] Later in the season she sang Papagena, Rosina and Cherubino as well as Oscar. She did not return to Covent Garden until 1892, in the interim appearing at the Paris Opéra and at the Met in New York; she was not re-engaged at either theatre. When she came back to London it was as Baucis in Gounod's charming *Philémon et Baucis*. Thereafter in all her Covent Garden roles she was well received, without achieving greatness. Once, however, greatness was almost thrust upon her, when, Calvé becoming indisposed, Harris translated Arnoldson from Micaëla to Carmen. Her courage, if not her interpretation, was commended. Much of the problem was Melba who, being the lioness of the season, had appropriated the best parts; all that was left for Arnoldson was an occasional Nedda, a solitary Queen in *Les Huguenots* and matters of secondary import such as Eudoxie in a revival of *La Juive*, and Gemma in Sir Frederick Cowen's *Signa*. When she did get to play the fitting

8 Sigrid Arnoldson as the Queen in *Les Huguenots*

role of Sophie in *Werther*, in spite of Eames and Jean de Reszké in the cast, it was given only once—to this day its only Covent Garden performance.

Still, Arnoldson might have gone on to better things had it not been for an incident at an extra-mural performance at Windsor Castle by command of Queen Victoria. It appears that Arnoldson's Danish husband, a Mr Fischoff, known as 'Fish-hooks' back-stage in the way of Victorian humour, was so put out of countenance when Harris did not introduce his wife to the Queen after the performance that he sent off a sharply worded letter of complaint to the Princess of Wales (herself Danish-born), in which he described Arnoldson as a Danish (sic) nightingale, and suggested that the slight might have international repercussions. The Princess dealt with the matter tactfully; she sent Arnoldson a brooch 'as a souvenir of her performance'. There things might have rested had not Harris got to hear about it. While he couldn't do without Melba, he could do without Mrs Fischoff (and her husband) and she was not re-engaged. The incident effectively brought her London career to an end. However, she continued to appear in Hungary, Sweden and Germany, with success.

Arnoldson's recordings were made in Berlin in the four years between 1906 and 1910. Her voice is still attractive, her interpretations stylish. The Jewel Song, for example, if scarcely brilliant in the way of Melba—there is little portamento, not even where it is specifically called for, as at the upward seventh on the word 'belle'—nevertheless, as an interpretation, has something of Patti's gossamer charm, with its well-judged rubato (from Strakosch?). The best is one of the last: from *Manon*, an excerpt from the St Sulpice scene. The voice, though obviously past its best, is still sweet and, for the most part, true. Especially well managed are the high As and B flats, where the method must have been from Artôt de Padilla; there is none of Marchesi's 'placement' here.

9 Emma Eames as Juliette

Like Melba and Arnoldson, EMMA EAMES (1865–1952) (it rhymes with Great Dames) also studied at the Ecole Marchesi. Unlike them, as her account of 'the Prussian drill master' quoted above suggests, her remembrances of it were scarcely affectionate. These were composed many years later, over forty in fact, and nearly twenty years after increasing vocal problems had obliged her, at the relatively early age of forty-four, to bow out of opera. Being an ambitious woman, it is hardly surprising that she felt cheated and decided to take the opportunity of her memoirs to settle a few old scores. There were two obvious scapegoats, neither in a position to defend herself: the first was Mme Marchesi, who was long dead and who, Eames quite incorrectly claimed, 'trained the voice to have three distinct registers, instead of one perfectly even scale, in which the tones of each register melt into the next',[7] and who, she further complained, 'did not have the faintest idea of my talent or what I had in me'. The other was 'another singer' whom, for fear of obvious legal retaliation, she carefully avoids mentioning by name. She might just as well have done so, for there is never the slightest doubt whom she meant. According to Eames, Melba prevented her making a debut at Brussels, tried to alienate her in the affections of Gounod, told tales about her to Marchesi, and even went as far as to call the day after Eames's debut as Juliette at the Paris Opéra, just to tell her how badly she had sung. No doubt there was some truth in all of it, for Melba never did care for other sopranos poaching on what she regarded as her preserves, and Eames was certainly poaching as Juliette, one of Melba's favourite and best roles, 'singing so splendidly throughout, and looking the most beautiful and youthful exponent of Shakespeare's heroine ever seen on the operatic stage'.[8] It would be easier to feel sympathy for Eames if she herself had not been so spiteful towards her colleagues—'Oh, Alda's fine for the chorus!'[9] Throughout *Some Memories and Reflections* she casts herself in the role of the virtuous pilgrim in Babylon, which does not square with a record that suggests that she was less like Juliette, and more like Gertrude—for she protested too much.

In her youth Eames's voice was a thing of 'exquisite purity, lovely in quality', the range from A below middle C to the high C sharp. At first she confined herself to the lyric repertory. From Juliette, Micaëla, Marguerite, Mireille, Pamina, the Countess in *Figaro* and Desdemona, she advanced to Aida, Elsa, Elisabeth, Eva, Santuzza, Sieglinde, Donna Anna, Iris in Mascagni's opera, and Tosca.

Contemporary criticism rated her an indifferent actress, like Melba: cold and lacking in temperament. When she sang her first Met Aida, James Huneker wrote: 'Last night there was skating on the Nile.' Her recordings do not confirm these opinions. It is true the voice itself is not warm, but she could use it in dramatic music with extraordinary intensity, as we hear in the Mapleson cylinders of *Tosca*. As Santuzza, a role on the face of it scarcely suited to her patrician make up, she suffuses 'Voi lo sapete' in an almost Stygian gloom; no tattered passions here, but Mascagni has become almost classical. Her grandeur was of the generalised rather than the specific kind, unquestionably effective in the opera, rather less so in concert. After a Carnegie Hall recital in 1906, Aldrich found much to admire but felt that—

> A warmer more intimate style, a greater power of detailed characterisations are needed for some of this kind of music. . . . her voice sounded inflexible, in the upper ranges she had difficulty in managing it, and in overcoming the metallic quality and molding it into fluent and connected phrasing.[10]

Her recordings date from about the same time, when decadence had set in. Though Eames would have it otherwise, Marchesi's method had contributed less to this than her own preoccupation with the dramatic repertory. What Tosca cost her may be imagined, when after four performances she came down with what Henderson described as an acute case of 'Toscalitis' and was obliged to withdraw for the rest of the season. In spite of this, of the weaknesses Aldrich notes and a prevailing hoarseness in the middle register, Eames left a number of very lovely records. The 'Chanson des baisers', which she must have got out of Bemberg when Melba's back was turned (it was in fact dedicated to Melba), is not only quite the best of Bemberg's songs, but finds Eames's voice at its freshest, the coloratura as fine as old lace. Especially beautifully vocalised is Micaëla's aria. Schubert's 'Gretchen am Spinnrade' is a very public interpretation, cast in the heroic mould. Is there here, ever so faintly, an echo of what so strongly stirred Wagner in Schroeder-Devrient's noble declamation? There are few other recordings in which the mood is sustained with such feeling, the extraordinary doleful effect created by the grand sweep of the downward portamenti.

Like Melba, Eames studied Juliette with Gounod (their recordings, not surprisingly, are similar), a fact she afterwards made much of. Her memory of just what it was he taught her, however, became increasingly vague through the years. In a broadcast talk, she denounced—on Gounod's behalf—those latter-day interpretations which are not 'absolutely in time and without meaningless holds and ritards'.[11] Needless to say, her recording is full of tempo changes, holds and ritards. One claim she made in her book has never been disputed: that she was once very good looking. Few opera singers have been so lovely; even in the frightful wig she dolled herself up in for *Aida*, nothing could disguise it. As a young woman her face had the cool dignity and sexless beauty of Waterhouse's Lady of Shallot.

Eames's first husband had been a fashionable portrait painter, Julian Storey. Apparently the Storey family was attracted to sopranos, and in particular, it would seem, to pupils of Mathilde Marchesi; Julian's brother, Waldo, married Bessie Abbot. Abbot, who came from Riverside, New York, had started as a vaudeville singer. After a few years she graduated to operetta. Then in 1898 she caught the attention of Jean de Reszké, who heard her sing and encouraged her to go to Paris for further vocal study. There she took lessons from Victor Capoul and Jacques Bouhy before arriving at the Ecole Marchesi. Like Eames, her debut was as Juliette at the Paris Opéra. In 1906, she appeared at the Met for the first time as Mimi, but the competition was too great (this was the year of Farrar's debut): neither then nor subsequently in other lyric parts did she make any impression. By 1911, her career was over.

A few years later another young American, LILLIAN BLAUVELT (1873–1947), had gone to Paris, to complete her studies with Jacques Bouhy. She was born in Brooklyn and made her debut at the Monnaie in Brussels as Mireille; subsequently she sang Juliette, Mignon and Marguerite. In 1898 she went to Rome, where she made a great impression as the soprano soloist in the Verdi *Requiem*. In London in 1903, for one season, she was at Covent Garden, as Marguerite and Micaëla, but it was as a concert artist that she revisited England almost every season until the First World War. She was regularly at the Proms and a particular favourite of Henry Wood, who thought her 'a fascinating and happy personality'.[12] In the United States for two seasons she appeared in operetta, as the heroine in Victor Herbert's *Magic Knight,* a spoof of *Lohengrin*. The *National Encyclopaedia of American Biography* describes her voice as—

> . . . a high soprano of very pure timbre, but dramatic in

10 Lillian Blauvelt as Marguerite

11 Suzanne Adams

quality; with this is united a musical intelligence which enables her to impart to the work its true interpretation. Her range is from the G below middle C to D in alt.[13]

She was also an accomplished technician, as her various recordings testify, though the voice itself was not of the first class. Her recordings include the Bolero from *Les Vêpres Siciliennes*, one of the very few in the original French, and a popular coloratura show-piece of the period by Dessauer, 'Le retour des promis'. This she does with much spirit and a certain hard-boiled charm, though the bottom of the voice already sounds worn.

The most successful, at least initially, of these American sopranos was SUZANNE ADAMS (1872–1953). She came from Cambridge, Mass., and like her countrywomen went to Paris to study, first with Bouhy, and then with Marchesi. Like Eames and Abbot, she too made her debut at the Opéra, as Juliette. Unlike them, however, she accepted the part in direct contravention of Marchesi's wishes and before her voice was properly ready. At first she was favourably received in Paris, and subsequently at Covent Garden and the Met. Philip Hale has left us an account of the effect she made in

those first appearances:

It was a pleasure to see a Marguerite who was so youthful; and the virginal attitude was unmistakably not a deliberate and laborious assumption. The impression was preserved in the Garden scene, where many Marguerites wonder too anxiously why the fine gentleman is so slow in coming. She sang with easy simplicity and a girlish charm that admirably suited the part.[14]

After her Met debut, Krehbiel wrote of her as 'one of the latest illustrations of America's capacity for producing lovely voices'.[15] She failed to follow up on these first successes. Later, at Covent Garden, where once she had been praised for her 'beautiful and liquid voice'[16] her singing was subjected to increasing criticism. In 1905, at a concert in the presence of King Edward VII, Albert Spalding was charmed by her good looks and the way in which before majesty 'she dropped into the deepest and most graceful curtsy I have ever seen', but he could not fail to notice that her voice was 'waning' and that 'she did not sing wisely'.[17] By 1907 she was appearing in variety. It was the end.

On 24 February 1902, at the Metropolitan, Adams

had been down to sing the short but brilliant role of the Queen, in one of those all-star—or almost all-star—performances of Meyerbeer's *Les Huguenots*. The day before she took cold, maybe fright; her voice was already over the top. After Grau had failed to cajole Sembrich into taking her place, he was obliged to try out another young American— yet another ex-alumnus of the Ecole Marchesi— Estelle Liebling. Neither that night nor subsequently did Miss Liebling's performances evoke any excited response. It was as a repetiteur and teacher of singing that she was to play an important part in New York's musical life during the next sixty years, her most renowned pupil being Beverly Sills. The Liebling editions of various coloratura favourites, which retain Marchesi's embellishments embedded in some of Madame's own very original flights of fancy, have been an inestimable boon to nearly three generations of 'coloraturas' who have felt that the composers were altogether too modest in their demands.

The strangest of Marchesi's American pupils was ELLEN BEACH YAW (1869–1947). Yaw had no real career. She sang Sullivan's *Rose of Persia* in London in 1899. There was a solitary *Lucia* at the Constanzi in Rome, another at the Met when Conried put her on in a vain attempt to combat Tetrazzini's enormous vogue at the Manhattan. Otherwise, apart from appearances in vaudeville and her own travelling road show, that was it. Still, her name has remained, in record collectors' circles, one to conjure with, or at any rate, one that could conjure up some extraordinary altitudinous notes. An extended falsetto in the female voice is not unnatural, but to make use of it, marry it into the rest of the voice so as to produce something musical, requires years of study. Perhaps only Lucrezia Ajugari (1743–1783) managed this with any real success. Mozart, charmed as well as astonished by her skill, notated some passage-work of hers that went all the way up to D in altissimo, more than an octave above high C. More recently Erna Sack and Mado Robin made recordings at least to B flat in altissimo, but in both cases pleasure was vitiated by the thin and piercing quality of the notes, and by the correspondingly weak and breathy middle register; nothing happens until the singer gets above high C, which is just where the music runs out. In Yaw's recordings there are, as well as cavortings in altissimo, a number of examples of another trick of hers more remarkable than pleasing—the trill in thirds. It calls to mind a comment by Spohr on one of Catalani's effects,

'sounding something like the howling of the wind in a chimney'.[18] Only one of her recordings warrants any particular comment, a piece of music the label is pleased to describe as being the work of Mozart, 'O dolce concento'; in fact it is a much abbreviated and much simplified version of a set of variations composed by Paer on a theme of Mozart for Catalani.

Perhaps the most complete exemplification of the Marchesi method, though scarcely the most successful, was her daughter, BLANCHE MARCHESI (1863–1940). Her voice was, like her mother's, nothing remarkable. She made a few appearances in opera at the German theatre, Prague, in 1900, and

12 Ellen Beach Yaw as Lucia

again at Covent Garden in the Moody-Manners autumn seasons of 1902 and 1903, as Brünnhilde, Isolde, Elisabeth and Santuzza. She was chiefly admired as a concert artist. One of her most devoted followers, the Indian composer Khaikhosru Sorabji, rather glib with a superlative, has written at length of her 'interpretative genius',[19] but even he could not forebear from quoting, if only to contradict it, what was so often said of her—that she was the greatest singer in the world without a voice. Richard Aldrich, after a concert in New York, wrote an appraisal of her voice and art which squares very well with the records:

> Her listeners were few, but Mme Marchesi's singing is hardly for the general public; it is for the public that appreciates the things she can do and is equally willing to forego the things she cannot do. Chief amongst the latter is the production of a beautiful tone. Mme Marchesi's tone is not merely unbeautiful, it is for the most part positively ugly, with a streak of commonness in the tones. Nevertheless, she is in many respects a consummate artist. What she can do in the way of interpretation, in characterising and expressing the mood and spirit of a song, is admirable. There is likewise much that is admirable in her vocal art, in her phrasing, the management of the breath and even in scales and trills.[20]

Marchesi made two series of records, in 1906 and again thirty years later in 1936. Of the products of that first session, Sorabji has a curious tale to tell. According to him they were all destroyed on the orders of another singer. Unlike Eames, he is not in the least coy about naming her; it was, of course, Melba. He states that Melba 'refused to record at all unless Marchesi was banned, or else, if any records of the latter had been made, she insisted that they should be withdrawn and they and the matrices destroyed'.[21] Unfortunately for all this, the disobliging facts are that the records were publicly issued in the ordinary way, indeed on Blanche's own initiative two of them were reissued in dubbed form at the time when she made the second series. Since Marchesi's few operatic roles were not in Melba's repertory and she was, as we have seen above, scarcely a popular recitalist, one cannot help wondering whether Sorabji did not get it round the wrong way when he wrote that 'Marchesi's paramount greatness was such gall and wormwood to Melba'.[22] From that first series, Adalbert Goldschmidt's 'Im Mai' is among the best. Here, the tone of the voice is pure if unlovely and there is much to admire in the skilful way she takes the high

13 Blanche Marchesi as Brünnhilde in *Die Walküre*

notes. Less admirable is a pronounced vibrato, almost a shudder that infects the tone, especially in piano passages. There is, too, about the interpretation a certain artfulness that does not seem entirely fitting. None the less the ending is, as she herself remarked to her pupil, John Freestone, 'une véritable tour de force',[23] something to rouse the enthusiasm of those 'who could appreciate what was given and for the moment divest themselves of a desire for what Mme Marchesi could not give'.[24]

3. Dramatic Sopranos

As Blanche Marchesi's two seasons at Covent Garden with the Moody-Manners company might have suggested, at that time there was no outstanding English dramatic soprano. One was, however, to emerge in the course of the next few years, a Miss AGNES NICHOLLS (1876–1959) from Cheltenham. In 1894, at the age of eighteen she began her studies at the Royal College of Music with Alberto Visetti. The very next year she made her first stage appearances, at the Lyceum Theatre, as Dido in Purcell's opera and as Anne Page in an English version of Verdi's *Falstaff*. Her concert debut took place during the season of Queen Victoria's Diamond Jubilee, at the Worcester Festival. Shortly afterwards she sang in front of the Queen at Windsor Castle (appropriately, in Delibes's *Le Roi l'a dit*) and on Jubilee Sunday was one of the soloists, with Albani and Edward Lloyd, in Mendelssohn's *Hymn of Praise*. In 1901, she made a modest debut at Covent Garden as the Dewman in *Hansel and Gretel*; the Sandman was another pupil of Visetti, Louise Kirkby-Lunn. Between 1904 and 1908 she appeared regularly, advancing from Micaëla, through Elvira and Elsa, to Sieglinde, where 'her beautiful voice and exquisite phrasing were heard to admirable advantage',[1] and eventually (in Richter's English Ring Cycle of 1908) to the *Siegfried* Brünnhilde, an interpretation that was especially acclaimed. She was not at Covent Garden again until after the First World War, when, for Beecham, she managed in one season alone Santuzza, Constanze, Mistress Page, the Countess, Elisabeth and Isolde. Thereafter she returned intermittently until her final season with the British National Opera Company, in 1924.

As a concert artist she followed in the great British choral tradition and was much liked in Handel and Bach, where her clean execution and purity of tone were particularly appropriate. Parry wrote parts for her in several of his choral works and for Elgar she created the Blessed Virgin in the first performance of *The Kingdom*. Later in her career she was a popular recitalist with her husband, the conductor Sir Hamilton Harty, at the piano.

Records have preserved Agnes Nicholls's lovely voice at its best, a good-sized instrument with a precise and forward production. Her account of Rezia's Ocean aria, in Planché's original English text, is a brilliantly exultant interpretation with

14 Agnes Nicholls as Brünnhilde in *Die Walküre*

clean declamation and pellucid diction; only in the concluding allegro does she sound a little overparted. The quality of her voice works an especial charm in Sir Frederick Cowen's song 'At the mid hour of night', where again we may note the clean attack and variety of dynamics, the smooth legato and portamento, which she uses with unfailing taste.

The greatest dramatic soprano at the turn of the century was, however, an American, and not a pupil of Marchesi. Miss Lillian Norton was the all-American singer. Born in Farmington, Maine, she went to the New England Conservatory to study with John O'Neill, whom she afterwards referred to as her only real voice teacher. In 1878, at the age of twenty-one, she was in London as soloist with the Gilmore band—one of many spawned in the era of Sousa—making a great hit, with 'her high C, powerful enough to vie with any trumpeter'. She did not immediately return to the United States, but instead continued her studies under Sangiovanni in Milan. In six months she was ready to make an operatic debut at Brescia, as Violetta. During the next eight years LILLIAN NORDICA (1857–1914), as she then styled herself, made the rounds of the leading European opera houses—Berlin, St Petersburg and Paris—gaining experience as Lucia, Ophélie, Philine, Marguerite, Gilda and Violetta. She used this last part again for her first London stage appearance, at Covent Garden in 1887. She joined Harris later that summer at Drury Lane in a season that introduced Sigrid Arnoldson, Fernando de Lucia and Jean de Reszké, and marked the return to London of Mattia Battistini, Victor Maurel and Edouard de Reszké. Even in such company, Nordica's triumph was complete:

> She had a soprano voice of bright, clear, sympathetic timbre, admirably produced (the range extends to the high D flat). It is of even quality and considerable power notably in the head register. As a singer, Mme Nordica possesses no slight agility, in addition to charm and purity of expression.[2]

She went on to Donna Elvira, Aida and Valentine. In the latter part she made a considerable effect as an actress, inspired by Jean de Reszké's Raoul; it was the beginning of a partnership that was to continue throughout the next decade in a variety of operas. From Valentine, Nordica began to move increasingly towards the dramatic repertory. Two years later she sang her first Wagnerian role, Elsa. In 1894 she created the same part in the first Bayreuth performances of *Lohengrin*. At the Met under the direction of Anton Seidl, she sang her first Isolde and all three Brünnhildes, often with de Reszké as Tristan or Siegfried.

If these artistic partnerships were notably productive, in affairs of the heart Yankee good sense seemed to desert her. She married three times. Her first husband was the engineer and aeronaut Frederick Gower, but they had been together less than three years when he went up in smoke—in a balloon experiment. In 1896, she married a certain Zoltan Döme, who claimed to be Hungarian, though his real name was Solomon Teitlbaum. An easygoing, good-looking fellow, he had made a nice reputation for himself (and a good living) with his renderings of gypsy friskas in the best drawing-rooms of London. After they were married he got ambitious. Jealous of de Reszké, he tried to convert his light-weight baritone into a heldentenor. When success was not forthcoming, he consoled himself with Nordica's money. She found out and he fled to Hungary. Unfortunately, it was not third time lucky when she married the banker George W. Young. The impresario Henry Russell describes meeting him one day: 'He had a very funny look, especially when I tried pressing him into financing a musical venture I was then involved with.'[3] Later Russell discovered that that morning Young had lost $15 million on the stock-market. Some of it was Nordica's money. So that marriage, too, came to an end. Afterwards, it was hardly surprising that she had a nervous breakdown. For a time she gave up the search for the ideal husband, taking emotional solace from increasingly heavy meals. The critic Huneker described the effects of her regime: 'She looked like a large heavily upholstered couch.' But is was only for a time. Hope springs eternal in the human breast, and Nordica, being amply provided for in that respect, was soon all set to take a fourth husband. It was not to be, however. On the way back from a tour of Australia, the boat was shipwrecked off the coast of Java. She was rescued but died from exposure.

Roberto Bauer lists over thirty titles Nordica recorded for the American Columbia company between 1907 and 1911. Only fourteen have survived, and those not too well. At that time Columbia's technical know-how was way behind the G & T company or Victor; even the best of its efforts were markedly inferior to its competitors, and the Nordica records were not among them. Her huge voice ('the biggest orchestra could not submerge it in its tidal waves of sound'[4]) was too much for the primitive recording trumpet; the breadth and power of her singing must largely be taken on trust. Her recording of the Liebestod is a paltry echo of a great assumption, even if the recording could not entirely ignore the ravishing tone, especially in the upper range, or miss the final F sharp, so perfectly modulated; but to her best it did its worst. Of the songs, 'Annie Laurie' is remarkable for the clear diction and eloquent phrasing; no diva's condescension here. The *Mignon* 'Polonaise' was probably intended to show what she could still do: it is pretty nimble, if

15 Lillian Nordica

spontaneous delivery and splendid natural quality that probably more nearly approached her great predecessor's. Undoubtedly the most sensational of her records is part of Elisabeth's aria from Erkel's *Hunyadi Laszlo*. Erkel was a genetic figure in the history of Hungarian opera, like Glinka in Russia, adapting the Italian style to suit the national music. This aria, originally composed for the French soprano Anna de la Grange, must have been the last surviving souvenir of Nordica's marriage to Döme. She often used it in concert, though it confounded the critics—'a strange piece with its explosive high notes'[5] (Aldrich). There are several of them on the record; also some other stunning vocalism, a passage of tremendous staccati and a trill on high B. The whole thing is a bit of a scream, as the voice, for a few fleeting moments, breaks out of the cubicle Columbia had locked it into.

If Nordica was the popular singer, the most naturally endowed of the great Wagnerian sopranos active at the turn of the century, it was OLIVE FREMSTAD (1871–1951), who enjoyed rapturous notices and the respect of her fellow artists, and even provided the inspiration for a novel—Willa Cather's *The Song of the Lark*—in which she appears, thinly disguised, as the heroine, Thea Kronberg. Fremstad was born Olivia Rundquist in Stockholm. She was brought to the United States as a girl and grew up in Minnesota. At first she took piano lessons, but when it became apparent she had a remarkable natural voice—a contralto she thought—she went to Berlin and put herself under Lilli Lehmann. Lehmann, whose own career was the most complete example of the triumph of mind over matter, at once decided she should be a soprano. This transformation was to take place in easy stages. Her debut was at Cologne, in the mezzo role of Azucena; thereafter she was Brangäne and Adalgisa to Lehmann's Isolde and Norma. After seven years spent in Germany she was engaged at Covent Garden, where she made an impressive debut as Ortrud: 'a superb dramatic voice, well produced and of unusually wide range, as well as rare histrionic ability.'[6] To this achievement she added Fricka in *Rheingold*, Venus and Brangäne. Next year she arrived at the Met, as Sieglinde. It was there that she attained true greatness.

In 1907, she created Salome in the first performance of that opera at the Met. The work, and Fremstad's interpretation, caused a furore. W. J. Henderson wrote: 'Fremstad coddled the severed head a good deal more at the dress rehearsal than she did on Tuesday . . . On Tuesday she moderated her

scarcely tossed off with the alacrity of youth, and not all the staccati quite hit the mark. It contrasts well with a powerfully declaimed 'Suicidio' from *Gioconda* (one of her last new roles), where the chest register is clearly established but not chewed out as in the style of the verismo school. The most interesting title is a truncated account of Leonora's 'Tacea la notte' from *Trovatore*. The voice flows more easily than elsewhere in the swelling phrases, where she adds some changes of Tietjens that Klein gave her. It was an appropriate gift: when Nordica was a girl Tietjens heard her sing this piece, and was impressed. If Lehmann inherited Tietjens's artistic mantle, it was Nordica's voice with its more

transports so that even little girls were not shocked. As for society women, they viewed the spectacle with perfect calmness.'[7] Aldrich acclaimed her performance as 'the crown to all that she has done at the Metropolitan'.[8] It was the following year, as Isolde, that she completed her transformation into a soprano:

> Mme Fremstad's voice is of indescribable beauty in this music, in its richness and power, its infinite modulation in all the shades and extremes of dramatic significance. It never sounded finer in quality and never seemed more perfectly under control. And her singing was a revelation, in the fact that the music was in very few places higher than she could easily compass with her voice. The voice seems, in truth, to have reached a higher altitude and to move in it without restraint and without effort.[9]

With Karl Burrian in the title role and Mahler conducting, these were the first complete performances of *Tristan und Isolde* at the Met. Fremstad was equally successful as Kundry, Santuzza, Carmen, Giulietta in *Hoffmann* and Armide in Gluck's opera; she sang this when the Met visited Paris. In all of these roles, wrote a critic years later, 'her most remarkable attribute as a singer was her ability to colour the tone so as to convey unambiguously its musical and poetic content'.[10]

Like Nordica, Fremstad recorded exclusively for Columbia, but her softer, warmer-toned, though less brilliant voice better suited the apparatus. Sieglinde's 'Du bist der Lenz' has something of Lehmann in its expressive but slightly squeezed-out legato, though the effect is more human. Her voice, notwithstanding Lehmann, sounds like what we should today call a mezzo-soprano, an impression confirmed by Brünnhilde's Battle Cry, where the high notes are taken with effort; here as elsewhere, her intonation is sometimes sharp. 'O don fatale' would have been a fine interpretation had it not been for the impossibility of fitting it all on one side of a record. Not even the reduced circumstances of the recording studio could diminish an impetuously vivid account of Elisabeth's Greeting from *Tannhäuser*. As Tosca too, though this was not generally regarded as one of her best parts, two excerpts are strongly felt. Only in Carmen's Séguedille does she disappoint. Nothing here of what was rated in its day 'a distinctive and highly original impersonation'.[11]

Fremstad bade farewell to the opera after a performance of *Parsifal* in 1914. She would have been re-engaged for the 1917–18 season if the war

16 Olive Fremstad as Brünnhilde in *Die Walküre*

had not eliminated the German repertory at the Met. After a few concerts, where she adapted her tones 'with a delicate charm that had yet the thrill of her great theatrical impersonations',[12] she retired absolutely.

There could hardly have been a more marked contrast between Lilli Lehmann's two great American pupils, between Fremstad, 'dark and gloomy . . . her life a vacuum to be filled until the next stage performance; her retirement thirty-five long sad years', and GERALDINE FARRAR (1882–1967) at her Met farewell, 'I don't want any tears in this house. I am leaving this institution because I want to go.'[13] Farrar was off to make a second career in the movies—silent ones. Not that she was lacking in determination; she had climbed to the heights with as much single-minded dedication as Fremstad, and a great deal less voice. It was—

> a full and rich soprano, lyric in its nature and flexibility, yet rather darkly coloured and with not a little of the dramatic quality ... Her singing is generally free and spontaneous in delivery, well-phrased and well-enunciated, yet she is not a wholly finished vocalist, and there were matters in her singing that could not meet with entire approbation.[14]

They never did. After her second season, Henderson wrote: 'She has an unjust conception of tone. Largeness, power and brilliance are what this young woman has sought, instead of mellowness, limpidity and perfect poise.'[15]

In spite of these misgivings, which time did not put right, Farrar's Met career was unrivalled by any other prima donna of her day. Her success was only in part, and decreasingly so, a vocal achievement. She was a beautiful woman. Neither statuesque like Fremstad, nor cold like Eames, hers was a theatrical glamour that she knew how to use to great effect as Juliette, Manon, Marguerite, Cherubino and Mimi, roles which suited her, and as Violetta, Margherita, Tosca and Carmen, which did not. Inspired by the example of Mary Garden, she attempted to put personality where there ought to have been voice. As Thaïs she never could reach the high Ds. In the title-roles of Dukas's *Ariane*, Leoncavallo's *Zazà*, Mascagni's *Lodoletta* and Giordano's *Mme Sans-Gêne*, she sported extravagant costumes and the manners of the movies, acquired, like her handsome film-star husband Lou Tellegen, from Hollywood. When she tried to import some of this new realism into the Met's *Carmen*, the impact was more than even she had bargained for; the chorus girls declined to be shoved about and Caruso, after she had slapped him in the face, told the management to get another Don José. All the histrionics could not stave off the inevitable; by the time she was forty, the hour had come to say farewell.

Cosmetic personality does not make any impression on wax; recordings merely demonstrate what Farrar tried so carefully to disguise: her voice could not cope with the demands of many of the roles she undertook, however lovely she may have

17 Geraldine Farrar as Manon in Massenet's *Manon*

appeared in them—Butterfly, for example (where she uses an earlier version of the score than the familiar Ricordi edition). Her first records, and the least demanding of those too, are the best; none more pleasing than a charmingly expressive account of Tosti's 'Mattinata'.

While all the weary and heavy-laden were taking up the Statue of Liberty's offer and crossing the Atlantic in droves, there was a small but not insignificant trickle running against the current. Most American singers came to Europe at some stage or other in their studies, and some of them, like

Suzanne Adams, settled in London. So too, did SUSAN STRONG (1870–1946) and Zélie de Lussan. The former was from Brooklyn, where her father was in turn a state senator and Mayor. She first came to London to study at the Royal College of Music with Francis Korbay. In the autumn of 1895 she made her debut at Covent Garden as Sieglinde. This was in a company organised by the American tenor Charles Hedmont, formerly a principal of the Leipzig opera; among the other artists were Rosa Olitzka and David Bispham, and Sir George Henschel conducted. On the strength of the impression she made, she was invited to return for the Diamond Jubilee season, repeating her Sieglinde, this time in German, and then adding Aida and the *Siegfried* Brünnhilde. *The Times* wrote:

> Her voice told well in the final scene . . . at some points she was very fine and the beautiful passage beginning 'Heilig Schied', was admirably taken.[16]

If it was not exactly an ecstatic notice, it was still praise; and she returned to Covent Garden several times thereafter, increasing her repertory with Venus, Donna Anna and Freia. During this period she made several visits to the United States, appearing at the Met in three seasons after 1897. Later on, however, she confined herself to a concert career.

Her records are mostly of songs. Particularly attractive is Paladilhe's 'Psyché'. She sings in good and clear French with measured restraint, contrasting the registers expressively. The tone of the voice is sweet if rather fluttery. Altogether, however, from her records it is hard to imagine her being able to encompass with any degree of ease or certainty the demands of a part like Brünnhilde. It is difficult to resist the conclusion that her decision to quit opera was not entirely a matter of artistic inclination.

After her retirement from the concert platform she opened a hand laundry in Baker Street, London, where she was affectionately known among her customers as Brünnhilde.

ZELIE DE LUSSAN (1861–1949) was also from Brooklyn. (Was the air so different then?) Her only

18 Susan Strong as Elsa in *Lohengrin*

19 Zélie de Lussan as Mignon in Thomas's opera

singing teacher was her mother. She made her first appearance in public at the age of nine, singing Mignon's 'Connais-tu le pays?'—it must be the only time this aria has been sung by a singer who was actually younger than Goethe's character. Her stage debut took place in Boston in 1884, and for some years afterwards she was the principal glory of the Boston Ideal Opera Company, appearing with great effect in Balfe's *Bohemian Girl* and in *The Daughter of the Regiment*. In 1888 she first came to Covent Garden, as Carmen. Subsequently she added Zerlina, Mistress Ford, Cherubino, Nedda, Musetta and Papagena, in all of which 'her insouciance and piquancy'[17] were much appreciated. In 1894 she returned to the United States to make her Met debut, again as Carmen; the cast also included both de Reszkés, and Melba in one of her rare appearances as Micaëla. Krehbiel, in the *New York Times*, confirmed de Lussan's success:

> She has gained much from her experience and study abroad—her voice in richness and expressiveness, her acting in unconventionality, variety and forcefulness. Her Carmen is an extremely interesting impersonation worthy of separate consideration and admiration, and if circumstances did not force a comparison with Mme Calvé, it would be looked upon as a striking performance. As it is though a reservation may be made as to its deficiency in some particulars, a hearty word of commendation must be spoken of it.[18]

In spite of this approval, both at the Met and at Covent Garden her career advanced no further. This had less to do with Calvé than her own voice: a short soprano, it could only manage a very limited and relatively undemanding repertory. More and more, as time passed, she appeared in second-class company: with Moody-Manners at Covent Garden, on tour with the Carl Rosa, and with the Metropolitan's English Grand Opera company in New York. Reviews suggest that her art and voice were not compromised by what were, after all, thoroughly respectable associations. 'The Zerlina of Mlle de Lussan was the finest piece of Mozartian singing; she understands how to put expression into the music without destroying its pattern and grace.'[19] 'Her rendering of Carmen [she sang it more than a thousand times in her career] was by subtle touches, placed as one of the most powerful interpretations on the stage.'

De Lussan made a short list of records in 1903 and 1906. They show a pretty and expressive voice, well-schooled and with admirably clear diction, but in none of them is there any particular character.

20 Louise Homer as Ortrud in *Lohengrin*

The impression is of an exceptionally accomplished soubrette. The song titles are the most attractive: Guétary's 'Lili', with its neatly executed gruppetti, and Landon Ronald's 'Rosy Morn', where she sinks into the chest register in the fashion then so much affected by ballad and operetta singers.

4. Three Contraltos

The two finest Anglo-Saxon operatic contraltos of this period were both Louises: Homer and Kirkby-Lunn. LOUISE HOMER (1871–1947) came from Pittsburgh. After some study in Philadelphia and Boston, during which time she kept herself as a stenographer, she travelled to Europe to be finished—which is what she was, almost completely, or so she claims in her autobiography, when

4. Three Contraltos   45

she went to the studio of Jacques Bouhy in Paris:
'He tried to muffle and contain my voice.' Dispens-
ing with Bouhy, she made an operatic debut as
Léonore in Donizetti's *La Favorite* at Vichy. In 1899
she was at Covent Garden, appearing there during
two seasons as Ortrud, Amneris, Mamma Lucia and
Maddalena. The following year she returned to the
United States to make her Met debut as Amneris,
where at first she was indifferently received:
'rather a hard voice of plentiful volume'[1] and not
'gifted with much temperament'.[2] It did not stop her
being re-engaged for every season until 1919 and
again between 1927 and 1930. To have a big and
secure voice was asset enough at the Met. Moreover
she was obliging, for there was nothing she would
not do, from Azucena and Fidès down to the Second
Lady in the *Zauberflöte* and the Witch in *Hansel und
Gretel*, 'a blood curdling . . . fearful and wonderful
appearance, capable of any iniquity towards rash
children; and she was willing to sacrifice something
of the beauty of her voice to the dramatic exigencies
of the character.'[3] Artistically her career gathered
momentum when she added to Ortrud other impressive Wagnerian interpretations. Her greatest
achievement, however, was in a revival of Gluck's
Orfeo, in 1909, of which Aldrich wrote:

> Mme Homer's impersonation of Orpheus was one of
> nobility, dignity and plastic grace for the eye and of
> full-throated and beautiful song for the ear. She was in
> this something other than a woman disguised. There
> was a true representation of the Greek singer . . . It was
> one of the finest and most artistic, as well as most
> original impersonations that Mme Homer has given
> here.[4]

Homer made a quantity of records that confirm
the strength of her voice; also its wide range,
enabling her to encompass mezzo-soprano roles
almost as easily as contralto. The earliest of them are
the best, when her voice was still fresh; later,
through overwork, it has become thick, the tone
still impressive but grey-sounding. Technically she
was secure, without quite matching up to the
highest standards then extant—no serious challenge to Schumann-Heink, who overshadowed her
throughout most of her time, and even at the end,
though ten years older, outdistanced her. She is at
her least successful in graceful and brilliant music:
in Delibes's 'Les Filles de Cadiz', who sound more
like puritan maids from Boston, and equally in a
transposed and humourless account of Urbain's
'Nobles Seigneurs' (in Italian). She is at her best in
matronly roles; which is not surprising, as she was

one of the few singers who successfully combined a
career with an American woman's first duty,
motherhood. Her solo and the two duets from
Trovatore with Caruso were appropriate selections.
The most interesting title is an abbreviated version
of 'Amour viens rendre à mon âme', the music
Viardot sang with such tremendous effect in
Berlioz's revival of *Orphée*. It was not included in the
Met version. Toscanini, supposing it to have been an
adaptation of an air by Bertoni—in fact, it was
originally by Gluck and only subsequently stolen
from him by Bertoni—put in its place Alceste's
'Divinités du Styx'.†

When Homer departed for New York in 1901,
Covent Garden engaged LOUISE KIRKBY-LUNN
(1873–1930) (the second k is silent). Kirkby-Lunn
was from Manchester. She studied in London with
Alberto Visetti and then went to Paris, where her
experience with Bouhy seems to have been happier
than Homer's. At Covent Garden she sang small
roles before progressing to Amneris, Ortrud and
Maddalena. The resemblance to Homer did not end
there; the range of their voices was similar, from the
low G to the high B flat. Kirkby-Lunn remained at
Covent Garden for the next fourteen years, until the
First World War, and, like Homer at the Met, played
a wide variety of roles. In 1905 she too sang *Orphée*,
an interpretation which 'had the beauty of tone and
all those strong expressive touches that she has
taught us to expect of her'.[5] Later she sang a notable
Dalila but her greatest triumph was as Kundry in
1914. It was this role she chose for her final
appearances at Covent Garden with the British
National Opera Company in 1921; thereafter she
continued to sing for some years on the concert
platform. As well as being a popular singer with the
public, Kirkby-Lunn was greatly admired by her
colleagues. Sir Charles Santley wrote of her: 'She
has become the greatest artiste on the lyric stage,
and the most accomplished English singer I have
ever heard.'[6] An equally high opinion of her was
held by Sir Henry Wood:

> a singer with a glorious voice and an even tone
> throughout a compass of well over two octaves, a
> singer with whom I never found fault in so much as a
> quaver all the years I worked with her, and who never
> sang out of tune. Her Brangaene at Covent Garden, her
> fine acting and singing as Kundry in America, and a
> marvellous rendering of Isolde's Liebestod . . . are
> among my most cherished memories of her.[7]

† This aria was added by Gluck for the tenor Legros, and does not
appear in the original castrato version. It was specially arranged
for Viardot by Saint-Saëns.

21 Louise Kirkby-Lunn as Dalila

Not everyone, however, was so fulsome in her praises. One critic wrote of 'a plentitude of thick and oily tone'.[8] Aldrich, while praising her 'nobly beautiful voice', thought some of her singing suffered 'from monotony and insufficient characterisation'.[9] Her records suggest something of this, and also a certain diffidence. As Laura, for example, duelling with Destinn's Gioconda, she may claim to love Enzo like 'the light of creation' but it seems to be burning rather low. At her best, in Adriano's great scene from Wagner's *Rienzi*, she declaims with fervour and passion; but even here, though the singing is sure and wonderfully composed, it is somehow inexpressive, and hardly a word of the English text can be made out. Her recordings of ballads and songs are often attractive, but like Homer with Schumann-Heink she was exposed to overwhelming competition, in her case from Clara Butt.

DAME CLARA BUTT (1873–1936) was a great British institution, coming forth at Imperial jamborees like Britannia herself, swathed in red-white-and-blue, to lead the community singing. Once upon a time there was scarcely a household in the country boasting a gramophone that did not have her record declaiming 'Land of Hope and Glory'—the one made in Hyde Park, where her voice rides the combined band of the Grenadiers and 10,000 loyal hearts, Lord Beaverbrook's and Nancy Astor's among them. On a clear day, Beecham claimed, you could have heard her across the English Channel. It was not a voice to everyone's taste. Reynaldo Hahn called it 'une voix obscène'. Compared with his own effete baritone, Dame Clara's mighty alto must have been shocking. Her range was just as remarkable. Sir Adrian Boult remembers a rehearsal when she sang through four B flats with ease: at the top it was sure and brilliant, in the lower reaches vast and powerful. On her first tour of the United States, Henderson acclaimed it 'the greatest contralto voice heard since Alboni'.

At her audition for the open scholarship at the Royal College of Music her singing of Hatton's song 'The Enchantress' created such a stir among the examiners that she mistook their genuine astonishment for amusement. Funny, was she? She'd show 'em! And, pulling out all the stops, she fairly hurled her great voice at them—'Kings have trembled when I came, reading doom upon my face'—letting

22 Clara Butt dressed as Britannia

out a low E like some tolling bell. 'I don't know about kings,' she remarked afterwards, 'but those examiners they certainly trembled.'[10] When they asked her to sing something else, quieter, she chose the solo from *Elijah*, 'Woe unto them'. They got the message; she got the scholarship.

Her career at the Royal College was crowned by an appearance as Orfeo, her first and, as it was to turn out, her only operatic role. Afterwards she went to Paris and Berlin for further study with Jacques Bouhy and Etelka Gerster, a pupil of Marchesi. Saint-Saëns wanted her to sing Dalila, but due to laws then extant forbidding the representation of Biblical subjects on the British stage, nothing came of it. One cannot help wondering how the usual stunted Samson would have made out with a six-foot-two Dalila. She would not have needed to wait until he was lying down to cut his hair off.

Her stage was the concert platform; her repertory, after the regulation Bach or Handel and a little Lieder, was the popular ballads of the day. She made a speciality out of those songs that, while hardly liturgical, are somehow not decently secular either: 'The lost chord', 'There is no death', 'O divine Redeemer', and perhaps the most notorious, a setting of 'Abide with Me' composed by her accompanist, Samuel Liddle. The text is an indifferent paraphrase of a passage from St Luke, the music surpassingly sentimental; yet so intense is the singer's utterance, the listener must steel himself against its awful power. There was another Clara Butt too who could support the thinnest thread of tone across the largest auditorium in 'A fairy went a-marketing', 'How pansies grow' and the 'Wee small bird'.

As in the case of her great contemporaries Caruso and Chaliapin, her voice recorded well, and she made a large number of records. In Handel's 'Ombra mai fu' and 'Rend'il sereno', we hear the real portamento style; if she imposes upon those secular pieces a sanctimonious fervour seemingly at odds with the text, this was not so much a lack of scholarship as a comment on the Victorian attitude to Handel. Handel 'as everyone knew' was the Church of England set to music, his operas a conformist gesture in a godforsaken age, but now they could be heard for what they really were— oratorio in wolf's clothing. 'Lusinghe più care' from *Alessandro* and Donizetti's Brindisi from *Lucrezia Borgia* contain indelible proof of the brilliance of her coloratura. Though there are no rapid divisions from the chest, and none of Senesino's fiery allegros,

the range is almost identical with his, and if her style is worlds removed from that of the great eighteenth-century virtuosi, there is something reminiscent of descriptions of the castrati in the affecting quality of the voice itself, especially in the power of the chest register. Her art could also be simple and intimate, as in Maude Valérie White's setting of her own translations of two poems by Heine that Schumann had previously used in his *Dichterliebe*: 'A youth once loved a maiden' (Ein Jüngling liebt ein Mädchen) and 'The tears that night' (Aus meinem thränen spriessen). There is no grotesquerie here, nothing of the mighty prophetess; how delicately and cleanly she executes the simple figurations in the first song, and how telling is the deliberate use of the vibrato to create a special effect on the words 'heaven help her lover now'. Here, as in all her records, her diction is not only abundantly clear, but beautiful as well.

5. Tenors

Clara Butt was one of the last of the great popular ballad singers. The ballad had played a dominant role in British musical life right through from the eighteenth century. Butt herself descended from Theodore Hook, a prolific composer of the early nineteenth century, whose 'Twas within a mile of Edinboro' town' Patti often included in her programmes. As the French and German vocal styles were in response to particular developments in the opera, so the English style evolved largely out of the ballad and oratorio; it was a concert rather than stage tradition.

One of the greatest ballad singers of the early nineteenth century was the tenor John Braham. Braham, of Jewish extraction, was trained in the Italian school by Rauzzini, a successful singing teacher who had settled in Bath and whose pupils included the Irish tenor Michael Kelly, creator of Don Basilio in Mozart's *Figaro*. From Rauzzini Braham acquired the basic precepts of the old Italian school. Then, like Rubini and Donzelli in Italy, and Nourrit and Duprez in France, he extended the traditional technique, retaining the brilliance of the eighteenth-century virtuosi (where he was supposed to have been surpassed by Catalani alone) and adding to it the dramatic accents in part acquired from his early cantorial training and partly from the inspiration of the great actors of that period, Mrs Siddons and John Philip Kemble. Like his contemporaries in Italy and France, Braham had mastered the falsetto:

Before his time the junction had always been very clumsily conducted by British singers. By falsetto his range extended from A in the bass to E above the tenor high C. It was so perfectly even and equal, he possessed so thorough a command over it, that he could give any given quantity or quality upon any part of it at pleasure; while if he ran through his whole compass by semi-tones it was impossible to point out at what precise interval he took or relinquished the falsetto.[1]

Some idea of the wide range and ready facility of his voice can be got from the exactingly difficult and, as we have noted, essentially unvocal music of Huon in *Oberon*, which Weber wrote for him. Braham was a minor composer himself and set several of Byron's Hebrew melodies. One of his ballads, 'The Death of Nelson', became a great favourite at concerts throughout the nineteenth century.

Braham's successor was Sims Reeves. Reeves seems by all accounts to have been a more tasteful singer but lacked Braham's stentorian brilliance. He was also handsome in the bewhiskered fashion of Victorian days, which Braham assuredly was not, and he had a great way with the public. In his best days, according to Klein, he made an unforgettable effect in Beethoven's 'Adelaide', with his 'faultless breathing' and 'beautiful phrasing'.[2] But what Klein only hints at, Hanslick spells out:

When I heard him in 1862, they told me his voice was gone but that he still sang well. One can pretty well imagine how it is now, twenty-four years later. Nevertheless, Sims Reeves still croons at all the fashionable concerts; he seems to enjoy it and what is more, is well paid for it. To win the favour of the English public is not easy; to lose it impossible! In Germany a singer like Sims Reeves would inspire merriment, at best; in all probability he would inspire much worse. But the English never let an old favourite down, once he has won their respect, least of all when he is an Englishman and lives in England. This is certainly most admirable. But Sims Reeves' struggle with nature has become too uneven, and it is about time he chose the course of wisdom.[3]

Reeves, in his turn, was followed by EDWARD LLOYD (1845–1927), who was also too long before the public, but we can be grateful that he stayed long enough to make, in his sixtieth year, some remarkable if not always pleasing records. Like Braham, Lloyd was short and unprepossessing in appearance; for this reason, it was said, he never sang in the theatre. In concert he was the ranking oratorio tenor, creating principal parts in Sullivan's

23 Edward Lloyd

Martyr of Antioch and *Golden Legend*, in Gounod's *Redemption* and *Mors et Vita*, in Parry's *Judith* and *King Saul*, and in Elgar's *Caractacus* and *Dream of Gerontius*. Klein describes his voice in the early years of his career:

It was one of the most exquisite quality. The smoothness of his legato was amazing; it was said to compare with Giuglini; and those who were fortunate enough to hear him sing Handel's 'Love in her eyes', could well believe it; it was absolutely unsurpassable. Such Handelian singing has not been heard since.[4]

Between 1874 and 1900, Lloyd took part in every Handel Triennial Festival at the Crystal Palace. There, in the largest greenhouse in the world, 16,000 people would assemble for London's greatest musical bonanza. Where small voices easily evaporated, his beautiful, clear and resonant tones carried through the vast spaces to grand effect. Yet, for all that he was much admired, he lacked the indefinable personal quality of a public idol. He succeeded to Reeves's repertory but never could quite replace him in the public's affections.

According to Shaw, if Lloyd sang Gounod's 'Lend me your aid' once in a season he sang it a hundred times. Allowing for Shavian hyperbole, it came very near to being his signature tune; he made two records of it—the first of the aria alone, the second an abridged version of the aria but with the long declamatory recitative, beginning 'How frail and weak a thing is man'. His voice underlines the point; the tone is cracked and old, but there is nothing feeble in the manner of delivery. Each word is put forth with the utmost conviction, the enunciation perfectly measured, the vowels and consonants clear but not separated. The soft consonants, indeed, retain almost as much tone as the vowels; the hard ones are attacked cleanly but without any ugly coup de glotte. In the aria there are remains of his amazing legato and perfectly judged portamenti, and though he can scarcely move in the upper reaches with the ease of youth, the flow is never interrupted.

'The mantle of Braham and Sims Reeves which was worthily borne by Edward Lloyd,' wrote Klein, 'rested more or less easily upon the shoulders of BEN DAVIES (1858–1943), a singer whose rare musical instinct and intelligence have always partially atoned for his uneven scale and lack of ringing head notes'.[5] Davies was from Pontardawe in Wales. Unlike Lloyd, who evolved from chorister to soloist without any formal training, he went to London to study with Alberto Randegger, a well-known conductor, repetiteur and singing teacher. Davies's stage debut was with the Carl Rosa Opera Company, and for the first ten years of his career he was principally an opera singer, with occasional appearances in operetta and musical comedy. By 1891, he was the leading 'English' operatic tenor. Sullivan selected him for the title-role in his *Ivanhoe*, which opened the Royal English Opera House, later to become the Palace Theatre. The following season he made his Covent Garden debut as Faust; two years later he sang there again in Cowen's *Signa*. Thereafter he turned almost entirely to concert work. In 1896, he sang in the first performance of Liza Lehmann's song cycle *In a Persian Garden*, subsequently making extensive tours of Great Britain, the Empire and the United States, where he was greatly admired at the Cincinatti Festival.

Davies was by no means the first British singer to desert opera for the concert hall. As Hanslick noted,

it was a matter of economics:

> It is difficult for an Englishman to commit himself to the theatre. Lloyd the tenor, and Santley the baritone, earn three times as much from concerts and oratorios as Carl Rosa can offer them.[6]

He made a large number of records, mostly of traditional and popular songs, and left one souvenir of his Covent Garden days, 'Salve dimora' from *Faust*, a forthright, rather unsubtle performance, the high C confirming Shaw's judgment: 'Mr Davies always a spendthrift in difficulties.'[7]

From the land of song, though less directly, came forth two other successful concert singers, Dan Beddoe and Evan Williams. The former, from Ameraman, Wales, emigrated to the United States while still in his early twenties; the latter was born in Ohio of Welsh parents.

DAN BEDDOE (1863–1937) was the elder by four years. At the age of 19, in 1882, he took first prize in a singing contest at the Eisteddfod. After arriving in the United States, he studied in Cleveland and later Pittsburgh, and then became a successful church singer in New York. By the time he made his official oratorio debut in 1903, he was already 40 years old. The following year Walter Damrosch engaged him

24 Ben Davies in Cellier's *Doris*

to sing the name part in a concert version of *Parsifal*, which was the nearest he ever got to an opera house. During the next ten years he travelled widely as a concert singer throughout the United States, and was particularly regarded for his singing of the tenor music in *Elijah* and the *Messiah*. It was in the former that he was invited to sing at a special Crystal Palace performance during the Coronation season of 1911. Thereafter, in his native country and throughout the rest of Great Britain, he was a popular and frequent visitor, giving recitals and taking part in concerts. From 1925 to 1929 his annual *Messiah* was one of the events in New York's musical calendar. At that time, as his later recordings prove, his voice was still amazingly fresh and responsive. His last appearance was in 1934, at the age of 71.

Beddoe visited the recording studios several times in the years between 1911 and 1914. His voice though not large had great natural charm and sweetness of tone; it also had a pronounced though not disturbing vibrato. In the solo from *Elijah*, 'Then shall the righteous shine forth', we can hear what was most characteristic of his best singing, the soft liquid consonants and beautifully clear diction. His affectionate delivery almost succeeds in disguising a want of breadth in the phrasing, of a really

25 Evan Williams

firm legato. There is something irresistably attractive about the way his voice does, literally, 'shine forth'; was it because of this that Caruso made Beddoe's recitals an exception and broke his golden rule of never going to hear other tenors?

While Beddoe began adult life as a coal miner, EVAN WILLIAMS (1867–1918) worked in a steel mill. He too, was discovered in an amateur singing competition and went to Cleveland to study. In the years between 1896 and 1911, he sang regularly at the Worcester Festival. In 1903 he undertook for the first time a recital tour of Great Britain and returned often in later years. In the United States his popularity was enormous; as a recitalist alone he is said to have made more than a thousand appearances, and he was equally in demand for oratorio and concert work. We can get some idea of the variety of his accomplishment from the programme of his New York recital in 1906. This included 'Waft her angels' from Handel's *Jephtha,* 'In native worth' from Haydn's *Seasons*, and the solo, 'The sorrows of death' from Mendelssohn's *Hymn of Praise*. His songs included Beethoven's cycle *An die ferne Geliebte*, as well as pieces by von Fielitz and Cécile Chaminade. Aldrich wrote:

> It is a voice of uncommon charm, of a lyric quality that is rare; yet, it is powerful withal, and he has equally rare qualities of intelligence, imagination, taste and sentiment. It is true that sentiment is sometimes unduly to the fore in his singing . . . but Mr Williams has ampler resources of a robuster and more vigorous expression; and they vitalised and invigorated his best work last evening.[8]

His recordings show a marked resemblance in style and voice to those of Beddoe. Williams also had a vibrato, though far less pronounced, and if his charm of manner is not as great, his voice seems to have been a more powerful instrument. In the ballad 'Love abiding' by Jordan, there is something of the sentiment Aldrich complained of, though less in Williams's simple and lovely singing than in the song itself, a typical period piece. It is a pity that his interpretation of Acis's famous 'Love in her eyes sits playing', from Handel's masque, had to be so drastically cut to fit the record; there is neither central section nor da capo. It is a shapely piece of legato singing, beautifully phrased with immaculate diction, the simple ornaments exactly and gracefully executed; only the passage notes sound a little squeezed.

26 Sir Charles Santley as Don Giovanni

6. Baritones and Basses

The greatest Victorian singer to survive to make records was the baritone, SIR CHARLES SANTLEY (1834–1922). Born nine years before Patti in Liverpool, his career was principally in the English speaking world, where he was first a renowned opera and oratorio singer, later a notable exponent of the ballad. He studied in Italy under Gaetano Nava and made his stage debut at Pavia, in 1858, as the Doctor in *Traviata*, later appearing at the Paris Opéra and La Scala. After returning to London he resumed his studies with Garcia (Santley was the only one of Garcia's great pupils to make records). His Covent Garden debut took place in 1859 with the Pyne-Harrison English Opera Company; it was

not until 1862 that he first appeared in the International season, when Gye engaged him for some performances of di Luna in *Trovatore*. He made a considerable impression. Thereafter he joined Mapleson's company, with which he remained for some years, appearing in a wide range of parts—as Hoël in Meyerbeer's *Dinorah*, Creon in Cherubini's *Medea*, Alfonso in *Lucrezia Borgia*, as well as Pizarro, di Luna and Valentin. For Santley, Gounod agreed to add the aria 'Even bravest heart'; the original words were provided by Chorley, and the French translation by Pradère, which does not fit too elegantly, was made later. It was not until quite recent times that it was included in performances in France, and it does not appear in many early French editions of the score.

In 1875 Santley joined Carl Rosa, one of the stalwarts in the campaign for opera in English, in his season at Drury Lane, afterwards at the Princes Theatre and on tour throughout the country. For Carl Rosa too, he showed off his versatility, in Balfe's *Siege of Rochelle*, Cherubini's *Water Carrier*, and, with suitable transpositions, the title-roles of Hérold's *Zampa* and Auber's *Fra Diavolo*, but his greatest success was reserved for Wagner's *Flying Dutchman*:

> Santley made a strangely mysterious and pathetic figure of Vanderdecken and sang his music with the requisite fervid energy.[1]

For Carl Rosa he was also Figaro in some English performances of the opera which Klein rated the best ensemble he had ever heard; this is the only one of his many roles of which he has left a sample of his interpretation on record. He continued to appear in opera from time to time until his farewell at Covent Garden in 1911, when he played Tom Tug in Dibdin's *Waterman*.

Santley was an outstanding oratorio and concert singer, his interpretative powers matched only by consummate vocal artistry. Hanslick heard him in 1886, and noted that though 'his hair and his voice too have turned grey, his singing is still effective, helped by refined vocalism and wise circumspection'.[2] Two years later Shaw found his singing 'as fresh and his method as unfailing as ever'.[3] Nearly twenty years after that, Klein wrote that his voice had lost its 'haunting beauty of tone', but there still survived 'perfect phrasing' and a remarkable 'measure of energy, vigour and feeling'.[4] About this time one of his concert favourites was the aria 'Del minacciar del vento' from Handel's *Ottone*; on one occasion, young John McCormack from Ireland heard him, and years after remembered 'Santley sang runs as I never heard man sing them before or since. It was a model of Handelian singing.'[5] An accolade from one champion to another. His singing made a similar impression on Sir Henry Wood:

Santley had the strongest rhythmic sense of any vocalist I ever accompanied. The technique of his Handelian vocalisation was clarity itself, and the phenomenal compass of his voice, from the low bass E flat to the top baritone G, was brilliantly even throughout. His performance of Handel's great aria 'Nasce il bosco' is one of my most cherished vocal memories. All his low Fs told—even to the remotest corners of the largest concert hall, while his top Fs were as a silver trumpet.[6]

Santley made two visits to the recording studio, the first of these in 1903, when he was already in his seventieth year. The voice, though by then dry and rather flat-sounding, is still superbly responsive. The selections are not especially interesting save that from Figaro, 'Non più andrai'. It is a matter of regret that he did not record either of the Handel arias referred to above, Schubert's 'Erlkönig' or Schumann's 'Ich grolle nicht', all of which he was still singing, instead of a group of unattractive Victorian ballads. Even so, they show off his exquisite art. In 'Thou'rt passing hence', the fine legato and beautifully clear but unaffected diction are some compensation for Sullivan at his most lugubrious. In 'To Anthea', we have an example of 'that sostenuto marcato style in which he excelled . . . He never broke the vocal line but always added the words to the tone and his marcato singing was never marred by shock of diaphragm, nor aspiration' (Sir Henry Wood). But it is the Figaro which is his finest legacy. Few pieces have become so vulgarised over the years by exaggerated marking of the rhythm. Santley's interpretation is a *jeu d'esprit*, contrived by a variety of rhythmic nuances that are never allowed to disturb an implicit legato; the dotted notes are retained for their proper length, not double-dotted. The embellishments too are in the correct style: a turn at the G, on the word 'contante', and a little flourish on the suspension immediately before the last reprise. In spite of the singer's age it is a lovely record, and he was obviously delighted with it himself; in the piano postlude we can hear him making approving noises.

In 1907, King Edward VII created Santley a knight; he was the first singer to be so honoured,

27 Sir George Henschel

and it was a just and timely acknowledgement. Sir Charles Santley was followed, in 1914, by SIR GEORGE HENSCHEL (1850–1934). Henschel, a naturalised British subject born in Breslau, was a remarkably accomplished musician, a composer, conductor, pianist and teacher as well as singer. At the Leipzig Conservatory he studied composition with Reinecke, singing with Goetze, piano with Moscheles and conducting with Richter. He was still a student when he made his first public appearance as a pianist. In 1868 he sang Hans Sachs in a concert performance of *Die Meistersinger*. In 1874 he took part in the Lower Rhine Festival and later sang in Bach's *Matthäuspassion* under the direction of Brahms. Three years later he made his London debut in a programme of Bach and Handel. He stayed on in London becoming soloist with the Bach Choir and, after marrying the American soprano Lillian Bailey, undertook with her joint recitals throughout Britain and the United States. In 1881, he was offered and accepted the position of Principal Conductor of the newly formed Boston Symphony Orchestra. Under Henschel's direction it quickly came to rank among the finest in the world. In 1884, he left Boston and returned to London. For the next twenty years he was Professor of Singing at the Royal College of Music, in succession to Jenny Lind. At the same time he founded the London Symphony Concerts. At these he revived a considerable amount of neglected music, as well as bringing out many new works. When these concerts failed to receive the public support he had hoped for, he went to Glasgow as conductor of the Scottish Orchestra.

Henschel composed a sizeable quantity of music—several choral works, more than a hundred songs and three operas. It was in a performance of one of them, *Nubia*, at Dresden in 1899 that he made his only stage appearance, stepping into the breach at the last minute, when one of the singers fell ill. None of his music has been revived in recent years and Shaw wrote scathingly of particular pieces. One song, 'Spring', was recorded by Melba and Eames. It is a harmless trifle—the singer persistently echoing the cuckoo—that would doubtless raise a few smirks today; yet the words are rather important—they are from 'Summer's last Will and Testament' by Thomas Nashe (*c.* 1600). As a conductor, Klein thought:

> His readings of the classical masterpieces might be conscientious and artistic, but they lacked individuality, force and warmth [whereas] the vocal recitals he gave with the aid of his accomplished wife never failed to attract by virtue of the unique interpretive charm with which the two singers invested their delightful selections.[7]

His conducting, not strictly our concern here, has been preserved by Columbia in a performance of Beethoven's First Symphony; it seems to confirm the opinion of Aldrich, 'a singer who could not make the orchestra sing'.[8] His vocal art survives in two series of recordings, the first made in 1908, the second in 1928, when he was seventy-eight years old. Even in the first there is not a great deal of voice, though it is doubtful if it was ever particularly strong, and it was certainly not a powerful instrument. However, he uses it with remarkable expressive skill, employing a wide variety of tonal colour. The only flaw—no doubt acquired

28 Harry Plunkett Greene

from his German training—is his constant employment of the voix blanche, a device which, if resorted to at all, should be kept only for very special effects. Draining the voice of colour and removing its natural movement can only be done by taking the voice off its breath support and in so doing not only whitening the sound but also flattening it; Shaw was quick to point out how often Henschel sang out of tune. It is therefore unmusical as well as sounding unlovely. Unfortunately, over the years, in the name of interpretation, it has become an accepted feature of lieder singing.

Henschel's interpretations have an almost improvisatory character, achieved by intensity of utterance and a free though never exaggerated treatment of the rhythm, contrived in part by playing his own accompaniments. Nowadays this is frowned upon, but the practice has some notable precedent; Rossini, Schubert, Gounod, de Lara and Hahn, among many, all delighted in singing to their own accompaniment. Today their songs are done very differently with the singer and the pianist in evening, or should we rather call it fancy, dress, presenting in the cold and formal atmosphere of the modern concert hall music for the most part written for informal occasions. Henschel's *voix de compositeur*, with his own piano playing, harks back to earlier, more intimate gatherings. His records preserve something of that informality when he juxtaposes two of Schumann's more popular songs, 'Ich grolle nicht' and the Smith's Song. He gets from one to the other by a succession of modulatory chords, the sort of thing that was once done by every important pianist; we can hear it still in recordings made by Busoni and Josef Hofmann. Just to reinforce that impression of informality, at the same time he clears his throat!

Another popular personality and noted exponent of the German lied and English ballads, from the folk song to the works of contemporary composers, was the Irish-born baritone, HARRY PLUNKETT GREENE (1865–1936). Greene studied in London with Blume and later in Florence with Vannuccini, a pupil of Lamperti. His first appearance was as soloist in Handel's *Messiah* at a popular proletarian institution of that day, the People's Palace, Mile End, in June 1888; he was 22. The following year he took part in a performance of Gounod's *Redemption* at one of Novello's Oratorio Concerts and he soon established himself as a leading soloist of the day. In 1890 he appeared at Covent Garden, as the Commendatore in *Don Giovanni* and the Duke of Verona in *Roméo et Juliette*. It was an experience he chose not to repeat; he was wise enough to realise his voice was unequal to the demands of an operatic career. In the concert hall he created the part of Job in Parry's oratorio, and was particularly associated with the works of Stanford, who wrote the *Songs of the Fleet* especially for him. He was also an impressive interpreter of the lieder of Schubert, Schumann and Brahms. Like Santley and Henschel before him, Greene made two sets of records, the first between 1904 and 1906. We may agree with Klein that had his vocal attributes only been on a par with his interpretive powers '[he] might fairly have been described as one of the finest concert vocalists of his time.'[9] His interpretive powers are indeed noteworthy. His voice, however, sounds dull and grey and he has difficulty in sustaining tones. As with Santley, the style is unmistakeably English, with the same beautiful diction. The only German song he recorded, the 'Abschied' from Schubert's *Schwanengesang*, is an interpretation of great charm. It goes with a wonderful swagger, the rhythm delicately but firmly marked and never breaking through the vocal line, the phrasing punctuated with seemingly careless grace.

Another pupil of Blume, nine years older than Greene, was the bass-baritone, ROBERT WATKIN-MILLS (1856–1930). He made his debut at a Crystal Palace concert in 1884. The following year, for Carl Rosa, he sang one performance of Baldassare in Donizetti's *La Favorita*. He was offered a permanent contract but turned it down in favour of a concert career. Thereafter he established himself as a leading oratorio singer. After 1894, he made tours of Australia, the United States and Canada, where he eventually settled.

Klein found him a 'safe singer' who deserved his reputation. Sir Henry Wood's description is more equivocal:

29 Robert Watkin-Mills

30 Andrew Black

Watkin-Mills' voice was of a penetrating quality and he sang Handel in what I call the sledge-hammer style. I found his singing rather dull and mechanical, but the Promenaders loved his Handelian runs which he executed with amazing force, each note being crystal clear. He was certainly able to give wonderful lessons in Handelian vocalisation.[10]

His recording of Simon's 'The Lord worketh wonders' from *Judas Maccabeus*, confirms Wood's opinion. It shows off a big, rather throaty voice. The singer appears to have difficulty in finding any head resonance, and from D upwards tones are not always pitched high enough, but the divisions from bottom A to the E above middle C are certainly hurled out with amazing force and clarity.

Of all Santley's successors in the oratorio and concert tradition, it was the Scottish baritone, ANDREW BLACK (1859–1920) who possessed the finest natural voice. Born in Glasgow, he came to London to study with Randegger. Like Watkin-Mills, he made his debut at the Crystal Palace, in the summer of 1887. The following year he sang there

again, as Lord Cranston in MacCunn's *Lay of the Last Minstrel*. This was the work of a twenty-year-old prodigy who had taken London's musical establishment by storm in a whole series of Gaelic epics, *Lord Ullin's Daughter, Land of the Mountain,* and *The Flood and Ship o'the Fiend*; perhaps some enterprising nationalist will address himself to the task of letting us hear what, if anything, these pieces are worth. In 1892, Black sang at the Leeds Festival in Dvorak's *Spectre's Bride*; in 1903, at Birmingham, he took the part of Judas in the first performance of Elgar's *The Apostles*.

Klein rated him—

> . . . one of the best male singers that Scotland has ever produced, the possessor of a superbly resonant voice, and notably impressive in music calling for pathetic sentiment and declamatory vigour.[11]

We can hear just how fine a voice it was in his recording of the Curate's song from *The Sorcerer*, a piece calling for precisely that pathetic sentiment he excelled in. Like most singers of this period, his diction is a model of clarity and this is managed without upsetting the line. In the upper range however the tone is sometimes rather constricted and the voice does not ring forth freely.

The concert and oratorio tradition was equally vigorous at this time on the other side of the Atlantic. One of its most celebrated exponents was born in Philadelphia two years before Andrew Black.

DAVID BISPHAM (1857–1921) came from a Quaker family. At first he was disinclined to yield to the temptations of a career in the theatre, but after his wife over-rode his objections he took some lessons from a local singing teacher, Edward Giles. A few years later he came to Europe, to Milan to study first with Vannuccini and then the elder Lamperti. From Italy he went to London, making his concert debut there in 1890. The following year he played the Duc de Longueville, in an English version of Messager's *La Basoche*, for d'Oyly Carte's short-lived English Opera Company. Henry Wood heard him about this time:

> His voice was of a real ugly, harsh quality. I told him not to attempt anything requiring beauty of tone for he simply had not got any. I suggested character singing.[12]

Whether on Wood's advice or his own initiative he went off to Bayreuth to study there. In 1892, he returned to London and sang for the first time at

31 David Bispham

recitalist. Seventy years ago his programmes must have seemed remarkable musical events; in 1904, the final group in his annual New York recital included ten songs of Hugo Wolf. Later he introduced works by Cornelius, Loewe and Brahms. In his autobiography he claimed to have sung more than 1400 different songs. All this activity had its rewards; he was one of only six singers who could be sure of a sold-out house at Carnegie Hall (the others were all women, Eames, Gadski, Nordica, Sembrich and Schumann-Heink). 'His versatility was extraordinary,' wrote Klein, 'alike in French light opera, Wagnerian music drama, Italian opera, oratorio and lieder.'[14] It went further than that. He frequently featured in his recitals a melodrama, i.e. verses declaimed to the accompaniment of a piano or orchestra, among these Longfellow's *King Robert of Sicily* with music by Cole and Tennyson's *Enoch Arden* with music by Richard Strauss. In 1898, he temporarily deserted the lyric theatre to play Beethoven in a Broadway production of Hugo Miller's play, *Adelaide,* though the title suggests he must have sung at least one song in the evening.

His recordings do not by any means preserve all these wide-ranging talents. There are few operatic arias, little oratorio and no melodramas, but he did make many interesting song titles, from Stephen Storace to Richard Strauss; the latter, like some Schubert songs, in translation, testifying to his ardent championing of the cause of opera and song in the vernacular. Aldrich's description of his performance in recital is borne out in many of his recordings:

> [Bispham] seeks to emphasise every characteristic touch and significant point in music or verse and make it tell to the utmost; the clearness of his diction, that makes his texts for the most part easily intelligible— one of Bispham's most admirable traits, though sometimes it is exploited at the expense of the musical quality of the phrase and melodic line; his fondness for lingering on the nasal and liquid consonants, and the individual timbre of his voice has much about it that is fine.[15]

In his method we may note again certain resemblances to Sembrich, the same rapid and narrow vibrato, the same slightly 'blown' attack, presumably the product of Lamperti's teaching. A recording of Gounod's setting of 'O that we two were maying' preserves his suave legato enlivened by a delicate use of messa di voce, the words firmly placed on the breath. It is a performance full of subtle vocal inflexions, yet quite without artfulness. Like

Covent Garden, as Kurwenal in *Tristan*; during the next ten years he missed only two seasons. His Met debut followed during the 1896–7 season. At both theatres he was acclaimed for his 'delineation of character', principally in leading baritone roles in Wagner's music dramas: the Dutchman, Wolfram, Telramund, Wotan, Beckmesser and Alberich. He was also admired as Escamillo, Alfio, Masetto, Pizarro, Iago and Falstaff. Altogether, in a stage career lasting little more than a decade, he sang fifty-eight different roles. From about 1903, he began to work principally in oratorio and concert. In 1904, Henry Wood heard him again while on a visit to the United States. He was amazed at the improvement in Bispham's singing—

> 'What have you been doing with your voice?' I asked him. 'Nothing, except listening,' Bispham replied.[13]

The example of his colleagues in the opera, the de Reszkés, Lassalle, Plançon and d'Andrade, had not been lost on him.

Like Sembrich, Bispham was an enterprising

Santley he was also a master of the sostenuto marcato style. We can hear it to great advantage in Schubert's 'Hark, hark the lark', (with Shakespeare's original words), an interpretation of much grace and eloquence, the rhythm well sprung, so that in the echoing lines, where he helps himself to liberal ritards, the effect is most expressive. All the portamenti are beautifully done. What lady could easily resist a lover who bade her 'Arise' so ingratiatingly?—even if his voice in itself was not a thing of loveliness. Except for one gruppetto on the last repeat of 'with everything that pretty is', it is sung as written.

EMILIO DE GORGORZA (1874–1949) was another of America's favourite concert artists at the turn of the century. Unlike Bispham, who had built up a reputation as an opera and operetta singer first, de Gorgorza's popularity derived from intense activity in the recording studio. The number of records he made during the first decade of this century covers more than eight pages in Bauer's catalogue, in itself a record. Under his own name he recorded for Victor; as Carlos Francisco and singing Spanish, Cuban and Mexican popular songs, for the Zonophone Company; as M. Fernand, French operatic arias and *mélodies* for the Eldridge R. Johnson Improved Record; and as Herbert Goddard, English ballads, for Climax Records. Nowadays, we might be tempted to think of such goings-on as an early example of tax avoidance; in fact it was a way of getting round an exclusive recording contract.

De Gorgorza, like Blauvelt, Strong and de Lussan, was from Brooklyn. Both of his parents were Spanish and at an early age he was taken to Spain, where he was educated and had his first singing lessons. As a young man he came back to the United States, to New York, to study with Moderati and Agramonte. In 1897, he made his concert debut at the Carnegie Hall, as supporting artist to Marcella Sembrich. Owing to a physical disability he was unable to make a career on the stage, though he sang with effect the title role in a concert version of Tchaikovsky's *Eugene Onegin* during the 1906 season. At that time he was married to Emma Eames and their joint recitals were popular events in New York and various cities throughout the United States. On these occasions it was husband rather than wife who enjoyed the critics' unqualified praises, a fact which may have proved a bone of contention between them; at any rate the marriage did not last. There are a number of souvenirs of the partnership: recordings of duets from *Figaro, Don Giovanni, Flauto Magico, Trovatore* and *Véronique*. In 'La ci darem', for example, Eames's rather matronly Zerlina (she sang Anna in the theatre) comes off less well than de Gorgorza's elegant-sounding Don.

His records have always been great favourites. All of them, whether operatic arias of Mozart, Rossini, Bellini, Meyerbeer or Verdi, songs from musical comedies, English ballads, or the *mélodies* of Debussy, offer the same polished singing, sensitive musicianship and good taste. Like many of the greatest artists he even turns his disadvantages to account: out of a rather small and throaty voice he produces an affecting quality that is wholly individual; a too prominent vibrato he transforms into a shimmer that gives the tone a special vitality. His interpretation of 'Deh vieni alla finestra' serves to remind us that though Don Giovanni went to the devil, this is not Méphistophélès's Serenade; it is done without exaggerating particular words at the expense of the vocal line—after all Don Giovanni could hardly have achieved all those conquests without having had, first and foremost, an ingratiating manner. His appropriation of 'Clavelitos' may seem odd; from his photographs—a little man, moustachioed with pince-nez—one can hardly imagine him sitting on a street corner selling carnations, but the singing is so enchanting it seems churlish to cavil.

David Bispham was the first American male

32 Emilio de Gorgorza

singer to gain an international reputation, and in several of his parts his place after his retirement from opera was taken by CLARENCE WHITEHILL (1871–1932). Whitehill was born in Iowa. He began his vocal studies in Chicago and then went to Paris, to the studio of Giovanni Sbriglia, a teacher who counted among his pupils Pol Plançon and Edouard de Reszké, and had helped 'convert' Jean de Reszké from baritone to tenor. In 1899, Whitehill made his debut at the Monnaie in Brussels, as Frère Laurent in Gounod's *Roméo et Juliette*. The following year he sang Nilakantha in *Lakmé* at the Opéra-Comique. Then he joined the Metropolitan English Grand Opera Company; the only other important artist on the roster was Zélie de Lussan. In 1902, he returned to Europe, to Frankfurt, for further study with Julius Stockhausen, one of Garcia's most distinguished pupils. In Germany he appeared in various Wagnerian roles at Frankfurt, Cologne and later Munich. At Bayreuth, his interpretations of Wolfram, Amfortas and Gunther received Cosima's seal of approval. When London first heard him as Wotan in 1905, 'he gave ample proof of the great reputation he had won for himself on the continent'.[16] He was the obvious choice for the role when, three years later, Richter determined on producing the *Ring* cycle in English. Higgins complained at having to pay Whitehill's fee but Richter insisted. Afterwards Whitehill returned to the United States for his first season at the Met. His Amfortas, Wotan, Wanderer and Gunther were well received by the critics, Henderson particularly praising 'his beauty of tone, musical phrasing and nuancing . . . nobility . . . and dignity of style'.[17] He remained a prominent member of the company until the year before his death, in 1931.

Whitehill was a fine-looking man with an impressive stage presence. His repertory included many unusual roles, Petruchio in Goetze's *Widerspenstigen Zähmung*, Ludwig in the Met's staging of Liszt's oratorio *St Elisabeth*, Altair in Strauss's *Aegyptische Helena*, Archibaldo in Montemezzi's *L'Amore dei tre Re*, the title-role in Thomas's *Hamlet* and Petronius in Nouguès's *Quo Vadis?*, in all of which he made a considerable impression. This, as Henderson revealed after his death, not without having to overcome a long-standing difficulty 'owing to the super sensitiveness of one vocal cord. When this was slightly congested the singer's tone acquired a little roughness . . . when the congestion was pronounced he became unmistakeably hoarse.'[18] The problem was hinted at in some reviews:

33 Clarence Whitehill as Amfortas in *Parsifal*

His voice did not seem to be at all times in the best condition. It sounded at its best when he sang with full power; in passages of less power, especially those of sustained character, it was not always under control, either in quality or intonation. He frequently sang flat. (Aldrich after a New York recital in 1911)[19]

Most of his records do not seem to have suffered from this infirmity. His interpretations are impressive, though they lack in the last degree any particular individuality. He delivers Wotan's 'Abendlich strahlt' from *Rheingold* with much dignity, but the declamation has neither the authority nor style of van Rooy. In the rushing divisions of 'Why do the Nations' the execution if not absolutely accurate is notably smooth, helping to explain why he was so highly accounted as an oratorio singer. An unusual title is the aria of Harés from Isadore de Lara's *Messaline*, 'O nuit d'amour', here sung in a German translation. Though there is some constriction in the higher notes at the climax, it shows off much of that 'beauty of tone' and 'dignity of style', of which Henderson wrote.

Part II

The French Tradition

7. 'Le Beau Idéal'

The greatest French tenor of the later part of the nineteenth century, in fact the greatest French singer of his day, was the Pole JEAN DE RESZKE (1850–1925), and if that sounds Irish we should remember that vocal style is the product of cultural identification, not the accident of birth—a baby born in a stable is not a horse. It was in Paris that de Reszké had his first great triumphs and in the music of French composers, sung in the French language. Like Nourrit, who acquired the classical Italian method from the elder Garcia, de Reszké was a pupil of Ciaffei and later Cotogni. His operatic career began as a baritone, in Venice in 1874, in the role of the King in *La Favorita*. He made a good impression, 'finishing off the cabaletta, 'De' nemici tuoi lo sdegno' with a ringing high A'.[1] In London, later the same year, in the same role, the *Illustrated London News* praised his

> voice of beautiful and even quality with an exceptionally high range, he phrases well, especially in cantabile passages and adds to his vocal qualifications the possession of a good stage presence.[2]

He went on to De Nevers, Almaviva in *Figaro*, Valentin and Don Giovanni; of his singing in this last role, the same critic gives the first clue as to the young man's real future. 'The voice,' he wrote, 'is more tenor than baritone in quality.'[3] A fact de Reszké himself was becoming increasingly aware of. Two years later he withdrew for a further period of study with Giovanni Sbriglia. When he returned to the stage, at the Teatro Reale, Madrid, in 1879, it was as a tenor, in the title-role of Meyerbeer's *Robert le Diable*. At first he made no effect at all. It was not until 1884 that the tide turned. His biographer, Clara Leiser, a lady not a little in love with her glamorous subject, gives a typically romantic account of how this happened. It chanced one day that de Reszké was in Paris, in the back room of a music store, running through some scores (apparently at the top of his voice), when who should come by but Massenet. It so happened that the composer was looking for a tenor to take the part of John the Baptist in his new opera *Hérodiade*. Responding at once to this cry from the wilderness, Massenet hurried into the shop and offered de Reszké the part. He accepted, created the role and a furore; within a year Massenet had written another opera especially for him, *Le Cid*. Two years later, as a result of the good offices of Herman Klein, Augustus Harris brought him to Drury Lane. He made his debut as Radames, a role in which, according to Henderson, he was only ever rivalled by Caruso. After that came Lohengrin, Faust and Raoul, each one quickening the pulse of London audiences. Years afterwards, Klein recalled the effect he made as Raoul:

> Alike in a vocal and histrionic sense, it was supremely great. His 'velvety' tones, fresh, clear and mellow as a bell, were emitted with an unsparing freedom that could thrill the listener not once, but twenty times, in the course of a single scene. Then, there was no saving up for the last act . . . And what tenderness, withal, in that famous grand duet of the fourth act! Not Mario himself had phrased the 'Tu m'ami, tu m'ami!' with a greater wealth of delicious surprise and pent-up adoration.[4]

It was the same story in New York, when he arrived there for the first time in 1891. Indeed wherever he went, from St Petersburg to Chicago, he quickly established himself as the beau idéal among tenors; as Shaw put it he was 'one of the beautiful ones'.[5] Whether in the pale moonlight of Gounod's *Roméo et Juliette*, to which the composer had added a new finale to the third act especially for him (the air 'O jour de deuil'), as the tragic José, the fine hero of *Le Cid* with his elegant postures and gracious demeanour, or in the title-role of *Lohengrin* (a knight in shining armour, if ever there was one), he was the perfect matinée idol, the

34 Jean de Reszké as Roméo

delight of every dowager. It would be tedious to enumerate all of his many triumphs; even in a role in which his success was equivocal, such as Verdi's Otello, where he could hardly trumpet out the tones to outsing Tamagno—instead 'he endowed the role with the chivalric and romantic element that had been lost in his great contemporary's almost hysterical savagery'.[6]

For all his enormous popularity, de Reszké was not content to rest on these laurels; he was an ambitious artist, and success stirred him to even greater achievements. Shaw, who was for ever encouraging him to undertake the great Wagnerian tenor roles, wrote:

When the rivalry of younger men and the decay of his old superficial charm with advancing years force him to make the most of all his powers, he may yet gain more as an actor than he will lose as a singer.

And so it was to be. Presently he appeared as Tristan and both Siegfrieds, evoking from the critics a fresh outbreak of superlatives:

> Tristan is a tremendous tragic hero, and the music in which his utterances are embodied is utterly different in style from that in which de Reszké has gained his world-wide fame. Today the tenor has to his credit an impersonation which, in vocal beauty, excels every Tristan known, and in dramatic power is a broad and commanding creation. Not only did he sing it in tune (a refreshing experience) but he sang it with declamatory power that was simply magnificent where power was necessary, and with such a wealth of yearning tenderness in the love passages that he almost eclipsed all memories of his own former fervour . . . It was a great performance of Tristan, and it revealed for the first time the complete musical beauty of Wagner's declamation.[7]

Alas, no commercial records of de Reszké have survived. Indeed it is a moot point whether he ever made any. The only surviving souvenirs of all his greatness are a few minutes captured by Lionel Mapleson in his last Met season, during which he gave an almost complete review of his repertory, appearing as Lohengrin, Faust, Radames, Le Cid, Vasco, Tristan, Walther, Roméo, Siegfried and Raoul, an achievement not equalled by any tenor since. The best of Mapleson's efforts are some excerpts from Vasco's 'O Paradis'. He takes this aria more slowly than we are accustomed to from most singers on 78 records. The grand manner is contrived less by large breath spans than by artful phrasing and expressive use of portamento. The tone of the voice, so far as one can tell, sounds attractive, the legato is suave and elegant. The graces to the vocal line are done with chiselled finesse; at the climax on the words 'tu m'appartiens' the mordent is turned more quickly than has been the fashion since Caruso's time. It does not seem to have been a brilliant or heroic-sized instrument and there is a very abrupt shift into the head register; the B flat having a large measure of falsetto, though to judge from the audience's reaction the effect was pretty stunning.

It has often been disputed that de Reszké was really a tenor. His teacher, Cotogni, denied it: 'He was only a baritone with a high enough range to sing tenor notes.'[8] Shaw, in a letter to Clara Leiser, gives us some idea of the difficulty he had with the upper range of his voice—

35 Emil Scaremberg

He could sing a ringing B natural when he was in good form; but he could only touch C, and was afraid of it. He could barely get through the duel scene from *Les Huguenots*, transposed half a tone down (in the score this goes up to high C sharp). Both Lohengrin and Meistersingers suited him exactly.[9]

Like his great predecessors Nourrit and Duprez, who had accommodated the new music of their age—the operas of Rossini and Meyerbeer—to the classical Italian method, de Reszké in his turn sought to extend that technique and embrace the works of Wagner as well. With a natural voice it would have been a hard enough task, but for a singer who had relied on art as much as nature, it was hardly surprising that the attempt ultimately cut short his career and kept him in a perpetual state of vocal self-consciousness. Emma Eames tells us:

> He was one of the most apprehensive singers imaginable, and wore an expression of terror in his eyes during the whole performance. He always had with him a laryngoscope and frequently examined his throat and larynx.[10]

He was also one of the first to keep a specialist ready

36 Charles Dalmorès as Jean in *Le Prophète*

to hand, throughout a performance constantly having his throat sprayed with this or that medication. De Reszké's Victorian good looks and his charm of manner were very much a part of the era in which he lived; his preoccupation with technique and the science of voice production indicative of the age which followed on.

EMILE SCAREMBERG (1863–1938), a tenor whose voice had the real heroic ring, made his debut in 1893 at the Opéra-COmique, in the title-role of Grétry's *Richard Coeur de Lion*; the following season he graduated to the Opéra. But he had none of the stylish attributes likely to commend him to audiences infatuated with de Reszké. During the next few years he withdrew to the provinces—to Nantes, Vichy, Marseilles, Nice and Bordeaux. Later he went abroad as a guest to the Monnaie, Brussels, and to Antwerp, Monte Carlo and Russia. For one season he sang at Covent Garden as Domique in a revival of Bruneau's *L'Attaque du moulin*, Raoul and Roméo; this last part he shared with de Reszké. Also at Covent Garden that Jubilee season were Salignac, Alvarez and van Dyck (then still in voice); in such company, Scaremberg made no impression. In 1903, after the retirement of de Reszké, the way at last

open, he made his rentrée into the Paris Opéra as Lohengrin, following it with Roméo and Renaud in Gluck's *Armide*. He was to remain unlucky, however, for before he could establish himself an accident brought his career to an untimely end; during a performance he was seriously injured by some falling scenery.

Scaremberg's records show off a strong, evenly produced voice. In spite of a marked vibrato, the tone is pure, the execution clean and mostly accurate. However, his technique is not remarkable; in Sigurd's entrance from Reyer's opera, the brilliant high notes make an effect but the declamation is not securely based. Elsewhere, in music calling for suave phrasing, there is no real legato. His manner is pedestrian and his style provincial.

Scaremberg began his career as a horn player in a military band, and so too did another and far more successful French tenor. CHARLES DALMORES (1871–1939) was from Nancy. For two years he played in the Colonne and Lamoureux orchestras. Then in 1894 he was appointed a professor at the Lyons Conservatory. At about this time his voice began to develop; he decided to give up the horn and go to Paris for vocal instruction. He made his operatic debut in 1899, at the Théâtre des Arts in Rouen. The next season he was engaged by the Monnaie, Brussels, where he remained for some years. In the summer of 1904 he came for the first time to Covent Garden, singing with Calvé in *Carmen* and *Hérodiade* and with Melba in *Faust* and Saint-Saëns's *Hélène*; his 'beautiful and artistic'[11] singing was greatly appreciated. The following year he was back again, adding Roméo with Kurz and creating Win-San-Luy in Leoni's oné-act *L'Oracolo*. He returned in 1909, 1910 and 1911, by which time he had progressed to more dramatic roles. In 1908, he went to Berlin to study the Wagnerian repertory with Emmerich (who had also given lessons to Sammarco and Matzenauer), and in the summer of that year he was engaged at the Bayreuth Festival as Lohengrin; he was one of the first French singers to be so honoured. In the autumn he joined the Manhattan company and thereafter was a regular visitor to the United States. Although he never sang with the regular company at the Met, he appeared there with the Chicago-Philadelphia company as Nicias in *Thaïs* with Garden and Renaud. Aldrich was impressed by his 'remarkably handsome and attractive' appearance, as well as by his 'superb'[12] singing. He even managed to get noticed as Cavaradossi in some performances of *Tosca* in Boston, during which Puritan susceptibilities were outraged by Vanni-Marcoux's frank representation of Scarpia's designs and Garden's equally explicit rejection of them; in the midst of all this Dalmorès's pre-occupation with merely vocal affairs seemed not only more decent but more musical as well. His Pelléas too, was more to the American taste than Perier's 'crooning', even if the impersonation had 'perhaps a trifle too much of the open air about it'.[13]

Records reveal a big, but rather dull and throaty sound, with nothing of Scaremberg's brilliant tone. He is at his best in such declamatory music as Samson's 'Arrêtez o mes frères', phrased in splendidly authoritative style with its incisive attack and expressive portamenti. Though the voice does not move with ease and the upper notes are produced with effort, without much head resonance, it does not detract from the effect.

Dalmorès's good looks and fine stage presence were rivalled, even surpassed, by those of LUCIEN MURATORE (1878–1954). Muratore was from Marseilles, from a family of Piedmontese immigrants. At first he had wanted to be an actor, but on the friendly encouragement of Emma Calvé he decided to move to the lyric theatre. He made his debut opposite Calvé in Reynaldo Hahn's *La*

Carmélite at the Opéra-Comique; to this he quickly added Don José, Guillaume in *Mignon*, Roméo, Rodolfo and principal roles in Fauré's *Pénélope* and Dukas's *Ariane et Barbe Bleue*. Later at the Opéra he sang Faust, Radames, Walther, Herod in *Salome*, and Renaud in *Armide*, as well as creating leading parts in Fevrier's *Monna Vanna*, Massenet's *Roma* and in Ravel's *L'Enfant et les sortilèges*. He sang in Brussels, Bordeaux, Nice and Monte Carlo, where he was Licinio in a memorable revival, in 1912, of Spontini's *La Vestale*. The following year he arrived in New York with his wife, the famous—even notorious—Lina Cavalieri. They appeared together in concert at the Hippodrome. It was an event for eyes as well as ears. Cavalieri, 'the most beautiful

37 Lucien Muratore

woman in the world', was only a singer afterwards. It was, moreover, her first appearance in New York since the breakdown of her second marriage to multi-millionaire Winthrop Chanler. The whole city was agog. So far as appearances went, she did not let expectations down, nor did her new husband. In spite of the fact that Aldrich judged it difficult to assess the worth of a singer in such a place, he nevertheless thought it was obvious that 'Mr Muratore has a good dramatic voice. Like most French singers, his enunciation was a delightful feature of his singing'.[14] However, when Muratore came to the Met, with the Chicago-Philadelphia company, to make his stage debut as Prinzivalle, in *Monna Vanna*, Aldrich was less impressed:

> Neither his tenor voice nor his style of singing can command high commendation. The voice is not devoid of quality, but its tones are unsteady and not always certain of the pitch, and there is an excessive use of 'open' tones that deprives it of some of the warmth and beauty that it might have. His best tones are to be heard only in fortissimo. Mr Muratore's presence is imposing and picturesque, and in certain of his scenes his acting was effective . . .[15]

Henderson did not agree:

> a French tenor of the best type, artistic and fervent. He is an excellent actor for a tenor.[16]

In view of Muratore's long association with the Chicago company—until 1929—it seems to have been Henderson's view that prevailed. Internationally, he was the most prominent French tenor of his time; whatever reservations were made about his singing, his artistry and good looks carried the day. In Paris, where he eventually returned and was for a few weeks at the end of the war made Director of the Opéra-Comique, he was held in especial regard and always referred to as 'Monsieur'.

The evidence of the gramophone suggests that the voice was not smoothly or evenly produced. The change in quality between the registers is too marked. Although it has an attractive timbre, especially in mezza voce, the unsteadiness Aldrich noted—a pronounced shudder—is very apparent as soon as tones are sustained. As an interpreter we can hear why Finck compared him to de Reszké: the manner is charming and the diction beautiful, and though his phrasing is only suggested, and not securely underpinned by a smooth legato, there is about it something of his great predecessor's

38 Charles Rousselière in Saint-Saëns's *Les Barbares*

expansive delivery.

Muratore's immense popularity rather cast CHARLES ROUSSELIERE (1875–1950) into the shade. Born in St Nazaire, he came to Paris as a student and made his debut at the Opéra in 1900 as Samson. In the course of the next decade he established himself in various French provincial theatres as Roméo, des Grieux, Gerald, Vincent in *Mireille*, Don José and Jean in *Hérodiade*. He took part in a number of world premieres: Saint-Saëns's *Les Barbares* at the Opéra in 1901, the same composer's *L'Ancêtre* at Monte Carlo five years later, and Fauré's *Pénélope* in the same theatre. In 1906 he made his Met debut as Roméo on the same night that Farrar was also appearing there for the first time, as Juliette. The *New York Times* wrote:

39 Victor Capoul in the title-role of Auber's *Fra Diavolo*

Mr Rousselière's success was not so unquestionable. As Roméo he is a manly and engaging figure. He has dramatic skill and authority of no mean order, and he filled out his impersonation with chivalrous ardour. His voice improved in its effect as the opera progressed. It is a powerful and vibrant tenor, but his art of singing is not impeccable. At the beginning his cantilena was not uniformly smooth and his voice sounded frequently strident; but he seemed to gain a better control of it, and in the duet in the second act and again in the fourth he did much that was beautiful and finely impressive.[17]

Later he appeared as Gounod's and Berlioz's Faust, Don José, Canio and Gerald in *Lakmé*, in which his singing was thought 'explosive': he was not invited again. After returning to France he gradually shifted to a more dramatic repertory, including Sigurd, Eléazar, Samson and later Lohengrin, Siegmund, Walther, Tannhäuser and Parsifal, which he sang at the Colon in Buenos Aires with much effect. He also appeared in Berlin as Boito's Faust.

Rousselière's recording career lasted a quarter of a century. There are arias from Flotow's *Martha* and Gluck's *Iphigénie en Tauride* as well as from Wagner's *Lohengrin* and *Tannhäuser*. The voice has something of Scaremberg's hard lustre but the rapid vibrato is less obtrusive and does not interfere with a firm legato. He moves smoothly through the difficult intervals and uncomfortable tessitura of Pylades's aria from Gluck's *Iphigénie*; in the duet of Blondel and Richard from Grétry's *Richard, Cœur de Lion*, with the baritone, Alexis Boyer, we can hear once again how the singers of that period were able to balance the weight of their voices and blend the tone in duets so as to create an effect that is musical in itself.

8. Lyric Tenors

Whereas Caruso, through his gramophone records, has remained the example for succeeding generations of tenors, de Reszké is only an ideal. Perhaps he was wise to leave it that way—wiser than VICTOR CAPOUL (1839–1924), the contemporary of Nicolini and Gayarré, who at the age of sixty-six, more than thirteen years after he had retired from the stage, allowed himself to be coaxed into the Fonotipia studios in Paris.

Capoul is the oldest French singer whose voice survives on records. At the age of twenty, in 1859, he became a student at the Paris Conservatory. In 1861 he graduated with the first prize and was soon engaged at the Opéra-Comique, where he appeared as Daniel in Adam's *Le Chalet*. He remained there as a principal tenor until the outbreak of the Franco-Prussian War in 1870, during which, like many of his compatriots, he sought asylum in England. There he joined the Mapleson Company at Drury Lane. His debut as Faust was somewhat overshadowed by the Marguerite of the evening, an American lady whom Mapleson had engaged without hearing her sing a note; in the event she proved quite unable to do so. Her fiasco eclipsed everything else. With Mapleson he went to the United States, where he was a regular visitor until 1884 and again at the Met in 1891 and 1892. Edith Wharton sets the first chapter of her novel *The Age of Innocence* at the Academy of Music in New York, during a performance of Faust with Christine Nilsson and Capoul, the stage action, as it were, providing a commentary on the activities in the auditorium:

> She sang, of course, 'M'ama!' . . . since an unalterable and unquestioned law of the musical world required that the German text of French operas sung by Swedish artists should be translated into Italian for the clearer understanding of English-speaking audiences . . . 'M'ama!', with a final burst of love triumphant, as she pressed the dishevelled daisy to her lips and lifted her large eyes to the sophisticated countenance of the little brown Faust-Capoul, who was vainly trying, in a tight purple velvet doublet and plumed cap, to look as pure and true as his artless victim.[1]

In London he appeared at Covent Garden for the first time in 1877, as Fra Diavolo, Lionel in *Marta*, Faust, Elvino and Ernesto, when his rendering of the famous Serenade was judged 'well nigh irreproachable'.[2] In Paris, he created Paul in Massé's *Paul et Virginie*, Roméo in *Les Amants de Verone* by the Marquis d'Ivry and Jocelyn in Godard's opera, for which he was in part responsible for the libretto. After his retirement he became a singing teacher in New York and later returned to Paris as a stage manager at the Opéra. He lived out his last years in the village of Pujaudron-du-Gers, where he died at the age of eighty-five, alone and destitute.

Capoul had a light-weight tenor voice which he used with much skill; he sang the lyric repertory with great success but he never ventured a part heavier than Faust. On the evidence of a recording of Godard's famous Berceuse, it would be stretching a point to suggest that his voice remained untouched by the hand of time, in fact very little of it remains at all; at this time he was almost stone deaf. Still there is an echo in the manner and style, particularly in the use of the head voice and enunciation of the text, that persuades us that here indeed was one of the great Victorian charmers.

One of the most successful of Capoul's successors in the lyric repertory, EDMOND CLEMENT (1867–1928), was a fine-looking man with—photographs suggest—histrionic talent as well. He was also a student at the Paris Conservatoire and made his first stage appearance at the Opéra-Comique, in Gounod's *Mireille*. Later he took leading parts in the world premieres of Godard's *La Vivandière*, with Marie Delna, in 1895, and in 1901 with Mary Garden in Pierné's *La Fille de Tabarin*. He remained at the Opéra-Comique until 1910, but made several visits abroad during this time. He never came to Covent Garden but was for one season at the Met in 1909 as Werther, Des Grieux, Fenton (he was the first Fenton at the Opéra-Comique) and, at the New Theatre, Domique in Bruneau's *L'Attaque du moulin*, this also with Delna. The critics were favourably impressed; but the public, which had grown accustomed to the Italian manner—to the magnificence of Caruso's voice even in French opera—found Clément merely dull, and he was not re-engaged. Between 1911 and 1913, Henry Russell took him for the Boston Opera and he continued to give concert and recital appearances in New York until 1923. Aldrich describes him at the Carnegie Hall in 1911 in front of 'a large audience of sympathetic listeners':

> His is one of the lightest voices, but it has a remarkably penetrating and carrying quality, much of which is due to the excellence of his production of tone. His diction has all the polish of the best style ... Mr Clément's style is one of much finish and poise, guided by most perfect taste and sense of proportion, and this does not mean he is devoid of true feeling, imagination and even passion ... His range of emotional expression is undoubtedly rather circumscribed by the nature of his vocal resources [and the] voice cannot be made to assume the widest variety of colour.[3]

Clément visited Brussels and Madrid, and in Paris continued to appear regularly in recital until 1927, the year before his death. On that last occasion the Australian baritone Edmund Burke heard him; 'a small voice but still an excellent artist and exquisite singer.'[4]

His recordings corroborate Aldrich's description. It is a small voice, the tone rather dry and the production constricted, especially in the head register, which is not managed without effort nor with complete security: B flat comes out in open falsetto. In Gerald's lovely air from Delibes's *Lakmé*, 'Fantaisie aux divins mensonges', although his is not the suavest legato, the line is smoothly shaped and he phrases with much affection and charm. The diction too is clear, without being exaggerated.

The Belgian tenor ADOLPHE MARECHAL (1867–1935) seems to have had a larger and more brilliant voice than Clément. After studying in Liège, he made his debut at Dijon in 1891. For the

40 Edmond Clément as Don José in *Carmen*

next few years he toured the provinces, singing in Rheims, Nice and Bordeaux; in 1895 he was invited to the Opéra-Comique. There he sang for several seasons, taking parts in various world premieres: as Julien in Charpentier's *Louise* in 1900, and the following year Alain in Massenet's *Grisélidis*. He was Danielo to Mary Garden's Orlanda in Leroux's *La Reine Fiammette*, and appeared in the first performance of the same composer's *Le Chemineau*. During these years he travelled to Russia and was a frequent visitor to Monte Carlo and Brussels. In 1902 he sang at Covent Garden; Faust, Don José and in Herbert Bunning's *Princesse Osra* which, in spite of Garden in the name part, was sung in French. The same year he created Jean in Massenet's *Le Jongleur de Notre Dame*, a part which subsequently, when Hammerstein produced it at the Manhattan, was appropriated by Garden. Her defence, in her autobiography, is superbly disingenuous:

It should always be a woman who sings the Jongleur. The part is so spiritual and so simple, and when a man sings it, it becomes too *terre à terre*. The role had been created by Maréchal, a charming man, but a man, not a boy. You needed to get the naive spiritual beauty of an unspoiled child into the role, and you did not get it in a man. And I had just the body for it. I was built like a boy . . . I don't have any hips. Only a woman with a body like mine could give any real semblance of realism to that role.[5]

Both Garden and Maréchal recorded Jean's apostrophe to freedom; either way—with or without hips—it is hard to hear anything in them of the 'unspoiled child'. Maréchal's voice is a bright-sounding, rather vibrant, instrument with an easy delivery and a correct management of the head voice. The interpretation is sensitive and attractively sung.

At the age of forty, Maréchal gave up his career and returned to Brussels. ALBERT VAGUET (1865–1943) retired at the even earlier age of thirty-eight. He was a graduate of the Paris Conservatory, where he had been a pupil of Barbot and Obin (the teacher of Escalaïs and Delmas). He made a successful debut at the Opéra in 1890 as Faust and remained there for thirteen years. His other roles included the Duke in *Rigoletto*, David in *Les Maîtres*

41 Adolphe Maréchal as Jean in Massenet's *Le Jongleur de Notre-Dame*

42 Albert Vaguet in Hué's *Le Roi de Paris*

Chanteurs, Cassio, Nicias in *Thaïs* and the title-role in Méhul's *Joseph*. In a concert performance of *L'Or du Rhin* in 1893 he took the parts of Loge, Froh and Mime, the unlikely accompaniment for the occasion being provided by a piano duo: Raoul Pugno and Claude Debussy.

Vaguet's records, which were made after his retirement, include a couple of duets with his wife Alba-Chrétien, who also had a short career at the Opéra. Among the solos are two pieces from Saint-Saëns's *Nuits Persanes* (a work fashioned in the style of Felicien David's *Le Desert*), in both of which his voice still sounds in fine condition. The first, the vigorous 'Air du Sabre', where local colour is suggested by roulades of coloratura, Vaguet despatches in full voice, accurately and with easy brilliance. In the second, the 'Air du Cimitière', he shows off his mastery of the head voice, this time in mezza voce, conveying the quasi-oriental manner of the music in a cleanly turned and expressive legato.

9. High Cs and Heroic Voices

There was nothing in the least glamorous in person, nor anything remotely reminiscent of Jean de Reszké, about the tenor LEON ESCALAIS (1859–1941). Like Duprez—whose voice his resembled in range and brilliance, if not in style—Escalaïs was a short man, hardly more than five feet, 'with the head of a bull and the legs of a basset hound'. Born near Toulouse, he went to Paris to study at the Conservatory, under Obin. In 1883 he took second prize, part of which was an engagement at the Opéra. He made his debut as Arnold in Rossini's *Guillaume Tell*, and created a great stir with the clarion quality of his high notes. He remained at the Opéra during the next nine years, taking parts in several Meyerbeer operas: the title-role in *Robert le Diable*, Raoul in *Les Huguenots*, Jean in *Le Prophète* and Vasco in *L'Africaine*. He also sang Reyer's Sigurd, Eléazar in *La Juive* and Samson. In 1890 he created the part of Lusignan in de la Nux's *Zaïre*, with Eames and Delmas. His Italian career began in 1888, at La Scala, as Eléazar; thereafter he sang throughout Italy and was especially admired in *Trovatore*. It was as Manrico that he made his only American appearances, at the French Opera in New Orleans in 1909. After he had hurled out three stupendous high Cs in 'Di quella pira', the audience absolutely refused to allow the opera to proceed until he had sung it again, and again, and again . . .

In all he sang it through five times that evening, producing fifteen high Cs!

Escalaïs was scarcely a subtle singer. He had none of the elegance or style that would have made him an effective Edgardo in *Lucia* or Elvino in *Sonnambula*, both roles in which Duprez had excelled; but though his singing was provincial it was not crude, and his voice was astonishingly secure and brilliant. In a recording of the Sicilienne from the First Act of *Robert de Diable* the execution is a thing of wonder. The wide-ranging music with its plethora of high notes is thrown off fearlessly to

43 Leon Escalaïs

stunning effect. All those expression markings of which Meyerbeer was so inordinately fond, from piqués to martelés, are clearly realised; like the florid figures and a well-turned trill, they are managed without diaphragmatic shock or aspirates. Freed from technical problems, the piece goes with a real swing. The equalisation of the registers and the strength of the high notes persuaded his contemporaries that these were taken entirely from the chest. The records show otherwise: he frequently makes use of 'la petite note inférieure' as a means of securely basing the head notes, and it is precisely their remarkable development which gives the top C such brilliance and facilitates the easy execution over the entire range of the voice. In the face of all this skill it is perhaps unkind to complain that the tone of the voice is unattractive and inexpressive, or that there is a want of sensitive musicianship.

AGUSTARELLO AFFRE (1858–1931) shared several of Escalaïs's roles. He had been singing for some years in the French provinces before he was 'discovered' by Pedro Gailhard, the Director of the Opéra; with Gailhard's support he was able to go to the Paris Conservatory to study with Duvernoy. His debut at the Opéra in 1890, as Edgardo opposite Melba's Lucia, was a great success. Hailed as the French Tamagno, he sang Arnold in *Tell*, Raoul, Vasco, Sigurd, Eléazar, Roméo, and Fernand in Donizetti's *La Favorite*. He created the leading tenor

44 Agustarello Affre

role in Massenet's *Le Mage* and was the first Canio at the Opéra. When Gailhard left the Opéra, Affre left too. In 1909 he sang at Covent Garden, as Samson and Faust, but made no particular impression; two years later he went to the United States, to the San Francisco opera. While in that city he took part in a famous public concert on Christmas Day, in which the principal artist was Luisa Tetrazzini. In 1912 he appeared in New Orleans and the following year was appointed Director of the company there.

Massenet greatly admired Affre:

La voix d'Affre est aussi pure et transparante qu'une goutte d'eau après un orage et vibrant comme un pur cristal.[1]

On records the voice does not sound especially pure; it is a heavy, rather dull sound—certainly not as brilliant or responsive as that of Escalaïs, though of great power.

In the fourth-act duet from *Les Huguenots*, with Antoinette Laute-Brun as a quavery, lightweight Valentine, he is a beefy Raoul with little elegance or finesse. The ascending phrases are done too strenuously and at the climax he has nothing left but a thin high C flat, almost completely in falsetto; there is little here of Tamagno's clarion quality. The scale is unequal and the shift into the head register far too abrupt. In such less exposed music as Eléazar's solo 'Dieu que ma voix' from *La Juive*, however, the powerful voice and imposing delivery are impressive.

GEORGES IMBART DE LA TOUR (1865–1911) and Albert Alvarez were both prominent dramatic tenors who left a number of recordings. Imbart, the younger, was another graduate of the Paris Conservatoire, where he studied with St Ives Bax. He made his debut as Raoul in *Les Huguenots* at Geneva and remained there for three seasons, after which he appeared at the Opéra-Comique (1894), Marseilles (1895) and at the Monnaie, Brussels where he was a principal for five years until 1904. He sang at Covent Garden in the 1900 season. His singing of Radames was well received, some of his stage mannerisms were not; and neither in London nor at the Met later that year did he succeed in establishing himself in the audience's affections. His repertory, though it included Roméo and Faust, was principally heroic roles: Jean in *Le Prophéte*, Masaniello in Auber's *La Muette de Portici*, Pylades in *Iphigénie*, Sigurd in Reyer's opera, Samson, Vasco in *L'Africaine*, Otello, Lohengrin, Loge and Tannhäuser. Whether it was too much for his voice, or whether his general health was poor, is not clear; but his career lasted less than fifteen years. He died in 1913, at the early age of forty-eight.

It seems to have been an especially brilliant voice: like Scaremberg's, but with a less pronounced vibrato. His singing of Masaniello's 'Du pauvre seul ami' shows a smooth and affectionate legato and also, as he sweeps up and down through the high-lying tessitura, a skilful management of the different registers at various dynamic levels. Like the best French singers of this period, his diction is notably clear with its beautiful liquid consonants and pure vowels.

ALBERT ALVAREZ (1860–1933) was far the more famous and successful singer. He was the leader of a military band before taking singing lessons from Martini in Paris. After some performances in Ghent, Lyons and Marseilles, he made his first appearance at the Paris Opéra in 1892 as Faust. In 1893 he was engaged at Covent Garden and returned regularly during the next ten years. Between 1899 and 1904 he was a member of the Met. His repertory included sixty different roles. In London, he created Helion in de Lara's *Messaline*, Leicester in the same composer's *Amy Robsart*, and Araquil in Massenet's *La Navarraise*, the last two opposite Emma Calvé. In Paris he was Walther in the French première of *Les Maîtres Chanteurs* and the first Nicias in Massenet's *Thaïs*. In New York he frequently deputised for Jean de Reszké as Don José, Raoul and Faust. He was a notable Tannhäuser, Radames and Otello, in this last part making an effect in spite of Tamagno. Aldrich described him—

> as a superbly powerful representative of Otello, a part in which his intensity of temperament fits to perfection. It is finely wrought in detail, subtly suggestive

of the growing obsession within him. His vocal qualities are on a lower plane than his dramatic; yet his peculiarities, as did Tamagno's, seem almost to enhance the significance of what he does.[2]

He declaims Otello's 'Ora e per sempre addio' (in the French version) in a very deliberate fashion, marking the rhythm strongly, but without undue exaggeration. The voice, which has the right heroic ring and mature timbre for Otello, still seems to be in a healthy condition.

10. The Successors of Faure

Two of the most feted baritones of the later years of the nineteenth century were Frenchman: JEAN LASSALLE (1847–1909) and Victor Maurel. Both

45 Georges Imbart de la Tour as Raoul in *Les Huguenots*

46 Albert Alvarez as Hercule in Leroux's *Astarté*

left recordings that, though made in their declining years, preserve aspects of their greatness.

Lassalle, six months the elder, born in Lyons, was the son of a silk merchant and would have gone into what was then a flourishing business had it not been for the early development of a remarkable voice. In Paris he became a student at the Paris Conservatoire and later a pupil of Novelli. He made his first appearance on stage as St Bris in *Les Huguenots* at Liège in 1868. During the next four years he sang in Lille, Toulouse, Brussels and The Hague. In 1872, the year after the Commune was finally suppressed and the Opéra re-opened, he made his debut there as Nelusko in *L'Africaine*. For over twenty years he was the company's principal baritone, the logical successor to Jean-Baptiste Faure. There, he took part in many world premieres: as Scindia in Massenet's *Le Roi de Lahore* in 1877; Sévère in Gounod's *Polyeucte* in 1878; Ben Saïd in the same composer's *Le Tribut de Zamora* in 1881; Malatesta in Thomas's *Françoise de Rimini* in 1882, and in 1883 the title role of Saint-Saëns's *Henri VIII*.

He sang at Covent Garden in 1879, 1880 and 1881 and again between 1888 and 1893. At his debut as Nelusko, when Patti was singing Sélika, Klein noted that 'the newcomer carried off a larger share of the honours than the prima donna, for Sélika was one of her few failures'.[1] In Paris, later the same year, Klein heard him again and was even more enthusiastic:

> A still greater joy for me . . . was the miracle of beauty that the Nelusko accomplished with his voice. This was the celebrated baritone Lassalle: young, fresh, scarcely yet in his prime—glorious to look upon and listen to—the possessor of probably the noblest male voice that France produced during the nineteenth century.[2]

At Covent Garden, as Scindia in *Le Roi de Lahore*, the *Illustrated London News* thought he 'displayed exceptional powers as an artist'.[3] when he sang Renato in *Ballo*, Shaw chaffed him for spending too much time over the prompt box, sword outstretched 'as if he were about to perform the feat of cutting an apple in two on [the conductor's] head'.[4]

In 1891 he repeated his Nelusko for his Met debut. Krehbiel, in the *Tribune*, wrote:

> Mr Lassalle, it is pleasant to say, brings something besides a reputation to the company. He supplies one of the wants that have been grievously felt ever since

the opening season—a baritone who can sing as well as act. His figure is herculean, his acting intelligent and straightforward. Under the fantastic picturesqueness of his interpretation . . . there was manifest an honest manliness that made a profound impression upon the audience last night.[5]

'Picturesque', a vogue word among critics of that era, was frequently used to describe various impersonations of Lassalle, in particular his Scindia and Escamillo.

At the Opéra, Covent Garden and the Met, with the two de Reszkés, Lassalle formed a famous trio. Klein has written at length of the warmth of their friendship and of its artistic distinction. Following the example of Jean de Reszké, Lassalle too became a noted interpreter of Wagnerian roles; in particular the Dutchman, Wolfram and Hans Sachs, all of them in German. Klein has left us an amusing and also

47 Jean Lassalle

instructive account of a vocal duel between
Tamagno and Lassalle which took place after a
performance in the de Reszkés' hotel suite in
London:

> Lassalle wagered Tamagno that he could sing higher
> with his falsetto than Tamagno with his voce di petto
> . . . Forthwith the two began a vocal duel . . . Out came
> Tamagno's As and B flats, as quickly responded to
> with the falsetto equivalents from Lassalle's sturdy
> throat. Then the Italian went 'one better'; and the
> Frenchman, in order, as he said, to help himself up the
> scale, mounted his chair and emitted the B natural;
> whereupon Tamagno also stood upon his chair and
> brought out not only a high C but a ringing D flat.
> Lassalle was now for mounting the table, but, this being
> 'ruled out' as an unfair advantage over a less athletic
> opponent, he proceeded to get the necessary notes
> from the eminence of his chair . . . Tamagno made a
> bold dash for a D natural, but did not quite succeed;
> and as Lassalle fared no better, we pronounced the
> result a 'dead heat'.[6]

Which, as Klein concludes, was no doubt to the
infinite relief of the other guests in the hotel.

At the very end of his glorious career, Lassalle
made a few recordings for the Odeon company; by
this time he was nearly sixty. In Massenet's Chant
Provençal his voice has retained much of its
beautiful silvery quality, and only in the lower
tones does there obtrude a vein of weakness. His
diction, the beautifully rolled Rs, the absolute
simplicity of his style, bespeak a great artist. At the
end, there is a sample of that famous falsetto.

But though Lassalle had the finer voice, it was
VICTOR MAUREL (1848–1923), who enjoyed the
surpassing career. Greater, perhaps, than any
native French singer before or since, he was a
popular idol, highly regarded by the critics,
respected by managements, held in awe by his
colleagues and admired, in spite of his strongly
accented Italian, by Verdi. In her autobiography,
Calvé calls him 'a man of genius':

> His dramatic gift was so extraordinary that it
> dominated the minds of those who saw him, and
> almost made them forget his voice, which was,
> nevertheless, of an unusual quality, full of colour and
> exceptionally expressive.[7]

Born in Marseilles in 1848—an appropriately
dramatic year—as a boy he wanted to be an artist.
Though he soon abandoned the ambition, many
years later, after he had finally retired from the
stage and concert platform, he provided the Met

48 Victor Maurel

with designs for Gounod's *Mireille*, an opera set in
his native Provence. At the age of eighteen he went
to Paris, to the Conservatoire, as a student of
Vauthrot and Duvernoy. Only a year later, he
shared first prize in singing and opera with the bass,
Pedro Gailhard. His debut at the Paris Opéra was in
Les Huguenots; but where Lassalle had sung St Bris,
he was de Nevers. After a guest season at the
Monnaie in Brussels, he decided to try his luck in
Italy instead of returning to Paris. He was immediately engaged at La Scala, to create Il Cacico in
the world premiere of the Brazilian composer
Gomes's opera *Il Guarany*, and so began a career
which in that theatre alone was to last more than
twenty-three years. The following season at the San
Carlo, Naples he was Roderigo in the first performances there of *Don Carlo*. From Italy he went to
London, to Covent Garden, as Renato in *Ballo*. The

Illustrated London News wrote:

> This artist possesses a baritone voice of agreeable quality and he phrases like a cultivated vocalist, his stage bearing likewise indicating good training. We shall doubtless have further occasion to speak of his merits.[8]

Repeatedly so, for more than thirty years. In his London seasons he sang Guillaume Tell, Assur in *Semiramide* with Patti, Valentin, Don Carlo, di Luna, Belcore, Nelusko, Mozart's Almaviva, Don Giovanni, Papageno and later on, at their Covent Garden premières, Telramund in *Lohengrin*, Wolfram in *Tannhäuser* and Vanderdecken in *Vascello Fantasma*.

In Paris at the Opéra, after 1879, and at the Opéra Comique after 1885, he established himself unequivocally as France's greatest singing actor. In 1883 he was a member of the directorate of the Théâtre des Italiens, but in spite of an outstanding company that included Nevada, Tremelli, Litvinne, Marimon, Gayarré, Edouard de Reszké and himself,

49 Maurel as Iago

after a couple of seasons this stewardship ended in financial disaster and the theatre never re-opened. Later that year he went again to Milan to create Simon Boccanegra in the revised edition, thus beginning an association with Verdi and Boito which was to give him the opportunity of creating Iago in *Otello* in 1887, and six years afterwards the title role in *Falstaff*. These parts he sang everywhere and always with tremendous effect, in Paris, St Petersburg, Vienna, at Covent Garden and the Met. He had made his first American appearances in 1873, as Amonasro in the local premiere of *Aida* at the Academy of Music, New York; when he eventually arrived at the Met, he chose Iago for his debut. The *New York Times* acclaimed him 'a truly great singing actor' even if 'his voice is no more than good'.[9] Later he appeared as Don Giovanni (an interpretation rated 'the perfection of dramatic art', in particular 'the inimitable manner in which he sang the Serenade, a performance of marvellous lightness and grace'),[10] as Valentin, de Nevers and Escamillo. However, the *Times* wrote: 'By this time (1895) his days of bel canto are over.'[11]

Other roles he created included Mathias in d'Erlanger's *Juif Polonais* and Tonio in *Pagliacci*. It was at Maurel's suggestion Leoncavallo composed the Prologue and so long as Maurel sang the part, Tonio had the last words: 'la commedia è finita.' His stage appearances continued well into this century, the very last of all in 1909 with his pupils at a private house in Paris, in Grétry's *Le Tableau parlant*, which Thomas Beecham conducted. As a singing teacher he eventually moved to New York and there from time to time emerged to give, as Aldrich tactfully put it, 'entertainments at the Carnegie Hall';[12] of his voice it was thought fairer to say as little as possible. In the songs 'there is still to be admired his skill in diction and the rhetorical expression he frequently gives to the music'.[13] In the operatic excerpts there was 'a really splendid dramatic intensity and conviction that transfixed the listeners' attention'.[14] We can hear some of this in a recording of Iago's narration of Cassio's dream, with its carefully measured tones—as if he were weighing the effect of his words—and the use of the head voice to quote what he claims to have overheard, 'Desdemona soave, il nostro amore . . .' It contrasts well with Falstaff's 'Quand'ero paggio' (repeated twice, the second time in French); Calvé's description, 'elegant fatuity',[15] seems apt; even if it isn't English we know what she means. As with Patti, the last words may be left to Albert Spalding;

50 Maurice Renaud as Zurga in *Les Pecheurs de perles*

after a dinner in London in about 1906, as chasse-café, Maurel sang through arias from *Otello, Falstaff, Don Giovanni* and several songs.

> His voice . . . had gone threadbare, but the majesty of an undying art was still there. He couldn't possibly have sung a real forte. He had to suggest it, but how he suggested it! After all these years it is Maurel's portrayal of the naked villainy of Iago, the sophistical and Rabelaisian philosophy of Falstaff, the elegant unscrupulous licentiousness of the Spanish Don that I recall each time I hear this music. He sang also a little song by Massenet—a rather cheap and sugar-coated morsel in which an old gallant recalls to his Marquise when and where she wore a dress of white satin. Maurel whispered this not too distinguished text with a kind of magical subtlety that was transfiguring. One could all but smell the perfume from that white satin dress and hear the swish of its flounces as it rounded a corner.[16]

In the generation that followed Lassalle and Maurel, undoubtedly the greatest French baritone was MAURICE RENAUD (1861–1933), a singer of remarkable accomplishment and an actor hardly less skilful than Maurel. Renaud was born in Bordeaux and studied first in Paris and later in Brussels with Dupont and Gaveart. He was a principal at the Monnaie, Brussels between 1883 and 1890, in which year he returned to Paris to join the Opéra Comique, making his debut as Karnac in Lalo's *Le Roi d'Ys*. During the 90s he sang regularly at both Paris houses, and at various French provincial cities; and he crossed the Atlantic for a season with the French opera at New Orleans. In 1897 he appeared at Covent Garden showing off his 'gloriously intelligent portrayal'[17] of Don Giovanni and 'taking the Champagne aria for once at a reasonable speed'. On this occasion he sang in French opposite Lucien Fugère's Leporello, and the same season he was Juan Mendo in d'Erlanger's *Inez Mendo*.

In the following years he repeated his Giovanni and added Wolfram, Escamillo, Valentin, Hamlet, Harés in de Lara's *Messaline* and one of Lassalle's creations, Henri VIII, in the first Covent Garden performances of Saint-Saëns's opera. Klein thought it 'an extremely picturesque embodiment of bluff King Hal viewed through a pair of French pince-nez'.[18] He did not return again until 1902; in the interim, he went to Monte Carlo and took the part of Boniface in the world premiere of Massenet's *Le Jongleur de Notre Dame* with Adolph Maréchal. Later he sang there in the premiere of another Massenet piece, *Chérubin*.

During three further seasons at Covent Garden, his Giovanni was enthusiastically received and he appeared in *Rigoletto* with Melba and Caruso in the latter's debut season. He was also Herod with Calvé and Dalmorès in the first London performances of Massenet's *Herodiade*. On Melba's advice, Hammerstein engaged him for the Manhattan in 1906. His debut was as Rigoletto—'a big man physically who has a voice of great power'. He remained with Hammerstein through all of his seasons in New York, and then joined the Met for two years. Later he made guest appearances with the Chicago and Boston companies and also took part in Hammerstein's brief and final inglorious episode at the London Opera House (later the Stoll Theatre) in 1911.

In New York, Renaud further expanded a considerable repertory: he was Petronius in Nouguès's *Quo Vadis?*; 'a perfect embodiment of the three evil spirits' in *Hoffmann*; Athanaël in *Thaïs*—'an impersonation of great nobility and fervour'[20]—and, perhaps his greatest triumph, Méphistophélès in Berlioz's *Damnation de Faust*. 'As Méphistophélès,' wrote Henderson, 'he was a brooding, world-weary devil who goes about his business with all the infinite pathos of despairing satiety.'[21] Krehbiel felt that 'with due respects to Plançon, Méphistophélès never had an adequate presentation here until last night'.[22] In this part his remarkable make-up was likened to a mediaeval drawing by Dürer.

At Carnegie Hall in 1911, he gave a song recital. By this time he was nearly fifty and his voice was no longer as fresh as it had once been.

> Renaud's greatest power as a dramatic singer has been manifested primarily through his genius as an actor, his remarkable versatility and extraordinary skill in characterisation, in the lyric drama, through art of the utmost finish and distinction. But his voice and his vocal style have also been potent factors only less noteworthy in his achievements in this field . . . his singing was full of artistic beauty and of truly imaginative quality. He has a full realisation of the meaning and value of legato singing, of the plastic modelling of the phrase, and in the music of the elder style this was a source of delight to the listeners.[23]

Renaud's recordings make it easy to appreciate why his art was held in such high regard. His voice seems to have been a good-sized instrument, not however as beautiful as Lassalle's even in that singer's decadence; the tone is greyer and the style, though suave, not as pure, for occasionally it becomes a little sentimentalised—too much expressive vibrato in moments of intensity. In two excerpts from Donizetti's *La Favorite* with the original French texts, in spite of a fine legato, the ardent manner and vocal colouring would better suit Gounod or Massenet. The style is not as smooth as Plançon, the imaginative detail less purely vocal than in the recordings of Battistini. On the other hand, in Herod's 'Vision fugitive' from Massenet's opera (shorn here in the acoustic recording of its picturesque saxophone obbligato), his impassioned phrasing and firm line produce the finest interpretation of this music on record. Don Giovanni's 'Deh vieni alla finestra' with its rubato will hardly commend itself to modern taste; whether Mozart would have been outraged by it is another matter. One can hardly believe he would have been upset by a performance so full of character, of such eloquence, and yet done without disturbing the vocal line; certainly he would have been pleased to hear all the appoggiaturas. About Méphistophélès's Serenade from Berlioz's *Faust*, there can be no reservations. It is a classic performance, partly contrived by artful but not exaggerated vocal colouring and partly the result of a cleanly focused tone and forward production which enables him to respond easily to every rhythmic nuance, to show clearly the difference between marcato and staccato and still maintain the poise of the voice.

11. Principal Baritones

HENRI ALBERS (1866–1925) from Holland and Jean Noté from Belgium, contemporaries of Renaud, were both ranking baritones in Paris: Albers at the Opéra-Comique, where he appeared regularly from 1899 to 1925 and Noté at the Opéra, between 1893 and 1922. Albers made his debut in Amsterdam in 1899, as Gounod's Méphistophélès, a role which following Faure's precedent was often undertaken by baritones. Two years later he moved to Antwerp, where he sang Escamillo, de Nevers, Albert in *Werther*, Guillaume Tell, Valentin, Aben-Hamet in Dubois's opera of that name—a part which had been created by Victor Maurel—and Jean d'Hautecour in Bruneau's *Le Rêve*. At this time he took part in a special Massenet season, after which the composer arranged for him to study with Faure. Throughout the 90s he was a regular guest at the leading French theatres: Bordeaux, Le Havre, Aix-les-Bains and Monte Carlo. After making a tour of the United States, in the autumn of 1898, he made his Met debut. Following a 'rather poor'[1] Wolfram, he appeared as di Luna, Escamillo, Valentin, de Nevers, Lescaut in *Manon*, Telramund and 'most stylishly of all',[2] as Mercutio in *Roméo et Juliette*; he did not return. In France again, the next season he began his long association with the Opéra-Comique as Zurga in *Les Pêcheurs de perles*; thereafter he took principal roles in Leroux's *Le Chemineau*, Saint-Saëns's *L'Ancêtre*, Massenet's *Thérèse*, *Pelléas et Mélisande*, *Dinorah*, *Le Roi d'Ys*, Bloch's *Macbeth*, Vidal's *Sur le front*, Leroux's *Les Cadeaux de Noel* (which he also sang in his only La Scala season in 1917), Hahn's *Nausicaa* and Laparra's *Le Joueur de viole*.

Perhaps his finest role was Hamlet in Thomas's opera. After some appearances at the Monnaie, a critic wrote that he had actually improved on Faure and Lassalle in the part, and had made out of Thomas's dull piece an interpretation of true

51 Henri Albers in Chausson's *Le Roi Arthus*

Shakesperian depth. His records do not suggest an artist of that calibre; although the quality of the voice is warm and appealing and the singing attractive, a rapid vibrato interferes with a really smooth line. In an unfamiliar piece from Gounod's *La Reine de Saba*, 'Sur les flots', the phrasing is merely routine and the upward portamenti are clumsily executed. The characterisation here as in Valentin's aria from the first act of *Faust*, is generalised rather than specific in the way of a Maurel of Renaud.

The career of JEAN NOTÉ (1859–1922) began at Ghent in 1883, then like Albers he was engaged at Antwerp. In 1887, Noté went to Brussels and stayed there for six years, at the end of which time he was invited to the Paris Opéra, where he remained a member of the company for almost thirty years. His repertory included Rigoletto, Amonasro, Telramund, Mercutio, Wolfram, Hamlet, the King in *Le Cid*, de Nevers, Valentin and leading parts in Massenet's *Roma*, Paladilhe's *Patrie*, Bruneau's *Messidor* and Reyer's *Salammbô*.

For one season, 1897, he sang at Covent Garden, but neither in London nor New York, in 1908, was he invited to return. His powerful but 'brutal and booming voice' was not very much appreciated; nor was his, frankly, provincial style. He made a large number of records, titles that reflect the preoccupations of the Paris Opéra repertory of three-quarters of a century ago: arias from Halévy's *La Reine de Chypre* and *Charles VI*, Dubois's *Aben-Hamet*, Rubinstein's *Nero*, Diaz's *Benvenuto Cellini*, Massenet's *Le Cid* and Saint-Saëns's *Henri VIII*. These show it to have been a big and dark-coloured voice, the timbre rather gravelly with a pronounced vibrato showing signs of loosening. In a short aria from *Le Cid* there is something to admire in the clear diction and strong delivery, even if he cannot manage a simple gruppetto without aspirating. Like Albers's singing, it is without much personality, wanting in dynamic range and entirely without subtlety.

LEON MELCHISSEDEC (1843–1925) was another prominent French artist who spent virtually his

52 Jean Noté as the High Priest in *Samson et Dalila*

53 Leon Melchissédec in the title-role of *Guillaume Tell*

entire career in Paris. He was equally successful in dramatic, character and buffo roles. In Paris in turn, he was a star at the Opéra, Opéra-Comique, Ventadour, Théâtre Lyrique, Gaîté and Les Bouffes Parisiens. His career began at the Opéra-Comique, in 1866; ten years later he went to the Théâtre Lyrique, and two years after that to the Opéra. He was a member of the company from 1879 to 1891 and again between 1905 and 1912. There his enormous repertory included Guillaume Tell, de Nevers, Nelusko, Valentin, Rigoletto, Amonasro, Gunther in Reyer's *Sigurd* and Le Gouverneur in Rossini's *Le Comte Ory*. He took part in a number of world premières; at the Lyrique in Massé's *Paul et Virginie*, in 1876; at the Gaîté, in Saint-Saëns's *Le Timbre d'argent*, which one critic called a 'five hour nightmare in four acts'; and at the Opéra as Hadjar in Gounod's *Le Tribut de Zamora* in 1879, Le Roi in Massenet's *Le Cid*, in 1885, and, three years later, in the first performance there of the revised version of *Roméo et Juliette*, as Mercutio (previously, at the Opéra-Comique, he had sung Capulet) with Patti, the de Reszkés and Delmas. In operetta he was at the Ventadour in 1878 in *Le Capitaine Fracasse* and thereafter at Les Bouffes Parisiens in a variety of works. He was still singing at the Trocadéro at the age of seventy-eight. From 1894 until his death he was Professor of 'déclamation lyrique' at the Paris Conservatoire and wrote several books on the art of singing.

Melchissédec's records were made when he was past sixty. Although the voice is old and quavery and without much quality, and there is no breadth of phrasing or smooth cantilena, he can still put over Belamy's drinking song from *Les Dragons de Villars* with the appropriate swagger and turn a trill neatly in the right style.

Like Melchissédec, LUCIEN FUGERE (1848–1935) rarely travelled beyond Paris and only once outside of France. His career too, was remarkably long and successful; he made his farewell in opera, as Don Bartolo in *Le Barbiere de Séville*, at the age of eighty five in 1933. Unlike Melchissédec, he was never a dramatic singer, his voice was a typical French light bass-baritone that changed very little over the years. His career began in 1874, at Les Bouffes Parisiens. In 1877 he joined the Opéra-Comique, appearing in Massé's *Les Noces de Jeanette*, and for the next thirty-six years was a principal member of the company specialising in buffo and character roles: Leporello, Papageno, Bartolo, Belamy, Comte des Grieux, Don Pasquale, the Marquis in Delibes's *Le Roi l'a dit*, Domingue in *Paul et Virginie*, the Duc

54 Lucien Fugère as the Devil in Massenet's *Grisélidis*

de Longueville in Messager's *La Basoche*, Le Philosophe in Massenet's *Chérubin*, Schaunard in the first French performance of *La Bohème*, Fritelli in Gounod's *Le Roi malgré lui*, Pandolphe in Massenet's *Cendrillon*, the Devil in the same composer's *Grisélidis*, the Father in *Louise* and Chorèbe in Berlioz's *Les Troyens*.

In 1897 he made his only trip outside France, to London, where he took part in the Jubilee Season at Covent Garden. There he sang Leporello to Renaud's Don. *The Times* wrote:

M. Fugère is an excellent comedian as well as a capital singer; every detail of business has been carefully thought out and very often has been suggested by the rhythms of the music. His delivery of the famous air in the first act, which has become 'Oui, Madame' roused the audience to enthusiasm.[3]

55 Gabriel Soulacroix as de Nevers in *Les Huguenots*

One of these, GABRIEL SOULACROIX (1853–1905) was born in Fumal, Lot-et-Garonne, five years after Fugère. After winning first prize at the Toulouse Conservatoire, he went to Paris to continue his studies; then, like so many French artists of that day, he made his debut at the Monnaie, Brussels, as Ourrias in Gounod's *Mireille* in 1879. He stayed in Brussels for seven years in all, taking many different parts: Papageno, Lescaut, Beckmesser, the Doctor in Saint-Saëns's *Le Timbre d'argent*, and Lord de Charolais in Delibes's *Jean de Nivelles*. He went to Covent Garden every season from 1881 to 1884, appearing in company with Patti, Albani, Sembrich and Lucca, as Pedrillo in *Seraglio*, Figaro in *Il Barbiere*, Escamillo, Daland, and in revivals of *L'Etoile du Nord*, *Le Pré aux clercs*, *Semiramide* and in the first London performances of Reyer's *Sigurd*. After 1885 he was a principal at the Opéra-Comique where, to the above repertory, he added Clément Marot in *La Basoche*, Zurga in *Les Pêcheurs de perles*, Camille in Delibes's posthumous opera *Kassya*, Ford, Frederick in *Lakmé* and Belamy in *Les Dragons de Villars*. In Monte Carlo, from 1889, he was a great favourite, running the gamut from Rigoletto, Enrico in *Lucia*, Germont and Iago, to Jean in *Les Noces de Jeanette,* Belcore, Don Pasquale and Bernabé in Paer's *Le Maître de chapelle*. In 1898, he sang Beckmesser at La Scala and the same season returned to Covent Garden. He died suddenly in 1905, at the early age of fifty-one.

Soulacroix's voice was a typical example of what the French call a baryton-martin—light in weight and with some of the characteristics of a tenor. It was by no means a heroic-sized instrument. It seems hard to imagine him singing Iago or Rigoletto except in a small theatre like Monte Carlo. Although his records were made at the end of a busy and strenuous career, the voice is still fresh and silvery, particularly at the top; only the lowest notes have become dulled. His technique is impeccable, and though there is not the personality that distinguishes the art of Maurel and Renaud, neither is there any of their exaggerations of style. In the air of Bernabé from *Le Maître de chapelle* the vocal effects arise out of a smooth and undulating legato, the imagination is in the singing itself and the colouring in the accurate and perfectly proportioned coloratura, which in music of this period is how it ought to be. For purity of style, an example of the canto di grazia—where the florid manner is at its most delicate and refined and the graces always subordinate—it ranks with the best of Plançon's records.

Fugère was over fifty when he made his first records and past eighty when he made the last of them. He has always been greatly admired by collectors, not so much for the voice itself as for those sensitive and refined aspects of French singing that were once relatively commonplace but are now difficult to find. A recording of an air from Isouard's opera *Joconde*, 'Dans un délire extrème', reveals a small dry baritone voice. In the upper range the singer makes much use of the falsetto, almost taking the breath support away. The style and manner are attractive, the voice caresses the line and the graces are done neatly except for a not very clearly articulated trill. In spite of the artistry, however, the voice lacks quality and the singing is without the vocal imagination we can hear in recordings of the greatest French singers of this period.

Another baryton-martin of this period, JEAN PERIER (1869–1954), though scarcely a singer of the distinction of Soulacroix, was a popular favourite at the Opéra-Comique for many years. Born in Paris, he studied at the Conservatoire with Taskin and Bussine. His debut was at the Opéra-Comique in 1892, as Monostatos in *La Flute enchantée*. There he created leading roles in Leroux's *La Reine Fiammette* and *Le Chemineau*, in Pierné's *La Fille de Tabarin* and in Rabaud's *La Fille de Roland* and *Marouf*. In 1902, he sang the role of Pelléas in the world premiere of Debussy's opera. It was in this part that he made his only appearances outside of France; at the Manhattan in New York. During his long career he was equally successful in operetta, at the Bouffes-Parisiennes and the Folies Dramatiques, and in later years, as an actor, in films.

He made no recordings from Pelléas, but we can hear him in another part he created, singing the Air de la lettre 'Adieu, je pars' from Messager's *Véronique*; the voice itself is not remarkable but the singing is of great charm, the music expressively phrased, the words tenderly inflected.

CHARLES GILIBERT (1866–1910), like Soulacroix, died when he was still young—he was only forty-three. Few artists better exemplify the saying: there are no bit parts, only bit players. Aldrich described Gilibert as 'an outstanding example of what art and intelligence can do with a voice not naturally beautiful'.[4] He was a student at the Paris Conservatoire before making his debut at the Opéra-Comique in 1888. Thereafter, he sang regularly in Paris and Brussels. He was at Covent Garden every season from 1894 until 1909, and in New York a member of the company at the Met from 1900 to 1903 and at the Manhattan from 1906 until the year he died.

His repertory embraced a great variety of character and comprimario roles: the Duke of Verona in *Roméo et Juliette*, Sulpice, Don Pasquale, Masetto, Bartolo and the Barber. His Boniface in *Le Jongleur* was deemed 'a perfect study', his Father in *Louise* 'a compendium of blighted love, blasted hope and human agony'.[5] He was the first Schaunard at Covent Garden, 'an inimitably humorous and unctious performance'.[6] As supporting artist he toured the United States with Melba; they have left us an appropriate souvenir of their travels in a recording of the duet, 'Through valleys and forests', by Blangini. Blangini, a Professor of Singing at the

56 Jean Perier and Mariette Sully in Messager's *Véronique*
57 Charles Gilibert as Don Bartolo in Rossini's *Barbiere*

Paris Conservatoire in the early part of the nineteenth century, was the teacher of three queens, twelve princesses and twenty-five countesses; his volumes of romances were the delight of generations of salon singers. As sung here, they still delight. The perfect balance of the voices, the poise in the 'a due' section with its beautifully sprung rhythm and the hushed ending—with such singing, that Gilibert's voice was not in itself beautiful seems of small account.

58 Pol Plançon as St Bris in *Les Huguenots*

12. Plançon, Edouard de Reszké and the Basses

Without question, the greatest 'French' basses of the closing years of the nineteenth century were Edouard de Reszké and POL PLANÇON (1854–1914). Of the two, it was de Reszké who had the more splendid voice and greater personality but Plançon was the finer singer. Indeed, his name has become a by-word for bel canto. Of all the French basses and baritones of his day, and there were many who could turn a deft trill or throw off runs and staccati to shame some of the leading sopranos, it was Plançon who was the most skilful and the most finished of vocalists. He was a student of Duprez and later Sbriglia. His operatic debut took place at Lyons, in 1877, as St Bris in *Les Huguenots*. After a few years spent in the French provinces, he arrived in Paris to take his rightful place at the Opéra. In 1891 he was invited to Covent Garden for the first time; there he was immediately appreciated and returned each summer for the next thirteen years. Two years later, he went to the Met, where he was equally successful.

Plançon's repertory, like his vocal range, was similar to that of Edouard de Reszké: Méphistophélès in Gounod's and Berlioz's *Faust*, Mefistofele, Don Fernando in *Fidelio*, Assur in *Semiramide*, Pogner, Balthazar in *La Favorite*, the King in *Lohengrin*, Frère Laurent, Marcel and St Bris in *Les Huguenots*, Vulcain in Gounod's *Philémon et Baucis,* the Landgrave in *Tannhäuser*, Sarastro, Plunkett in *Marta* and Escamillo. He created Astolat in Bemberg's *Elaine*, Ariofarne in Mancinelli's *Ero e Leandro* and Le Comte de Gormas in Massenet's *Le Cid*. After his London debut, Klein wrote:

> Plançon is among the most accomplished and distinguished artists that France has ever sent here. He is a basse-chantant with a superb voice trained by Duprez, allied to a style that is at once elegant and impeccable, a splendid actor who adorns every part he plays.[1]

In New York, he was similarly acclaimed. At his debut there, Krehbiel welcomed 'his sonorous voice ... suave and finished style'.[2] Henderson commended him for 'singing the modified vowels of his native tongue without abandoning that noble sonority of tone which is one of the most admirable characteristics of his art'.[3]

There were, it is true, some dissenting voices. The New York critic Huneker disliked 'his mincing gait' and complained of 'a lack of virility in his impersonations'. Whether this was fair comment or merely a Puritan critic's reaction to what was then hot gossip, is hard to know; it was widely rumoured that Plançon had been caught in his dressing-room with the composer Herman Bemberg in flagrante delicto.

Plançon made more than sixty records between 1902 and 1908, all of them testifying to the beauty of his voice and its purity of tone, and to his mastery of every facet of vocal art; they also reveal considerable and often subtle interpretive gifts. The most stunning, and perhaps the best-known, is the air of the Drum-Major from Thomas's *Le Caïd*, where he fires off a whole fusillade of effects; trills, runs—from bottom F to the E above middle C—and ornaments in staccato and marcato, all of them contained within a beautifully pointed but never inflexible rhythm. He shows as much vocal imagination in a simple legato aria, 'Vi ravviso', from *Sonnambula*, here by suave phrasing and subtle nuance perfectly capturing the pensive and reflective mood of the music. The two solos from Gounod's *Faust* are far from the coarse yet characterless ranting we are too often accustomed to. He does not attempt to impose on Gounod any grotesque diablerie which may be effective in its own terms but is quite unstylish. His effects are contrived by exact attention to rhythm, as at 'et Satan conduit le bal' in 'The Calf of Gold', and by appropriate colouring in the insinuating phrases of the Serenade. Among the songs, it would be hard to choose any one to the exclusion of another. Less familiar, but all showing off the grace and charm of his style, are Massenet's 'Si tu veux', Bemberg's 'Le soupir' and Godard's 'Embarquez-vous?'. In general, the earliest of his records are the best; by 1908 the high notes had lost their silvery quality, are only produced with some effort and are often attenuated. In the later recordings there are also occasional lapses of intonation.

EDOUARD DE RESZKE's (1853–1917) voice was discovered by his elder brother Jean; on his encouragement the younger man went to study, first in Milan and Naples, and later in Paris with Giovanni Sbriglia. He made his debut at the Paris Opéra, in 1876, in the first performance there of *Aida*, as the King. Verdi was in the audience and afterwards congratulated him, 'even if you did look more like Amneris's son than her father!'[4] Three years later, he went to La Scala to take the part of

59 Edouard de Reszké

the Wanderer, Hagen and Hans Sachs. As great as was Edouard's popularity in London, it was even exceeded in New York, where his career continued for a couple of years after Jean's retirement in 1901. The list of roles he sang in his first New York season is astonishing: Frère Laurent, Marcel, Rodolfo, Zacharias, Plunkett, Rocco in *Fidelio*, Heinrich in *Lohengrin*, Leporello, Don Pedro in *L'Africaine*, Nilakantha in *Lakmé*, Le Roi in *Hamlet*, Daland, Ramfis and Méphistophélès! In this part, the *New York Evening Post* wrote—

[He] is the ideal Méphistophélès unquestionably. Whether in the demoniac or the ironic moments, he always suits his mien to the situation, his words to his actions and his tones to his words. Singing is no impediment to his speech; he repeatedly moved the audience to laughter.[6]

Edouard de Reszké was a genial giant of a man— Shaw thought him a stupid one, too. He was certainly without the artistic dedication and his singing without the finesse that had secured his brother a unique place in the history of opera. On the other hand, nature had been far more generous to him; his voice—it is difficult to resist the weight of evidence—was a much more remarkable instrument, a splendid basse-chantant. Of his Sachs, David Bispham wrote:

[His] was the best, more completely in nobility of voice and of personal appearance realising the part, to which he brought a greater degree of bonhomie, than any of the other numerous artists with whom I have sung ...[7]

And even in a role where his great height and physical bulk was a handicap—Leporello, for example, according to the *New York Times*—he was—

simply superb. It is a joy without alloy to hear him read the recitative with all the skill of a perfect actor and vocalist, and with such brimming and unctious humour that every line is funny. As for his 'Madamina', it is one of the most admirable of all achievements in the art of buffo singing.[8]

And in a part which called precisely for 'a powerful and sonorous voice' and an imposing physique, as the baleful Hagen, in *Götterdämmerung*:

His portrayal would have represented a signal achievement for an artist who made a speciality of cheerless, tragic roles, it was even more so for one who

Indra in the first performance there of Massenet's *Re di Lahore*. Later in the season he appeared in Gomes's *Maria Tudor*, Verdi's *Simon Boccanegra* and *Ernani*, after which the conductor Faccio wrote to Verdi:

It is not for many years that we have heard here a bass with such a vigorous yet affecting voice, one at the same time with a fine technique and artistic sensitivity.[5]

His career at Covent Garden began in 1880 and continued until 1900. During that time, he sang a bumper of parts: Indra, Giorgio in *I Puritani*, Rodolfo, Don Basilio, St Bris, Frère Laurent, Prince Gudal in Rubinstein's *Demone* (the composer conducted the performances), Alvise, Ramfis, Daland, Assur, in which he was compared favourably with Tamburini, Alfonso in *Lucrezia Borgia*, Méphistophélès and Mefistofele, King Henry, Zacharias in *Le Prophète* and Don Pedro in *L'Africaine*. In the later part of his career, he sang König Marke in *Tristan*, Heinrich in *Lohengrin*,

... had made immortal his conception of comic characters ...[9]

Edouard de Reszké's three records made for the Columbia company in 1903 are, perhaps, the most disappointing ever made by a famous singer. Even allowing for the frailty of Columbia's recording system, his voice sounds in very poor shape. At the time he was forty-nine, not a great age for a bass; Chaliapin at fifty was at the height of his career. That the records are a fairly accurate impression of his voice, we may assume from the fact that this was his last season in America; though he was re-engaged for the Manhattan company three years

60 Pedro Gailhard as Méphistophélès in Gounod's *Faust*

later, when Hammerstein heard him he was so shocked at the state of his voice he at once tore up the contract. Unlike brother Jean, Edouard sang naturally and had never much concerned himself with technique or worried very much about keeping his voice. His life-style was hardly conducive to it; he sang too much, too often; he smoked too much and drank too much. No singer can expect to get away with that kind of regime far into middle life. In all fairness, however, it must be added that some Mapleson cylinders, in particular fragments of the Valentin-Marcel duet from Act 3 of *Les Huguenots*, where he seems to be making an impressive sound, present a somewhat different picture, and these were made only a short time previously. Of the three commercial recordings, the best is Plunkett's Porter Song from *Marta*, though it hardly compares with Plançon. The breath control has gone and the voice seems to have lost most of its quality; yet there lingers still something of the grand manner, and in the fine trill and neat coloratura evidence of good schooling. On none of them, however, is there any trace of that 'bonhomie', or of 'a powerful and sonorous voice'.

The oldest French bass on records, PEDRO GAILHARD (1848–1918), was born in Toulouse where he took his first singing lessons. In due course he went to Paris to study at the Conservatoire. He graduated in 1867 sharing with Victor Maurel the first prize in singing and opera. His stage debut was at the Opéra-Comique later the same year, in Thomas's *Le Songe d'une nuit d'été*, as Falstaff (the opera has nothing to do with Shakespeare's *Midsummer Night's Dream*).† He remained there until 1870 taking part in many different pieces, including premieres of Offenbach's *Vert-Vert* and Auber's *Rêve d'amour*. It was the eighty-seven-year-old composer's forty-seventh and final work for the stage. 'The title is too youthful and the composer too old,' he lamented. 'I'm making a mistake but what of it: it is my last!'[10] After the Franco-Prussian war was over, Gailhard sang at the Salle le Pelétier as Méphistophélès, and then when the Palais Garnier was opened in 1879, appeared there as Le Roi in *Hamlet*, St Bris, Leporello and in the world premieres of Mermet's *Jeanne d'Arc* and Thomas's *Françoise de Rimini*.

In 1879 he came to London, and returned to Covent Garden regularly during the next five seasons, as Méphistophélès 'proving himself an

† Barbier and Carré used the title for a romantic drama in which the principal characters include Shakespeare, Queen Elizabeth and Falstaff.

accomplished actor and singer'; as Girot in *Le Pré aux clercs*, 'he sang and acted like a true artist'.[11] He was also Osmin, Alfonso in *Lucrezia Borgia*, Assur in *Semiramide*, Lothario in *Mignon*, Rodolfo in *Sonnambula* and most effectively of all, Mefistofele. In 1884 he became a joint Director of the Opéra, first with Ritt, later with Bertrand, and from 1899 to 1906 he was in sole charge. Like Maurel he had ambitions to be a painter and designer and frequently created the mise-en-scene at the Opéra, including that used for the famous production of *Roméo et Juliette* with Patti and the de Reszkés, which Gounod himself conducted.

Gailhard's four recordings were made in 1905, at the age of fifty-seven. He sings Mephistophélès's Serenade in French and Italian, a short excerpt from *L'Africaine* and Yradier's La Paloma. The voice has become horny and dull with age. As Mephisto his interpretation is without excesses of any kind; even the laughs are sung precisely as notated—on the three Fs—and the phrasing is shapely with the characteristically fine diction of singers of that era.

While de Reszké and Plançon were the French school's greatest international basses, JEAN FRANÇOIS DELMAS (1861–1933) was the dominating figure at the Opéra. A big barrel-chested, six-foot giant, he sang there every season for forty-one years—a record. In Paris, he was a student of Bussine and Obin. He made his debut at the Opéra in 1886. Two years later he was Capulet in the all-star *Roméo et Juliette* when the work was brought to the Opéra for the first time. With an unusually wide-ranging voice, his repertory included baritone as well as bass roles: Mephistophélès, Wotan, Iago, Bluebeard in Dukas's *Ariane et Barbe-Bleu*, Marco in *Monna Vanna*, Gurnemanz, Hans Sachs, the Landgrave, Athanaël in *Thaïs*, König Marke, Tonio, Hagen and Narr-Havas in Reyer's *Salammbô*.

Recordings have preserved an imposing, rather cavernous voice, with a darker colour than its range would have suggested. In the famous Bénédiction des Poignards from *Les Huguenots,* he declaims with exactly the right sombre intensity. In Paladilhe's 'Pauvre martyr obscur' from *Patrie* the manner is appropriately lugubrious. It is not refined or imaginative singing, there is little variety of dynamics, few subtleties, nothing of Plançon's shapely legato; but in Bizet's mock-Meyerbeer 'Quand la flamme' from *La Jolie Fille de Perth*, the voice itself is so impressive, the manner so assured, it is not hard to hear why he enjoyed the approval of the Parisian public through two generations.

In spite of Delmas's monopoly of many of the leading roles at the Opéra, his supremacy, especially in later years, did not go unchallenged—in particular, after 1900, by JUSTE NIVETTE (1865–19??). Nivette first joined the Opéra-Comique, making his debut as Sarastro in *La Flûte enchantée*. In 1900 he moved to the Opéra, where he sang Méphistophélès, the Duke of Verona and Frère Laurent in *Roméo et Juliette*, the Cardinal in *La Juive*, Cardinal Campeggio in *Henri VIII*, Ferrando in *Il Trovatore,* Abimelech and the old Hebrew in *Samson et Dalila*, St Jacques in *Le Cid*, Zacharias in *Le Prophète*,

61 Jean-François Delmas as Iago

62 Juste Nivette as Sarastro in *La Flute Enchantée*

Fafner, Hagen, the Landgrave, Lodovico in *Otello* and many other, particularly small parts. In 1902, he took the role of Le moine peintre in the world premiere of Massenet's *Le Jongleur de Notre Dame* at Monte Carlo, and was thereafter a frequent and popular visitor. In 1907, he was invited to La Scala and the following summer to Covent Garden, as Méphistophélès and was also an 'impressive' St Bris in *Les Huguenots*. The next year, he went to the United States, to join the Boston company. There his fine voice and splendid presence were much admired. In the role of Alvise, one critic described him looking as if 'he might have stepped out of one of van Dyck's Italian (sic) paintings'.[12]

As we hear him on records, Nivette's voice is dark in colour, and even through two octaves from F to F. He is equally sure plumbing the depths of the Cardinal's aria from *La Juive*, or Bertram's Valse Infernale from *Robert le Diable*, where the top has a clean focus and heady ring; at the end of this piece are some runs which he manages smoothly, if not with absolute clarity. Though his phrasing is not expansive and the interpretations without much character, it is certainly an outstanding voice.

HIPPOLYTE BELHOMME (1854–1923) made his debut at the Opéra-Comique at the age of twenty-five in 1879 in Félicien David's *Lalla Roukh*, and except for five years between 1886 and 1891, when he was at Lyons and Marseilles, remained with the company until 1916. During that time he made occasional guest appearances elsewhere in France and appeared at the Monnaie, Brussels. In Falstaff's couplets from Thomas's *Le Songe d'une nuit d'été*, we hear a typical French voice, well-schooled with some remarkable if not especially lovely trills.

63 Hippolyte Belhomme

13. Dramatic Sopranos

The leading native-born French soprano of the later years of the nineteenth century, EMMA CALVE (1858–1942), was one of the great personalities of her day. In France she was a national figure, in that respect at least—though utterly unlike her in every other way—what Clara Butt was on the other side of the Channel. In her autobiography she has reproduced a striking photograph of herself, halberd in hand, draped in the tricolour, just about to launch into 'La Marseillaise'. Throughout the rest of the world she was a by-word for her greatest role, Carmen; even the original dumb blonde, Anita Loos's Lorelei Lee, knew her name, though she could not quite remember how to spell it!

Calvé was from the Aveyron province in the South of France, a rugged and mountainous district; from her forebears she inherited a healthy constitution and a healthy respect for money. When she died at the ripe old age of eight-three, she had reigned for years in solitary state, chatelaine of the castle that towered over the town where she was born. As a girl, at convent school, she developed a remarkable voice. When she was twenty-one, she went to Paris to study singing with Jules Puget. After three years, she felt she was ready to make her debut: at the Monnaie, Brussels in 1882, as Marguerite in *Faust*. Years later, Clara Louise Kellogg, the American prima donna, remembered hearing her in the part; 'her Marguerite', she wrote, 'was a mixture of red pepper and vanilla blanc-mange'.[1] Whether Kellogg's strictures were fair or not, the Monnaie did not re-engage her. She went back to Paris for further study. In the interim, Puget having died, she was obliged to look around for another teacher. She joined a class at the rue Jouffroy, as Mme Marchesi recalled in her memoirs:

> I tried the voice and found it so tired and overworked that I advised her to rest it for some time before beginning lessons.[2]

Calvé stayed only six months with Marchesi; in her autobiography she is reticent about the whole episode, but we may assume that she did not find the Marchesi method appropriate to her particular gifts. At about this time, she joined the Opéra-Comique, remaining a member of the company for two years but earning only indifferent reviews. In 1887, Marchesi claimed on her recommendation, Calvé was engaged for La Scala, to create the leading role in Samara's *Flora Mirabilis*. Her reception in

Milan was certainly not indifferent, it was down-right hostile; she was very nearly booed off the stage. Once more she returned to Paris; this time, at the suggestion of the publisher, Heugel, she went to work with Rosine Laborde. It was third time lucky—Laborde gave her the confidence to make a new start. In six months she was able to go again to Italy, to the San Carlo, Naples, and this time she was enthusiastically received. When news of her success filtered through to La Scala, she was invited back, as Ophélie in Thomas's *Amleto*, opposite Mattia Battistini. She was determined to erase the unfortunate memory of her previous visit:

> I attacked a cadenza which I had never before attempted in public. It was an extremely difficult piece of vocalisation, going from low A to the F above top C . . . I held the note as long as I could, but when my breath gave out, I had to descend the chromatic scale. I did it with such brio, such perfection, that the audience burst into a thunder of applause. Seldom have I had such an ovation![3]

If this was scarcely the voice of modesty, from that time forth she had little need of it.

Though she was to become the greatest exponent of Carmen and Santuzza of her day, her voice, as her own description above suggests, was essentially a high-lying and brilliant instrument. She was a dramatic singer in manner rather than in weight of tone, and she did not make the kind of sound we associate with these roles today. Her effects were to some extent contrived by clever stagecraft and a highly individual personality, though she never relied on them to the extent that Geraldine Farrar and Mary Garden did. When she sang Ophélie at the Met, Henderson noted that 'she did most of her acting with her voice, she was first and last and all the time a singer'.[4] It was this skill that enabled her, especially in later years, to enjoy a considerable success away from the theatre, as a concert singer and recitalist. In 1905, after a two-year absence, she reappeared at the Carnegie Hall; Aldrich wrote:

> . . . she chose to seek no effects outside the magic of her voice and the charm of her style. The voice has always been one of the most searchingly poignant in its quality, wonderfully potent in its expression of emotion and in the variety of colour it could assume in heightening and enforcing the emotional significance of the music. At its best, her style has a certain intangible charm and her enunciation the grace and crisp clearness that we have learned to associate with the best French diction.[5]

64 Emma Calvé as Carmen

Calvé's repertory was considerable; apart from Sapho, which Massenet composed especially for her, she created Anita in his *La Navarraise* and the title-role in Reynaldo Hahn's *La Carmélite*. Among her other unusual parts were Amy Robsart and Messaline in de Lara's operas; she sang in Félicien David's *Lalla Roukh*, Thomas's *Songe d'une nuit d'été*, Lalo's *Le Roi d'Ys*, and Massé's *La Nuit de Cléopâtre*. She also sang both Salomé and Hérodiade in Massenet's opera, Margherita and Elena in

Boito's *Mefistofele*, and in her youth Cherubino, Susanna and the Countess in *Figaro*. And, when she was still in possession of some high notes, Ophélie, Lucia, Amina and Lakmé.

As Henderson and Aldrich suggest above and her records abundantly confirm, her singing was the result of very careful and thorough tutelage. There was none of that roughness of execution and nasal and acidulous tone so common among Gallic sopranos; only in her management of the registers is it possible to be critical. We have seen before how impressed she was by the castrato Domenico Mustafà's skill with the head voice and how she contrived something similar herself. In concert and on records it was successful, but in the theatre there survives by chance a striking record of its ineffectiveness. Mapleson caught her out, at the Met, during a performance of *Faust*, in the final phrases of the Jewel Song; everything seems to be going well until she gets to the last note, a high B, when all at once, from an appropriately full tone, she shifts into a disembodied falsetto. The effect is, to say the least, disconcerting.

If the passage of time eventually obliged her to relinquish the altitudinous roles of her youth, she continued to sing Carmen and Santuzza and to make regular concert tours. In 1912, on one such, she brought with her to America her husband, a tenor, by name Galileo Gaspari; from whence he emerged or where he went later is not sure. According to Olin Downes, his singing 'must be the true and final test of conjugal affection'[6]—a test evidently that proved too much for Calvé; she makes absolutely no reference to him in her autobiography. She was still in good voice on her final concert tour of the United States, in 1922. She felt she would like to sing Carmen again at the Met, and sent word to Gatti accordingly, but he demurred. A public increasingly enchanted by the new, and silent, idols of the moving pictures would, he felt, not take kindly to a sixty-four-year-old temptress, no matter how well-preserved her voice.

Landon Ronald has left a diverting account of how he got her into the studio to make her first records for the G & T company, in London in 1902. Apparently it was not in a very salubrious part of town. When the cab stopped in a dingy alley, Calvé positively refused to budge; she was convinced it was a plot to kidnap her. To prise her out, Ronald sent one of the company's employees to the nearest bank, drew a cheque and poured a stream of golden sovereigns into her lap. In a trice Calvé had gathered them up—'Allons mon petit Ronald!'—grabbed her

65 Calvé in the title-role
of Reynaldo Hahn's *La Carmélite*

mantilla and swept into the studio. The records she made then and later in America confirm the opinion of her contemporaries; the voice is still astonishingly fresh and silvery in quality. David's 'Charmant oiseau', the Mysoli bird, may not have been quite the virtuoso one Tetrazzini knew but, from a famous Carmen and Santuzza, the record is a tour de force. As Carmen, there is none of that chesty growling nowadays thought so seductive. In the Habanera, it is the pure tone of the voice itself that is attractive, the subtle, teasing rhythmic nuances that she uses to vary each verse, and the beautifully turned graces (how many famous Carmens have fallen over them?) that make her interpretation irresistible. In the dramatic roles—Santuzza, for example—there must have been some intensity in her stagecraft which the gramophone was not able to preserve. All of her recordings show a typical peasant husbanding of

66 Félia Litvinne as Armide in Gluck's opera

years later she went to New York, taking part in Mapleson's last stand at the Academy of Music. She was civilly received, but the critics' attention was elsewhere; at the new Metropolitan Opera House. Back in Europe, she made the usual progression through the principal houses, to St Petersburg and Moscow, Brussels and the Paris Opéra. In 1890 she reached La Scala as Gertrude in the same *Amleto* that gave Calvé the opportunity of putting things right with the Milanese audience.

Three years later she married a certain Dr Emmanuel Depoux, and for a time withdrew from the stage; but it did not prove to be a lasting affair. She went back to the stage in 1895, to the Met as Aida, Donna Anna, Gertrude (this time playing second fiddle to Melba), Sélika in *L'Africaine*, Chimène, the *Siegfried* Brünnhilde and Isolde. In this last part the *New York Times* commented that though she was an earnest artist she nevertheless performed—

> with all the faults which we used to bear so patiently in those German days [a reference to the all-German seasons at the Met during the 1880s] following the departure of Lilli Lehmann.[7]

Where New York was concerned Litvinne timed things badly. In matters of artistic conviction and authority she could not compare with Lilli Lehmann or Milka Ternina, and by all accounts her acting was conventional stuff, and her voice, though impressive, was never the equal of Nordica's in brilliance or size. She was not invited to return. Back in France she took part in a variety of leading Wagnerian occasions with the Lamoureux concerts and at the Opéra. It was as Wagner's Isolde that she made her Covent Garden debut in 1899. The London *Times* commented:

> Hers is a powerful dramatic soprano, she is evidently well experienced both in the stage business of the part and in the declamatory style of her singing . . . in the Liebestod she made a wholly favourable impression, though her voice is not of the most sympathetic quality imaginable.[8]

At Covent Garden she later sang Aida, Gioconda and Donna Anna, but it was in Wagnerian roles she was 'heard to greater advantage', in particular, as the *Walküre* Brünnhilde, 'where her voice is well-suited to the requirements of the music, with its full tone and clear enunciation'.[9] Though her range easily encompassed the high C, the dark mezzo colour of her voice belonged to the French tradition

resources; she never squandered her capital when the interest was so productive. Although she claimed she so much wanted to sing Senta and Isolde, she was too shrewd to risk her voice in the attempt.

Perhaps the greatest 'French' dramatic soprano voice of this period was FELIA LITVINNE (1860–1936). Born in St Petersburg, her real name was Françoise-Jeanne Schutz; her father was Russian and her mother French-Canadian. As a girl she went to Paris to study, first with Mme Barth-Banderoli, and then with Sbriglia and Viardot-Garcia. Her debut at the Théâtre des Italiens, in 1883, deputising for a famous diva of the day, Mme Fidès-Devriès, as Amelia in *Simon Boccanegra*. After some further appearances on her own account as Elvira in *Ernani*, the theatre's co-director, Victor Maurel, invited her to join him on a tour of the French provinces. Two

of Stolz, Falcon and Fidès-Devriès; the Wagnerian dramatic soprano roles, written predominantly in the middle of the voice, with only occasional flights over the top of the stave, were indeed well-suited to her voice. In addition to Sélika and Chimène, she sang other so-called Falcon roles: Katherine in *Henri VIII* by Saint-Saëns, Rachel in *La Juive*, Valentine, and towards the end of her career, in Paris, Gluck's Armide and Alceste, in the latter role leaving an unforgettable impression in the memory of Ernest Newman. She retired from the Opéra at the time of the First World War, but made occasional appearances in concert during the 1920s.

Her first series of gramophone records were all accompanied by the great French pianist, Alfred Cortot—a partnership that had commenced sometime previously when he conducted some performances with her at the Théâtre Château d'Eau. The tone of her voice is not especially pure, nor, as the London critic noted, of the most sympathetic quality, but her interpretation of Chimène's lament from *Le Cid* is delivered in appropriately noble style, she observes most of Massenet's phrase markings, and the many examples of martellato are managed without breaking the vocal line. Hers was not a front-ranking personality, to equal those of Ternina, Lehmann or Nordica, but she did have an outstanding voice, and her singing on record is never less than highly accomplished.

The Finnish soprano, AINO ACKTE (1876–1944), was also French-trained. She was from a family of singers: her father a successful baritone, her mother for many years a principal of the Finnish opera, a pupil of Massé and the elder Lamperti; and in due course her younger sister became a noted contralto. Ackté's first lessons were from her mother; then in 1895 she went to Paris to study with Duvernoy, afterwards coaching with Girodet and Vidal. Two years later she made her debut at the Opéra as Marguerite in *Faust*. She remained with the company until 1903, taking such lyrical roles as Juliette, Nedda, Micaëla and Elsa. At the Opéra-Comique she sang in Massenet's sacred music drama *Marie-Magdalène*. In 1904 she was engaged by the Met where, too, her first appearance was as Marguerite. Subsequently she sang Juliette, when Henderson described her singing as 'intolerable'.[10] The following season she seems to have worked some improvement:

She has bettered the impression she made last year. The character of Micaëla is a colourless one, but she made all there was to be made of it, and sang . . .

beautifully, especially in the Third Act, in which she showed a freedom and a warmth that have not always characterised her work.[11]

Her singing and acting were in the process of development. When she arrived at Covent Garden, in van Dyck's German season in the autumn of 1907, she had graduated to a more dramatic repertory, adding to her Elsa, Eva, Elisabeth and Senta. In this last part the *Times* critic commended

67 Aino Ackté as Tosca

her 'finished art and perfect conviction'.[12] But it was not until 1910 that she at last found a role exactly suited to her talents, when she undertook for the first London performances, the title-role in Strauss's *Salome*. Her assumption provoked all sorts of critical hyperbole, and for more than a generation it remained the interpretation by which all others were judged. That same season she sang in a couple of Promenade concerts: the first time the 'Herbstabend' by Sibelius and the closing scene from *Salome*; the second time as soprano soloist in the Verdi *Requiem*. According to Henry Wood:

> She simply electrified the audiences. Hers was one of the clearest and brightest sopranos I have ever heard. Rarely has a woman been endowed with the full equipment that goes to make what a really great opera singer needs—looks, figure, voice and brains. Added to which she was a great and really convincing actress.[13]

Praise indeed. Was the great man perhaps, ever such a little bit, in love with her? At any rate, her career does not seem to have amounted to much thereafter; she made guest appearances in Stockholm, Leipzig, Warsaw and Copenhagen, scarcely the world's great operatic centres. Eventually she retired to her native Helsinki. Thereafter she became a successful authoress, turning out several novels, a couple of volumes of memoirs, even opera libretti. In 1938, she was the Director of the Finnish opera.

Her records are all of lyrical music. An account of Elsa's dream, in French, displays little of the temperament Wood describes—perhaps she thought it would have been inappropriate here. The voice was of a good size with an attractive natural quality, but the support is not ideally firm, it detracts from a really sure legato and she has a disagreeable way of falling off a note—not a true portamento but a slide. Nevertheless, in Grieg's 'Je t'aime' the passionate and ardent manner suggest something of an artist.

But it was not Ackté with her temperament, nor Litvinne with her impressive voice, who was the greatest of the alien-born French artists: that was little Miss MARY GARDEN (1874–1967) from Aberdeen, Scotland, only five-feet tall and weighing less than a hundred pounds. She had gone to Paris via the United States and was to return there for the best part of her career. Yet, in spite of the years spent in America and her Scottish birth, Garden was a French artist, and her training was French—from Trabadello and Lucien Fugère. It was

the French language she spoke with complete idiomatic mastery, though she never did deign to suppress a 'celtic' burr, and it was in the French repertory she appeared, from Debussy's *Pelléas et Mélisande* to Février's *Monna Vanna* and Leroux's *La Reine Fiammette*, and when she did sing Strauss's *Salome* or *Tosca* (save for 'Vissi d'arte') she sang them in French, too. When she made her unannounced debut as Louise at the Opéra-Comique in 1900, at twenty-six, she was an instant success. It was not just her voice; indeed it hardly had to do with her voice at all. As she herself put it, 'People went to hear Melba and Caruso, they came to see Garden.'[14] In six years at the Opéra-Comique she created leading roles in Massenet's *Cherubin*, Pierné's *La Fille du Tabarin* and d'Erlanger's *Aphrodite*. But it was as Mélisande that she found a part to reward her talents. In 1907, she sang it at the Manhattan with the Hammerstein company:

> Miss Garden made it a new disclosure of her art and of the power of her dramatic personality. She is the dreamy wistful maiden, wandering, uncertain, unhappy; and her denotement of the veiled and mysterious character is of much beauty and plastic grace. In places she rises to a height of tragic power that ought to put her among the greatest of lyric actresses. It was difficult to believe this statuesque maiden was of the same stuff as Thaïs, as Louise.[15]

If Garden's stature as an actress was never in any real doubt, during her three years at the Manhattan and thereafter with visiting troupes, the New York critics nevertheless subjected her singing to merciless criticism:

> Interest . . . was . . . added by Miss Garden's . . . gay and jocular manner upon the platform which seemed . . . to cover a certain embarrassment . . . Miss Garden's embarrassment, if it really was such, was, under the circumstances, easily understood and perfectly justifiable, especially after she had begun to sing . . . Discussion of it is not agreeable.[6]

Nevertheless, Aldrich went on to discuss it in great detail, noting the particular 'deficiencies in her voice and vocal art'.[17] And he was one among many. It is an interesting fact, however, that her various recordings do not show 'the kind of hysterical display one might have expected',[18] but 'a lyrical voice of excellent natural qualifications schooled according to the best canons of art'.[19] In this they accord far more with the opinion of the *Chicago*

68 Mary Garden as Jean in *Le Jongleur de Notre-Dame*

brilliance. It cascaded through dazzling cadenzas of coloratura, trilled and fluted in the canzonette.[21]

Perhaps it was not a first-class voice, but it was not, the evidence suggests, half as bad as some writers have declared. Its range was the two octaves from C to C. In her own words 'It never gave me any trouble . . . I never had to rest because it was tired . . . whether the critics liked it or whether they didn't . . .'[22] Her recording of 'Ah! fors' è lui' and 'Sempre libera' (in French), though not perhaps to be compared to Melba's or Tetrazzini's, does indeed reveal 'unsuspecting elements of brilliance'; it is surprisingly accurate and sung in the original key, though she dodges the high D flats. We can hear much of that sympathetic tone too, and expressive phrasing, in the famous Statue Aria from *Thaïs*; a good deal more, may it be said, than in some modern accounts of this music. Perhaps her loveliest records are of Scottish and Irish airs, in particular 'Bluebells of Scotland' and the 'Irish Love Song', both sung with delicate tenderness and haunting tone. And her voice bore up well. She sang into the 1930s, and when she was in her late fifties made some recordings which show it much as it had been in earlier years, with only the kind of wear to be expected after a career of more than a quarter of a century.

After Paris and New York, Chicago was the centre of her activities. Even today, over the Director's head, in the principal offices of the Auditorium Theatre, a full-length portrait of her keeps a watchful eye on things. It is an appropriate place for it; for twenty-one years she sang with the Chicago Opera, and for one unforgettable season she was its Director, the supreme mistress of its fortunes, and it was a fortune that she disposed of, even in those halcyon pre-Depression days. 'If it cost a million,' she told her biographer later, 'it was worth it.' Certainly it was one of the few things Chicago had any right to be proud of in the hey-day of Al Capone. In that latter-day Babylon, where the police chief offered his protection to gangsters and bootleggers, it was a nice irony that his susceptibilities should have been outraged by Garden's Salome. 'It was indecent, disgusting, Miss Garden wallowing around like a cat in a bed of cat mint,' he told the *Tribune*. Garden retorted that indecency, like beauty, was in the eye of the beholder. Even today in Chicago they still remember her ripostes— to the elderly dignitary at a city banquet who demanded to know what it was that kept up the diva's dangerously low decolletage: 'Two things,'

Tribune critic, who noted, after her Thaïs:

> . . . she proved she can sing with unfailing sympathy of tone that is so variedly expressive that it compensated for lack of purity.[20]

The same critic wrote again of one of her rare appearances as Dulcinea in Massenet's *Don Quichotte*:

> Her singing disclosed unsuspecting elements of

69 Garden as Aphrodite in d'Erlanger's opera

she snapped, 'your age and my discretion.'

Her career was unique. In the first place the operas she sang were mostly French, and outside France, French opera had never equalled in popularity the Italian or German repertory; then too, she sang for the most part what was at that time new music; she had that much in common with Caruso; she was one of the last great singers to identify herself with the works of her contemporaries. Since her retirement, nobody has managed to revive with any lasting effect those operas of Massenet with which she had been specially identified: *Chérubin, Grisélidis, Thaïs* and *Le Jongleur de Notre Dame*, and nobody has even tried to breathe life back into the compositions of d'Erlanger, Pierné, Leroux and Février—it is not desirable that anyone should try. These pieces were products of a long-since spent tradition, when interpreters were not the dutiful junior partners of our own day, used to treating with acknowledged masterpieces: artists like Bernhardt and Garden were dominating personalities, able so to charge quite second-rate material with their own peculiar genius that Sardou's *Madame Sans-Gêne* became Bernhardt's and Février's *Monna Vanna* became Garden's.

14. Lyric Sopranos

When Garden quit the Opéra-Comique in 1906, there were several contenders waiting to slip into her roles. One of these was JULIA GUIRAUDON (1873–19??) who had been the first French Mimi at the Comique in 1897. Two years later she created Cendrillon in Massenet's opera. She was frequently chosen to appear in other Massenet pieces; whether this was on account of genuine talent and suitability or perhaps the consequence of her marriage to Henri Cain, one of the composer's favourite librettists, it is difficult to be certain. In one of her rare recordings, 'Depuis le jour', though her vibrato is more prominent, the style is reminiscent of Garden's, and the tone appealing without the usual Gallic acidity.

Which is more than can be said for MARGUERITE CARRÉ (1881–1947), born Giraud, who went one better than Guiraudon and married, not the composer's librettist, but his employer, the Director of the Opéra-Comique, Albert Carré. She was from Bordeaux and was a student there at the Conservatory before coming to Paris. Early in 1902 she joined the Opéra-Comique, at first without anyone taking much notice; but Miss Giraud was ambitious, she was set on becoming the company's principal soprano, and if this could not be accomplished on stage, it would have to be managed backstage. Garden was the main obstacle in her way; she was not only the public's favourite, she was also Carré's. Giraud figured that though the public might be able to resist her charms and prefer Garden, the Director could not. She was beautiful, and she was right; she quickly became his mistress, and before the year was out, when they were married, mistress of the house, too. One day, soon

70 Julia Guiraudon in the title-role of Massenet's
Cendrillon

71 Marguerite Carré in the title-role of Leroux's
La Reine Fiammette

afterwards, she came face to face with Garden in one of those opera-house corridors too narrow to let both ladies pass without some accommodation: for a moment there was an impasse. Then Carré took a step forward and glared at Garden:

> 'Let me pass,' she demanded, 'don't you know who I am? I am Mme Carré!' 'O ma chère,' replied Garden, 'but I was Mme Carré long before you were.'

She remained at the Opéra-Comique for the rest of her career, until the First World War; but though she took over most of Garden's roles, and, as that lady remarked, everyone else's as well, she never did make a great name for herself. From first to last and all the way, she was a house soprano. She never travelled outside France and rarely beyond the Salle Favart. At the Comique, she was the first Pamina and the first Butterfly.†

† Puccini is said to have complained of her inability to sing his music.

Her records are also particularly rare but they reveal nothing more than a routine French lyric soprano, the tone tremulous and hard, especially the high notes.

LUCETTE KORSOFF's (1876–1955) background was polyglot. She was born in Genoa, but her parents were Russian and it was in St Petersburg that she made her first stage appearance, in Pergolesi's *La Serva Padrona*, when she was only sixteen. Soon afterwards she travelled to Paris to study with Frederick Boyer and made a second debut in 1901 at Toulouse. For three seasons she was a principal 'lyric-coloratura' at the Monnaie, Brussels, where she sang Musetta, Philine, Norina, Rosina, Sophie in *Werther*, Rose Friquet in *Les Dragons de Villars*, Isabelle in *Le Pré aux clercs*. In 1905 she joined the Opéra-Comique and was especially renowned there for her Queen of the Night. Later, in the United States, she sang with the Boston, New Orleans and Chicago companies. After

72 Lucette Korsoff in the title-role of *Amaryllis*

73 Lise Landouzy as Gounod's Mireille

her career was over, she retired to Brussels.

Korsoff made a large number of recordings that preserve a very French style and vocal technique, save that the tone is without the characteristic nasality—the mitigating effect of her Russian blood, perhaps? She was an accomplished singer and the voice is notably secure, especially the head register. If the quality is a little hard, the manner is not without charm; in her recording of Manon's entrance music she carefully observes Massenet's subito pianos at the end of the ascending phrases. Altogether in this piece the phrasing and the use of rubato show a correct mastery of the style. She prefers the upward alternatives, including a cadenza that touches the E in alt, which she does in a single proficient gesture. The 'éclat de rire' on the repeated Gs may strike us as rather quaint, but this was the fashion in which these notes were taken in Massenet's day. She was a fine soubrette when the term was descriptive rather than abusive.

LISE LANDOUZY (1861–1943) belonged to the previous generation of Opéra-Comique sopranos. Her debut took place in 1889, as Rosina, and in the course of the next decade, like Korsoff, she a principal 'lyric-coloratura' at the Monnaie, roles. She was a French Anne Ford in the Paris première of *Falstaff*. She was a regular guest at Aix-les-Bains, Monte Carlo and the Monnaie, Brussels.

Hers was a typically Gallic sound: hard driven, with piercing high notes. Unlike Carré, she made a great number of records; in appropriate music, such as the rondo 'Vive le marriage' from Thomas's *Le Caïd*, though shortened and simplified, she has the right vigour and rhythmic élan, even if there is no special personality. There have always been singers like this in France, from the days of Grétry to Poulenc. In the eighteenth century their voices made Dr Burney wince; these days, standards being relative, they seem less objectionable.

A voice of lovely quality has always been a

refreshing treat at the Opéra-Comique; one such at the turn of the century was ALICE VERLET's (1873–1934). She made her first appearance there in 1894, after making a debut in her native Belgium. She sang Philine, Lakmé, Rosina, Mireille, Manon, Violetta and Jeanette in Massé's *Les Noces de Jeanette*. In 1900 she appeared at the Théâtre des Folies Dramatiques as La Reine Elisabeth in Thomas's *Le Songe d'une nuit d'été* and Caroline in Adam's *Le Toréador*. The following season she was engaged at the Monnaie as Gilda, the Queen in *Les Huguenots*, a Rhinemaiden, Elvira in Auber's *La Muette de Portici*, Baucis in Gounod's *Philémon et Baucis* and Constanze in the *Seraglio*. In this last part, a critic wrote:

> . . . we have seldom heard the formidable vocalisation demanded throughout, performed with such absolute virtuosity.[1]

She sang the part again, in her London debut with the Beecham company at Her Majesty's during the 1910 season. From 1903, she appeared regularly at the Paris Opéra. In the First World War she was in the United States, making concert tours and appearing with the Chicago company as Philine to Supervia's Mignon.

Her many records are mostly attractive. By the highest standards, perhaps, there is a want of individuality—she has a way of reminding the listener of other, and greater singers, a two-edged compliment. Technically, she is proficient rather than brilliant and the highest notes are done with caution, but the singing is always attractive. We can hear her at her best in the Almsgiving scene from *Le Cid*; Massenet is at his most sanctimonious, but her smooth delivery and pure tone are heard to advantage, especially in the perfectly managed upward portamenti to the soft high B flats, at the end of the repeated 'Alleluias'.

BLANCHE ARRAL (1865–1945), née Clara Lardinois, was another Belgian soprano; an accomplished vocalist and a very piquant and original personality. After studying with Marchesi, her career began at the Opéra-Comique in 1880 when, by her account of things, she was only sixteen. Four years later she took the part of a serving maid in the world premiere of Massenet's *Manon*. At the Opéra-Comique, she sang in opera: Mignon, Manon, Ophélie, Philine, Juliette and Lakmé, and in operetta, appearing in the first Paris productions of works by Strauss and Millöcker. From the turn of the century, however, she gave up the stage for concert tours, which she undertook throughout Europe, the United States, South America and the Orient, styling herself 'Prima Donna of the Five Continents', and carrying with her a variety of distinguished supporting artists, the greatest, her own countryman, the violinist Eugène Ysaye. In 1909, when in New York, Richard Aldrich heard her:

> The voice is powerful and well under her command, and she has a certain amount of skill in the delivery of the florid passages of the music. It is not a voice in the freshness of youth not of beautiful quality, nor is it one of many refinements of shading and emotional colouring . . . It has the penetration and carrying power of abundant sonority. Mme Arral's experience enables her to make these things count to their utmost. To music such as that of Massenet and Thomas, she gives a brilliance which, though rather hard, is effective. In that of a more sustained sort . . . she was less at home.[2]

Her operatic recordings are not to be numbered among the best. In operetta, however, her wonderfully vivid personality gets free rein. The 'Valse d'oiseau' from Varney's *L'Amour mouillé*, a real

74 Alice Verlet as Baucis in Gounod's *Philémon et Baucis*

period piece with its birdy noises, is quite irresistible; equally charming is Vasseur's 'El bolero grande', a typical example of 'espagnolerie' with its castanets and 'Oh la la', owing everything to France and *Carmen* and pretty well nothing to Spain.

15. Three Contraltos

Although Patti, Albani, Lilli Lehmann, Capoul, Lloyd, Lassalle and Kaschmann survived to leave (with varying degrees of success) accounts of their art for posterity, the only records we have today of a contralto born in the first half of the nineteenth century are the three titles, made in 1905, by the then sixty-three-year-old Marianne Brandt, a pupil of Pauline Viardot. Of Sofia Scalchi, Giulia Ravogli and Antoinette Sterling, all of whom might have left us echoes of their erstwhile glory, there is nothing. It would be too much to expect a souvenir of Viardot herself, although she lived until 1910, for her voice had passed away nearly fifty years previously; but it is sad that Marietta Alboni, a favourite singer of Rossini, died in 1894, only a few years before the gramophone was keeping records. According to

75 Blanche Arral as Carmen

Emma Eames, who heard her several times in the last years of her life, she was still singing with memorable effect. The distinguished American critic Max de Schauensee tells how he took Eames to hear Supervia in *Cenerentola*, and after the performance he asked her how she liked it. 'Oh, my dear,' Eames replied, with infinite expression, 'I heard Alboni sing that music.'[1]

As Viardot and Alboni both settled in Paris, it is appropriate that the former's influence as teacher and the latter's example should have had an effect on the style and method of the French contralto singers of the early years of this century. The oldest of them to make records was born BLANCHE DESCHAMPS (1857–1923) in Lyons. After finishing her studies at the Conservatory there, she came to Paris. Then, like many another French artist, she made her stage debut at the Monnaie, Brussels in 1879. In the course of the next few years she created the title role in Massenet's *Hérodiade* and Ufa in Reyer's *Sigurd*. Upon returning from Brussels she joined the company at the Opéra-Comique, where she stayed until 1902. During those years she took part in an impressive list of world premieres: in Massé's *La Nuit de Cléopatre* (1885), Gounod's *Le Médecin malgré lui* (1886), as Margared in Lalo's *Le Roi d'Ys* (1888), Mme de la Haltière in Massenet's *Cendrillon* (1891) and the mother in Charpentier's *Louise* (1900).

In 1889 she went for the first time to Monte Carlo, where she met Louis Jehin, principal conductor there, and soon afterwards they were married. Two years later she made her Covent Garden debut, in the autumn season, as Carmen with Jehin conducting:

> Merely to listen to such a beautiful voice would be a source of delight, but when combined with a perfect command of expression and pathos it held every listener spellbound.[2]

In two seasons in London, she sang Fidès with Jean de Reszké and principal roles in Bruneau's *Le Rêve* and Bemberg's *Elaine*, the latter with Melba, Plançon and both de Reszkés. She added a new dimension to her Paris career when she joined the Opéra, there she was admired as Fidès, Léonore in Donizetti's *La Favorite*, Amneris, Ortrud and Dalila (she was the first Dalila at the Palais Garnier). After 1902 she occupied herself increasingly with concert work, making only occasional operatic appearances and usually in Monte Carlo, there she sang for the last time on stage, as Martha in Boito's *Mefistofele* with Chaliapin and Smirnov, in 1909.

Her few recordings were made at the end of her career, when she was over fifty. Although the voice is still a fine instrument, especially at the top, the chest register has become dull and worn. A performance of Azucena's 'Stride la vampa', with the French text, is done cleanly, the rhythm strongly marked, though the voice itself is sometimes hoarse and her intonation is not always precise, Dalila's 'Mon coeur s'ouvre' is less successful, the tone rather tremulous, and the phrasing short-breathed.

Many of Deschamps's best roles at the Opéra and the Opéra-Comique were subsequently taken over by MARIE DELNA (1875–1932) (an anagram of her real name, Ledan). She was from Meudon. In Paris she studied with Rosine Laborde, the teacher of Calvé. Her debut took place at the Opéra, in 1892, as Dido in *Les Troyens.* Thereafter she sang at both theatres until after the outbreak of the First World War. At the Opéra-Comique she was Charlotte in the first performances there of *Werther,* and Dame Quickly in *Falstaff.* At the same theatre she created the role of Marcelline in the world premiere of Bruneau's *L'Attaque du moulin.* It was this part she took in her only appearance at Covent Garden, in the summer of 1894. Klein recalled that she made 'an ineffaceable

77 Jeanne Gerville-Réache as Dalila

impression . . . her Marcelline was a superb creation'.[3] In 1907 she sang Orfeo at La Scala, under Toscanini, and appeared in the same role for her Met debut, succeeding Homer, again with Toscanini in the pit. Though her beautiful voice was much praised, not everything in her performance pleased; Henderson complained that 'her respect for rhythm was slight . . . which must have taxed Toscanini's skill to keep the accompaniment in union with her'.[4] After some performances in the Met's New Theatre Season, as Marcelline, she went back to Paris; it was her only visit to the United States. When the Met came to the Théâtre du Chatelet, in 1910, and Toscanini conducted the opening performance of *Aida,* at the beginning of Act II he was roundly booed by a section of the audience; a reprisal, it was said, organised by Delna. In the later years of her career she sang mostly in the French provinces. She died in 1932, a pauper, and had to be buried by the state.

Delna's records confirm that hers was a fine

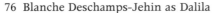

76 Blanche Deschamps-Jehin as Dalila

78 Marie Delna in the title-role of Massenet's *Hérodiade*

voice, smoothly produced through a wide range, but it was also a monotonous one; there is a lack of personality and a want of rhythmic energy. In an account of Cassandra's address to the Trojans (she sang this role in the first performance of the first part of Berlioz's epic at the Opéra, in 1899) she sings cleanly but without much authority.

Another pupil of Rosine Laborde, JEANNE GERVILLE-REACHE (1882–1915), was also the possessor of a fine contralto voice. Later she went to Viardot-Garcia to study, especially the roles of Fidès and Orphée. It was as Orphée that she made her debut at the Opéra-Comique in 1899. Three years later she created Geneviève in *Pelléas et Mélisande*. Subsequently she sang with success in Brussels, and in 1905 at Covent Garden, deputised for an ailing Kirkby-Lunn in some performances of *Orphée*, 'arresting the attention of the house from the first with the fine quality of her singing and the breadth and assurance of her acting'.[5] In spite of enthusiastic reviews, or perhaps because of them, she was not invited again. Hammerstein took her as part of the package when he presented the first performances of *Pelléas et Mélisande* at the Manhattan. For him she sang a number of different roles but with only qualified success. As Carmen, Henderson thought—

> she presented a charming appearance but seemed to be unable to get into the picture on the stage at all, and so little command had she of her voice that on several important parts it almost failed her entirely.[6]

It never became a famous impersonation. She had a greater measure of success with Anita in *La Navarraise* and that in spite of Calvé's supreme example, but it was as Dalila that she really came into her own. Hale put it on a par with de Reszké's Roméo, de Lucia's Canio, Ternina's Isolde, Calvé's Carmen and Maurel's Iago.

In 1910 she married the Director of the Pasteur Institute in New York and settled in the United States. She appeared there with the Chicago and Philadelphia companies and undertook extensive concert tours. In these her programmes included much unfamiliar material: arias from Mercadante's *La Vestale*, Gounod's *Sapho* and *La Reine de Saba*, Massenet's *Roma*, and from Delna she inherited Marcelline's Battle Cry from Bruneau's *L'Attaque du moulin*. This she brought out at a New York concert at the beginning of the First World War, rousing the audience to a fine old frenzy. Aldrich, by no means easy to please in the concert hall, preferred her here:

> [her voice] has the greatest beauty in its middle register, though her deep tones of a true contralto, such as are seldom heard, are very effective and cannot fail to impress the listener.[7]

How her career might have developed must remain a matter for conjecture. She died at the age of thirty-two from ptomaine poisoning.

As well as familiar pieces from *Carmen* and *Samson*, her recorded repertory includes arias from Debussy's *L'Enfant prodigue*, Gounod's *Sapho* and *La Reine de Saba*, Godard's *La Vivandière* and Massé's *Paul et Virginie*. It is an unusual voice, powerful but not always agreeable. The registers are strongly contrasted, more in the German fashion—like Marianne Brandt, for example—perhaps this was the result of Viardot's teaching. In Dalila's music there is a firm legato and the voice has the right dark colour, but here, as elsewhere, the tone is rather throaty and the execution, especially in the chest register, often coarse and vehement. Like the Germans she had a certain skill in coloratura as we can hear in Chaminade's picturesque 'Chanson Slave'.

PART III

The Emergence of Verismo

16. 'La Gloria d'Italia'

In Italy the classical Italian method, that taught by Garcia and exemplified still in the art of Patti, was irrevocably compromised by the changing repertory. Though Verdi still gave the singer his head, his principal concern had been to write vocal music that was dramatically effective. Unlike his predecessors, Rossini, Bellini and Donizetti, he had not bothered himself with whether it was gratefully written; the singer's vocal comfort and health were beside the point. Boito and Ponchielli went a stage further, putting the singer in the front line in direct combat with the orchestra, which inevitably led to a more vehement and dramatic vocal style. These developments culminated in the verismo school with its exaggerated and often unmusical pathos. The effect of it all on Italian singing can be heard readily enough on any number of records made in the first two decades of this century: impure tone, obtrusive vibrato, crude attack and rough execution, all too familiar features that are not only unlovely but, in the interpretation of music of earlier periods, unstylish as well.

Apart from Patti, there survived into this century at least one other indubitably great singer whose art was formed before the excesses of the verismo had taken root—the baritone MATTIA BATTISTINI (1856–1928). Happily the gramophone preserved his voice while he was still in his prime. Battistini was the son of a Professor of Anatomy at Rome University. From the beginning he showed a remarkable musical talent; like Patti, it is said, when still quite a small boy he clambered on top of a table and launched into an operatic aria. What the piece was legend has not recorded; since it could hardly have been Rigoletto's 'Cortigiani' or Nelusko's 'Adamastor', perhaps he too chose 'Casta Diva'. After parental resistance had been overcome when he declined to become a doctor, he was allowed to take lessons from Venceslao Persichini, a famous teacher whose pupils included Francesco Marconi and later Giuseppe de Luca and Titta Ruffo. His debut took place at the Teatro Argentina, Rome, in *Favorita* in 1878. During the next decade he sang extensively in Italy and made his first appearances at Covent Garden in 1883, as Riccardo in *Puritani* with Marcella Sembrich; later he sang Telramund, di Luna, and, with Patti and Nicolini, Germont in *Traviata*. He was cordially but not ecstatically received; no doubt the presence of an old favourite, Antonio Cotogni, in the company the same season had something to do with London's failure to capitulate at once.

Battistini's greatness was achieved in spite of the fact that he never sang in the United States—he didn't like sea-trips—and appeared in London and Paris not more than a handful of times each. His biggest triumphs took place in Italy, Spain and Portugal, Germany, Austro-Hungary, Poland and most of all in Russia, where he went for the first time in 1888 and returned every year until 1914. His operatic career continued well into the 1920s. In 1926, in Vienna, he sang Rodrigo in *Don Carlo*:

> This septuagenarian is an incomprehensible miracle whose splendid voice is almost wholly untouched by age. He can compete as to brilliance and power of singing, with the youngest vocal celebrities whom, however, he surpasses in musical culture, artistic mixture of registers and technical perfection. Physically too, this incomparable artist has preserved his freshness and elasticity, whilst histrionically he always fascinates and moves his audiences.[1]

In the course of fifty years, he disappointed only once; he had proposed to celebrate his golden jubilee by appearing again at the Argentina in Rome as Alfonso, but less than a month before the event he died from an attack of asthma.

Battistini belonged to the same generation as Jean de Reszké, when opera was still grand and it was unthinkable for a great singer to play anything less than a king, nobleman, cavalier, or at the least a romantic hero. In the days when singers wore their own costumes, he travelled with over thirty pieces of handmade luggage each one embossed with the initials, 'M.B.', and each containing a wardrobe of different stage costumes. Except for Rossini's Figaro, buffo roles he regarded as infra dig and he declined to undertake Falstaff—who, though a knight, was a buffoon, and a fat one at that. In the repertory of his choice, however, he was without equal: in Meyerbeer's *Ugonotti* and *Africana*, Tchaikovsky's *Eugenio Oneghin* and *Dama di Picche* (which he sang in Italian and Russian), Massenet's *Werther*—a part which, with some adjustments, he appropriated to particular effect—in the great Verdi roles from Carlo Quinto in *Ernani* to Iago, and in Donizetti's *Roberto Devereux, Maria di Rohan* and *Torquato Tasso,* which he continued to sustain long after they had slipped from the general repertory. Lauri-Volpi has described the effect of his virtuosity in a performance of *Favorita*:

> At the cadenza (in the Giardini del Alcazar scene) on the words 'il cor' he took a deep breath, releasing it sparingly in a prolonged and accented 'i', repeating the note to the front, to the left, to the right of the stage, to the various sections of the audience,† who would not let him end, filled as they were with delight at his audacious virtuosity.[2]

When asked why he did not teach, Battistini replied: 'My school is in my records.' During a period of twenty-two years he made a great many, and they must be numbered among the best and most revealing of any singer of that era. The first date from 1902, when he was forty-six and still at the height of his career, the last from 1924, when he was sixty-eight—although the voice is older and less responsive, it is still in fine condition. His was a brilliant high baritone, extending with consummate ease to the high A, only the lowest notes being weak and undeveloped. As the Vienna critic above noted, the registers were perfectly blended. Battistini was a master of breath control of the art of messa di voce and, if his trill was not clearly defined, otherwise his skill in fioritura rivalled the greatest French singers and he managed it with a virile ring and cutting edge more appealing to modern taste. His style in the music of Bellini and Donizetti was less pure than Tamburini's or Ronconi's must have been. In Riccardo's 'Bel sogno beato' from *Puritani*, for

79 Mattia Battistini in the title-role of Rubinstein's *Demone*

example, the coloratura is an impression rather than an actual account of the notes, not because he could not have done it literally, but because he was trying to inform the earlier music with the more dramatic style of the later nineteenth century and, unlike so many of his contemporaries, achieve this entirely by vocal means. That edge on the tone which at climaxes he developed into what Desmond Shawe-Taylor has called 'a splendid snarl'[3]—sometimes even pushing the note sharp—was, like his passion for sudden sforzandos and seemingly endless diminuendos, a mode of expression, an affecting device. No singer, not excepting Patti, excelled him in the portamento style. In Rodrigo's 'Io morrò', for example, he shapes the grave cantilena with all kinds of nuance, gradation of dynamics and range of

† This device, which was a particular feature of the old Italian style, was much used by Battistini to give especial rhythmic emphasis and as a way of punctuating phrases without breaking the vocal line.

80 Antonio Cotogni as Nevers in Meyerbeer's *Ugonotti*

the utmost affection and charm, the whole piece dying away in a hushed and prolonged F, the voice leaning on the breath (what the Italians call 'appoggio'), and not a scrap of it wasted. Like Patti's records, so Battistini's inspire superlatives; unlike hers they need no apology.

In his day he was enormously admired by the public and critics, but perhaps most of all by other musicians. Frances Alda, a lady usually sparing in her praises of her colleagues, heard him only once, but the impression he made she never forgot; 'he was the greatest singer I have ever heard.'[4] Albert Spalding thought so too, after hearing him in the early 1920s in Rome, in Lorenzo Perosi's oratorio *Resurrezione di Cristo*:

> The baritone role of Christus was sung by the veteran Battistini ... The passing years had brought no impairment to the effortless production of golden tone, which poured itself forth with astonishing opulence. He phrased like an instrumentalist; breathing became an expressive punctuation rather than a physical necessity; and he had a sustained legato that was unbearably beautiful. . . . He was, I think, the greatest vocalist I have ever heard.[5]

Listening to his records today, it is easy to agree.

Battistini's great predecessor, ANTONIO COTOGNI (1831–1918), had a very brief and scarcely revealing relationship with the gramophone; at the age of seventy-seven, in 1908, with the tenor Francesco Marconi, he recorded Masini's duet 'I Mulatieri'. Not surprisingly Marconi gets the better of it. Still, however difficult it is to make out Cotogni's contribution, it is all that we have left of a singer who for over forty years dominated the stages in London, Madrid and Lisbon, St Petersburg and Moscow and throughout Italy. During all that time he most completely exemplified the tradition of Tamburini and Ronconi, of the school of Bellini and Donizetti. As Vivian Liff has written, 'It is fascinating to be able to recall the art of a singer, active before Verdi had written *Trovatore* or *Traviata*, who at Covent Garden kept company with Tietjens, Tamberlik, Scalchi, Mario and Nicolini.'[6] Cotogni's voice is the oldest to survive on records. As a boy he had fought at the barricades on the side of the short-lived Roman Republic of 1849, against Louis-Napoléon's 'chasse-pots'. His pupils included Jean de Reszké, Mariano Stabile, Benvenuto Franci, Gigli, Mario Basiola and Giacomo Lauri-Volpi, who is still, at the time of writing, making gramophone records.

tonal colour. Yet there is nothing contrived, fussy or self-regarding about it: like the cadenza Lauri-Volpi describes above, it always seems spontaneous, the sound itself vital, animated throughout by the unceasing support of the breath. He was especially effective in the operas of Meyerbeer; in Nelusko's 'Figlia di Regi' every section is strongly contrasted. The opening cantabile con portamento with the allegro vivace, 'Quando amor m'accende', where he hurls out the marcato passages yet without breaking the line; then at the end in the swelling phrases 'O Brama, o Dio possente', he spins a legato of incomparable eloquence and intensity. Sung like this, Meyerbeer would not be difficult to revive. He brings the same resources and skill to bear in a miniature, Tosti's 'Amour, amour', phrasing with

GUISEPPE KASCHMANN (1850–1925) was senior to Battistini by six years. He studied with Alberto Giovannini at Udine before making his debut in 1876, also as Alfonso in *Favorita*, at Turin. His success was considerable, and the following season he sang at the Fenice in Venice, Rome, Bologna and Trieste. In December 1878 he made a triumphant debut at La Scala in *Don Carlo*; 'His wonderful voice, elegant style and splendid acting, riveted everyone's attention'.[7] Unlike Battistini, who only ventured across the Atlantic twice (on both occasions to South America), Kaschmann was a regular visitor in Rio and Buenos Aires, and for two seasons appeared at the Met. The first time he sang Enrico in *Lucia*, on the second night of the inaugural season, and returned in 1894, adding Rigoletto, Don Giovanni, Valentin, Amonasro, and, in German language productions, Kurwenal in *Tristan*, Wolfram and Telramund. His reception was equivocal: his acting and stage presence were very much admired and his singing too, up to a point—the point being a rapid and very pronounced vibrato which was not to the taste of public or critics.

81 Giuseppe Kaschmann as Carlo Quinto in *Ernani*

Though he never sang in London when most of the important Italian singers were regular visitors, his career continued at Bayreuth in *Parsifal* and *Tannhäuser* with great success, and in Italy at all the leading theatres. Until he was nearly sixty, he was still singing Amonasro, Rodrigo, Macbeth and the title-role in *Guglielmo Tell*. Thereafter, he began a second career in buffo and character parts in Mozart's *Bastiano*, Cimarosa's *Astuzie Femminili*, Pergolesi's *Serva Padrona* and Monteverdi's *Orfeo*, as Bartolo in *Barbiere* and Malatesta in *Don Pasquale*. He sang this for the last time in the 1920s, with his pupil Salvatore Baccaloni in the title-role.

By general consensus, Kaschmann's greatest role was Hamlet in Thomas's opera—

> when his voice seemed like thunder so impressively did it reverberate. In the duet with Ophélie it was veiled with tenderness, in the Brindisi clear and brilliant . . . a miracle of beautiful sounds, with infinitely subtle emphasis and affects.[8]

The Brindisi was one of the five titles Kaschmann recorded in 1903, and by that time his voice was on the wane, the 'miracle of beautiful sounds' passed; the vibrato is omnipresent and there is an effortfulness in the execution, the voice not moving easily. The patrician manner, however, remains untouched in Carlo's 'O dei verd' anni miei' from *Ernani*, its finely wrought phrasing and legato broadening out in appropriately regal style. A particular feature of his singing, a by-product of the vibrato, is in the clean and precisely turned ornaments, which are always done on the beat yet remain properly subordinate. Only the rather hard attack presages the new realism.

A contemporary of Kaschmann and Battistini, the Portuguese baritone FRANCESCO D'ANDRADE (1859–1921), was a pupil of Ronconi. He made his first stage appearance at San Remo in 1882 as Amonasro. In the years immediately thereafter, he appeared in a variety of roles at many of the leading Italian houses, including La Scala. At Covent Garden he was a member of the company between 1886 and 1889, making his debut as Rigoletto, when 'he sang in finished style and displayed a voice of remarkably beautiful and sympathetic quality'.[9] Later came Carlo Quinto, Barnaba, Valentin and Renato:

> His 'Eri tu' was sung with such beauty of tone, excellence of phrasing and impassioned pathos that the audience was moved to an unusual display of

enthusiasm, and prolonged their applause until the artist consented to repeat the final section.[10]

In later seasons he added Alfonso, an Italian Telramund, Riccardo, Germont, Amonasro, when Shaw thought he ranted too much, Nevers, in which his intonation was questioned, and Don Giovanni. It was this last part he sang everywhere, throughout Germany (where he eventually settled), Holland, Austro-Hungary, Russia, in Scandinavia and once as far afield as Australia, in a company organised by Etelka Gerster. It was 'an unrivalled and fascinating characterisation', to which a certain zest was added by the knowledge that—

in real life he is a Don Juan himself. If the list of his victims has not reached *mille et trois* the fault cannot be laid at his door. His stage victims were all fat *frauen* [at a performance in Munich, in 1910]. Zerlina wore a blond wig, showed very black eyebrows and red lips. Her golden molars shone from afar.[11]

His last Don Giovanni was his last stage appearance, in 1919, when he was sixty. A recording of the Champagne aria made in 1906 has nothing special to recommend it, for the voice already sounds tired and old and the execution is slapdash; familiarity seems to have bred contempt.

ANTONIO MAGINI-COLETTI (1855–1912) was a debutant of the 1880 season; at the Costanzi, Rome, where he appeared as di Luna in *Trovatore*. In the course of the next seven years he sang in various provincial Italian theatres, and everywhere he went his powerful voice and artistic versatility were appreciated. In the 1885 season in Lisbon he sang in Rossini's *Mathilde di Shabran*, Donizetti's *Poliuto* and in *Aida*. The following year he was invited to La Scala, to replace Maurel as Amonasro; thereafter he was Zurga in *Pescatori di Perle* and took part in the Greek composer Samara's *Fiora Mirabilis*, in which Calvé made her first and most unfortunate impression at La Scala. In 1889, he was in the world premiere of Puccini's *Edgar*. Although Magini-Coletti's career was principally in Italy, he made the customary summer tours in South America, with

82 Francesco d'Andrade as Figaro in Rossini's *Barbiere*

83 Antonio Magini-Coletti

84 Giuseppe Pacini

Toscanini conducting; these were the first performances of the opera at La Scala. Later that season and in the next came Belcore in *Elisir d'amore* with Caruso, Wotan in *Valchiria*, Hares in de Lara's *Messalina*, Miller in *Luisa Miller*, Renato, di Luna and Lysiart in Weber's *Euriante*.

Magini-Coletti's wide ranging repertory is reflected in recordings, though strangely he left no souvenir of his many Wagnerian interpretations. The voice was of good quality, secure and well-schooled, and if his singing is wanting in those original touches that distinguish a great artist, as a colleague his excellence is never in doubt. In the Figaro-Rosina duet from *Barbiere*, with the Polish soprano Regina Pinkert rather out of her depth, we hear Figaro's roulades for once sung in full voice, each note clearly defined. He is also an important contributory factor in a remarkable performance of the great septet from *Ugonotti*, with Escalaïs, Ferruccio Corradetti, Oreste Luppi, Giuseppe Sala, Angelo Algos and Giovanni Masotti, which quite explodes the myth that there was no such thing as fine ensemble singing until modern times. In spite of the cramped circumstances of the early recording studio the singing is not in the least inhibited, and the careful observance of the traditional interpretive devices—holds, ritards and rubati—essential in a stylish and expressive performance of this music, is evidence of thorough rehearsal and preparation.

GIUSEPPE PACINI's (1862–1910) career began in Florence in 1887, with a performance of the Doge in Verdi's *I Due Foscari*. In the course of the next few years he toured the Italian provinces, appearing in *Puritani, Favorita, Aida, Trovatore, Lucia* and *Rigoletto*. Between 1892 and 1899 he was a regular visitor to South America, where he sang Carlo Quinto, Don Carlo, Nelusko in *Africana*, Barnaba and Alfio. In 1895 Mascagni brought him to La Scala to create leading roles in his *Silvano* and *Guglielmo Ratcliff*, two of a stream of works the composer poured forth in a vain attempt to repeat the triumph he had won with *Cavalleria*. Neither work made much impression, but Pacini did; he came back the following year as Zurga in *Pescatori di Perle* and the High Priest in *Sansone e Dalila*. He returned to La Scala in after years, as Scindia in *Re di Lahore* and Valentin. In 1900 he sang in Warsaw and Moscow, and eight years later visited Spain. He died in 1910, at the early age of forty-eight.

Pacini's voice was a big, ringing, high baritone, with a characteristic timbre. His singing provides a link between the old school and the generation that

guest appearances at the Imperial opera in St Petersburg and Moscow, and in Warsaw. His repertory also included buffo and character roles; during his only visit to New York, at the Met, in 1891, he sang Capulet in *Roméo*, Don Fernando in *Fidelio*, Amonasro, Figaro in *Barbiere* and Hoël in *Dinorah*. At the Argentina in Rome in 1899, he took these last two parts opposite Luisa Tetrazzini. The following year he returned to La Scala, as Kurwenal in *Tristano* with Amelia Pinto and Giuseppe Borgatti,

came to maturity during the first years of this century. Although his style already has traces of the latter's vehement and forceful manner, in the aria 'Il balen', in his management of the graces and ornaments in the high-lying tessitura, in the very free almost improvisatory treatment of the rhythm, there lingers an echo of Battistini. Renato's 'Eri tu' is done in a more vigorous fashion; here the influence of the verismo is stronger. In the Prologue from *Pagliacci*, on the other hand, the beautifully clean and forward-sounding declamation makes something almost noble out of it.

MARIO ANCONA (1860–1931) was two years older than Pacini, but his career began later: in 1890, when he was already thirty years old. His voice developed slowly and he had spent some while in the diplomatic service before starting to study in earnest. After a year with Giuseppe Cimi, he was ready to make a debut at Trieste, as Scindia in *Re di Lahore*. Within a year he was engaged at La Scala, as the King in *Le Cid*. The next year he came to London for a short season at the Olympic Theatre, which according to Klein was notable for little other than Ancona's performances of Alfonso and Telramund. Harris lost no time in signing him up for Covent Garden. His first role was Tonio in the local premiere of *Pagliacci* with Melba, de Lucia and Green; he made 'a tremendous hit with the prologue'.[12] Klein recalled years after:

> He had a voice of peculiar charm, sang like an artist and was a good actor, qualities which secured him another engagement at Covent Garden the following year and for many years thereafter.[13]

It also led to his first visit to the United States, to the Met, where he repeated Tonio with the same effect. During seventeen seasons at Covent Garden he took leading roles in *Les Huguenots*, *Favorita*, *Traviata*, and in the one and only performance of Stanford's *Veiled Prophet*, with Nordica and Vignas, and in Sir Frederick Cowen's *Signa*, which, much to Harris's ire, got the regulation three performances ('These English composers *are* artful, they compel you to agree beforehand to play their operas three times.')[15] He sang Figaro and Germont with Patti in her farewell season and was Marcello in the first Covent Garden performances of *Bohème*, again with Melba and de Lucia. It was said his popularity in London had to do with a remarkable physical resemblance to King Edward VII. No such explanation could account for his triumphs in the United States. He sang there again in 1906, on the opening

night of Hammerstein's first season at the Manhattan, with Pinkert and Bonci in *Puritani*. In 1908, he went to Paris, to the Théâtre Sarah Bernhardt, as Figaro in *Barbiere* with Elvira de Hidalgo, Dmitri Smirnov and Chaliapin, returning in 1914 for *Ballo in Maschera* with Destinn, and *Pagliacci* with Martinelli. One evening the 'divine' Sarah herself came round to congratulate the singers; after Ancona had warmly embraced her, she wrote in his

85 Mario Ancona as Hoël in Meyerbeer's *Dinorah*

autograph book:

> It's true dear Mr Ancona that I have been slightly hurt by your beard, but I have been cured by your singing![16]

Jean de Reszké rated him the finest baritone after Lassalle, and the best schooled. He was still singing well when he retired in 1916 and a Chicago critic praised him for 'his lack of mannerisms, for the freshness of his voice'.[17] As an actor he made a less profound impression. Indeed Shaw wrote of his Rigoletto: 'It made no impression at all.'

Records confirm Ancona's voice, when he was nearly fifty, to have been fresh and mellow-sounding, the legato smooth and the high notes effortlessly produced. In Alfonso's 'A tanto amor'

86 Antonio Scotti as Scarpia in *Tosca*

there are no crudities of style, no attempt to fashion Mascagni out of Donizetti. Yet for all its admirable qualities the singing is bland, without much variety of dynamics or vocal colour and none of those personal touches that make the records of a far less gifted artist, Antonio Scotti, so much more attractive.

17. Scotti, de Luca and Pini-Corsi

ANTONIO SCOTTI (1866–1936) was a pupil of Esther Triffani-Paganini. He made his debut in the role of Cinna in Spontini's *Vestale* in Naples in 1889. During the next ten years he gained experience throughout Italy, travelled abroad to St Petersburg, Moscow, Odessa, Warsaw, Madrid, Lisbon and South America, taking leading parts in *Favorita, Lucia, Puritani, Ernani, Ugonotti, Carmen, Faust, Don Giovanni, Falstaff, Maestri Cantori,* Gounod's *Mirella* and Bizet's *Fanciulla di Perth*. In 1899 he sang at La Scala, the following year at Covent Garden, where he quickly established himself a prime favourite, returning every year except 1912 and 1913 until the outbreak of the First World War. He was Amonasro, Rigoletto, 'a noted'[1] Don Giovanni and London's first Scarpia in 1900. According to Klein it was a creation which has won him universal recognition as an ideal presentation of 'one of the most subtle and malevolent figures in modern opera.'[2] To this he added in the course of the years a whole gallery of impersonations. In the autumn of 1899, he made his Met debut and began a career which was to be among the longest ever at that theatre, lasting more than thirty-three years. There too his Scarpia was acclaimed. Henderson wrote: 'a brilliantly vigorous and aggressive interpretation with a full appreciation of character.'[3] He was pronounced a 'superb'[4] Don Giovanni, a 'fine'[5] Germont and 'set standards'[6] as Mozart's Almaviva. In a revival of *Ernani*, with Sembrich and de Marchi, however, Henderson was more critical:

> He failed to fit his manner to the music . . . His delivery was acquired in the interpretation of the modern Italian school.[7]

As Iago, Aldrich wrote:

> Scotti's [performance] is full of characteristic detail and eminently realises the unlovely spirit, the sinister and malevolent motives of the character, while vocally he is extremely efficient.[8]

And efficient he remained through all the years;

87 Giuseppe de Luca and Rosina Storchio as Malatesta and Norina in *Don Pasquale*

long after his voice was gone he was still an imposing Falstaff , Scarpia and Chim-Fen in Leoni's *L'Oracolo,* a piece which had been specially written with his talents in mind. He brought it out for his farewell in January, 1933.

We have mentioned before Scotti's Scarpia on the Mapleson cylinders. His commercial recordings abundantly testify to the individuality of his style.

Though the voice is unlovely and rather wooden, especially at the top, and the range of colour is restricted, the tone is firm and in everything he does there is evidence of a strong personality. Malatesta's 'Bella siccome un angelo' goes with an ingratiating lilt, the line beautifully shaped with many expressive nuances; this is a souvenir of a popular impersonation. Even finer, perhaps, is Belcore's

'Come Paride vezzoso' from *Elisir,* a performance of exceptional sensitivity, the phrasing contrived by graceful portamenti, the fioritura a fitting part of the whole. The duets with Caruso from *Don Carlo, Forza, Bohème* and *Butterfly* are justly famous, the singers balancing their voices so perfectly that they once changed about in *Forza* without anyone in the audience noticing. Two excerpts from *Rigoletto* suggest that he never allowed histrionics to disturb the vocal line. Even in Scindia's 'O casto fior' the interpretation is so expressive and tasteful that it seems churlish to complain that such highly perfumed music ideally needs a more glamorous voice. Like Battistini, he knew how to turn a song to advantage.

GIUSEPPE DE LUCA (1876–1950) was ten years younger than Scotti; his career too lasted well over thirty years and embraced a wide range of parts. After studying with Persichini he made his debut at Piacenza as Valentin in 1897. In the following years he sang at Genoa in *Le Cid, Pescatori di Perle* and Leoncavallo's *Bohème,* in Trieste, *Traviata* and *Puritani* and at the Sao Carlos, Lisbon and in Naples, before he reached La Scala in the 1903 season. At first he had to cope with powerful competition from Scotti, Titta Ruffo, Sammarco and Pacini. In the long run he was to outdistance them all, the result of skill and wise circumspection in the use of a good but not first-class voice, remarkable neither in size nor quality. From the beginning, however, his ebullient personality, intelligence and stage presence enabled him to make great successes out of character and buffo roles, as des Sirieux in Giordano's *Fedora,* Michonnet in *Adriana Lecouvreur* (which part he created at the Lirico, Milan, with Caruso and Angelica Pandolfini), and later at La Scala as Sharpless in the world premiere of *Madama Butterfly.* There too, he took part (as Gleby) in the first performances of Giordano's *Siberia,* in which La Scala virtually exhausted its entire stock of singers on a work that proved only how exhausted its composer was. The great years of his career began after his first visit to the United States, in 1915.

A comparison between de Luca's early records and those he made later, in the 1920s, shows a voice only a little greyer after a career lasting nearly thirty years. In one of the finest of the first group, the duet 'Cheti, cheti' from *Don Pasquale,* he is joined by Ferruccio Corradetti. Corradetti was a well-known buffo and character artist who sang for many years in Italy and later went to New York to teach singing. It is a performance of contagious humour, overflow-

88 Antonio Pini-Corsi

ing with high spirits yet without compromising the music or the singing. As with the great buffo, Antonio Pini-Corsi, the score is a ground plan rather than a rule book; the improvisation is not in the form of elaborate vocalises or interpolated high notes, but in the free treatment of the text, a tradition which formed a part of opera buffa back to the eighteenth century. It would be hard to imagine a performance more vivid or sharply characterised.

ANTONIO PINI-CORSI (1859–1918), the most famous buffo of his day, was from a family of singers, his brother being a well-known tenor who appeared with him on various occasions at La Scala and elsewhere in Italy. Buffo singers are generally remarkable more for their histrionic skill than vocal prowess, but in his debut at least, as Dandini in Rossini's *Cenerentola,* it was his singing that impressed one critic:

> Pini-Corsi is a baritone of much distinction. His voice is fresh, sufficiently strong and equalised in all registers. He sings and phrases with grace like a true artist, and he executed the agility passages with such perfection and cleanness that he was able to sing note for note all the complicated and difficult passages.[9]

During the first ten years of his career he sang extensively throughout Italy, succeeding to much of the repertory that had made Giuseppe Ciampi so popular in the previous generation, appearing in *Barbiere* (as Figaro and Bartolo), *Elisir, Don Pasquale, Figlia del Reggimento, Cenerentola, Italiana in Algeri, Conte Ory* and *Forza del Destino*. In 1890 he joined the contralto Guerrina Fabbri in Rossini seasons in Rome, Turin and Milan. Three years later at La Scala he was the first Ford in Verdi's *Falstaff,* a part he subsequently introduced in Trieste, Genoa, Madrid, Berlin, Vienna, London and New York. He was a frequent guest at La Scala, as Gessler in *Tell,* Don Pasquale, Lord Rocburg in *Fra Diavolo,* Beckmesser in *Maestri Cantori,* and Alberich in *Sigfrido* and *Oro del Reno*. He took part in the first Scala performances of Franchetti's *Cristoforo Colombo*, Massenet's *Griselda*, and Hérold's *Zampa*. At Covent Garden, he was a member of the company From 1894 to 1896 and again in 1902 and 1903. There he was Lescaut in the first London performance of a Puccini opera, later came Schaunard, Tristram in Flotow's *Marta*, Mozart's Leporello and Rossini's Figaro. His final London appearances, like those of Ancona and de Lucia, were with the Russell company at the Waldorf in 1905, when he had a field day in the title-role of Paer's *Maestro di Cappella*. In New York he took the role of Masetto in *Don Giovanni*, the Sacristan in *Tosca* and created small parts in Puccini's *Fanciulla del West*, Humperdinck's *Königskinder*, Damrosch's *Cyrano* and Victor Herbert's *Madeleine,* none of which entered the repertory. He was also a regular visitor at Monte Carlo.

By the time he came to make recordings the voice has become dry, and sustained notes soon develop a wobble. But in all of his records there is an abundant wit and personality. Dulcamara haranguing the peasantry is an interpretation of wonderful unction, the difficult patter music full of delightful touches and taken at a tremendous lick, but not so fast he cannot articulate every word clearly. Both here and in Bartolo's 'Manca un foglio', an aria of Romani's that was formerly substituted for 'A un dottor', there is no slavish adherence to the score;

yet the departures are always in the right spirit. In Bartolo's aria at one point he actually reinforces the musical line, altering the declamation to echo the melody in the accompaniment. He is a master of the florid style, never resorting to the kind of aspirated mugging that is too often passed off as the real thing, and any changes he makes are deliberate, not the result of incompetence, or over-familiarity.

18. Verismo Triumphant

With EUGENIO GIRALDONI (1871–1924) and Mario Sammarco, we find the verismo style fully developed. Giraldoni's parents were both singers: his father, also a baritone, had appeared at La Scala in several Verdi roles, whereas his mother, a soprano, was the first Italian Selika in Meyerbeer's

89 Eugenio Giraldoni
in the title-role of *Simon Boccanegra*

Africana and created the title-role in Catalani's *Loreley*. The younger Giraldoni made his debut at Barcelona as Escamillo in 1891. Two years later he went to Russia and Poland, appearing as Alfio, Barnaba and Valentin. After singing in various Italian theatres, in the summer of 1898 he was invited to South America, in a company that included Tamagno, Borgatti, Virginia Guerrini, Sammarco, Tetrazzini and Torresella. He took the roles of Amonasro, Severo in Donizetti's *Poliuto*, Telramund and the title-role in *Guglielmo Tell*; he returned in 1899 and 1900. During the winter season he sang at the San Carlo, as Monforte in *Vespri Siciliani* and Amonasro. On a visit to Barcelona, he gave an 'impassioned'[1] portrayal of Gerard in *Andrea Chenier*. It was no doubt his success in this and other new works that decided Puccini to give him the opportunity of creating Scarpia in *Tosca*. Appropriately the work was first staged in Rome, at the Costanzi, with Hariclea Darclée and Emilio de Marchi as Tosca and Cavaradossi. The opera was a success, but Giraldoni's performance drew qualified reviews; one critic recommended him to re-study Scarpia's death scene. Primo Levi complained that he had Scarpia 'in a permanent rage', portraying him as—

> a bloody monster instead of a cold-blooded creature who must be a super-refined police officer, elegant and fond of women, who never admits his brutality except when he is alone, while by nature and profession he loves to be cruel with voluptuous art.[2]

Later Giraldoni introduced the role in Turin and Buenos Aires. In 1904, he made his Met debut as Barnaba 'singing in a disappointingly crude manner'.[3] He was also heard as Rigoletto, Alfio, Valentin, Amonasro and Scarpia, but was not invited to return. At La Scala, in the 1905 season he created Lazzaro di Roio in Franchetti's *Figlia di Jorio* and added Falstaff to his repertory, an interpretation which does not seem to have been greeted enthusiastically. In the autumn of 1906 he sang Germont at Covent Garden with Melba, and Scarpia again, but here too his lack of finesse was criticised and he did not secure another engagement. Thereafter, his career was principally in Italy and South America where, the verismo school being more appreciated, he was more popular. There he remained a firm favourite, as Gerard, Sharpless, later adding Boris Godounov, Telramund, Hans Sachs and even Baron Ochs in *Cavaliere della Rosa*. In Rome he was the first Golaud in *Pelleas e*

Melisande. In Paris, he repeated his Boris and Scarpia. He continued to sing in the Italian provinces until after the war, the last time as Raimondo in Mascagni's *Isabeau*, at Genoa. After his retirement he went to Helsinki to teach; he died there in 1924.

Giraldoni's records provide striking proof of the change in style in one generation (in fact, he was only fifteen years younger than Battistini). There is little on them of the smooth tone and shapely legato which was still apparent in the singing of Ancona and Scotti, the voice is impressive but rather gruff and with a big vibrato. Nor is there any of that individuality of style which makes Pacini's recordings, in spite of certain crudities, of great interest. In an unsubtle piece, Amonasro's 'Quest' assisa', where a strong voice and a clean delivery are important, he makes an effect, but Rodrigo's 'Per me giunto', notwithstanding a fine trill, is sung in a monotonous mezzo forte, the phrasing short-breathed, without real eloquence. He did not record anything from *Tosca*, but in Gerard's big scena from Act Two of *Andrea Chenier*, the strenuous accents and exaggerated pathos, characteristic features of the verismo style, seem more fitting.

The career of MARIO SAMMARCO (1873–1930) covered much the same ground but he was more successful in London and in the United States. Born in Sicily, he studied first with Antonio Cantelli, who had once toured the United States with Carlotta Patti, Adelina's elder sister. Sammarco's debut was in Palermo, as Valentin. After some other provincial engagements, he was called to Parma to substitute for an indisposed Kaschmann as Carlo Quinto and had a great success. Instead of continuing with his career he resumed his studies, this time with Franz Emmerich. A year later he re-emerged at the Alhambra, Milan, in Berrutti's *Evangelina*. There followed a tour of the principal Italian and Spanish theatres. In 1895 he came to La Scala, making his debut in the title-role of *Enrico VIII* of Saint-Saëns, in the opera's first performance there. Sammarco was a short, thick-set man with a shock of black hair, very much the Sicilian, and it must have needed considerable skill in make-up to transform him into anything at all like Bluff King Hal, but vocally at any rate his impersonation was deemed appropriate. He made further appearances as Hamlet and Escamillo, and created the role of the revolutionary servant, Gerard, in Giordano's *Andrea Chenier*. From this time wherever he went he was praised for 'his beautiful and robust voice',[4] 'correct singing style and musical intelligence'.[5] In

90 Mario Sammarco as Valentin in Gounod's *Faust*

earning golden opinions from critics, public and colleagues. At Covent Garden he sang twenty-six different roles, appearing in the local premieres of *Adriana Lecouvreur, Loreley, Germania*, in d'Erlanger's *Tess* (from Hardy's novel) and in Wolf-Ferrari's *Segreto di Susanna* and *Gioielli della Madonna* (Huneker called them paste!). In New York, though he did not get to the Met, he sang at the Manhattan. He made his debut in *Pagliacci*; the public and critics greeted him enthusiastically. Later he sang Marcello—'a splendid Bohemian',[8] Rigoletto, Germont, Renato and Enrico, his colleagues including Melba, Tetrazzini, Russ, Bonci and McCormack, who remembers him with affection in his memoirs, particularly as Don Giovanni. After Hammerstein quit, Sammarco joined the Chicago-Philadelphia Company, and made several concert appearances in New York. On one of these occasions, Aldrich wrote:

> Mr Sammarco's singing was beautiful, in both voice and style; that of a true and accomplished artist. He was doubly to be admired for putting on his programme, the Lamento and Inno from Monteverdi's *Orfeo* . . . music of noble and eloquent simplicity which he sang with poignant declamatory fervour.[9]

He sang the role of Orfeo at the Milan Conservatory in 1919. The previous year he had been appointed to the board of La Scala. His last stage appearances were at Covent Garden in 1919 and later the same year at the San Carlo. As a teacher his most successful pupil was the bass-baritone, Paul Schoeffler.

It is hard to reconcile Sammarco's reputation with his records. Perhaps there was something about his presence on stage that caused critics like Henderson and Aldrich to overlook those transgressions which in other artists they were quick to point out. It was a good voice, and in some verismo pieces, such as Cascart's 'Buona Zazà' from Leoncavallo's opera, there is an authenticity of style—the real thing, but the singing itself remains fundamentally unattractive. Among the artists of that era, in the main, contemporary criticism seems to be sustained by the recorded evidence that has survived: Sammarco is an exception, and no doubt there must be exceptions.

The last two outstanding Italian baritones to come to maturity in the period immediately before the First World War were both better singers and finer artists than Giraldoni or Sammarco. The younger, whose international career got under way

the wake of his Scala successes he travelled to Russia, appearing in Moscow, Kiev and Odessa. In 1898, in the summer he crossed to South America in the same season as Giraldoni, the two dividing the principal baritone roles. Sammarco came off best with Marcello, Nevers, Rigoletto, Enrico, Iago and Sachs in *Maestri Cantori*. In 1900 at the Lirico, Milan, he created Cascart in Leoncavallo's *Zazà* and the same season shared the honours with Tamagno in *Otello*. In the autumn of 1904 he was engaged for the first time at Covent Garden, as Scarpia. Klein thought it a 'sinister and impressive'[6] impersonation, while his Rigoletto 'accomplished all that was expected of him by those who knew his Italian reputation, though his voice had not the quality we remember in such artists as Lassalle'.[7] Indeed it had not; on records it sounds powerful enough, but the tone is unlovely, the execution approximate and the style coarse. Even in Scarpia's music it seems exaggerated, and in the operas of the earlier period, wholly inappropriate. Yet the fact is he was a great success in London, returning year after year,

91 Pasquale Amato

sooner, PASQUALE AMATO (1878–1942), was born in Naples. He was a student there at the Conservatory of San Pietro a Majella, first under Beniamino Carelli, the father of the soprano Emma Carelli, and later Vincenzo Lombardi, teacher of the tenor Fernando de Lucia. His debut took place in Naples, at the Teatro Bellini, in 1899 as Germont. During the next few years he sang in Milan and Genoa, and on tour with an Italian opera troupe in Germany. In the summer of 1904 he went to South America and in the autumn appeared at Covent Garden in the same season as Sammarco. He sang Amonasro, one of his most successful impersonations, Escamillo, Marcello and Rigoletto, the last in succession to Maurel and Sammarco. He does not seem to have been able to rival the former's histrionic skill or the latter's forceful vocal manner. He never again sang at Covent Garden. In Italy, however, Toscanini secured him an engagement at La Scala, where his vocal range and artistic versatility very much impressed Giulio Gatti-Casazza. In one season he was Golaud in *Pelléas*—

the first performance of the opera at La Scala—Barnaba, Kurwenal, Don Carlo, Scarpia, and Gellner in *La Wally*, as well as taking principal roles in Franchetti's *Cristoforo Colombo* and Cilea's *Gloria*. In November 1908 Gatti introduced him to New York, at the Met, where he was a great success. During twelve busy seasons, to the more conventional repertory he added Wolf in Puccini's *Le Villi*, Hidraot in Gluck's *Armide*, Worms in Franchetti's *Germania*, Cascart in *Zazà*, Prince Igor, Antonio in Mascagni's *Lodoletta*, Manfredo in Montemezzi's *L'Amore dei tre Re*, Giovanni in Zandonai's *Francesca da Rimini* and Athanaël in *Thaïs*; in the world premiere of Puccini's *Fanciulla del West* he created Rance, in Damrosch's *Cyrano* Gaston, and in Giordano's *Mme Sans-Gêne* Napoleone. It was a remarkable achievement, if scarcely a recipe for vocal longevity. From the beginning he was overworked. In the thirteen days between 23 November and 5 December 1910, he sang Barnaba, Amfortas (in German), Tonio, Hidraot in *Armide*, di Luna, Tonio again and Amonasro. Small wonder that after four or five years of this the effects were noticeable; one critic wrote that the voice had 'acquired a harshness and the intonation began to suffer'.[10] Following his departure from the Met in 1921, though he was only forty-three his career was relegated to appearances in provincial theatres and on tour with various second-rate companies. He spent the last years of his life as Professor of Voice and Opera at the Louisiana State University.

Amato's was a splendidly firm and ringing voice; in his best days the top, up to high A, made a great impression. On records it is almost impossible to confuse it with any other baritone, for there is a bell-like and plangent quality that is wholly individual, a rapid but narrow vibrato that is only rarely obtrusive and which he is able to make use of for effect. Though it is a slightly throaty voice and the vowels are not equally forward, the scale is correctly developed and the tone always precisely focused; in duets with Gadski and Hempel, when deferring to the ladies his contribution is still clearly audible; in a thrilling account of the Enzo-Barnaba duet from *Gioconda*, he even seems able to match his vibrato to suit Zenatello's. As with Ancona, Amato's style resisted the excesses of the verismo; exposure to Mascagni, Leoncavallo, Giordano and Franchetti did not prevent him from making a proper effect in Verdi's music. Renato's 'Eri tu' and Rigoletto's 'Cortigiani' are justly famous interpretations in which the unusually pure vowels, which are never covered even on the highest notes, make each word clear and telling, alike in trenchant declamation and smooth legato. The Doge's romanza from Act One of *I Due Foscari* is a beautifully composed piece of cantabile singing, the high Fs coming out just as Verdi ordered—dolce.

For all their many and admirable characteristics not one of the baritones above who followed Battistini made a name to equal TITTA RUFFO (1877–1953)—or a noise either. De Luca called his voice 'a miracle'—then the sting in the tail—'which he bawled away'.[11] It was a phenomenon: in that respect more like a great modern singer, where nature has had a bigger hand in it than method. Ruffo's studies were scant and his experiences with teachers not especially happy. As a boy he went to the Liceo Musicale di Santa Cecilia in Rome.

I was assigned to Persichini, who kept me during the first months simply as a listener. The lessons began at 9.30. Persichini always arrived punctually. He was a handsome man, about sixty-five, tall with wavy hair, carefully parted in the middle; with a big white moustache—he twisted it continually—and a pointed beard in the manner of Napoleon III. He usually wore a black coat and waistcoat, striped pants pressed to look in front like two razor blades and shoes also black that announced his arrival beforehand. He was the prototype of the man of the ottocento. The pupils were very obsequious. They rose when he came into the room, one took his gloves, another the stove hat, a third his stick. Then he would ring the bell for his coffee.[11]

92 Titta Ruffo in the title-role of Franchetti's *Cristoforo Colombo*

Ruffo did not like Persichini, who at that time, he claims, was mostly interested in de Luca, and wanted to turn him into a bass; he was having none of it and left. Later he tried Sparapani and Lelio Casini, but he remained essentially self-taught. His stage debut took place at the Costanzi, Rome, in 1898, as the Herald in *Lohengrin*. In the next couple of years he sang in Genoa and Parma, and in the summer in South America, as Germont, Amonasro, di Luna, Nelusko, Rigoletto and Cascart. In 1903 he was invited to Covent Garden as Figaro, Enrico and Rigoletto, but he never did get the opportunity to sing the last part. He fell foul of Melba. At the dress rehearsal when he pulled out all the stops, the diva lost no time in getting him put out—'I'm not singing with him, he's too young to be my father!' Ruffo claims that years later, when he was at the top of his career, he took revenge on Melba, declining to have her as his Gilda—'She's too old to be my daughter.'[12] In fact, their paths never crossed again. Melba continued to sing in London

and the United States, and by the time Ruffo reached there, her days as Gilda were long passed. He kept Rigoletto for his Scala debut in the autumn of the following year. For the next eight years he travelled extensively throughout Europe, to St Petersburg and Moscow, Paris, Lisbon, where his Hamlet was received with tremendous acclaim, Berlin, as Figaro, to Spain and South America, adding Renato, Rodrigo, Barnaba and the title-role in Franchetti's *Cristoforo Colombo*.

His United States career began with the Chicago company in 1912, when he sang Hamlet. The company gave one performance in New York:

Expectation had been laid in trains of gunpowder all through the Met last night . . . all, of course, for Titta Ruffo, the very expensive Italian baritone . . . His voice is of immense power and sonority. It is still young, fresh and vibrant . . . It is a voice of rather metallic quality; a voice of bronze until it is forced to extreme power in its upper tones, when it is a brazen clarion. Mr Ruffo's vocal style allows little variety of colour and little variety of emotional or dramatic expression . . . it is a voice that soon exhausts its effect. As an actor . . . his style is vivacious, restless and uneasy. He made certain strongly marked and obvious points; but for subtlety or suggestiveness or consistently and definitely conceived and skilfully executed delineation of character his impersonation was not notable.[13]

A week later he appeared in concert:

The general impression of Mr Ruffo's style and voice was not greatly changed . . . he is at his best, as it seemed, in the broad and sonorous and emphatically dramatic music of the young Italian style . . .[14]

Henderson, in a perceptive article entitled 'Get Rich Quick Singing', lamented the urge to make a big sound and 'the hurried preparations for short careers';[15] he felt a house in which the 'moderato of Sembrich or the finest spun mezza voce of Bonci could be heard' had no need of the kind of shouting Ruffo was offering. He went on prophetically:

Only a few singers today are provided with a real vocal technique, and even some of these sacrifice their voices to big tone. The others go to pieces anyhow in a few brief seasons, most become teachers of that which they never knew, namely the art of bel canto.[16]

To Ruffo's credit, in later years when things turned out as Henderson had predicted, he declined to teach, candidly admitting his ignorance of vocal technique. A voice of such elemental power did not immediately wear out, but the singer's inability, or unwillingness to accommodate to less lavishly endowed colleagues upset not only Melba; it is said Caruso used his influence to prevent Ruffo being invited to the Met and this notwithstanding good personal relations between the two singers. It is certainly a matter of fact that in spite of Ruffo's enormous popular success in New York, he did not become a member of the company for another ten years, until the very season after Caruso's death. Between 1922 and 1929, he appeared there regularly, as an 'impressive'[17] Carlo Quinto, a 'sinister'[18] Barnaba, and using 'much unction and colour'[19] as Figaro. In the later 1920s, when Henderson's prognosis became increasingly apparent and his voice had coarsened and the tone spread, he was very often indisposed; by 1929, it was obvious his career was over.

Most of Ruffo's records are successful in giving an impression of the splendour and power of his voice. He was not an elegant vocalist to compare

with Battistini, and had little of the grand manner of Kaschmann, but his singing was not crude like Sammarco's. His dramatic effects were imposing rather than subtle, he knew how to use the 'voce bianca' and tremolando without the voice losing its support—for example, in the central section of the Hamlet Brindisi, 'la vita e breve'; then, as it modulates back into the major, 'via da noi', the execution is clean and accurate, the cadenza tossed off in a single superbly defiant gesture. With such a voice it is hardly surprising he liked showing it off; so for this reason his style is not so completely an exemplification of the verismo as Sammarco's, being less histrionic and more vocal. He had, in his best days, a firm and expressive legato; in the *Pagliacci*

93 Francesco Navarini

Prologue, for example. Unfortunately, his preoccupation with volume of tone eventually proved his undoing, and as Henderson prophesied, has had a baneful effect on generations of baritones since.

19. The Basso

The turn of the century was not a period rich with Italian basses. There was no one at that time comparable with the great singers of the early part of the century, Filippo Galli or Luigi Lablache, no one in Italy whose prestige was on a par with Edouard de Reszké or Pol Plançon. The Italian bass, in spite of Rossini's Mosè, Boito's Mefistofele and Verdi's Filippo, had yet to be emancipated; mostly he was still confined to playing lay figures, elders and priests, at best Zaccaria in *Nabucco*, Silva, Fiesco, Ramfis and Alvise. Whereas a popular tenor might earn a couple of thousand dollars for a single performance, a basso would be lucky to get that much for a whole season's work, singing four, sometimes five times a week. It was not until the Russian repertory came to the West and, in particular, when Chaliapin in *Boris Godounov* proved he could create an effect to equal, indeed to surpass most tenors, that the bass finally came into his own.

The most outstanding Italian bass of his day, FRANCESCO NAVARINI (1855–1923), studied in Milan with Carlo Borroni, and then made his debut at Treviso as Alfonso in Donizetti's *Lucrezia Borgia*, in 1878. In the following years he sang in Lisbon, Florence, Naples, Turin, Palermo and Bologna. In 1883 he was engaged at La Scala, where he appeared in nine seasons during the next ten years as Alvise, St Bris in *Ugonotti*, Oberthal in *Profeta*, Don Pedro in *Africana*, the Cardinal in *Ebrea*, Giorgio in *Puritani*, Baldassare in *Favorita*, Fiesco, Basilio, Silva, Gessler in *Guglielmo Tell*, Don Roldano in Franchetti's *Cristoforo Colombo* and the King in *Lohengrin*. He took leading roles in the world premieres of Gomes's *Condor* and Franchetti's *Fior d'Alpe*, and created Lodovico in Verdi's *Otello*. In 1887 Harris engaged him for his famous Drury Lane season; in that stellar ensemble, not surprisingly, a mere bass made little enough impression, though sufficient to secure an engagement at Covent Garden the following year. There, as Alfonso 'he made good use of a powerful voice',[1] which at that time was equally remarkable for its range, extending from the C below the bass stave to the baritone A flat; but for whatever reasons, after some appearances as Leporello, and Raimondo in *Lucia* with Melba, Navarini left London and did not return. Though he continued to sing in Italy with some effect for several years thereafter, it would appear that before he was forty the voice had begun to deteriorate. By the end of the century his career was reduced to appearances in provincial theatres or with touring companies.

Navarini's recordings were all made in 1907, and include souvenirs of many of his best roles. Basilio's 'La Calunnia' is a fascinating performance and gives us an inkling of how Lablache made an effect in this music. The continuous use of parlando, very strange to our ears, is nevertheless done in a shapely and musical fashion, without destroying the form of the piece. The voice is imposing and sometimes, at the top, as we hear it in Alfonso's aria and cabaletta from *Lucrezia Borgia*, still a beautiful instrument; he makes several upward changes in a line that is already practically into the baritone range. The lower octave has become weak and quavery and the tone is sometimes cracked.

The bass GIOVANNI GRAVINA (1872–1912) was a Sicilian. He went to Milan to study with Giovanni Laura. After some appearances in Palermo, Rome and Naples, he was heard by an agent of Giulio Gatti-Casazza, who invited him to La Scala. After a successful debut as Ferrando in *Trovatore*, he was cast in the role of Giovanni Palm in the world premiere of Franchetti's *Germania* with Amelia Pinto, Caruso and Sammarco, both operas being conducted by Toscanini. In the next few years he sang extensively in Russia and Spain, and again with Caruso in Monte Carlo, where he was Colline in some performances of *Bohème*. In 1908 Gatti took him to the Met, but illness prevented his making more than a single appearance, as Sparafucile. Four years later he returned to the United States, as a member of the Boston Company. He had sung Alvise and Ramfis when he succumbed to a heart attack; he was just forty.

Gravina's records show us a fine voice but at the age of thirty an immature artist. The Evocazione from *Roberto il Diavolo* is rather short on characterisation and there is little of the grand manner. In Fiesco's 'Il lacerato spirito', where he omits the last revealing phrase which carries the singer from middle C sharp down to the bottom F sharp, the tone does not seem to be ideally smooth and the phrasing lacks authority.

ANDREAS DE SEGUROLA (1873–1953) was born in Valencia, Spain. He studied with Varvaro in Barcelona and made a successful debut there in 1898. In the course of the next few years he sang at

94 Andreas de Segurola as Colline in *Bohème*

various Italian and French theatres. Then in 1902 he was invited to the Met by Maurice Grau; he appeared at the very end of the season in two performances of *Aida*. The following season he was engaged at La Scala. His career continued in Europe until 1908, in that year he was booked by Hammerstein to appear at the Manhattan. There he sang a particularly memorable Basilio in a cast that included Tetrazzini, Sammarco and Gilibert. In 1909 he returned to the Met and was to remain a member of the company for the next eleven years. To begin with he sang Basilio, Méphistophélès, Rodolfo in *Sonnambula*, Colline and Alvise but gradually competition from other bassos, chiefly Léon Rothier and Adamo Didur, reduced him to comprimario roles: Lodovico in *Otello*, Sparafucile, Samuel in *Ballo*, Ramfis, Arontes in *Armide*, Arlecchino in Wolf-Ferrari's *Donne Curiose*, Fouché in Giordano's *Mme Sans-Gêne*, Didier in Victor Herbert's *Madeleine*, Skoula in *Prince Igor*, Franz in Mascagni's *Lodoletta* and many others. He created Jack Wallace in the world premiere of Puccini's *Fanciulla del West* and Nicolao in *Gianni Schicchi*. After he left the

Met, he continued to give concerts. Later he taught singing in Hollywood and appeared himself in the film *One Night of Love* with his pupil Grace Moore.

In a recording of 'Vi ravviso' from *Sonnambula* we hear a rather light-weight bass voice. The tone is pleasant but shaky and he cannot draw a firm legato. The phrasing is routine and the graces, which are of the essence of the style, are mumbled over. He sang Rodolfo at the Met just four years after Plançon's final appearances in the same role; the recording gives us an idea of how far standards had fallen in such a short space of time. He was a conscientious and dutiful singer but basically a comprimario; as his art was scarcely up to the standards of Plançon, so his voice was no match for Didur's.

ADAMO DIDUR (1874–1946) was born in Galicia, but we shall consider him here; for during the major part of his career he identified himself with the Italian repertory. He studied first in Lemberg with Wysocki and later in Milan with Franz Emmerich. He made his debut in 1894 in Rio de Janeiro. Between 1899 and 1903 he was a principal of the Warsaw Opera, there he took leading roles in *Les Huguenots, Aida, Faust, Bohème* and *Mefistofele*. At La Scala in 1903 he appeared in *Oro del Reno, Rigoletto* and *Germania*. In the autumn of 1905 he was engaged at Covent Garden; there he sang Sparafucile, a 'powerful'[2] Méphistophélès, Colline, the title-role in *Mefistofele* and a Leporello 'conceived in a spirit of broad comedy'.[3] He returned in 1914 and after repeating his 'clever and interesting'[4] Mefistofele added Archibaldo in Montemezzi's *Amore dei tre Re*. Like de Segurola he arrived at the Met by way of the Manhattan. His debut role was Ramfis in *Aida* on the opening night of the 1908 season; the rest of the cast were Destinn, Homer, Caruso and Scotti; the opera was conducted by Toscanini. Didur made a great impression, reminding older members of the audience of Edouard de Reszké in his best days. It was the beginning of an association that was to last twenty-five years, until his retirement in 1933. During that time he sang a great variety of parts: Colline, Sparafucile, Méphistophélès and Mefistofele, Philip II, Basilio, Figaro and Almaviva in Mozart's *Figaro*, Tomsky in *Pique Dame*, Kezal in *Verkaufte Braut*, Tonio in *Pagliacci*, Klingsor, Oberthal in *Le Prophète*, Mustafà in *Italiana* and many other smaller parts. Boris, which he sang in Italian and regularly between 1913 and 1921, was probably his finest achievement. In the latter year, however, Chaliapin made his triumphant come-back in the role; Didur sang it only once again. The wheel had gone full circle; Didur had been engaged originally after Chaliapin's unsuccessful first season at the Met in 1907. By the 1920s Didur's voice was on the wane. After leaving the Met he returned to Poland, first as Director of the Cracow Opera and later as Professor of Singing at Lvov (as Lemberg had become) and Katowice.

Didur's voice at its best was a magnificent instrument of fine quality and imposing throughout its entire compass. Though the top was the strongest part, ascending easily to F sharp, he could still make a good effect in the lower range. He is most impressive in declamatory music, in Cardinal

95 Adamo Didur

Brogni's 'Voi che del Dio vivente' from Halévy's *L'Ebrea*, hurling out the imprecations. 'Infelice' from *Ernani*, which requires as well a mastery of the legato style, reveals some chinks in his technical armoury. The actual voice production is rather rough with too much loose vibrato. It is a fact of some interest that in spite of certain eccentricities of style—principally in the way he executes the ornaments—Chaliapin outsings as well as out-acts Didur in this music. In the swelling phrases of the aria his voice is smoother with its silvery quality and his legato style has far more tension. In the recitative 'Che mai veggio', of course, there is no comparison, where Didur is merely incisive in a literal way, Chaliapin's altogether freer treatment enables him to contrive at once a characterful and also more musical effect.

20. Tradition and the Italian Tenor

By the close of the nineteenth century it was the repertory that dictated to the singers; the days had long passed by when a Manuel Garcia or Adolphe Nourrit felt it necessary to appropriate Don Giovanni. Tenors had their work cut out just coping with what had been explicitly written for them; from the brilliant coloratura of Rossini, through Bellini and Donizetti, and the lyric Verdi of the Duke and Alfredo, to Manrico and Radames, and finally Otello. As we have seen, in the days of Rubini and Donzelli there had been some discrimination between the lighter and heavier roles, but this had been the direct consequence of composers like Bellini suiting their music to the voice of a particular singer. It was not until the repertory had expanded considerably that it came to be the other way about, and the singer was forced to realise, by a process of trial and error, that not every part was suited to his voice. Then it was that the younger generation, out of self-defence, began to classify voices according to their different characteristics in the manner we are familiar with today. Even in the first years of this century, however, this process was not complete, and there were still singers like the tenor Marconi, whose repertory embraced what seems today an astonishing range of parts.

FRANCESCO MARCONI (1853–1916) was a pupil of Ottavio Bartolini and later of Venceslao Persichini. From his debut at the Teatro Reale in Madrid, in 1878, as Faust, 'his bright voice of singular beauty'[1] created an excellent impression. Within two years he was at

96 Francesco Marconi as Enzo in *Gioconda*

La Scala, as the Duke, Enzo and Faust, and in the fashion of the day took his summers in South America, where his Enzo was especially admired and he managed to hold his own against Tamagno in *L'Ebrea*, when he took the short but difficult high-lying role of Leopoldo. In his two seasons at Covent Garden in 1883–4 he sang Arturo in *Puritani*, Enzo, Don Ottavio, Don José, Elvino in *Sonnambula*, Radames, the Duke, and Gounod's and Boito's Faust. He seems to have been successful in most of these, though Radames he found heavy going. That he wasn't really a dramatic tenor was confirmed when he went to New York in 1888, to appear as Otello in the first performances of the opera given in the United States, and failed to make any impression whatsoever. Though here it was not only a matter of his being overcome by the heavy orchestration and the heroic demands of the role, critics like Krehbiel felt that Verdi too had been overcome by the Wagnerian example, and it took them some while to change their minds. After his return to Europe Marconi directed his attention eastwards, like Battistini, and was a regular visitor to Russia and Poland, where his repertory ran from Arturo in *Puritani* to Lohengrin. His career ended around the turn of the century; among the last engagements he undertook was a tour of Verdi's *Requiem* with Virginia Guerrini and Navarini.

He made two series of recordings, the first in 1904, the second four years later. Even in the earlier of these the effect on the voice of singing too much dramatic music is all too obvious; it has become stiff, the tone is often flawed and the breath support far from certain. There remains, however, a beautiful style and finish on the singing. He is no longer successful in brilliant music, in 'Questa o quella', where there is no lift to the rhythm and little elegance in the phrasing. More attractive is the tenor finale to *Lucrezia Borgia* 'Madre se ognor'; here the long arching phrases are done—at least in intention—with beautiful control and much intensity; it is a pity that he rather spoils the ending by becoming maudlin. Perhaps the finest of his records is of the recitative and aria from the last act of *Lucia* 'Fra poco a me ricovero'; it is a wonderful performance. The recitative is sung with lovely tone and vocal poise and with a great variety of expression: first resignation—'Tombe degl' avevi'; then anguish—'ingrata donna'; and finally fury—'al felice consorte'. The aria is sung freely and with great feeling, the cantilena full of genuinely musical nuances and with particularly elegant portamenti.

The repertory of the Spanish tenor FERNANDO VALERO (1854–1914), though it did not go as far as Otello, embraced Lohengrin and Nadir in *Pescatore di Perle*. He was a pupil of Vidal, the teacher of the famous Gayarré. Valero was supposed to have resembled his predecessor, though his voice was considered less impressive. During his career he took further instruction from Mario, Tamberlik and the younger Garcia. He made his debut at the Teatro Reale, Madrid in 1878 as Nadir. He visited Italy for the first time in 1881; then two years later was invited to La Scala to sing Faust. In 1882, in Berlin, he sang Arturo and the Duke. The following year, in Russia, he appeared in a season of French operas: as Gerald, Corentin in *Dinorah*, Guillaume and Philé-mon in Gounod's *Philémon et Baucis*. In Spain he toured in Breton's *Los Amantes de Teruel* with the contralto Guerrina Fabbri. Harris brought him to Covent Garden for the 1890 season—he sang the Duke, Nadir and Don José—but this was in the hey-day of Jean de Reszké and he was not engaged for the following season. When he did come again in 1901, it was as Turiddu, a part in which he had great successes at La Scala, Florence and Palermo, at the Met, Chicago, Boston and Philadelphia. He was also much admired as des Grieux in Puccini's *Manon Lescaut*. After a performance in Warsaw, a critic wrote:

> His voice, sympathetic and responsive, was perfectly suited to the sweet and passionate melodies ... he made each phrase clear and brought out the most subtle shades of beauty.[2]

In later years he became a teacher in St Petersburg.

Valero's records (there are only four) were made in London when he was forty-nine and virtually at the end of his career. The voice is still in good shape. The most characteristic feature is the vibrato; though he is able to exercise a certain control over it, it is always present in some degree. The tone is pure but not fresh, there is little variety of colour or dynamics, and the prevailing white quality soon becomes monotonous. To some extent this is offset by an engaging manner and limpid execution. The Siciliana from *Cavalleria* with its plaintive charm and neatly turned ornaments is quite without the strident and over-wrought manner that later became so fashionable in this piece.

Two years after Valero's first season at Covent Garden, in 1892, Harris engaged the Neapolitan tenor FERNANDO DE LUCIA (1860–1925) to create Turiddu in the Covent Garden premiere of *Caval-*

97 Fernando Valero as Don José in *Carmen*

leria Rusticana. According to Shaw—

> De Lucia succeeds Valero . . . as artificial tenor in
> ordinary to the establishment. His thin, strident forte
> is in tune and does not tremble beyond endurance; and
> his mezza voce, though monotonous and inexpressive
> is pretty as prettiness goes in the artificial school.[3]

Rather faint praise. It is an interesting fact that the
image of de Lucia that has been fostered by record
collectors, as a paragon of bel canto, an artist who
was universally admired and acclaimed, hardly
squares with the record.

After studying at the Naples Conservatory with
Vincenzo Lombardi and Beniamino Carelli, his
debut took place at the San Carlo in 1885 in the title-

role of *Faust*; it was the beginning of an association
with that theatre which was to last for more than
thirty years. During the next couple of seasons he
sang in *Linda di Chamounix, Dinorah, Elisir
d'amore, Fra Diavolo* and *Sonnambula* at the smaller
Italian houses, in Spain and South America, and like
Valero was favourably compared with Gayarré. His
first appearance in London was at Drury Lane in
1887, but in the company of Jean and Edouard de
Reszké, Nordica, Arnoldson and Battistini, he was
quite put in the shade. After praising Arnoldson's
Rosina, *The Times* pronounced against 'Signor de
Lucia, a more than indifferent Almaviva, [who] sang
the serenade in a truly detestable manner'.[4] It was
not for another five years that he came again to
London, to Covent Garden. In the interim, in Italy,
he began to expand his repertory into the verismo
roles, in particular enjoying considerable successes
as Turiddu and Fritz in *L'Amico Fritz*, which he
created at the Costanzi, Rome, in 1891. Both of these,
with Calvé, he sang at Covent Garden. *The Times*
wrote that though the voice 'is not of very agreeable
quality . . . at least he sings in tune with a good deal
of effect'.[5] More faint praise. It was only after he
returned the following year and created Canio in the
local premiere of *Pagliacci* that the reservations, or
at any rate almost all of them, were put aside. Klein
thought that—

> despite his tremolo [his] was just the kind of passionate
> tenor for the role . . . his portrayal of the hapless
> Canio's anguish and suffering was a triumph of
> realism. His touching soliloquy at the end of the first
> act was delivered with an abandonment of feeling that
> completely carried away his audience.[6]

In 1893, in the London company of Melba and
Ancona, de Lucia made his Met debut as Canio. Hale
ranked it an impersonation on the level of de
Reszké's Romeo and Ternina's Isolde. About the
rest of his interpretations opinions were by no
means as favourable; his Duke was thought
'inadequate',[7] his Ottavio 'miserable'.[8] He was
never invited back. In Italy, at his La Scala debut in
1895, he reaffirmed himself in the verismo repertory, creating the leading role in Mascagni's *Silvano*
and appearing in the first performances there of
Massenet's *La Navarrese* and Puccini's *Bohème*. In
London, too, he was the first Rodolfo, but the part
had to wait for Caruso and it was Melba who got the
notices. The following year he was Cavaradossi and
then tried Almaviva once more, but 'the strident
quality of his voice'[9] was thought 'far better suited

to the modern music'.[10] Again in Italy, he created Osaka in Mascagni's *Iris*, a precursor of *Madama Butterfly*. His final London season was at the Waldorf with the Russell company in 1905. In 1916 he bade farewell to La Scala as Rodolfo in *Bohème*. The following year he made his last appearances at the San Carlo. The very last time he sang in public was on the mournful occasion of Caruso's funeral, in August 1921.

The pronounced vibrato or tremolo which we hear in the recordings of de Lucia, Valero, Bonci and Giraud, and in other tenors of this period, was a decadence in technique as well as style; it is impossible to separate the two, for the obtrusive vibrato had its origins in the abuse of an affecting device. Rubini and Mario were the first to be rebuked for resorting to it to excess; in the course of the nineteenth century it came to be, particularly in Italy, an accepted feature of singing. That it was not an intrinsic part of the voice, as is sometimes suggested, is apparent from the fact that we find it hardly at all among the French and German singers and to a much lesser extent among the post-Caruso Italians. This kind of rapid vibrato is only one, if usually the most obvious, symptom of inadequate breath control. In de Lucia's records we can hear other signs: the registers are not properly blended nor is the scale fully equalised, and he has two distinct methods, one for singing in piano, another for forte. In piano, in the middle, the quality is attractive but at the top the head register tends to separate off in the fashion of a crooner. In forte, there is insufficient support to carry the voice above B flat, in spite of excessive recourse to the long 'ee' vowel to try and focus the tone and keep it forward (it was this that produced that 'strident quality' for which he was so much criticised).

De Lucia's recording career began in 1903, for the G & T company, and continued under his own imprimatur, Phonotype, until 1919; by that time, though he was nearly sixty, the voice had changed very little. His recorded repertory ranges from a complete *Barbiere* to excerpts from Marchetti's *Ruy Blas, Pagliacci* and *Andrea Chenier,* taking in on the way arias and duets from such varied operas as *Lohengrin, Traviata* and *Carmen*. The biggest problem is to find the right speed to play them at. Most acoustic records involve some adjustment up or down from the standard 78 rpm, for the recording turntables were simply not reliable; but today with a continuous speed motor, the score and a good ear, it is usually a simple matter to put right. When—as happens from time to time—the singer transposed a

98 Fernando de Lucia

piece, the change in vocal timbre should make it obvious. In the case of de Lucia, however, to whom transposition was the rule, until the key for one piece can be definitely established, it is not easy to be sure that what we are hearing is the voice as it really sounded. Until quite recently his records were played (and often re-recorded on to LPs) too fast, the results were reminiscent of Larry the Lamb, with the vibrato coming out almost a trill. At first it seemed incredible that he was transposing familiar arias down often a minor or major third, but when this was accepted what came out was almost a different voice, darker and more virile; the idea of him as Canio no longer seemed so odd.

Undoubtedly his best-known records are from

Barbiere; to most ears the objections raised by his contemporaries will seem more than offset by the graceful delivery and limpid execution, even if the suspicion lurks that much of the fioritura is contrived by—as it were—running up and down the vibrato. Almaviva, written for the elder Garcia, is a low part in spite of the elaborate coloratura and ideal for de Lucia's voice, though even in this he made some transpositions. In other Rossini operas— Lindoro in *Italiana*, for example, where the tessitura is extremely high—to have got it down far enough would have created too many problems for the rest of the cast, and he never attempted it. In Bellini's *Sonnambula*, which he did sing on occasion, at least at the beginning of his career, he was obliged to make some profound adjustments; a recording of Elvino's cabaletta 'Ah! perche non posso odiarti', which extends as written to a high D, and for that reason is often cut from performances, he takes down a major third to B flat. Since Bellini countenanced Malibran's transposing 'Ah! non giunge' a fourth, perhaps this would not have seemed so remarkable once upon a time: after all, transpositions were invented for singers. In this piece in spite of the lack of a really smooth legato, he finds the right pathetic accents and the graces are all executed neatly. In his lifetime, though de Lucia's histrionic skill was highly regarded, he did not enjoy a reputation, like de Reszké, as a charmer; yet on records it is surely this quality above all that has endeared him to collectors. In the songs of Tosti, Denza, Costa and di Capua, he is irresistible, and when he applies the same affection to a work that never gets it any more, Wagner's *Lohengrin*, the agogic lingerings reveal a quality in the music we had quite forgotten was there.

The Spanish tenor FRANCESCO VIGNAS (1863– 1933) was another pupil of Melchiorre Vidal. Like de Negri, he was a leading exponent of Wagner in Italian; at his debut, at the Teatro Liceo in Barcelona, in 1888, he sang Lohengrin, repeating it soon afterwards in Valencia and the following spring at La Scala. He was a regular visitor at most of the leading Italian theatres; at the San Carlo for seven seasons between 1893 and 1910, at Genoa where he took part in revivals of *Africana* and *Simon Boccanegra*, and in Rome as Radames and Lohengrin. In Spain and South America he was a great favourite for more than twenty years. It was said there was hardly a theatre of importance in which he had not sung Lohengrin or Tannhäuser. His repertory also included Andrea Chenier, des Grieux in Puccini's *Manon Lescaut*, Faust in Boito's *Mefistofele*, Don

99 Francesco Vignas in the title-role of Wagner's *Tristano*

Carlo, Walther in *Maestri Cantori* and the title-role in *Profeta*. In 1891 Lago brought him to the Shaftesbury Theatre to create Turiddu in the local premiere of *Cavalleria*. On the opening night the opera was rapturously received and Vignas had to encore both the Siciliana and the Brindisi. The following year when Harris introduced it at Covent Garden, de Lucia was not liked so well. Eventually, in 1893, Vignas was invited to Covent Garden to sing *Lohengrin* with Melba, Turiddu and Fritz with Calvé and *Tannhäuser* with Albani. When Queen Victoria decided a little Cavalleria Rusticana was needed at court, Calvé, Vignas *et al* were commanded to take it down to Windsor. The Queen was ecstatic; being unable to show her appreciation in the usual way—at that time royalty only clapped their hands for the servants—she gave each member of the company a signed photograph as a souvenir. Vignas returned to London the following season, adding Don José, but after that did not come again until the autumn of 1904, when the critics were pleasantly surprised to find 'his brilliant voice was unimpaired'.[11] In 1893, he appeared at the Met; there, as well as Turiddu, Lohengrin and Tannhäuser, he sang Radames and Edgardo. He was at La Scala again in 1896 and 1904, succeeding Caruso and Zenatello as Federico in Franchetti's *Germania*. His final stage appearances were in Barcelona, as Parsifal, during the 1913 season.

On records Vignas's voice has something of Valero's rather plaintive quality, but it is an altogether firmer and more brilliant instrument. Although his style and method antedate the verismo, and his singing is without the cruder

100 Florencio Constantino as Raoul in Meyerbeer's *Les Huguenots*

mannerisms we find in many of his Italian contemporaries, he is not at his best in the early music. In Gennaro's 'Di pescator ignobile' he moves easily enough through the high tessitura, but in a very matter of fact way; the piece is a narrative, but it still requires shapely phrasing, some variety of colour and expression. Meyerbeer's 'Sopra Berta' is more successful; here the ringing high notes make a great effect. He scales the difficult wide-ranging music with complete security, and at the end the run down from high D flat is done with dazzling aplomb. In the opening of Enzo's romanza from *Gioconda*, on 'Cielo', there is a perfect glissando from E flat to B flat, each note correctly marked in the interval. Of all his operatic recordings perhaps the most eloquent are those of Wagner. In Walther's 'Am stillen Herd' ('Nel verno al piè') and the Prize Song with the distinctive quality of the voice, the tone firm and smooth, the pure vowels and clear diction—here, indeed, is a master singer. Some songs prove he was also capable of more intimate effects; Alvarez's 'La Partida', for example, where the typical Spanish graces are done to a turn, or Guétary's 'Mi Nina' with its teasingly drawn-out rhythm.

Unlike his compatriots Vignas and Valero, FLORENCIO CONSTANTINO (1869–1920), though he appeared in Italy, made his reputation in South America and the United States. His career began in Montevideo, in Breton's opera *Dolores*, in 1892. After spending some years in South America, he returned to Europe and sang in Spain, Italy and Germany, mostly in provincial theatres. At this time his repertory seems to have been drawn principally from works of the older school: *Barbiere, Ugonotti, Lucia, Puritani, Rigoletto* and *Traviata*. In 1905, he was engaged at Covent Garden, as Alfredo, the Duke and Ottavio, sharing the last two roles with Caruso. In other circumstances he might have made a better impression, but in such company the *Daily Telegraph* thought him 'scarcely a singer of the highest distinction'.[12] There followed a season at the French opera in New Orleans, then in the autumn of 1908 Hammerstein brought him to the Manhattan. Henderson wrote of his debut in *Rigoletto*: 'a voice of lovely quality'[13] and 'with many charming morendo effects and other ornaments of the lyric art'. Subsequently he sang in *Carmen, Bohème* and *Lucia* with Tetrazzini:

He is a typical Italian [sic] tenor of the lyric variety and his emotional flights are not lofty, but there is so much excellence in his tones that he is certain to become a favourite with audiences.[14]

The 'excellence in his tones',[15] however, was not matched in his character. He was a stupid, disputatious fellow. After winning $100,000 (a very meaningful sum in those days) in a suit against a cabaret artist, he abruptly left the Manhattan to join Russell's company in Boston; Hammerstein responded by suing him for breach of contract and took thirty thousand of it. In Boston, too, his singing was well-liked, but there he got involved in a punch-up with the bass Gravina and lost another fifty thousand. When Hammerstein had withdrawn from New York he was allowed back to appear at the Met, with Melba in *Rigoletto* and Tetrazzini in *Lucia*. Aldrich thought him 'a tenor of Italian opera absolutely true to type ... consequently there could not be a better exponent of Edgardo'.[16] A couple of seasons later, he left New York and went off to South America, where he appeared at the Colon and other theatres in the heavier repertory: as

101 Alessandro Bonci

Radames, Ernani, Lohengrin, Canio, Sinodal in Rubinstein's *Demone* and Dick Johnson in *Fanciulla del West*. Some time in 1915, he returned to the United States and sang on stage in Los Angeles, apparently for the last time anywhere. He died in 1920, destitute in a Mexico City poorhouse, after being picked out of the gutter.

Constantino's records reveal a lyric tenor voice with an exceptionally attractive and individual quality. And it is in lyrical music, an aria from Breton's *Dolores,* for example, that he is heard to best advantage, phrasing with the most persuasive portamenti and 'those morendo effects and other ornaments'. In more brilliant and exacting music, 'Spirito gentil' from *Favorita*, at the end in the cadenza a break in the registers is apparent; he takes the top C too forcibly, more in the style of Puccini, and as the voice tightens under pressure, a slight flutter in the tone turns into a disagreeable shudder. Much of his popularity is explained in his singing of a sentimental little ditty, 'Adorables tourments' by Caruso's accompanist, Barthélemy (with some assistance from the great man himself); Constantino's lovely voice and affectionate delivery are quite irresistible.

21. Lyric Tenors

ALESSANDRO BONCI (1870–1940) was another 'tremulous' tenor. Born near Bologna, he studied with Felice Coen in Pesaro and then went to Paris to the studio of delle Sedie, a prominent teacher of the day. His stage debut took place at Parma, as Fenton in *Falstaff,* in 1896. Within a year he was at La Scala, in *Puritani*, making a great effect with the high notes in 'A te o cara' (though it was transposed down a semi-tone). It was Arturo he chose for his New York debut ten years later at the Manhattan on its opening night. Aldrich wrote:

> ... a small voice delicately and exquisitely modulated, although the tone was sometimes nasal or white. His art is finished in all that relates to phrasing, to the technique of the breath. His diction is exquisitely polished and clear. The emission of his tones is of the utmost ease and spontaneity, and the perfect repose and balance of his singing in Bellini's smooth cantilena was a joy. So too, was the flexibility with which he took the florid passages.[1]

Hammerstein had conceived Bonci as an answer to Caruso at the Met, but for all his virtues and high Cs, Bonci had neither the size nor quality of voice to compare with his great contemporary. After a season he was wise enough to realise it and on the good old principle of when-you-can't-beat-'em-join-'em he joined the Met. He stayed there for three years and after the war returned to the United States for a couple of seasons touring with the Chicago company.

In London, Bonci sang in four seasons after 1900. At about this time, Lilli Lehmann heard him:

102 Giuseppe Anselmi as Maurizio in *Adriana Lecouvreur*

Bonci has won my hearty admiration for his splendidly equalised voice, his perfect art and his knowledge of his resources and notwithstanding the almost ludicrous figure he cuts in serious parts, he elicited hearty applause.[2]

From so knowing and stringent a critic it was praise indeed. At Covent Garden, as Almaviva, Rodolfo, Edgardo, Nadir and perhaps most of all as the Duke in *Rigoletto* he was a great favourite. *The Times* acclaimed him in this role, for 'his lovely voice with its wonderful sweetness of quality',[3] but urged him also to resist the temptation to try and out-sing Sammarco, so producing 'the bleating tone that used to be heard from the average Italian tenor a few years ago'.[4] In Spain and South America, as in Italy, his career was a long succession of triumphs well into the 1920s.

Bonci was a prolific but not always satisfying recording artist; often it sounds as if he did not heed the advice above, for the tone is driven in climaxes, the intonation false. On such occasions the vibrato seems particularly obvious, whereas at other times, though it never completely disappears, the listener is hardly aware of it. We can hear him on his best behaviour in the aria 'Spiagge amate' from Gluck's *Paride ed Elena*, one of his favourite concert pieces. In spite of the rather strenuously produced top notes, not in the purest style, his beautiful enunciation and expressive cantilena, enlivened by many delicate touches, are in the finest classical tradition. He is very affecting too, in a souvenir of one of his best roles, Ernesto's 'Cercherò lontana terra', where he keeps the doleful mood in check by giving the rhythm the right kind of forward impetus; the phrasing is made eloquent by suave portamenti and marking the words firmly on the breath but without disturbing the line.

GIUSEPPE ANSELMI (1876–1929) followed in the de Lucia and Bonci tradition. Born in Catania, he was first a child prodigy on the violin, and then in his late teens decided on a career as an opera singer. He made his first stage appearance in 1896 at the Royal Opera, Athens, as Turiddu. During the next four years he sang elsewhere in Greece and at various provincial theatres in Italy. At one of these he was heard by the composer-conductor Luigi Mancinelli and brought to the San Carlo, Naples. In 1901, again through Mancinelli's influence, he was engaged at Covent Garden. He sang the Duke at his debut, showing off 'a voice of considerable range and strength but somewhat marred by vibrato'.[5] He returned in the autumn season of 1904 and in the summer of 1909, as Turiddu, Cavaradossi, 'a graceful and unaffected'[6] Maurizio in *Adriana Lecouvreur*, Edgardo and Almaviva opposite Tetrazzini, and Rodolfo 'singing with finished art and glorious tone'.[7] He appeared in Spain with great success, evoking comparisons with Gayarré in a repertory that ranged from Nadir in *Pescatori di Perle*, Almaviva and Lensky, to Loris, Osaka in *Iris* and Turiddu. In Russia, after 1904, he was a regular visitor until the First World War. In Warsaw too, he was a great favourite, as one opera-goer remembered many years later:

> He was a very tall [for a tenor], slight, handsome man. The voice was of lovely quality, his use of the diminuendo ending on the softest pianissimo had a devastating effect on his audiences.[8]

On records too, it is the lovely quality that is immediately striking, though it was an exceptionally throaty voice and in the lower range he was not able to support it properly. It seems to have been a problem that obviously preoccupied him; time and again on his records we can hear him nervously trying to clear his throat, in the piano introduction to Loris's 'Amor ti vieta' from *Fedora*, for example. This is an inspired performance, beautifully phrased, the words clearly and deliberately enunciated, the kind of graceful and dignified singing rarely heard in Giordano's operas. In Handel's 'Va godendo' he shows off his spirited coloratura rippling through the divisions with some accuracy; even if the high notes—like Bonci's, taken too strenuously—overweight the line, the emission is smooth and there is much here consonant with surviving descriptions of singing in the baroque era. Less successful is 'Un'aura amorosa' from *Cosí*; the cantilena, though full of genuinely musical nuances, is spoilt by aspirates; much of this piece, like 'Ecco ridente', which suffers from the same fault, lies in the lower and throaty part of his voice where he had an incomplete control over the supply of breath.

ARISTODEMO GIORGINI (1879–1937), another Neapolitan tenor, was perhaps not in the Anselmi class but at his best his singing had something of the same sweetness and charm. After studying at the Accademia di Santa Cecilia in Rome he made an unsuccessful debut in 1903, following which he returned to Naples and there renewed his studies under Massimo Perelli. When he reappeared, at La Scala as Ernesto in 1905, he had a considerable success, and he returned there on several occasions; in 1910 he was Elvino to Storchio's Amina in a

popular revival of Bellini's *Sonnambula*. In these years he sang at most of the leading Italian houses, and at Barcelona, Madrid, Lisbon, Warsaw, St Petersburg and Moscow. In the autumn of 1905 he appeared at Covent Garden succeeding de Marchi's Rodolfo opposite Melba's Mimi, singing a 'gifted' Duke, and with Battistini as Don Giovanni his 'pretty voice'[9] was thought 'of great service as Don Ottavio'.[10] In the United States he sang with the Chicago Opera. His career continued until the later 1920s.

Giorgini made his first records in 1904; twenty-four years later he sang Rodolfo in a complete *Bohème*. As we hear it in Arturo's 'A te o cara', it is an attractive lyrical voice with a rapid but not unpleasant vibrato. The registers are well blended and he has no difficulty with the high C, though he is inclined to make too much of a feature of it and it does not arise smoothly out of the line. There is a want of a really persuasive legato, or expressive phrasing; it is a sound but rather provincial interpretation.

EDOARDO GARBIN (1865–1943) was another pupil of Alberto Selva and Vittorio Orefice. He made his debut as Don Alvaro in *Forza del Destino*, at Vicenza, in 1891. In the next two seasons he sang in Naples, as the Duke, and at Genoa created the role of Guevara in Franchetti's *pièce d'occasion Cristoforo Colombo*, written to commemorate the 400th anniversary of Columbus's discovery of the New World. The following February, he took the part of Fenton in the world premiere of Verdi's *Falstaff*, at La Scala; the Nanetta, Adelina Stehle, eventually became his wife. During the next ten years, usually in company with his wife, he was especially associated with the

103　Aristodemo Giorgini　　104　Edoardo Garbin

operas of Puccini, singing des Grieux, Rodolfo, Cavaradossi and Pinkerton. He travelled to Warsaw, Madrid, Lisbon and Buenos Aires. In 1900, at the Lirico, Milan, he was the first Dufresne in Leoncavallo's *Zazà*. Five years later he created the title-role in the world premiere of Montemezzi's *Giovanni Gallurese*. The same year he went to Paris, appearing as Maurizio in *Adriana Lecouvreur* and Dufresne in a company organised by the publisher Sonzogno to show off his wares. When Garbin arrived at Covent Garden in 1908, it was to face the same stiff competition that had overwhelmed Bassi. Caruso, it is true, was absent, but there was Bonci; also Zenatello and McCormack. As Loris, Cavaradossi and Pinkerton, the critics found him 'poor' and 'inadequate'.[11] It was his only visit. In Italy, he

105 Francesco Tamagno as Otello

remained a popular artist until the outbreak of the First World War. At La Scala he sang Osaka in *Iris* and *Andrea Chenier*, and in the Verdi centenary celebrations, in 1913, he repeated his Fenton; his last appearances there were in 1918, in Renzo Bianchi's *Ghismondo*.

Garbin's voice has something of the quality of Valero, both singers having pronounced vibratos, but from different causes. Whereas Valero's, like de Lucia's, is a rapid quaver—what Garcia called a bleat, the consequence of inadequate breath support —Garbin's derives from a too forceful style; it is less regular and particularly obtrusive on high notes. Dufresne's 'E un riso gentil' is another souvenir of the premiere of *Zazà*; in spite of the strenuous delivery of the climax, there are some delicate gruppetti. He interpolates several of these, too, into the Brindisi from *Cavalleria Rusticana*. This he delivers as if it were recitativo parlante—the prosody governing note values, and then before the final reprise a seemingly interminable corona. An interpretation of considerable historical interest.

22. Dramatic Tenors

The voice of FRANCESCO TAMAGNO (1850–1905) was unique. Henderson described it as 'a magnificent "tenore robusto", reaching to the high C sharp and full of a pealing quality that overcame, if it did not move the hearer.'[1] It was a natural voice, so powerful—it was claimed—that it could set the whole of the great chandelier at Covent Garden vibrating. (Is that why the object is no longer there?)

Tamagno's origins were humble, a fact of which he was proud. Unlike some of his illustrious contemporaries, he neither claimed nor sued for noble lineage; it might have cost him money and that he was determined to hang on to. His parsimony was a byword, the number of stories about it legion. In her memoirs, Melba recalls a dinner she and Tamagno were at when he asked the hostess for a paper bag so that he could take home a cutlet for his dog. As soon as it was brought to him, he promptly went round the table gathering up all the left-overs. By chance Melba happened to call at his villa the next day and found him with his daughter at lunch; it would not be hard to guess what they were eating.

His career began in the chorus at the Teatro Reggio in Turin, his home town. One night he was sent on as Nearco in Donizetti's *Poliuto*; although the part is not much more than a cough and a spit, the young man got an ovation. The conductor Carlo Pedrotti at once offered to give him lessons. He made his real debut in 1874 as Riccardo in *Ballo* at Palermo. There followed engagements at Ferrara, Rovigo and Venice, where he was Edgardo opposite Albani's *Lucia*. At that time his singing was not what it was to become later on:

> He took engagement after engagement leaving no time to arrive at that artistic perfection in his art to which his natural gifts would eventually enable him to attain.[2]

Within three years he was invited to La Scala for the first of nine seasons. He appeared in *Africana* and Gomes's *Fosca*, in both of which his natural gifts made an enormous impression, but the critics thought much as did Albani: that his singing was 'undisciplined' and his acting 'ineffective'.[3] From that time, however, his progress was sure and steady. The next season he returned for forty-three performances, as Don Carlo, Alim, in the first La Scala performances of Massenet's *Re di Lahore*, and in the world premiere of Gomes's *Maria Tudor*. After visiting South America for the first time in the summer of 1879, the following autumn he was again at La Scala in Ponchielli's *Figliuol Prodigo*, Verdi's *Ernani* and *Simon Boccanegra*. In later years he added Don Carlo (in the revised edition), Raoul, Faust in *Mefistofele*, Radames, Arnold in *Tell* and the title-role in *Profeta*. In South America he was soon earning $2,250 a performance; even then he didn't care to spend too much of it, preferring to take the sea voyage steerage and pocket the difference between the first-class fare he always demanded.

The pinnacle of Tamagno's fame came when Verdi and Boito invited him to create the title-role of *Otello* at La Scala in 1887. Tamagno's performance created a furore only surpassed by that of the opera itself; every opera house wanted to put on the opera and everybody wanted to have Tamagno in it. He sang it in Rome, Naples, Venice, Palermo, Genoa, Nice, Lisbon, Madrid, Moscow, Buenos Aires, London and New York. In London, at the Lyceum theatre, so great was public interest that Covent Garden shut for the night so that their own singers and musicians might attend. From Tamagno's opening 'Esultate' he showed off a voice 'of remarkable compass and resonance'[4] and acting abilities to go with it. Though Shaw dissented about his singing, finding the voice 'shrill and nasal', he

had only praise for his 'original and real'[5] acting. In New York it was the same story, according to Henderson:

> It was one of the great masterpieces of the modern stage. Only Salvini's Othello could vie with it in poignant despair or puissant passion.[6]

Soon no one was criticising his acting, though there were still those who found fault with his singing. Vannuccini, a colleague of the Lampertis who had given some instruction to Tamagno, told David Bispham that 'Tamagno bleated like a goat',[7] and added that he was a musical illiterate, who had never heard of Rossini's *Stabat Mater* until he was asked to sing in it.

In his first New York season Tamagno appeared twenty-three times in nine different roles: Arnoldo, Radames, Edgardo, Manrico, Otello, Turiddu, Vasco in *Africana* and the title-roles of *Profeta* and *Sansone*. In Paris, in 1897, he sang—in French—his four-hundredth Otello in just a decade. In later years he created Hélion in de Lara's *Messaline* at Monte Carlo, where he was a regular visitor and paid $5,000 a performance; he repeated it in London and at La Scala. From that time, however, ill-health obliged him to cut down the number of performances he gave, though he continued to sing until 1902, and even emerged the following year for one last Otello, at the Argentina, Rome, at a gala given to honour Kaiser Wilhem II.

Tamagno's first records were made that same year at his villa; 'to minimise the strain',[8] in his own words. He was fifty-two at the time and in spite of the heavy schedule of performances he had undertaken over the years, and failing health (he was to die in less than two years), the voice is still astonishingly brilliant and powerful. It is no longer quite as responsive as it must once have been and we can hear something in the tone of that nasality Shaw complained of, but neither this nor a very narrow and rapid vibrato are distracting (it actually gives an added brilliance to the tone). The excerpts from *Otello* are invaluable historically; 'Esultate' is thrown off with amazing force, the high notes still have plenty of that 'pealing quality'. The Death scene is an interpretation very much in the grand manner; with its pellucid diction, a monumental piece of declamation. In 'Re del ciel' from *Profeta*, there are some remarkable examples of martellato, the voice literally hammering out the notes, yet remaining firm and steady. In them all there is an intensity of utterance and expressive phrasing that

106 Giovanni de Negri

is unique.

After Tamagno, GIOVANNI DE NEGRI (1850–1923) was the most important Italian dramatic tenor. A pupil of Guasco and Abbadia, he made his debut at Bergamo in 1878. During the next four years, in Zagreb, he sang Faust, Pollione in *Norma*, Alfredo, Riccardo in *Ballo in Maschera* and Don Alvaro in *Forza del Destino*. At Venice, he added Enzo and the title-role in *Profeta*. It was not, however, until 1887, when he sang Otello for the first time, that he found a part really to suit him. He sang it first in Turin, and then Genoa, Venice, Trieste and Buenos Aires. Though he was not able to trumpet forth 'Esultate' with Tamagno's unrivalled power, elsewhere, in the love duet, he was considered to have excelled him in the expression of the more tender emotions. In 1890 at La Scala, as Gabriele Adorno in *Simon Boccanegra*, after one performance a critic wrote:

> De Negri came, sang and conquered. The Scala public has finally discovered a tenor with a voice, a tenor who sings, who touches the emotions, and it was not restrained in showing its approval. He sang with feeling and passion, making the best use of his rich and ample resources.[9]

He returned for five seasons thereafter, as the first

Scala Tannhäuser and Siegmund, as Samson in Saint-Saëns's opera and taking part in the world premieres of Gomes's *Condor* and Mascagni's *Guglielmo Ratcliff*. But 'rich and ample' as his resources may have been, the heroic repertory proved too taxing; in 1896 he was obliged to undergo an operation for the removal of nodules on the vocal cords. It was unsuccessful, and though he sang occasionally thereafter, it effectively brought his career to an end.

His four records were made in 1902, when the voice was only a shaky remnant of its former glory. The opening phrases of Otello's death are declaimed with a measured restraint that contrasts effectively with his more overtly emotional manner in the passage 'un bacio ancor', where he is quite different from Tamagno.

Italy's greatest Wagnerian tenor, GIUSEPPE BORGATTI (1871–1950), was chipping stones in a mason's yard when a local Marchese, an aficionado of the opera, chanced by and heard the young man singing away at the top of his voice. He offered to pay for him to have some formal instruction. After a period of study with Alessandro Busi and Elena Cuccoli, whom he later married, Borgatti made his debut in 1893 in *Faust*, at Castelfranco Veneto. There followed performances of Fra Diavolo and Ernesto in *Don Pasquale*. It was not, however, until after he went to Milan and took some lessons from Carlo d'Ormeville† that he was engaged at an important theatre for the first time; at the Dal Verme, Milan, in 1894, in the title-role of *Lohengrin*. During the next couple of years he went to St Petersburg and Seville, singing in *Falstaff*, *Lucia* and *Manon Lescaut*. In Milan, at the eleventh hour, he was called in to replace Alfonso Garulli and create the title-role in Giordano's *Andrea Chenier*. At the dress rehearsal, when he finished the 'Improvviso', the librettist Luigi Illica jumped to his feet shouting 'Finally, here is Andrea Chenier'. The performance was a great event for the cast and the composer. As soon as it was over, Giordano cabled his publisher, Sonzogno: 'Chenier triumphant. Last act aroused fanatical enthusiasm. Boom! Boom! Boom!' Borgatti consolidated his success with appearances in most of the principal Italian theatres and in South America. There he was specially admired as Faust in Boito's *Mefistofele*, but from this time it was the challenge of Wagner that was to preoccupy him. In 1896, at a concert given in La Scala under Toscanini, he sang in the Prologue of *Crepuscolo degli Dei*. Three years later, in 1899, he

† The librettist of Marchetti's *Ruy Blas* and Catalani's *Loreley*.

took the title-role in the first performances of *Sigfrido* at La Scala, the following year came Tristan, and in 1903 Loge in *Oro del Reno*; all of them conducted by Toscanini. He did not relinquish his Italian repertory, for he sang Cavaradossi, Enzo and Radames at La Scala, Alfredo, Canio, Loris, and Vassili in Giordano's *Siberia* in other Italian opera houses; but most of his activities during the next thirteen years, from St Petersburg to Santiago, Chile, were directed towards Wagner. In Naples he was the first Tristan and the first Siegfried in *Crepuscolo degli Dei*. The high-water mark of his career came with some performances of *Parsifal* in 1913, at La Scala. 'The Wagnerians have found their St Paul,'[10] declared D'Annunzio, but it was an unfortunate analogy; *Parsifal* had been staged in spite of dire threats from Cosima—till then it had been the prerogative of Bayreuth. Whether her fulminations had anything to do with it or not, Borgatti's sight, which had been deteriorating for some while, became so bad that he was eventually obliged to give up his career.

Borgatti's Wagner recordings, though all of them are in Italian, are among the finest ever made. Toscanini's assistance in promoting his career at La Scala helps us overlook the famous conductor's latter day aberrations in taste where singers were concerned. It does not seem to have been an instrument of heroic proportions, and demonstrates once and for all that a good-sized voice, well-produced and properly modulated will still sound out effectively over a Wagnerian orchestra. His singing exemplifies those older Italian virtues that Wagner so much admired and wanted to hear in his music. Each word is clearly articulated and placed in a poised and limpid legato (what Dr Burney would have called portamento): each vowel and consonant—to use the composer's own words— takes place 'in the Musical Tone',[11] and not separate from it, as we are accustomed to hearing. In Siegmund's 'Spring song' and Lohengrin's 'Atmest du nicht' ('Deh! non t'incantan', in Salvatore Marchesi's translation), there is beauty of tone, a wide variety of vocal colour and sensitive phrasing, achieved without imposing the manners of the verismo school, or compromising the style of the music.

When La Scala staged *Crepuscolo degli Dei,* in 1907, it was not with Borgatti; the role of Siegfried was taken by FIORELLO GIRAUD (1868–1928). Giraud, born in Parma, was the son of a tenor and, like Vignas, he made his debut as Lohengrin, in 1891. Within a year, at the Dal Verme, Milan, he

107 Giuseppe Borgatti in the title-role of Wagner's *Sigfrido*

played a principal part in one of the great operatic events of that period; he was the first Canio in *Pagliacci*. In the course of the next few years, he sang with success in various Italian theatres: in Spain, at the Liceo, Barcelona; in Portugal, at Lisbon's Sao Carlos; and in Chile, at Santiago. He specialised in the verismo repertory. As well as Canio, he created Giasone in the world premiere of Tommasini's *Medea* at Trieste in 1906, and in the following year appeared at the Teatro Massimo,

Palermo, in the first performances of Donaudy's *Sperduti nel Buio*. At La Scala, in 1908, he was the first Pelléas in Debussy's opera.

Giraud's vocal style, in spite of his close relationship with the works of the 'modern' school, was formed in the previous generation. In one respect it resembles de Lucia—there is a strong vibrato—but the quality and the pure vowels remind us more of Valero; the registers too, are closer knit, and the top of the voice freer and more secure. Once the quavery tone is forgotten, Rodolfo's 'Quando le sere' from *Luisa Miller* with its elegant phrasing has a decided charm; it also has something to tell us of the style of the earlier Verdi. Just as Verdi's music itself developed and changed greatly in the forty-odd years that separate *Oberto* from *Otello*, so did the interpretive style of its singers; the intense and ardent delivery appropriate to *Otello*, which we can hear in the recordings of Tamagno, is out of place in the brilliant music of *Luisa Miller*, *Ernani*, *Rigoletto* and *Trovatore*. Although these operas are more melodramatic than Donizetti's, less purely vocal, Verdi retains in them much of the language of the old florid style, albeit debased; feeling is still expressed in a flowing cantilena, in an essentially vocal grammar of effects: mordents, appoggiaturas, portamenti and so forth. What has come to be called 'Verdian' style today is unhistoric: too literal, even bald, and at the same

108 Fiorello Giraud

time full of extra-musical dramatisation, the legacy of the verismo style. The hard attack (coup de glotte), dynamic excesses, strenuous high notes taken from the chest, and covered tone which makes it impossible to pronounce words clearly are all features of singing now so much a part of the norm that we accept them unquestioningly. Whether Verdi would have approved of them or not, he could not but have been surprised by them; contemporary criticism and descriptions of the singing of Strepponi, Mario, Piccolomini and Ronconi, and the earliest recordings that survive, by Patti, Bellincioni, Battistini and Maurel (all of whom Verdi admired), are suggestive of something quite different. Freer, more elaborate and refined, they show that it was the style to embellish the vocal line with graces and mordents, to introduce not only high notes but also cadenzas (at the end of 'La donna e mobile', for example), and to make other changes in notation and rhythm.

The image of Verdi as his biographers describe him—a rigorous genius—has encouraged critics to draw an altogether too facile equation between his character-traits and the performance-style in his music. Standards in Verdi's day were very different from our own; what we may feel extravagant would to him have seemed chaste in the extreme.† And Verdi's music cannot be divorced from the manners of his own age, though Toscanini made a great attempt to do so. At La Scala and the Met, he set out deliberately to eliminate tradition, calling it the last bad performance. Though he claimed to exalt nothing but the letter of the score, this completely new, revolutionary idea was not only undesirable but unrealisable. The 'letter' will not suffice to make a performance, and where once tradition and the singer filled out the bare outline he now imposed his personality in their place. As his recordings show, in such matters as rubato and cuts he was quite as whimsical as any singer. The singing we hear on records made by artists who worked with him— Rethberg, Martinelli, de Luca and Pinza for example—so often held up by critics as authentically Verdian, for all its fine qualities, in matters of style and interpretation only tells us about performance practice in the first half of the twentieth century, and little or nothing of the real Verdi

† A case in point: although Verdi objected to Tadolini's creating Lady Macbeth—he asked for a singer with a 'hollow' and 'stifled' voice—he eventually accepted Mme Barbieri-Nini, a high soprano whose voice could hardly have satisfied those requirements as we should have imagined them; her repertory, which included Amina and Gilda, was much the same as Patti's.

Elio (Corradetti)   Chopin (Bassi)

109 Amadeo Bassi and Ferruccio Corradetti in Orefice's *Chopin*

tradition. For an echo of that we should turn to the records of Giraud and his contemporaries.

After Borgatti's enforced retirement, many of his Wagnerian roles were taken over by AMADEO BASSI (1874–1949). Bassi's career began in 1897 at Castelfiorentino, in the title-role of Marchetti's *Ruy Blas*. He soon became one of Italy's leading lyric dramatic tenors; as Rodolfo Celletti has described him as 'a vigorous champion of verismo, a versatile actor, at once dynamic and picturesque'.[12] After appearances in Genoa, Verona, Florence and Venice, as Leandro in Mancinelli's *Ero e Leandro*, the Duke, Rodolfo, Loris, Faust and Cavaradossi, he was invited to South America, where he was a regular visitor between 1902 and 1907. In Monte Carlo he created Lionello in Mascagni's *Amica* with Geraldine Farrar, and Angel Clare in d'Erlanger's *Tess* at the San Carlo, Naples. The same year he arrived at Covent Garden, sharing Canio, Riccardo and Cavaradossi with Caruso, and Rodolfo with Bonci. Though Bassi's voice was a fine one it was not exceptional: unfortunately for him, in a company that included Caruso, Bonci and Zenatello,

exceptions were the rule. He returned again that autumn and for some performances in 1911, but without making any lasting impression. At the same time he was invited to New York, to the Manhattan. His Radames was commended for 'tonal beauty and brilliance of technique',[13] and as Alfredo, first with Melba and later Tetrazzini, although the ladies dominated the notices, the *New York Times* got in a line praising his 'opulent outpouring of voice'.[14] After Hammerstein left, he made a solitary appearance at the Met in lieu of an ailing Caruso, as Dick Johnson, but it led to nothing else. Instead he went to Boston, where he was well enough received, though curiously Hale found little to enjoy in his acting. In Chicago it was Dick Johnson again, but unfortunately Caruso's only two performances there in recent years had been in *Fanciulla del West*, and this made sure Bassi's impersonation took second place. In Italy he continued to make the rounds of the principal houses, though by this time his voice was showing all too evident signs of the results of trying to make out of it more than nature had put in. With Borgatti gone, he moved over to Wagner, offsetting vocal decline with a greater skill in stage-craft. According to Augusto Carelli, the stage designer and brother of Emma Carelli—

He who has seen and heard Bassi as Siegfried, lying under a tree in the whispering forest, dreaming of his unknown mother, and heard his wild question after Mime's exit will remember poetry that can never return.[15]

He sang this role for the last time at La Scala in the 1925 season.

Bassi was the complete verismo tenor. In a recording of Loris's 'Amor ti vieta' from *Fedora*, he gives an exhibition of the style: each phrase stretched out, ending in a note with a wide and loose vibrato, an attack often pitched from below, and in the last phrase, 'Non t'amerò', a catch in the breath inserted for 'realistic' purposes. Caruso too, in this aria, uses the vibrato for effect and sings in an intense and emotional manner, but, in contrast to Bassi, the voice is kept on the breath and remains under complete control. All that Bassi seems to have managed is to age it prematurely; the tone is already dry and hoarse, and in the lower notes he often has a 'frog' in his throat.

After Tamagno by far the most successful dramatic tenor of the younger generation was GIOVANNI ZENATELLO (1876–1949). His career began as a baritone, but after some performances at Naples and Bassano, as Silvio and then Tonio, he quickly graduated to Canio. Within a few months he added such unequivocally tenor roles as Manrico, Edgardo and Faust. Subsequently his progress was swift and sure. In 1901 he sang in Trieste, Lisbon and Palermo, and the following summer he made his first visit to South America. In the autumn of 1902 he appeared at La Scala in the *Faust* of Berlioz, returning for the next seven years in a variety of parts: Federico in *Germania,* Hermann, Don José, Enzo, Radames and Faust. There too he created Vassili in Giordano's *Siberia*, Pinkerton in *Butterfly* and leading roles in Franchetti's *Figlia de Jorio* and Cilea's *Gloria.* In the autumn season of 1905, he made his Covent Garden debut as Riccardo:

> It is not often that a singer having a great reputation in his own country shows at once the grounds for that reputation on his first appearance at Covent Garden, and although in the earlier part of the opera his voice sounded a little small, its beautiful quality was immediately apparent, while once having felt his way and accustomed himself to the new surroundings he sang superbly ... His tenor voice is a happy combination of the lyric and heroic, robust yet delicate when delicacy is required and full of colour, and he is singularly free of the excessive exuberance of many of his race. As he acts with firm liveliness he is certain to earn the greatest credit here.[16]

And so it was to be. That autumn he was also Andrea Chenier, Faust, Radames, Pinkerton and des Grieux; the following year he added Maurizio, Rodolfo, Loris, Don José and Cavaradossi. In 1908 London heard him for the first time as Canio, Raoul and Otello. In this last role he established himself the finest interpreter of the part since Tamagno. After many years' absence from Covent Garden, he returned to sing it once again, in 1926. Though his voice was somewhat dimmed by the passage of years, his interpretation remained as potent as ever. His first London Desdemona, Melba, was responsible for bringing him to Hammerstein's attention. After the opening Manhattan season Bonci had defected to the Met, and Hammerstein needed a new tenor; he engaged Zenatello. His New York debut was as Enzo in *Gioconda*, and he followed this with Alfredo, Edgardo, Canio, Vassili and Otello, of which the critic Henry Lahee wrote:

> It is admirable. He lacks physical bulk—his Moor is tall, spare, quick of glance and alert of elastic movement. His voice has penetrating intensity. By every token of physical aspect this Otello has the sensitive and tense passions that such a frame often encloses.

110 Giovanni Zenatello as Riccardo in *Ballo in Maschera*

Later, in the United States, Zenatello sang with the Boston and Chicago companies. In the summer of 1909, when Caruso was indisposed, he went on the Met tour in his place, but for whatever reasons (Caruso's jealousy, perhaps) he never appeared with the company in New York. He did, however, return to the Manhattan as a member of the Boston company, singing Otello, Cavaradossi and Masaniello in *Muta di Portici*, in which Pavlova danced the title-role.

He was still singing well into the 1920s, in Central and South America, in Berlin and Leningrad. After his retirement he became a successful teacher of singing with his wife, the Spanish born mezzo-soprano Maria Gay. He was a moving spirit in the restoration of the ancient Roman amphitheatre at Verona, and sang there in the inaugural season in 1913. In later years he was a Director of the company on more than one occasion, and after the Second World War was able to use his influence to effect the debut of Maria Callas, who made her first appearance in Italy at the arena in the summer of 1947 in the title-role of *Gioconda*.

Zenatello made many records over a period of more than twenty-five years. The voice we hear on them is a brilliant lyric dramatic tenor, the production somewhat constricted but even throughout its range, and with a particularly penetrating quality. The neat and narrow vibrato is reminiscent of Tamagno's and gives the voice a hard glitter, which he uses to telling effect in *Otello*; his singing has a considerable range of dynamics and colour and even in what we think an unlikely piece for him, Alfredo's 'Dei miei bollenti spiriti', the interpretation is surprisingly sensitive. He is at his best in Andrea Chenier's 'Improvviso', with its urgent declamation and expressive phrasing, making a thrilling climax not by shouting but concentrating the sound, sustaining the intensity through until the last note.

The Puerto Rican tenor ANTONIO PAOLI (1870–1946) first appeared on stage at the Paris Opéra, in 1899, as Arnold in *Guillaume Tell*. The following year he went to Italy and made a great effect with his brilliant high C in *Trovatore* at Parma. Thereafter, with his forthright if rather unsubtle

111 Antonio Paoli

singing, he was a popular favourite at many leading Italian houses; also in Spain and Portugal, and in South America. There he sang Samson, Canio, Alim in *Re di Lahore*, Raoul, Vasco, Andrea Chenier and Otello. In 1910 he appeared at La Scala as Vasco and Samson.

The voice on records is remarkably brilliant and powerful, with something of the clarion quality of Escalaïs at the top, though there seems less head and more chest resonance and it is not as responsive. He has a disagreeable way of letting a note go—the coup de glotte backwards, as it were. Otello's 'Esultate' gives a good idea of his strengths and weaknesses. The high notes are certainly exultant, but it is hardly necessary to compare him with Tamagno to hear how crude is the declamation—not securely based, full of exaggerated effects inserted into the line, rather than arising out of it.

23. Caruso

It is fitting to conclude this survey of Italian tenors with the most famous of them all. ENRICO CARUSO (1873–1921) was the last great operatic tenor to be a part of a living musical tradition. Until the First World War, the bulk of the repertory in the major opera houses was still made up of works, broadly speaking, contemporary; little of it more than fifty or sixty years old, much of it written in the previous quarter of a century. Today, when the world's leading singers are careful to give modern operas a wide berth, it may seem hard to believe that Caruso and Melba, for example, actually popularised contemporary music. Yet, in order to get *Bohème* an audience in its first season at the Met, after one performance Melba came out in front of the curtain at the end and sang Lucia's Mad Scene; a sop for those who expected Puccini to have written one for Mimi. Caruso created leading roles in Cilea's *Arlesiana* and *Adriana Lecouvreur*, Giordano's *Fedora*, Franchetti's *Germania* and Puccini's *Fanciulla del West*. In spite of the increased size and importance of the orchestra and the more dramatic manner of much of this music, the style was still a vocal one, in this respect not radically dissimilar from the popular music of the day. In the generation before the arrival of American jazz, when it was still possible for a classically trained singer to have a foot in both camps, Caruso was as famous as a singer of popular ballads and Neapolitan songs as he was in the opera.

He was born in Naples, a city renowned for its singers and its poverty. His family was poor, but not as poor as some; he was never one of those urchins who even today can be seen roaming the streets, cadging a ride hanging on the back of the trams or begging from the tourists. He went to school, and it was while he was still a boy that he first showed musical talent, singing treble in a church choir. Later, when his voice broke and he began to work, he started studying singing in earnest. In 1891 he was brought by a friend to the studio of Guglielmo Vergine; after three years of study he made his first stage appearances, at the Teatro Nuovo, Naples, in two performances—probably the only two—of Morelli's *Amico Francesco*. He did not create a sensation. In spite of the natural beauty of his voice, his art was crude and his technique incomplete. In particular, he had difficulty with the high notes, finding it hard to manage a top A without its shattering. In the course of the next eight years, singing in most of the Italian theatres, in Egypt, Russia and South America, by dint of hard work and experiment in a wide-ranging repertory, he began to forge his own technique. During that time he sang the Duke, Faust, Turiddu, Enzo, Fernando in *Favorita*, Araquil in *La Navarrese*, Tebaldo in *Capuleti ed i Montecchi*, Rodolfo, Arturo in *Puritani*, Alfredo, Canio, Don José, Faust in Boito's *Mefistofele*, Radames, Osaka in *Iris*, Ernani, Riccardo, Nemorino, Lohengrin, des Grieux in Puccini's and Massenet's *Manon*, Nadir, Cavaradossi, Riccardo in Donizetti's *Maria di Rohan* and Marcello in Leoncavallo's *Bohème*. At first his reception was equivocal, partly because of vocal problems, partly because the critics accustomed to the old school found it difficult to accept his vehement and frankly more vulgar style. By 1902, however, when he made his first records for the G & T company, the operas of the verismo were triumphant. Two years previously, at La Scala, in *Bohème*, after the critics and the box-holders had withheld their approbation, Caruso appealed over their heads to the gallery; it was a new century and the age of the common man. From that time dates the beginning of his greatness.

After his first appearances at the Met in 1903, in spite of a few initially dissenting opinions, he soon established himself as the world's greatest tenor. From that time New York became the centre of his activities. At the Met he appeared in seventeen seasons, six-hundred-and-twenty-two times, in thirty-seven different roles. Here as in so much else during his career, Caruso's timing was perfect. Jean de Reszké, who had charmed the Diamond horseshoe and the exclusive society of the old New York of Edith Wharton's novels, had been retired for more than two years. The Met was ready for someone new. In its first years it had been a German theatre; then in the 90s, under the sway of the de Reszké brothers, Lassalle, Plançon and others, it was the French repertory that predominated. From the turn of the century a new influence began to manifest itself: that of the city's half a million Italian immigrants. It was appropriate that the new idol should have been one of their countrymen.

At the Met Caruso continued to appear in the traditional repertory, adding Manrico, Gennaro in *Lucrezia Borgia* and Elvino in *Sonnambula*. For the first time too, he sang in French opera in the original language, albeit translating it into the modern Italian style. Among new roles were Pinkerton, Dick Johnson, Julien in Charpentier's sequel to *Louise*, Flammen in Mascagni's *Lodoletta* and Avito in Montemezzi's *L'Amore dei tre Re*. Though he did his best, the Charpentier and Mascagni failed to make any impression, and Avito was one of his rare failures; it stretched his technique to its limits and was in fact the last role from a new opera he undertook. Instinctively realising there was nothing left for him in the contemporary repertory, that from a singer's point of view, it had gone as far as it could, he began to switch his attention to revivals. Under Toscanini's direction, he had already taken parts in Donizetti's *Elisir d'amore* to great effect, and Gluck's *Armide*. During the last years of his life he added Samson, Jean in *Le Prophète*, Don Alvaro in *Forza del Destino* and Eléazar in *La Juive*. All of these pieces he virtually created anew; his is the performing tradition still extant today. By this time the hegemony of his style was complete; it not only succeeded the old Italian school, which, in any case, had never been popular outside Italy, but very soon the traditional French and Russian styles were in retreat. Singers like Alessandro Bonci, Edmond Clément and Dmitri Smirnov with their elegant and refined but unfortunately small-scale art, when they visited New York, failed to make any headway with a public infatuated by Caruso's magnificent outpourings.

By the time he came to make records, he had secured the high notes by trial and error; the B flat and B natural had become the splendid and formidable things they were to remain for the rest of his career. Above that, though he had a top C and C sharp, there was a very obvious shift in gears, and these notes were not completely married with the rest of the voice.† Even after his technique was firmly based, it was never wholly completed; throughout his entire career it was a dynamic thing, developing and changing in response to his artistic ambitions. In the eighteen years of his recording career we can hear his technical development fully documented. The timbre darkened dramatically, though perhaps too much has been made of this; he was not a tenorino in 1902, nor a baritone in 1920— not at least, if the records are reproduced at the correct speeds. The voice was conditioned by the style, not the other way about; Caruso was the ultimate tenor, his art the consummation of a tradition that extended back via de Lucia, Gayarré, Nicolini and Mario, to Rubini; he did not reject his predecessors' style, rather he transcended it. His whole technique was founded in a portamento of the breath, much as that was understood in the days of Mancini and Agricola, except that he increased the tension so as to thrust out the high notes and produce the big and full tone his public came to expect of him. Yet the voice remained responsive, as in recordings of 'Una furtiva lagrima' and the brilliant cadenza to 'La donna è mobile', and he was skilled in the traditional modes of expression: mordents, trills—there is a fine example in Handel's Largo—and gruppetti, at the end of the opening solo in 'Bella figlia dell'amore'. In spite of 'the vulgar demand for huge sounds' (as W. J. Henderson puts it), 'the quality of his voice, floated on a deep and perfectly controlled stream of air, is something beautiful beyond description'.[1] We can hear in the trio 'Qual voluttà' from Verdi's *I Lombardi* (unquestionably one of the most magnificent pieces of singing on record) that it is the perfect control of the breath that makes possible and also disciplines those new affecting devices that are particularly associated with him: the forceful attack and a similarly violent way of relinquishing a note; the aspirate which, like the sob and catch in the breath, is introduced deliberately and is not the consequence of technical infirmity. Though extravagant, and decadent too, they were spontaneous devices and arose out of a genuine musical feeling, all of a piece with his prodigious natural talent. Caruso glorified the verismo and, unlike most of his successors, who copied only his mannerisms, his technique was still sufficiently informed by tradition to illuminate the music of earlier periods.

† A recently issued computerised re-recording of Caruso's 'Salut demeure' suggests that the acoustic system may have been exaggerating this.

112 Enrico Caruso

Though certain aspects of his style have been modified over the years, his has remained the example among tenors, not only in Italy, but in France, the United States, Great Britain, and, after the Second World War, in Russia too. Giovanni Martinelli, Beniamino Gigli, Giacomo Lauri-Volpi, Alfred Piccaver, Georges Thill, Jussi Björling, Richard Tucker, Placido Domingo and Virgilius Noreika, are all descendents of Caruso. When he arrived in New York, Caruso was just another Italian tenor; ever since, he has remained *the* tenor. More than a half a century has elapsed since his death and still his name is a byword. Traditionally, it had been the prima donna—Mrs Billington, Catalani, Pasta, Malibran, Patti and Melba—who enjoyed universal fame; brilliant voices, by their very nature, are more affecting. Since the eighteenth century and the disappearance of the castrati, no male singer had challenged their supremacy: Rubini, Mario and Jean de Reszké were greatly admired, but their reputations had not extended far outside the opera house or beyond the society that patronised it. Indeed, Jean de Reszké rarely appeared in concert, and then only in excerpts from opera; throughout his entire career he never sang a song. Undoubtedly the gramophone was a potent factor in translating Caruso into an international figure; it took his voice into the homes of millions of people who were never likely to hear him in person. Caruso was a man of the people; certain critics in the early years, Klein among them, lamented his lack of 'poetry and romance' and 'that rare nobility' that had so distinguished de Reszké's art. They discounted his instinctive musicianship and exceptional voice—by all accounts, a far finer instrument. Yet it was precisely Caruso's glorious natural talent that was so appealing, while his humble background enabled him to communicate with a far wider spectrum of people than ever de Reszké did. As a singer of songs, he replaced the intimate and genteel accents of the salon singers of the late nineteenth century with something more expansive, better suited to the large popular audiences he sang to in America, and via the gramophone throughout the world. It was not subtle, but grand and overwhelming; and unlike Gigli and Tauber, before electrical recording, it was uncorrupted by the influence of the microphone; nor did it compromise his performances in the opera.

In sincerity, in fervour, in devotion to his art, he was the peer of any opera singer in history . . . He was an indifferent actor and a supreme singer when he came here [to New York]. He finished his career a singer less flawless, but an operatic interpreter who commanded the respect and sympathy of the sternest critics, even when they could not credit him with triumphant success.[2]

Caruso personified the musical idiom of the times, at once the general particularised, how Everyman would have liked to sing had he the voice; in the bathroom it was Caruso he fancied he heard.

24. Sopranos 'B.C.'

The Italian tenor and baritone sound of the 'new' school, as typified by Caruso and Ruffo, proved an irresistible example and came to prevail over the earlier style of Marconi, Battistini and Kaschmann, and eventually, too, over other national schools. The Italian sopranos of the later nineteenth century, however, remained provincial singers. Patti's rivals and successors, though they were often Italian-trained, were none of them Italians: Nilsson, Lucca, di Murska, Gerster, Albani, Sembrich and Melba. In the male singer, the preoccupation with tone, quantity rather than quality, the emphasis on the development of the chest register, though in the long run it would deprive the voice of much of its flexibility and eloquence, nevertheless suited contemporary notions of dramatic realism; in the female singer, however, the forceful attack, coarse chest tones and exaggerated vibrato to simulate intensity and passion, like the *vino di campagna*, were too earthy to travel well. With the notable exception of Tetrazzini, the Italian sopranos at this time were a breed apart, their careers confined almost entirely to Italy and the Italian operatic empire.

The first generation of Italian sopranos to leave records of their art, as it were B.C. (Before *Cavalleria*), though we can hear in their singing much of what later turned into the verismo style, are noticeably more restrained in manner. The eldest, INES DE FRATE, was born in 1854. Very little is known of her early career. She was over forty when she appeared for one season only at La Scala as Leila in *Pescatori di Perle*. At the time she made her few records, she had graduated to 'Casta Diva', the 'Inflammatus' from Rossini's *Stabat Mater*, Abigaille's 'Anch'io dischiuso' from *Nabucco* and 'M'odi, m'odi' from *Lucrezia*

113 Elena Teodorini as Carmen   114 Fanny Torresella

Borgia. In this last piece, from an opera which was still regularly performed in Italian theatres, we can readily identify salient characteristics of the late nineteenth-century style. The voice, in the middle register particularly, has a white, rather open quality, the head and chest notes are clearly differentiated, the scale equalised in weight but not in colour, and not every join smoothed over. Though she was fifty-four at the time, the voice is still quite fresh, the high notes brilliant, if a little hard. Hers is not the most remarkably suave or limpid legato, but it is smoother than we can hear from at least one of her contemporaries, the Roumanian born ELENA TEODORINI (1858–1926), who recorded the same piece. She was four years younger than de Frate but the voice is already worn; excessive recourse to the coup de glotte and a temperamental manner had something to do with it. The phrasing is altogether freer than de Frate's, the tone more lachrymose; to audiences already won over to Mascagni and Giordano her gusty and approximate way with the coloratura probably seemed meaningful. She studied in Milan and took lessons from one of Nordica's teachers, Sangiovanni; then she made her debut, in 1877, in the travestie role of Gondi in Donizetti's *Maria di Rohan*, a mezzo soprano part; thereafter, she sang Rosina, Leonora in *Favorita* and Amneris, only gradually moving into the soprano repertory. She appeared with success in South America, Spain and Italy; though at La Scala, when she sang Valentine and the title-role in the Italian premiere of Massenet's *Erodiade*, she was not liked. Lago brought her to

Covent Garden in 1886, where she made five appearances in all, her first role being Valentine. The *Illustrated London News* wrote:

> The debutante occasionally sung [sic] with pathos and dramatic feeling, especially in the grand final duet (with Gayarré), in which she produced a favourable impression. The prevalent use of the tremolo was probably the result of extreme nervousness.[1]

Afterwards came Gioconda, apparently 'with less tremolo'[2] and later Zerlina, 'to small advantage'.[3] She was not invited again.

The year following Teodorini's visit, FANNY TORRESELLA (1856–1914) came to London, to Drury Lane with the Augustus Harris company. After she sang Gilda, *The Times* critic wrote:

> The lady has vocal and dramatic merits which were effectively displayed in several instances and will probably be more manifest when she discards the tremolo which was too frequently apparent.[4]

Whether they would have been, she did not get the opportunity; it was her one and only London performance.

Torresella, though Italian, was born in Tiflis, Georgia; at the time her father was Director of the opera orchestra there. She took lessons from him and made her debut as Fenena in *Nabucco*, at Trieste, in 1876. Subsequently she sang the Shepherd in *Tannhäuser*, Eudoxie in *Ebrea*, Siebel in *Faust*, the Queen in *Ugonotti* and Berthe in *Profeta*, the last two at La Scala in 1884. For the next twenty years she travelled throughout Italy and visited Spain, Portugal and South America; she sang the title roles in *Lucia, Fanciulla di Perth* and *Mirella*, Ophélie in *Amleto*, Elvira in *Puritani*, Oscar in *Ballo*, Zerlina in *Don Giovanni* and Leila in *Pescatori di Perle*. In 1904, again at La Scala, she was still able to hold her own as Gilda opposite Ruffo's Rigoletto. By that time she had ventured a little into the verismo repertory with Nedda, Musetta and Suzel in *Amico Fritz*. Her few gramophone records, made in 1900, unfortunately suffer from temperament; not hers, the turntable's. She was a typical lyric-coloratura of that period. There is little bloom left on the tone. An efficient technique extends to the high D, in the Polacca from *Puritani*, but does not enable her to discriminate very clearly between a trill and a tremolo. There is nothing especially characterful or admirable in her singing. However, she did record Adina's 'Prendi, per me sei libero' from *Elisir d'amore*, not Donizetti's setting but the one Malib-

115 Medea Mei as Tosca

ran sang; although accredited to the diva's husband, the violinist, Charles de Bériot, it seems more likely to have been her own work. It lies low in Torresella's voice, and she makes a number of upward changes in the line.

Opera in Imperial Russia until the turn of the century was still dominated by the Italians. Many of the greatest Italian singers, Battistini and Marconi, for example, were regular visitors; at least two sopranos, Medea Mei and Olimpia Boronat, married Russian citizens and settled in St Petersburg. Of these, MEDEA MEI (1858–1952) was far the more important. Born in Florence, she studied there with Bianchi, Carozzi-Zucchi and Panofka, whose vocalises are still staple diet for students today. At the age of sixteen, she sang the mezzo part in the Verdi *Requiem*, soon afterwards making her stage debut, as Azucena. During the next nine years she appeared in various Italian theatres, and visited Russia, South America and London. At that time her repertory included Ulrica, Gertrude in Thomas's *Amleto*, Amneris, Leonora in *Favorita* and Carmen, all mezzo soprano roles. By degrees, she began to shift into the soprano repertory; after Charlotte in *Werther* came Valentine in *Ugonotti* and Margherita in *Mefistofele*. She married the famous Russian tenor, Nicolai Figner; with her husband, she created leading roles in Tchaikovsky's *Queen of Spades* and *Iolanthe* and in Napravnik's *Doubrovsky* and *Francesca da Rimini*.

In spite of the forty-odd years she spent in Russia and her association with many leading figures in musical life there, she remained an Italian singer. She appeared mostly in Italian and French opera. In recordings the voice is warm and attractive, and if the tone is not always ideally steady it is quite without the obtrusive vibrato of the ladies above. In other technical respects, however, there are points of similarity: the registers are equalised, but the chest voice is not blended in and has a habit of separating off. To get over this, she makes frequent use of the coup de glotte, though less forcefully than either de Frate or Teodorini. Her interpretation of Lisa's air from the *Queen of Spades* is of great interest historically, particularly the alternate low ending sanctioned by Tchaikovsky. Here, and in Tosca's 'Vissi d'arte', she achieves a considerable intensity and without exaggeration. Her very first record, Tosti's 'Penso', with its refined style and charm of manner reminiscent of Patti, gives us, as it were, a glimpse into the great drawing-rooms of old Russia, where she and her husband were such special favourites.

OLIMPIA BORONAT (1867–1934) sang in most of the leading theatres of Italy including the San Carlo and the Teatro Bellini at Catania. She travelled to Spain and Portugal and South America. Her roles were drawn principally from the lyric-coloratura repertory: *Faust, Puritani, Hamlet, Capuleti, Roméo et Juliette, Traviata* and *Rigoletto*. In 1891, six years after her debut, she visited Russia for the first time. In the following year she married a Polish nobleman and thereafter she sang only intermittently, principally in Italian seasons given at the Aquarium Theatre, St Petersburg.

Records suggest a typically Italian voice, similar to Torresella's but in better condition. Although the tone is not especially fresh, it is still attractive. The wide variety of nuance and imagination in the phrasing, which we can hear to particularly charming effect in Amina's 'Come per me sereno', with her partiality for lengthy morendos and high

116 Olimpia Boronat

born Chapman, studied in Paris with Giovanni Sbriglia and Pauline Viardot, after which she went to Italy, where she made her debut at Casalmonferrato as Elvira in *Puritani*. Subsequently she sang Dinorah at Varese and then other lyrical roles. By 1884, when she arrived at the San Carlo, Naples, her voice had developed sufficiently to undertake Lucrezia Borgia and Paolina in Donizetti's *Poliuto*. At this time, she made frequent trips to South America, appearing in Buenos Aires and Rio. On a brief visit to Berlin she met the famous tenor Antonio Aramburo; in spite of an age difference of nearly twenty years, they were married.

In Paris, between 1886 and 1891, as a principal soprano, she sang Valentine, Selika and Chimène in *Le Cid*, and there too created the Duchesse d'Etampes in Saint-Saëns's *Ascanio*. In 1893 she made her La Scala debut as Brünnhilde in *Valchiria*. The following year she was at Covent Garden for the first of four visits, during which she sang Aida, Venus, Valentine, Brünnhilde and Donna Anna. She was not much liked, *The Times* complaining of 'a perpetual tremolo':

> Mme Adini is a very energetic Donna Anna but her singing is not of the finished quality that is required in Mozart's music, while her peculiar vocal method does not add to the attractions of her performance.[5]

pianissimi, reminds us of de Lucia; like him too, she makes out of each of these something of beauty in itself. In full voice the tremolo is often distracting, the tone driven against the hard palate, a less than attractive feature we shall hear again in other Italian sopranos of this period. Her coloratura is not absolutely accurate—the trill, in particular, far from perfect—and she is noticeably circumspect in the production of the highest notes. At the end of 'Sempre libera', which is transposed down a semitone, she is careful to lead up to the interpolated D in alt, by vocalising the preceding measures. She is at her most affecting in Tosti's delightful 'Senza l'amore', 'The last rose of summer' (here sung in Italian) and 'E lo sapevi', from a totally forgotten work—Giannelli's *Olga*—delivered with exactly the right fervour yet without overdoing a good thing. A constraint not felt by all of her contemporaries.

The American soprano ADA ADINI (1855–1924),

In the nineties, she travelled to Vienna, Turin and Rome, made tours throughout Germany, and took principal roles in a variety of novelties, including Leoncavallo's *I Medici* and Paladilhe's *Patria*. She returned to Paris in 1902 and spent the last years of her career at the Opéra. After divorcing Aramburo, she married the librettist Paul Milliet. In her retirement she taught singing; one of her pupils was the Spanish mezzo soprano Maria Gay.

Adini's records were made pretty well at the end of her career. The voice is strong and the quality still sweet, especially at the top. The vibrato is most obvious in the middle register and when she is singing at less than a forte; even then it does not sound as disturbing as the London critics suggest. An abbreviated account of Aida's Nile aria, 'O fresche valli' (in French), takes in the high C easily enough; in the chest register, however, she has a tendency to bray and the phrasing is shortbreathed. She seems more in tune with Salome's 'Il est doux' from Massenet's *Hérodiade*, where, some tremulousness and a hard attack notwithstanding, her delivery suits the music's sentimental style.

117 Ada Adini as the Duchesse d'Etampes in Saint-Saëns's *Ascanio*

25. After Cavalleria

The origins of the verismo style have been traced back as far as the middle of the nineteenth century. Gino Monaldi claims Verdi's *Traviata* as the first verismo opera. Till then, like Donizetti, Verdi had treated historical dramas; those of Shakespeare, Byron, Schiller and Hugo. With Dumas fils's *La Dame aux Camélias*, he abruptly shifted to the 'real', or at any rate contemporary world, to subject matter which so scandalised bourgeois morality that, at first, to mollify the censor it had to be cloaked in the decency of period costume. Though it quickly became one of his most popular works, and has remained so ever since, it was an experiment he did not choose to repeat. He retained in later operas many of its formal and musical innovations, the use of motifs, for example, but abandoned 'real' people and returned again to the world of the historical melodrama.

Similar claims have put forward on behalf of Boito's *Mefistofele*, though here it is not the subject matter so much as the musical style that is prophetic of things to come: the strenuous vocal writing, in particular the awkward setting of words in high-lying climactic phrases and the heavy orchestration, are all prominent features in the music of Mascagni, Giordano and Leoncavallo. In Margherita's Mad Scene, one of the last in Italian opera, the outbursts of coloratura, though written in the traditional modes, to make their proper effect need to be expressed in a more anguished and dramatic style than would be appropriate to Lucia or Ophélie. Boito was the author of the libretto of another precursor of the verismo: Ponchielli's *Gioconda*. With Verdi's *Aida*, it is the most successful Italian adaptation of the French Grand Opéra, of Scribe's recipe, but if its architecture looks backwards—one show-stopping number after another—the impassioned style, which keeps going at full tilt all evening, points the way to verismo: Mascagni, as it were, out of Meyerbeer. Listening to La Cieca's 'Voce di donna', Enzo's 'Cielo e mar' or Gioconda's 'Suicidio', we hardly need to be told that Puccini was a pupil of Ponchielli. In this last piece Ponchielli has contrived most of its dramatic effect in the chest register, encouraging the kind of ventriloquism the gramophone has abundantly preserved for us, where the soprano alternates between a thin, often tremulous head register and masculine-sounding chest notes forced up to G, even A flat.

It was not, however, until 1890 that all the

118 Gemma Bellincioni

ingredients of verismo were finally brought together, under one act, in Mascagni's *Cavalleria Rusticana*. Here was a realistic subject, a contemporary setting, stark passions expressed in appropriately perfervid vocal writing, a scenario moving swiftly and inexorably to its climax through a series of instantly appealing arias and duets. Not surprisingly it created a sensation. If imitation is the sincerest form of flattery, there never was an opera more admired. In Italy, Mascagni's example was followed by Giordano, Puccini, Cilea and Franchetti, while Leoncavallo with *Pagliacci* provided its *alter ego*. Abroad it had its imitators too; Massenet, an established composer of ten years, lost no time in abandoning the erotic, legendary and heroic subjects which had hitherto preoccupied him and contrived his own recipe, which, as Shaw noted, proved entirely efficacious.

With a sidelong glance at Bizet, he set *La Navarraise* in Spain. Instead of the military being concerned with putting down a strike in a tobacco factory and getting their officers out of the clutches of gypsy girls, he chose a setting in the middle of the Carlist wars, and instead of one man killing another for honour, a concept rather abstruse outside of Sicily, a woman kills a man for money, which in France doubtless seemed far more realistic.

Of all the sopranos who identified their careers with the new repertory, none was more famous in her life-time, or more important historically than GEMMA BELLINCIONI (1864–1950). Her career began in Naples in 1877 when she sang in Orefice's *Il Segreto della Duchessa*. In the course of the next few seasons she undertook Dinorah, Amina, Desdemona (in Rossini's *Otello*), Oscar, Elvira in *Puritani* and Lucia, which she sang in San Sebastian, opposite the Spanish tenor, Gayarré, and was acclaimed for 'la sincerità di espressione'.[1] At the Teatro Argentina in Rome, her Violetta caused a furore, as the impresario, Gino Monaldi, remembered years afterwards:

> Words cannot describe the fanaticism aroused by Bellincioni. It seemed as if no one had ever seen or heard Violetta before these performances, so different from other impersonations did hers appear. It is of little consequence to discuss whether her singing and acting were in unison, or if the first had gaps in its execution and the second went too far in its search for histrionic and vocal effects; what is certain is that her suggestive powers were extraordinary.[2]

In South America, the critic of the Buenos Aires *Le Razon* wrote:

> It was a voice of beautiful quality, secure and extensive, which she could colour to suit the drama and emotion. It was not big, but so velvety, so correct in intonation and so sweet that she more than made up in beauty of timbre what she lacked in volume.[3]

Today, when a big soprano voice, though the singer is without temperament, is automatically labelled a dramatic soprano, and a high and brilliant voice, a coloratura, even when the singer's florid technique is sketchy, it may seem odd that Bellincioni, a skilful executant of coloratura roles, with a smallish, light-weight voice should have been considered a dramatic soprano. But if her voice was hardly of dramatic proportions, her manner of singing and acting, like that of Calvé, was highly dramatic.†

† Undoubtedly Bellincioni's most remarkable, if not most plausible, impersonation was Figaro in *Barbiere*, which she sang in Madrid and Stuttgart, in a cast that included Eva Tetrazzini (Luisa's elder sister) as Count Almaviva!

She did not, however, appeal to everyone; not to Boito who heard her in her first season at La Scala in 1886. In a letter to Verdi, he wrote:

> this attractive young woman is not yet an artist and I do not know if she will ever be one. Her voice is agreeable and slender, like her figure, but it is not a true voice of the theatre; it has a thin timbre which passes through the crowd without occupying a place. The almost pastoral role of Alice (in *Roberto il Diavolo*) suits her well enough and some phrases here and there she sings well enough, and even with a certain élan, or rather with a certain boldness which derives, I fancy, from the faith she places in her physical attractions. True dramatic feeling, true spontaneity and power of accentuation she does not, in my opinion, possess; her gestures have been taught by masters of mimicry and her phrasing must be the faithful imitation of what some Lamperti or other has taught her. Everything she does seems to be copied from somebody else. She shows two good qualities. She pronounces well (though not superlatively well) and she rarely looks at the conductor. If I were the conductor [Faccio] I should protest against this, but it is a sign there is something musical in this young lady. But true artistic inspiration eludes her. I was in a box on the stage and so in a rather good position to judge the strength of voice and clarity of enunciation. At the end I realised that I had been looking at her for the whole evening, that is a tribute to the charm of her face and figure and the whiteness of her teeth—nothing more. A pity! But I do not believe that Bellincioni was destined to be strangled in the Isle of Cyprus.[4]

Probably as a result of this letter, Verdi himself went to hear her in her next role at La Scala, Violetta, and formed an altogether more favourable impression of her talents, but whether out of deference to Boito or not, she was not invited to create Desdemona. From the evidence of gramophone records and the strongly dramatic nature of so much of her later repertory, the part would probably not have suited her anyway. It was not until 1890 that she was offered a role that did exactly fit her particular talents. In that year, with her husband, the tenor Roberto Stagno, she created Santuzza in *Cavalleria* and 'by the singularity of her performance, by its vocal ardency, and rustic delineation of character, she laid claims to a place in operatic history'.[5]

In her autobiography, she describes her enthusiasm for what remained throughout her career her most popular role, though she was subsequently to take part in at least another dozen world premieres:

It seemed to me that the music was so wedded to the story, so much a part of it, that together they became a single homogenous entity, enabling me to reveal to the public my own artistic ideals. I broke away from every outmoded tradition of the lyric stage, abandoning myself to 'recitar cantando', in a complete and harmonious unity, so that I was able to express fully all the grievous sorrow in Santuzza's heart.[6]

In Latin countries where the sincerity of her performances carried all before it, her vocal inadequacy was overlooked. On her only visit to London,† at Covent Garden, in 1895, she was not enthusiastically received as Santuzza or Carmen. David Bispham, who was the Alfio in *Cavalleria*, admired her 'superbly controlled emotion' but noted 'her voice was not of the best quality and was already in decline';[7] at that time she was only thirty. *The Times* felt much the same:

It is as an actress she will mostly be judged, for it must be at once admitted her voice is not particularly sympathetic or remarkable in any way, nor does any exceptional skill in its use make up for natural defects . . . her vocal powers do not encourage the idea that she will supplant Mme Calvé in the affections of the English audiences.[8]

Nor did she. Of all her defects, again it was the tremolo which was found the most distracting. From 1890 onwards, in her gradual desertion of the lyric repertory for dramatic parts her voice was the inevitable sufferer. Perhaps she realised it too, when at Turin in 1906 as Salome, under Strauss's own direction, she chose to do the Dance of the Seven Veils herself.

She recorded for the G & T company and Pathé; though she was not more than forty, there is little left except a rather hoarse and tremulous intensity. Fedora's 'O grandi occhi', and 'Voi lo sapete' remain suggestive; a compelling authenticity of style is some compensation for the uncertain intonation. In 'Ah! fors' è lui' this is less easy to ignore, though the interpretation has some interesting details and there is a lovely piano high C in the cadenza. Even at her best, however, it is doubtful if a gramophone record could ever have given us more than a keyhole glimpse of her art. Given only the voice in decay, without her extraordinary personality and hist-

† The 'Signora Bellincioni' who sang at Her Majesty's in 1889 was her elder sister, Saffo.

119 Bellincioni at the age of sixty

rionic gifts, we shall never know which of her contemporaries was right, or whether perhaps they all were.

Bellincioni's personality enabled her to triumph over a modest vocal endowment. Like Duse, to whom she was often compared, the separation between her real and stage personality was never very clear; she inhabited a theatrical limbo, half way between reality and the melodrama. Henry Russell's description of Duse the day after a performance sitting alone in a darkened room in order to recharge her depleted emotional reserves, gives us some inkling of what this self-indulgent style cost, and Duse did not have to worry whether she would be able to sing the next night. We may imagine its effect on an instrument as delicate as the human voice: Bellincioni, Storchio, Pandolfini,

Carelli and Ferrani all lost their voices at a relatively early age.

Pandolfini and Carelli were both personality singers, both from musical families and both outstanding representatives of the verismo style. Pandolfini's father had created Amonasro in the Italian premiere of *Aida* at La Scala in 1872. Carelli's father, a Professor of Singing at the Conservatory of San Pietro a Majella in Naples, included among his pupils Fernando de Lucia, Pasquale Amato and Francesco Bonini. Though ANGELICA PANDOL-FINI (1871–1959) made her debut as Marguerite in *Faust*, in 1894, she was soon singing Santuzza, Manon Lescaut and Mimi, the latter in many Italian theatres: the San Carlo, the Argentina and Costanzi in Rome, at Florence, Venice and Bologna. In 1900 she succeeded Hariclea Darclée as Tosca in Milan and Rome. Two years later at the Lirico, Milan, she created the title-role in Cilea's *Adriana Lecouvreur* with Caruso and de Luca. Following her marriage in 1909, she retired at the early age of thirty-eight. Her singing was frequently subjected to strong criticism: as Violetta at the San Carlo 'she sang the high lying passages harshly and out of tune', and Aida was thought 'to tax her to the limits'.[9]

Her recording of the entrance aria of Adriana has always been a super rarity; though of historic importance, as an interpretation it seems quite unremarkable. The voice is sweeter and the manner altogether more attractive in Godard's delightful, and undemanding, 'Chanson de Florian'.

EMMA CARELLI (1877–1928) was a handsome and intelligent woman, but her singing too was not of the first class:

Her voice was a short one, but of warm timbre, most fluent and easy in the middle and lower registers. By skilful and careful teaching, and hard work, she conquered the high notes necessary for the great dramatic roles of verismo opera. She had a good legato style and clarity of diction. It was the sincerity of style

120 Angelica Pandolfini

121 Emma Carelli

and vivid dramatic acting rather than sheer beauty of voice that gained her reputation in Italy and South America.[10]

Like Pandolfini she began with lyrical roles from the earlier repertory. At her debut she appeared as Giulia in Mercadante's *Vestale*, and later that same year sang Giulietta in Bellini's *Capuleti ed i Montecchi,* in which Caruso was Tebaldo. In 1899, in Rome, she had graduated to Margherita in *Mefistofele* (again with Caruso); according to one critic, her interpretation, though vivid in the fashion of the verismo school, was lacking in taste and exaggerated in style. Later that year she made her Scala debut as Desdemona opposite Tamagno's Otello. Subsequently, she sang there Elsa, Mimi, Margherita, and Tatiana in *Eugenio Oneghin*. In South America she appeared as Iris and Santuzza; in Spain and Portugal as Tosca; and in Russia as Fedora, Zazà, Gioconda and Adriana Lecouvreur, all to great effect. In 1910 her husband, Walter Mocchi, a prominent political figure of the day who was responsible for establishing the Società Teatrale Italo-Argentina, an organisation through which Italian interests were made to prevail in the South American theatres, was appointed Director of the Costanzi in Rome. After Carelli's final season there, in the title-role of Strauss's *Elettra*, she joined him in the artistic management, and remained in charge until 1926. Two years later she was killed in a car smash. Duse sent a wreath, with the message 'I thank her as a sister with love and admiration.'

A recording of Stefania's 'Nel suo amore' from Giordano's *Siberia*, one of the few agreeable pages from a score in general as grim as the title suggests, shows her to her best advantage. It is a typically Italian voice, white and open-sounding in the middle register; at the top, the head notes though secure are rather pinched. She phrases attractively enough, lingering affectionately on the high notes but without being able to make anything like the effect Giannina Russ does in the same piece.

By no means all the principal verismo roles needed dramatic singers, even if most of them were capable of a dramatic interpretation. Nedda and Mimi, for example, as Melba proved outside Italy, could make quite as much effect sung by a lyric soprano whose voice still exemplified most of the virtues of the old Italian school of Patti. In fact, both of these roles were created by lyric sopranos, Nedda by Adelina Stehle and Mimi by Cesira Ferrani. The latter, the elder by two years, was a pupil of a

famous Austrian soprano, Antonietta Freich, alias Fricci, one of Marchesi's Viennese pupils. Ferrani's career began in Turin, her birthplace, as Gilda in 1887. During the next six years she progressed through Elsa, Desdemona (opposite de Negri in Genoa), Inez in *Africana*, Amelia in *Simon Boccanegra*, Anna in Catalani's *Loreley* and Suzel in *Amico Fritz*. In 1893 she was invited to create the title-role in Puccini's *Manon Lescaut* at the Teatro Reggio, Turin; it was the composer's first big success, and we may believe that sentiment entered into it when, three years later, he selected her again to create Mimi, in the same theatre. Whether Ferrani had anything to do with it, initially *Bohème* was not so successful; not until 1898, at the Massimo, Palermo, when the roles of Rodolfo and Mimi were taken by Garbin and his wife, Stehle, did the work find its proper niche in the repertory. The couple had previously created Fenton and Nanetta, in 1893, and Stehle had been the first Walter in Catalani's *Wally,* as well as the first Nedda with Giraud and Maurel, at the Dal Verme, Milan, the previous year. Like Ferrani, her other roles included Gilda, Elsa, Violetta, the Queen in *Ugonotti*, Ophélie in *Amleto* and Mathilde in *Guglielmo Tell*. Later in her career she ventured as far as Fedora and Adriana Lecouvreur. After retiring from the stage, she became a teacher, one of her best-known pupils being Giannina Arangi-Lombardi. Unfortunately Stehle made no solo recordings; she can only be heard in the spaces left by her husband in a duet from *Adriana Lecouvreur*, and with him Sammarco and Camporelli in the third act quartet from *Bohème*. Ferrani's last appearances at La Scala were in 1908, as Mélisande with Giraud and Amato; as Gatti recalls in his memoirs, the performances were a humiliating experience as much for the singers as for Debussy. The reception was, if anything, even worse when she ventured the role again, in Rome, the following year: they were her last stage performances.

The recordings of CESIRA FERRANI (1863–1943), made in 1903, include two solos each from *Bohème* and *Manon Lescaut*. Hers is a typical Mimi voice, with the characteristics we should expect to hear from a singer in this music today. The quality is pleasing though she has little support left and there is not much legato; the phrasing lacks breadth and the tone has become quavery. For all that, Mimi's 'racconto' has the right girlishness; though she must have sung it time out of number by then, it is still an expressive interpretation with even a suggestion of improvisation. As Manon, she is

122 Cesira Ferrani as Melisande

in many of her contemporaries, nor is the tone of the voice as open-sounding. Perhaps, albeit diluted, the example of Marchesi reached down to her via Fricci.

A lyric soprano with a rather different reputation but whose voice was not so dissimilar was the remarkable LINA CAVALIERI (1874–1944)—'La donna piu bella del mondo', as she liked to style herself. It was said that she began her career in the Piazza di Spagna, Rome, selling flowers—well, if so, not for long. At the age of twelve or thirteen (as she would have it), she moved indoors, into a famous café of those days, La Torre di Belisario. There she was already able to titillate the young swells with what she put into her saucy songs and what she largely left out of her dresses, covering over instead with rhinestones. Within a few years she had graduated to the variety stages of the Eldorado and Alhambra in Rome, the Empire in London and the Folies-Bergères. By this time the home-made dresses had given way to creations by Worth and the paste was replaced by the real thing. But Cavalieri was an ambitious young woman, and in 1900 she quit Variety to take up a career in opera. She took lessons from Mme Mariani-Masi and made her debut at the Teatro Sao Carlos in Lisbon in 1900 as Mimi. She was instantly successful. There followed performances in Warsaw and St Petersburg, where she met and quickly married a wealthy Russian nobleman, Prince Bariatinski. Once she had secured the title and part of his fortune she left him and Russia. In the course of the next few years she appeared in Monte Carlo (there she created Ensoleidad in the world premiere of Massenet's *Chérubin*), and in Paris with Caruso and Ruffo. In the autumn of 1906 she made her Met debut in the first performance there of Giordano's *Fedora*. Henderson thought she 'justified her reputation as a beauty . . . Her voice is a light lyric soprano, very pretty in quality but not rich or vibrant'.[11] Her other roles included Manon Lescaut, Mimi, Nedda and Tosca (in lieu of an ailing Eames). But the biggest sensation she created was when she married the multi-millionaire Winthrop Chanler and cajoled him into making over his entire fortune to her; then, within a week, she left him too. Chanler's brother, whom he had had committed to an institution, sent him the short but apposite note: 'Who's looney now?' After this Cavalieri was obliged to withdraw to Europe. London was agog to see her and was pleasantly surprised by what they heard too:

> Everyone was surprised to find her voice, though not in its first freshness, was quite effective in grand opera and of remarkably agreeable quality. If she seemed last

unable to float the opening phrase of 'In quelle trine morbide', and the climax extends her to the limits, the high B flat collapsing into an unsupported slide. However, she sings entirely without recourse to the cheap, extra-musical effects that later became so familiar in these works. Rodolfo Celletti has written that her vocal style lies somewhere between the colder northern singers and the more neurasthenic modern Italian school; it is true that the registers, though clearly marked, are not as separate as found

123 Lina Cavalieri

third husband, Lucien Muratore, the French tenor. She failed to fulfil an engagement with him at the Chicago Opera but she appeared in concert in New York at the Hippodrome. Her encore was a little number by Harry von Tilzer with the apocalyptic title 'Last night was the end of the world'. It was an appropriately theatrical choice, fitting in well with her life style; after retiring from the opera she had another career in the cinema and yet another husband, but with him she stayed right to the end. They were killed together in bed in their Florence palazzo during an allied raid on the city in 1944.

In reputation though not repertory, Gemma Bellincioni was succeeded by ROSINA STORCHIO (1876–1945). Hers too was a light voice, almost a soubrette, but unlike Bellincioni, though her style was conditioned by the verismo roles she sang, she did not abandon everything else. Throughout her career she balanced Butterfly, Wally, Zazà and Mimi with Amina, Norina, Violetta and Manon. A pupil of Melchiorre Vidal, she made her first stage appearance at the age of sixteen, in the title-role of Arnoldo Galliera's *Trilby*. Her formal debut took place later that same year, as Micaëla at the Dal Verme. In less than three years she reached La Scala, as Sophie in *Werther* with Adini and Valero. In 1897 Leoncavallo invited her to create the other Mimi in his *Bohème* in Venice, and three years later at the Teatro Lirico, Milan, she was the first Zazà. After extensive tours in Russia, and then Spain and Portugal and Central and South America, she returned to La Scala in 1902 as Linda. During nine seasons and until her final appearances there, as Norina in 1918, she was a 'creatura della Scala'. There she sang Hansel, Euryanthe, Wally, Susanna, Zerlina in *Fra Diavolo*, Violetta, Amina, Mimi, Manon and Mignon. At La Scala she took part in two world premieres, as Stefania in Giordano's *Siberia* with Zenatello and de Luca under Toscanini and, in the same company, the title-role in the first version of *Madama Butterfly*, in 1904. The performance was a fiasco. From the beginning the gallery was restive and there had been intermittent booing, but when Butterfly came out with the child, 'Trouble', the audience took the cue and Storchio was greeted with derisory laughter and a stream of ribald remarks. She vowed she would never sing the part again at La Scala, and kept her word, but the incident had no lasting effect on her relations with the audience or the management. For Giulio Gatti-Casazza, as a rule rather restrained in his praises of prima donnas—not surprisingly for he married one of the most difficult,

night to have rather less power than is wanted in Covent Garden . . . she sings excellently in tune and phrases well and musically.[12]

Records substantiate these judgments. In Manon's 'In quelle trine morbide' we hear a warm and attractive lyric soprano, occasionally a little under-powered, when the voice has a tendency to slip below the centre of pitch, but having no difficulty rising to a good B flat. She phrases appealingly and without overemphasis.

After an interval of a few years, in 1913, she returned to the United States arm-in-arm with her

Frances Alda, and had to deal with many others in a long career as an impresario—Storchio was an exception:

> . . . the best rounded and perfect artist. Her voice was suave and penetrating; she was an interpreter full of taste; she had impeccable diction, facial expressiveness to the highest degree and an artistic temperament of the greatest versatility.[13]

Since Gatti, at the same time, was also Director of the Met, and Toscanini was conducting there too, it must remain a mystery why she did not go to New York at the height of her career, when her interpretive powers were at their peak and her voice was still fresh. Her only New York appearances were at the Manhattan in 1921, as Butterfly, and though she was only forty-four, her voice was already worn out. However, Henderson noted 'the childish prattle in Act One had never been done with such artistry'.[14]

In the opinion of Rodolfo Celletti, the gramophone hardly does Storchio justice. She was only in her early thirties, but the voice, especially in the middle register, is already threadbare. Her remarkable personality made such an effect in the theatre, but little of it gets through to the records. She is at her best in a pretty number from Leoncavallo's *Bohème*,† more operetta than opera: a captivating performance, even if the impression that lingers is of an operetta singer past her best. We cannot know how she sounded in her youth, but by this time at any rate, Linda's 'O luce di quest' anima' and Norina's 'Quel guardo' lay outside her range.

Only six months after that unfortunate premiere Puccini had rewritten *Madama Butterfly* to produce what is essentially the work we know today. The revised version was given for the first time in the autumn of 1904, at Brescia, with SALOMEA KRUSCENISKI (1872–1952) in the title-role and was the success it has ever after proved to be. Krusceniski, born near Lemberg, in what was then Austro-Hungary, now Lvov in Russia, studied at the local Conservatory with Valery Wysocki, one of Poland's leading teachers whose pupils also included Janina Korolewicz-Wayda and Adamo Didur. She made her debut at Lemberg in 1892, soon afterwards appearing in Odessa and Cracow. In 1896 she sang in Italy for the first time, at Trieste, as Leonora in *Forza del Destino*. She was much liked and returned for performances at the Costanzi,

† Curiously this aria, 'Mimi Pinson', is sung by Musetta, though Storchio had created the part of Mimi.

124 Salomea Krusceniski as Desdemona

Rome, the San Carlo and La Scala. Between 1898 and 1903 she was a member of the company at Warsaw, but in the latter year after becoming involved in a political demonstration she settled in Italy and did not sing in Poland again for many years. There, she was particularly associated with the new repertory; as well as Butterfly, she was the first Francesca in Mancinelli's *Paolo e Francesca,* took part in the world premiere of Cilea's *Gloria* in 1907, and in 1915 created the title-role in Pizzetti's *Fedra*. She made regular visits to Spain and Portugal, and South America. Of her Wally in Catalani's opera, in Buenos Aires in 1906, the critic of *Prensa* wrote:

The singer is above all an artist of great talent and heart, an interpreter as fine as her intentions are profound. She has made a meticulous analysis of the role of Wally which she performs with great veracity . . . this was not Krusceniski on the stage but Wally.[15]

If her artistic dedication was in accord with the ideals of the verismo, her singing was open to the usual objections:

She had a very good voice but it was slightly inclined to be shrill; she compensated for this by her acting.[16]

At La Scala she was one of the leading figures in the introduction of the German repertory, singing Isolde, Brünnhilde, Elektra and Salome, all of them in Italian, and in the last named, like Bellincioni, doing the dancing herself 'with a discretion that did not exclude refined sensualism'. Gatti thought her Salome 'an interesting performance and better than all the others'. But, like Storchio, she never went to the Met and sang only once in New York, long after her best days were over; in a concert at the Mecca Auditorium in 1928, when she was fifty-six. Her very last public performance took place in her native Poland. While on a visit to relatives in 1939, the Second World War broke out; stranded for the duration, she became a teacher at the Lvov Conservatory and there, in 1945, sang in a victory concert.

On records we hear a warm and beautiful voice of a much better quality than some of her contemporaries. Her account of Margherita's Mad Scene is done in typical verismo style: the vibrato is exaggerated for dramatic effect in the climaxes, the coloratura delivered in a forcefully affecting manner—though more accurately than in some other versions—the whole piece suffused in a doleful tone. To an extent it works, but ultimately the tearfulness makes it impossible to give the

expansive phrases their proper measure. She is more restrained and therefore more affecting in Catalini's 'Ebben ne andrò lontana' from *Wally*, which is one of the finest interpretations of this aria.

Krusceniski is usually included among Polish singers, though, in fact, she was Ruthenian. As her name suggests, TERESA ARKEL (1861–1929), née Blumenfeld, also from Lemberg,† was of German extraction. As a result of conquest and re-conquest, this part of Eastern Europe had become, by the end of the nineteenth century, a polyglot of different nationalities. Arkel, eleven years older than Krusceniski, was also a graduate of the Lemberg Conservatory. She made her debut in 1884, thereafter singing in Prague, Hamburg, Bilbao, Madrid and Lisbon, from the beginning in dramatic roles: Norma, Valentine, Elsa and Aida. In 1891 she was invited to La Scala to take the part of Venus in the first production there of Wagner's *Tannhäuser*, with Darclée, de Negri and Scheidemantel. Later she sang Norma with Virginia Guerrini as Adalgisa and Desdemona opposite Tamagno. As a result of her Italian successes she moved to Milan, though still returning fairly regularly for performances in Poland. In Italy, she specialised in the Wagnerian roles: Isolde, Brünnhilde and Sieglinde. After she retired from the stage, she taught singing in Milan. Her pupils included Lucette Korsoff, Claire Dux and Eugenia Bronskaya.

By the time she made her recordings Arkel was on the verge of retirement, and her voice is hardly as attractive as Krusceniski's. Though her career was less closely associated with the 'modern' Italian school, she adopted, records suggest, many of its mannerisms. In 'Spunta l'aurora' from *Mefistofele*, she relies heavily on the coup de glotte and an agitated vibrato. The high notes have that very Italian 'squillante' that might be spelled more suggestively 'squealante'. Years of driving up the chest register have produced a patch of breathy tones between F and A above middle C. The supercharged emotionalism is self-defeating; the phrasing is so chopped and jerky that she is unable to knit the piece together, and the music disappears through the gaps.

The growing interest in the operas of Wagner in Italy during the first decade of this century, the introduction of these works into the repertory at La Scala, the Costanzi, the San Carlo, and in South

† Before the First World War Lemberg was in Austria, after which it was renamed Lvov and included in Eastern Poland. In 1940, following the Ribbentrop-Molotov Pact, this region was annexed by the Soviet Union.

125 Teresa Arkel

126 Amelia Pinto as Isolde

America, offered a new challenge and one that Italian singers (the works were given in the vernacular) met with varying degrees of success. The first Isolde at La Scala, AMELIA PINTO (1878–1946), who sang opposite Borgatti's Tristan under Toscanini's direction, made a speciality out of the role during a short career, singing it in Rome, Trieste, Naples, Lisbon, Cairo, Alexandria and Buenos Aires. A pupil of Cortini Falchi at the Liceo di Santa Cecilia in Rome, she made her debut as Gioconda at Brescia in 1899. After some performances of Tosca at Lucca, she was invited to La Scala. In spite of her successes as Brünnhilde in *Valchiria* and Isolde, she did not neglect the Italian repertory. At La Scala she was Ricke in the world premiere of Franchetti's *Germania* with Caruso and Sammarco and also appeared as Elena in *Mefistofele*. Elsewhere she sang Tosca, Stefania in *Siberia* and Desdemona.

In her first series of recordings, made in 1902, Pinto's voice is at its freshest; not as warm as Krusceniski's, but more pleasing than Arkel's. In Ero's romanza from Bottesini's *Ero e Leandro* she makes a fine effect, rising easily and impressively to the climax. Although she is very much a verismo singer, and despite some tremulousness and a hard attack, she is more restrained than some of her contemporaries. Bottesini, a virtuoso cellist, better known as a composer for his own instrument, used a libretto by Boito; later on it was re-set by Luigi Mancinelli.

JANINA KOROLEWICZ-WAYDA (1875–1957) though of Polish birth was principally associated with the major roles of the international repertory. She was a student of Wysocki, the teacher of the bass Adamo Didur. She made a precocious debut while still in her teens, as Hanna in Moniuszko's *Haunted Castle* in 1893. During the next ten years she sang extensively in Poland, principally coloratura roles: Gilda, Rosina, Juliette and Dinorah. By 1904, when she made her Covent Garden debut, she had advanced to a more lyric repertory: Marguerite, Nedda and Elsa. She returned in the autumn of 1906 but without making much impression. Was that why Melba engaged her for one of her Australian tours in 1911? In her memoirs, Korolewicz-Wayda has left us an engaging account of her travels—and her relations with Melba. In Warsaw again she had moved on to Rachel, Gioconda, Aida, Amelia, Elisabeth, even Brünnhilde. In 1917 she was appointed Director of the Warsaw Opera; she was the first woman to become manager of an opera house. She held the job twice,

between 1917 and 1919 and again between 1934 and 1936.

The voice we hear in a recording of Eudoxie's aria from *La Juive* (sung in Polish) is a full lyric soprano, brilliant at the top but less impressive in the lower range and without a completely developed chest register. It has a slightly throaty quality; certain intervals are not managed without the help of aspirates. On this evidence she does not seem to have had a good legato style or to phrase expressively; though it would take a great deal of eloquence to make anything out of such meretricious music. In part of the third act duet from *Aida* with the tenor Tadeusz Leliva (also in Polish), though the high notes make a thrilling effect, her attack is hard and not always exact. With Leliva again in a duet from Orefice's *Chopin* (a not very felicitous arrangement of the famous E Flat Nocturne), she shows the same healthy voice, but such expression as there is comes mostly from him.

127 Janina Korolewicz-Wayda

128 Maria de Macchi as Aida

129 Giannina Russ

26. Four Dramatic Sopranos

During the first decade of this century there were four outstanding Italian-born dramatic sopranos: Maria de Macchi, Eugenia Burzio, Celestina Boninsegna and Giannina Russ, who, though they often sang in what were then contemporary works, were noted exponents of the great roles of the traditional Italian repertory. All four recorded 'Casta Diva'; two, de Macchi and Boninsegna, had a direct link with the so-called ottocento period; they were pupils of Virginia Boccabadati, a favourite singer of Verdi's and daughter of Luigia Boccabadati, a noted prima donna of Donizetti's day.

MARIA DE MACCHI (1870–1909), the eldest, began her career in 1889 as a mezzo, singing Laura in *Gioconda*, but she soon moved up to soprano roles. She appeared throughout Italy and on tour in Russia, Spain and Portugal. In 1901 for one season she was at La Scala in the title-role of Goldmark's *Regina di Saba*. As a result of Caruso's good offices, three years later she secured an engagement at the Met. Her debut was in the title-role of Donizetti's *Lucrezia Borgia*, the one and only performance given of it there. Later she sang Santuzza, Valentine and Aida, but without enjoying a success. She died at the early age of thirty-nine in 1909. In a recording of Paolina's 'Di quai soavi lacrime' from Donizetti's *Poliuto*, though she shapes the cantilena

130 Celestina Boninsegna as Elena in Boito's *Mefistofele*

131 Eugenia Burzio as Gioconda

expressively, containing the ornaments within a good legato, the voice itself is rather hard driven, especially the top notes—Santuzza looking over Paolina's shoulder?

EUGENIA BURZIO (1872–1922) did not sing in the United States or in Great Britain. Born in Turin, she made her debut there in 1903. During the next couple of years, at various theatres in Italy and South America, she sang in Cilea's *Arlesiana, Tosca, Fedora, Andrea Chenier* and *Gioconda*. In 1906 at La Scala she created Caterina in Alfano's *Resurrezione*, afterwards appearing in Franchetti's *Figlia di Jorio* and Catalani's *Loreley*. The following season came *Wally, Santuzza, Aida* and *Gioconda*. In the summer of 1907, in Buenos Aires, she sang Valentine; at La

Scala in 1911, Norma, and the title-roles in Gluck's *Armida* and Pacini's *Saffo*. Her career was cut short by ill-health and she died in 1922. GIANNINA RUSS's (1878–1951) career also began in 1903, at Bologna, where she appeared as Semiramide, Abigaille in *Nabucco* and Elena in *Vespri Siciliani*. In the summer of 1904 she sang Aida and Amelia at Covent Garden, both opposite Caruso; 'her dramatic gifts were appreciated but her voice did not possess the necessary suavity that the music requires.'[1] In 1905 she made her debut at La Scala as Aida, after which she appeared as Elisabeth in *Tannhäuser* and the Contessa in *Nozze di Figaro*. Later that year she visited Paris, Monte Carlo and South America. She was a member of Hammerstein's company at the

Manhattan during his first two seasons, where her roles included Donna Anna, Elvira in *Ernani,* Valentine, Gioconda and Santuzza. She sang Norma for the first time, in Florence, in 1908.

Of this quartet, CELESTINA BONINSEGNA (1877–1947), though she was not especially successful in any major theatre, is undoubtedly the most renowned today, because of her records. As a girl she sang Norina and Marguerite in *Faust.* After her official debut, however, she specialised in Verdi's *Ballo, Aida* and *Trovatore,* in which she appeared at various Italian theatres. In the autumn of 1904 she sang at Covent Garden, taking the same roles—Aida and Amelia—that Russ had sung the previous summer. In 1904 she sang at La Scala, but without success. At the end of the following year she went to the Met as Aida:

> Her voice of light calibre was pleasing but scarcely big enough for the dramatic requirements of the part; her vibrato was pronounced and once or twice she sang flat.[2]

Riccardo Stracciari, who sang Amonasro with her, offers a different explanation for why she failed to impress the New York critics or public:

> She was the only one who sang Aida the way I thought it should be sung ... Her voice was so big and beautiful, sheer velvet, but she had no charm, no elegance of person, and when she appeared in her Met debut, her ample form swathed in chocolate-coloured underwear, New York could not forgive her.[3]

One can imagine that Boninsegna must have appeared crude and provincial to audiences used to Eames's Aida. Even if Eames's voice was not ideally suited to the role, her singing was pure and eloquent—and she was gowned in costumes created in Paris from designs by her husband, the fashionable portrait painter, Julian Storey. Not surprisingly these were thought more seemly for Aida than Boninsegna's 'chocolate-coloured underwear'. She may have been in captivity, but she was, after all, a King's daughter!

Whatever reservations were made about Boninsegna by her contemporaries, we can readily hear why her records have appealed to generations of collectors. The voice is important-sounding, extending from bottom A to the high C, the scale fully equalised though the registers are not always blended together smoothly. Her singing is of the verismo school but without its more extravagant manifestations; the emission of tone is suaver and,

pace the New York critics, there is less vibrato and she rarely forces the tone. Yet it is difficult not to feel these to be only negative virtues, that her restraint is not a matter of taste, only a lack of temperament. In Santuzza's 'Voi lo sapete', though the singing is absolutely in the right style—the voice's sharply defined registers enabling her to contrast a plangent middle register with some brassy chest notes and paper over the cracks between with a few suitable sobs—as an interpretation it is without character and wanting in real feeling. It is interesting to compare her to Eames in the same piece: locked into Marchesi's ruthlessly high 'placement' (the voce fissa, as the Italians called it) her voice does not easily come by the wide range of tonal colour which Boninsegna has at her command and which the music ideally calls for. To compensate for this, Eames uses a strongly marked declamatory style, communicating anguish through intensity of tone; in spite of her method, the passion seems more genuine.

Eugenia Burzio's records divide opinions sharply and are more difficult to appreciate in an age that has long since rejected the tenets of the verismo. The quality of the voice is not as attractive as Boninsegna's. In other respects, range and power, there is a considerable resemblance. Both recorded Leonora's 'Pace, pace mio Dio' from *Forza.* Boninsegna's is the more conventional performance, well sung, though not to be numbered among the best, and with rather a narrow range of dynamics. It is a curiously detached account of what is very dramatic music. From the start she fails to capture the right atmosphere, hurrying over the opening 'Pace'; the phrasing is conventional and lacks eloquence, and key words are let pass without receiving their proper due. As Henderson put it in another context, 'not an interpretation, merely articulation'. Burzio, by contrast, fairly gorges herself on Leonora's distress, taking a very free view of the notation and helping herself abundantly to rubato. It may seem extravagant to our more chaste notions of the way this sort of thing ought to be done, but it is undeniably effective. The words are all made to tell—from the beginning we know the lady to be in extremis—and the ritards and accelerandi are not mere caprice, they are used to make the maximum contrast between Leonora's prayer and her anguished outbursts against fate. It is a vivid interpretation, very much of its times; but in view of Verdi's known affection for dramatic singers—Strepponi, Tamberlik, Tamagno, Maurel and Bellincioni, among many—and his oft-

breath support, and many of her later records (made when she was only just turned thirty) are spoilt by dubious intonation. It is a moot point whether her voice was really equal to all the demands she made of it. She seems so much more at home as Mimi than scaling the heights of Norma. Her soft warm-grained timbre is affecting in 'Mi chiamano Mimi', where she has quite sufficient resources to fill out the climactic phrases. A recording of 'Casta Diva' (one verse, but with two of 'Ah bello a me ritorna') though pleasingly vocalised, is rather lacking in authority. She transposes the cabaletta.

27. Tetrazzini and some 'Coloraturas'

There was at this time, however, one Italian soprano whose fame was universal, who sang with equal success in Moscow and Mexico City: that was LUISA TETRAZZINI (1871–1940). For years she made the rounds of the provincial Italian opera houses, visiting Russia, Spain and Portugal, and, with her own company, organised by the first of three husbands, touring extensively in Central and South America. As well as the 'Patti' repertory, she sang Leonora in *Forza del Destino*, Ophélie, Mathilde in *Guglielmo Tell*, Philine, Oscar, Musetta and even Aida, in which she created a sensation, capping the great ensemble at the end of the Triumphal scene with a stunning full-throated high E flat. Through all these peregrinations she earned golden opinions and matching fees. Then in 1907, when she was already thirty-six and might be thought to have passed her best days, she became, literally overnight, a great star: she was engaged to sing Violetta in the unfashionable autumn season at Covent Garden. Bookings being sparse, Higgins, then the theatre's managing director, tried to get out of the contract at the last minute, but Tetrazzini insisted on coming. So it was to a bleak house, the fog inside as well, that she came, sang and conquered. Those years that she had spent on the periphery of the Italian opera scene had been invaluable; she had developed a phenomenal florid technique and acquired a vocal poise that no passing mishap could shake. To this she added an intuitive musicianship, a feeling for the shape of a phrase, where to interpolate a trill, mordent or high note, so as to make it sound appropriate, spontaneous and inevitable—if the composer did not put

132 Luisa Tetrazzini as Gilda

expressed concern for effect, we may believe he would have found much in it to approve of.

Of the quartet, Russ's voice was the most attractive, less powerful than Boninsegna's and without the shrill quality of either de Macchi or Burzio. The fluttery tone easily accounts for her relative failure outside the Latin opera centres. Recordings suggest that she had a tendency to oversing, in particular at the top of the voice—indeed, when she appeared at the Manhattan she was rebuked for shouting the high notes. This habit gradually undermined her technique, especially the

it there then he should have!

Her London engagement had followed from a 1905 season in San Francisco, when she had come into the United States, so to speak, through the back door. On that occasion Conried, then the Met's manager, had taken an option on her services, but for some reason failed to avail himself of them and missed the chance of a lifetime. It fell to Hammerstein to introduce her to New York in his second season at the Manhattan. There she repeated her Violetta to a clamorous audience. A critic described the effect she made with the high E flat at the end of 'Sempre libera':

> Singing that magnificent note, Tetrazzini bent to gather up the long train of her gown and proceeded to walk off the stage, all the while affecting the utmost insouciance and all the while holding on to that phenomenal E flat till she had disappeared from view. This tour de force brought the house down.[1]

Generally, however, the critics were less than unanimous; perhaps, as has been suggested, they did not like to take their stars ready-made from London, preferring to find their own. They did so some years later when the Chicago company brought Galli-Curci to town, an amiable vocalist with a sweet voice and an engaging manner but not in the Tetrazzini class. On that occasion they broke out in a rash of superlatives, which within a few short years Galli-Curci's increasingly indifferent vocalism made to seem ridiculous.

The main criticism of Tetrazzini was that the middle of her voice 'sounded like the wailing of a cross infant'.[2] And certainly her singing, though largely free from the excesses of the verismo style, had still one aspect of its vocalism: the registers were very clearly delineated and not properly equalised like those of Patti, Melba or Sembrich. In the opinion of John McCormack, who sang with her often, the comparative weakness of the middle register was the result of overwork and an uncongenial repertory in her youth.[3] In fact this does not seem likely, for Tetrazzini always sings well within her means on records, and it is more probable that her voice was late maturing; the middle, which develops with experience, always takes the longest time to compose itself. This is borne out in Richard Aldrich's review of a concert she gave in New York in 1919:

> The inferior quality of her lower tones, which on her first appearance here had a singular infantile quality

133 Tetrazzini

that many will remember, she had succeeded to some extent in bettering before her departure. This quality seems now almost wholly to have disappeared, and the whole range of the voice is more nearly equalised.[4]

It is also confirmed in some unpublished recordings, made a few years later, which have only recently come to light. Apart from anything else it would seem logical that an infantile quality is the result of a lack of development, rather than an over-development. Paradoxically, what upset the critics appealed to the public; though Tetrazzini's singing hardly had the polish of the eighteenth-century virtuosi, it did contain to a greater extent than is customary in a female voice that irresistible combination we have mentioned before in connexion with the castrati: the child's naturally affecting quality, powered by an adult's bellows.

Tetrazzini's astounding technique was founded in complete control of the breath; the voice, as it were, sitting on top of it. Above the high A, where most lyric soprano voices turn sour, hers remained rounded—indeed, seemed as it ascended to take on a new strength and surety. In this altitudinous region, she cavorted with ease, tossing off the most intricate patterns of staccati, as in the Mireille waltz, and running up and down chromatic scales; at the end of Proch's variations there is a perfect marvel, from E flat in alt down an octave and back up again, all in one breath. She was renowned for her ability to conjure a high C out of the air, swell it to forte, and then diminish it to the merest thread of tone. But all these effects she used in a musical way; they were not only astounding, they were beautiful too, and entirely appropriate in their setting. She was a considerable vocal actress, however incredible she may have looked as Amina, Violetta or Rosina. Not surprisingly, 'Sempre libera' is a knock-out, but 'Addio del passato' is just as wonderful with its sorrowful tone, beautifully drawn portamenti and dolce high As. If her recordings of 'Pace, pace mio Dio' and 'Ritorna vincitor' are not among her best, many another soprano would have been well satisfied with them. They show she was no soubrette, for her voice was big as well as brilliant, but the drama was always in the singing; even in such a display piece as Venzano's 'Grande Valse', the way she launches into the second verse, the attack powerful and clean with no trace of the coup de glotte, imparts a dramatic thrill. This piece exemplifies the rhythmic brio which was characteristic of all her singing.

She was a natural comedienne. 'Una voce poco fa' (sung in the original key of E) not only dazzles us, but by genuinely musical touches, at the same time, encapsulates Rosina's character—it is a classic performance and has not been equalled since. On occasion, when no one could stop her, she even clambered into hose for Verdi's Oscar; photographs look as if her corset was suffering from whalebone fatigue. But when she sang 'Saper vorreste' it was of small account. There is no other performance on record that so perfectly marries wit to prodigious vocalism. How roguishly she teases—'Oscar lo sa ma nol dirà'. And then, that cadenza with its repeated staccato high Ds! Those who complain that

it holds up the action should know that that is what it is supposed to do, for the fermata marked in the score means just that. In the middle and lower range, though she had not the refinement of Patti nor the polish of Melba, the voice is still expressive and 'she could get an amazing amount of *larmes dans la voix*'.[5] This is well heard in Ciampi's old song 'Tre giorni son che Nina'; it would be hard to imagine a more eloquent cantilena, tenderly and delicately inflected. And she was a great charmeuse, in Tosti's 'Aprile' just singing the melody simply and unaffectedly and at the end interpolating a lustrous high B flat—'Ah vieni. E l'April!'—bewitching art.

Until the First World War Tetrazzini appeared regularly in opera throughout the United States, at Covent Garden and in various European capitals. Later, she confined herself almost entirely to concert tours and from these amassed a very substantial fortune, but alas, like many another prima donna shrewd in her business affairs, those of her heart proved ruinous. She was obliged to continue before the public well into the 1930s, according to those who heard her then still singing all her old pieces and refusing to compromise their keys. When she died in 1940, she had to be buried at the state's expense: her career a fond memory, her husbands gone and her fortune spent.

At the same time as Tetrazzini, there were three other sopranos still busying themselves with the older lyric coloratura repertory; two were Spanish, the third Portuguese. The eldest, REGINA PACINI (1871–1965), born in Lisbon, was from a musical family, her father a well-known baritone and later Director of the opera. She took lessons from Vallani and made her debut in 1888 at the Sao Carlos, Lisbon, as Amina. The following year she came to London and took part in Mapleson's last season at Her Majesty's; this came to a sudden end when he found himself without the wherewithal to pay the pipers. In the course of the next few seasons she sang in Milan (at the Teatro Manzoni), Palermo, Madrid, Barcelona, Warsaw, St Petersburg, Florence, Monte Carlo, the San Carlo, Naples and in Buenos Aires. Her repertory included Annetta in Ricci's *Crispino e la Comare*, Lucia, Linda, Elvira in *Puritani*, Gilda, Rosina, the Queen in *Ugonotti*, Ophélie in *Amleto*, Leila in *Pescatori di Perle*, Dinorah, Adina, Zerlina in *Don Giovanni* and Massenet's *Manon*. At Covent Garden, in 1902, she was Adina and Lucia opposite Caruso. In 1907 she married Marcello Alvear, an Argentine diplomat who later became President of his country; she

134 Regina Pacini

Elvira in *Puritani*. The following year, opposite Florencio Constantino, she sang Mimi for the first time in Bilbao. During the 1901 season she appeared at the Fenice, Venice as Violetta, and at the San Carlo, Naples, as Amina in *Sonnambula*.

From 1903 onwards, Huguet recorded prolifically: arias from *Dinorah, Lakmé, Mignon, Puritani, Faust, Traviata, Vespri Siciliani*, and in duets with de Lucia, Giorgini, Pini-Corsi and de Segurola. She was Nedda in a complete recording of *Pagliacci*, made in 1907 under the composer's direction, which despite some rival claims was probably the first complete opera recording. Her voice, similar in range and type to Pacini's, was sweeter and more ingratiating, the tone forward and well-focused and the registers used to charming effect as we hear in Rico's pretty waltz 'Stella'. In an Italian version of the Bridal duet from *Lohengrin*, she is the perfect partner for de Lucia, echoing his phrasing in the same tender and affectionate manner. It is easy to

135 Josefina Huguet

then retired from the stage.

Though she was only in her early thirties when she made her records, Pacini's voice already sounds worn, the tone curdled in the middle register. Hers is a rather mature Gilda, in 'Caro nome' feeling her way cautiously and not always successfully through the staccato passages. Mireille's 'O d'amor messaggera' also lacks real brilliance and at the end, in an unlovely cadenza, the intonation is vague. The top of the voice is the best part, and she is effective in the finale to the first act of *Puritani* 'Ah vieni al tempio' (here done as a solo), taking up the bass melody two octaves to an easy, if piercing, D in alt. The phrasing is attractive, but we can hear traces of the verismo style in some exaggerated marcati and the hard attack.

JOSEFINA HUGUET (1871–1951) was another debutante of the 1888 season. That year, at the Teatro Liceo in her home town of Barcelona, she sang Micaëla, and Inez in *Africana* with Gayarré. In the course of a dozen or so years she made the rounds of the principal theatres in Spain, South America, Russia and Italy. In 1896, at La Scala, she sang Ophélie in *Amleto* with Sammarco. In Russia, she was Ophélie and Rosina with Battistini. At the Teatro Argentina, Rome, in 1899, she took the role of

136 Maria Galvany

hear why her records were so greatly enjoyed.

The youngest of the trio was also from Spain, MARIA GALVANY (1878–1949). She was a student at the Madrid Conservatory under Puig, then Verger. She made her debut at Cartagena in 1897 as Lucia. Thereafter, she sang in Madrid, Valencia and Lisbon, as Amina, Elvira in *Puritani*, Isabella in *Roberto il Diavolo,* Inez in *Africana,* the Queen in *Ugonotti* and Violetta. In 1901 she appeared in Italy for the first time at the Dal Verme, Milan. She was a regular visitor in Russia and South America. In 1908 she had a success in the role of Ophélie at the Fenice. The following year, with an Italian touring company, she came to England. When the tour was done, the company did a short stint at Drury Lane. Galvany sang Amina, Rosina and Dinorah, and seems to have had quite a success in spite of the fact that Tetrazzini, then at the height of her fame, was appearing at the same time in the first two roles at Covent Garden. After her debut, as Amina, *The Times* critic wrote:

> Her voice is not of a very pleasing quality in the lower and middle registers and though her high notes are neither very powerful nor very round she sings her

brilliant passages with considerable skill . . . she has a youthful appearance and acts with animation and sincerity, her success was not in doubt for an instant . . . she sang a high F and had to repeat 'Ah non giunge'.[6]

These were not her only London appearances. According to P. G. Hurst, she sang in Harrods![7] What the occasion was, or in which department, sadly he does not record.

Galvany made a considerable number of records. On these we hear a hard little voice of no particular quality, the tone fluttery but secure, the range extending easily to the high F, and with quite an extraordinary facility in staccato, which she takes the opportunity to show off wherever she can, no matter how inappropriate; it is surprising to find a cadenza at the end of the Bell Song, outrageous in the Queen of the Night's aria, the staccati chattering away like machine-gun fire. Her records are amusing party pieces. Perhaps the most characteristic, and one that will cause little offence, is of a waltz by Arditi, suitably entitled 'L'Incantatrice'. In duets with de Lucia and Ruffo she is on her best behaviour, no doubt, perforce; but shorn of her tricks, there is little else of interest in her singing.

28. Italian Contraltos

The most outstanding Italian contralto of the last years of the nineteenth century, GUERRINA FABBRI (1866–1946), was in the great tradition of Marietta Alboni, Barbara Marchisio, Sofia Scalchi and Giulia Ravogli. She studied in Florence and made her first stage appearance in 1885 at Viadana. During the next two seasons, she sang in Madrid: La Cieca, Frederic in *Mignon*, Martha in *Mefistofele* and Arsace to Patti's Semiramide. In the summer of 1887, she came to Drury Lane, but Klein was 'not impressed'[1] and Harris did not invite her to Covent Garden. In 1890, first at the Costanzi, Rome and later in Turin and at the Dal Verme, Milan with Pini-Corsi, she took part in revivals of Rossini's *Italiana* and *Cenerentola*. In 1891 she was Lola in the Scala premiere of *Cavalleria Rusticana*, and afterwards

137 Guerrina Fabbri in the title-role of Gluck's *Orfeo*

took the title-role in Gluck's *Orfeo*. In the autumn of that year she returned to London with Lago's company, to the Shaftesbury Theatre. Her notices were good but the public's attention was focused elsewhere; at the first London performances of *Cavalleria*. She sang Orfeo and the title-role in Rossini's *Cenerentola*, and—

> by the beauty of her voice throughout its great compass, and by her almost perfect vocalisation, . . . won a distinct success, not only in 'Non più mesta', which was sung to perfection, but in many of the earlier scenes.[2]

Like other Italian singers of that era she was a regular visitor to Russia, where she sang Siebel, Orsini in *Lucrezia Borgia* and Leonora in *Favorita* with Battistini. In Spain too, she was a popular favourite, whether as Amneris, Laura or Fidès. In 1901, in Florence she appeared as Rosina in *Barbiere* and the following year at Venice, Romeo in Bellini's *Capuleti*. From that time, however, she seems to have concentrated increasingly on character roles: Mme de la Haltière in Massenet's *Cendrillon*, Dame Quickly, Natalia in *Zazà*, which she created, and Margarita in Wolf-Ferrari's *I Quattro Rusteghi*. Her last stage appearance was in this part, at Genoa in 1925.

Fabbri's voice on records, is a striking instrument, the chest register especially, of remarkable power and quality. Her manner is uninhibited not to say self-indulgent and quite unlike that of any of the contraltos active at the same time north of the Alps. She was not a refined or particularly sensitive artist, and the influence of the 'new' music is apparent in the violent attack and other exaggerations. Nevertheless, though her use of the middle register taken up to high G and with a considerable amount of vibrato, looks forward to the mezzo-soprano technique of later generations— to Stignani and Castagna—the very brilliant and open tone reminds us of descriptions of the singing of Alboni and Scalchi. She is especially fine in Romeo's 'Se Romeo t'uccise' from Bellini's *Capuleti* at both ends of the voice, declaiming the words strongly and with a splendid intensity in the chest register, especially at the end—a deliberate attempt to sound masculine, perhaps?

The Portuguese contralto EUGENIA MANTELLI (1860–1926) was six years older than Fabbri. She made her debut at the Sao Carlos, Lisbon, in 1883, as Urbain. During the next decade she travelled extensively throughout Italy, Spain, Germany,

138 Eugenia Mantelli in the title-role of Gounod's *Sapho*

[She] has a powerful mezzo-soprano voice which she habitually forces after the manner of most Italian singers; it is of fairly agreeable quality when not thus misused and she sings in tune and without any tremolo.[3]

Scarcely an overwhelming reception and it was the best she was to get; as Ortrud, the same critic thought 'she hardly confirmed the favourable impression she made at her debut',[4] and she was not liked as Amneris or Brünnhilde in *Valkyrie*, when 'the bad habit of forcing the voice ruined much of the performance'.[5] By 1902, she was reduced to singing in vaudeville; a couple of years later she retired to Lisbon.

By the time she made her records, the voice is worn, the tone small and light-weight. At the top she is uncomfortable on high A, at the bottom, in the famous downward runs in Cenerentola's Rondo Finale, she dodges back up again before the low G sharp. The narrow range of dynamics, like a tendency to settle on the flat side of a note, suggests that the support is going. Nevertheless there is still much to enjoy in the charm of her delivery; the coloratura, though not brilliant, is neatly done and in Leonora's 'O mio Fernando' and Siebel's Flower song (complete with cadenza), she shows off a graceful portamento style. It is singing that falls agreeably on the ear, delicately and expressively phrased, in spite of rhythmic sluggishness and a lack of characterisation—Angelina, Urbain and Rosina come out sounding pretty much the same as Dalila, Carmen or La Cieca.

The career of ARMIDA PARSI-PETTINELLA (1868–1944) never took her to London or New York, but she was much admired in Italy and the outlying areas of the Italian operatic empire. Born in Rome, she made her debut there at the Teatro Costanzi in 1892 as Azucena in *Trovatore*. In the next few years she appeared at Ravenna, Brescia, Piacenza, Florence and in Chile. She was engaged at La Scala in 1895 to take part in the world premiere of Mascagni's 'English' opera *Guglielmo Ratcliff*, with a cast that also included Adelina Stehle, Giovanni de Negri and Giuseppe Pacini. The following season she sang Anne Boleyn in Saint-Saëns's *Enrico VIII*, with Litvinne and Sammarco, then Dalila in *Sansone* and finally Gertrude in *Amleto* with Huguet and Sammarco. She repeated her Dalila at the Liceo, Barcelona in the spring of 1897. One critic wrote:

[She] was an excellent Dalila who possessed a homogenous voice—equal, velvety-clear diction and

South America and Russia. In 1894 she was invited to the Met, where she sang a variety of parts including Dalila, Amneris, Emilia in *Otello*, Martha and Pantalis in *Mefistofele*, Ortrud, the Second Lady in *Flauto Magico* and Leonora in *Favorita*. Though the critics were equivocal, she survived altogether six seasons; at the time the Met was short of good contraltos, for Scalchi and Ravogli were nearing the end of their careers, Schumann-Heink and Homer had not yet arrived on the scene, and the only other ranking artist was Rosa Olitzka. In the summer of 1896, she came to London, to Covent Garden. Her debut was in *Favorita*. *The Times* critic wrote:

139 Armida Parsi-Pettinella

what is more important, she interpreted the Biblical personality effectively and idiomatically.[6]

Between 1897 and 1901 she visited South America, Venice, Lisbon, Trieste, Odessa and Madrid, adding to her repertory Leonora in *Favorita,* Laura, Amneris, Ortrud, Mignon, Fricka in *Valchiria,* Fidès, Carmen, Ulrica and Urbain. In 1903, she was again at La Scala, as Loretta in Franchetti's *Asrael,* and Ulrica in *Ballo* with Zenatello under Toscanini's direction. Three years later she returned to the Costanzi, again as Azucena. Her final appearances at La Scala were as Dalila in 1910. The following season she bade farewell to opera in the role of Dame Quickly in *Falstaff* at the Reggio, Turin.

The voice we hear on gramophone records resembles Fabbri's in range and general character, though the quality is by no means as good : there is a great deal of vibrato and the tone is worn. One of the titles, Urbain's 'No giammai' from *Ugonotti,* is the aria Meyerbeer added for Alboni when she sang the role—originally written for high soprano—in the famous Covent Garden production of 1848. Parsi-Pettinella sings it nimbly enough but with too many aspirates and several of those Tyrolean effects as she gets in and out of the chest register. Not, on the evidence, a refined or eloquent singer.

MARIA GAY (1879–1943), the youngest of these contraltos, was from Barcelona. She studied in Paris with Ada Adini, and then made her debut at the

Monnaie, Brussels in 1902, as Carmen. It was to remain the most important role in her career. In the next few years she sang it at various theatres in France and Italy before securing an engagement at the Opéra-Comique in 1906. Her first appearance at Covent Garden took place later that same year, again as Carmen. She repeated it the following season when the *Illustrated London News* wrote :

Her Carmen can be compared with Ternina's Isolde and Jean de Reszké's Tristan, even Calvé's performances pale next to it.[7]

By all accounts it was a visual as much as aural interpretation, strikingly picturesque to look on and full of what were then considered aggressively realistic touches. It owed a great deal to her nationality and was probably, until that time, the most completely Spanish conception of what is, after all, French opera. That the drama came first for her we can gather from the reception meted out to her Amneris, which was considered dramatically exciting but not well sung. She made her New York debut in the following autumn, in 1908, when the *Sun* thought her a 'no more than tolerable'[8] Carmen. She went on to sing Dame Quickly in *Falstaff,* Lola in *Cavalleria,* Amneris and Azucena, in none of them reversing the initial impression she had made. A year after leaving the Met she joined the Boston Company, remaining there for two seasons until 1912. In 1913 she married the tenor Giovanni Zenatello and that summer appeared with him at the Verona arena in the first season of opera held there, singing Amneris to his Radames. The following year she was Carmen. During the later part of her career she toured in Central and South America and then was for a time a member of the Chicago Company. After her retirement, with her husband, she taught singing in New York.

In part of Alceste's 'Divinités du Styx' beginning 'J'enlève un tendre époux' she reveals a light vibrant voice not absolutely smooth with a good but not individual quality. The top seems easy and secure; the chest register however sounds dry and not fully developed and middle C is a weak note. It is a dramatic interpretation. She makes the maximum contrast between the different sections, phrasing eloquently with an appropriately urgent rhythm and obviously chooses her own tempi; nowadays conductors have usurped what was once the singer's prerogative, but no conductor-led performance could get as much variety of expression in this music as Gay does. It is a free but stylish performance; she is scrupulous in making holds and rubato only where fermatas are marked in the score. She is also careful to observe the many portamento markings; altogether the execution is notably accurate, especially in the tricky presto section—'Je sens une force nouvelle'—which she nips through with clarity and great élan.

140 Maria Gay as Carmen

PART IV

Wagner and the German Style

29. The Instrumental Example

For all the proliferation of German state opera houses these days, and of the court theatres with their princely endowments three quarters of a century and more ago, Germany has never been a Land of Song. There have been great German singers, but that greatness has lain in artistry and musicianship, very rarely in the singing itself. In the eighteenth century, when the vocal art was almost by definition an Italian prerogative, the Germans were not thought to be able to sing at all. By all accounts it needed a great deal of persuading to get Frederick the Great to give Elisabeth Schmäling a hearing, and when he eventually gave in what he heard so much surprised him that he immediately appointed her a 'kammersängerin' and refused to let her leave Berlin. To escape his clutches, she contracted a marriage with a cellist, Mara by name, and under the cosmopolitan-sounding cover of his name did a moonlight flit. Mme Mara, like her predecessor Mingotti, sang in the Italian style; they were taught by Italians. The German style, of which abundant examples survive in early recordings, evolved during the nineteenth century and was a direct response to the works of the great German Romantics, an attempt to accommodate vocal music that had largely been inspired by the instrumental example.

The German singers tried to produce an instrumental purity of tone and to control the emission of the voice so that they could manage the most unvocal intervals. That they were only partially successful need not surprise us; the fact is, the voice is not an instrument like any other, it cannot be divorced from the body. Whereas the organ can be shut down to a flute stop without any deleterious effect and the fiddle player can contrive enharmonics by manipulating the strings, the voice is not at the singer's direct disposal and it can only be controlled by mastering the breath. It is the breath that both supports and frees the voice and when properly and completely utilised produces its naturally affecting quality, that tension that lay at the basis of the old Italian style, which Hanslick noted in Patti's singing as a pleasure independent of the music. As soon as any attempt is made to engage extraneous muscles to interfere with the vocal mechanism's liberty to follow its own movement, the natural tension disappears, the sound is constricted, the tone becomes not pure but emasculated—what the old teachers called the 'voce bianca'—the flow of the voice (portamento) is interrupted and there is no legato. At least in the short run, the German singers of the late nineteenth century were able, by 'stopping' the sound down, to manage a surprising variety of roles and different musical styles, to execute awkward tessitura and unvocal intervals with clarity, and coloratura with remarkable fluency and seeming ease. But the effect, though sometimes amazing, was rarely pleasing or musical. It was not the art that disguises artifice, the mechanics were exposed for all to hear; however lovely the natural quality of a particular singer's voice, the sound was too constrained to be really expressive. Worse, it proved virtually impossible to sing in tune. The grip put on the larynx prevented the vocal cords from vibrating fully, head notes were shallow and thin; without the lower harmonics to round out the tone, the pitch was almost invariably sharp, sometimes excruciatingly so. And when the grip was relaxed in downward passages, in the middle register the pitch tended to sag below the note. The long-term effects of imposing on the fragile vocal mechanism a stronger muscular system than the one intended by nature for the purpose proved terminal. Of the first six sopranos we shall consider here, none of them was still singing with any success at the age of forty; records suggest that several of them were already way past their best at thirty.

IRENE ABENDROTH (1872–1932) was not the

eldest, but she, perhaps best of all, typifies the virtues and vices of the German method. She was, like Sembrich, Arkel and Krusceniski, from Lemberg. According to one account, as a child she was taken to Milan to study with the elder Lamperti. Later on, in Vienna, she was a pupil of a pupil of Lamperti—Aurelie Jager-Wilczek. After completing her studies, she made her debut at the Vienna Imperial Opera, in 1889. Hanslick was present on the occasion:

> Irene Abendroth, a barely seventeen-year-old frail-looking girl, survived yesterday her debut as Amina in *Sonnambula*. The youthful singer possesses a remarkable agility, which she disclosed in staccato, as well as in legato passages, especially in long held trills with secure ease. Her intonation is clear, her interpretation betrays the best Italian school. She has no tremolo and knows how to produce her headtones, beautifully and securely. The real soul of singing, emotion and dramatic expression still remain undeveloped and in the bud—musical talent and a remarkable musicality she has without a doubt.[1]

Her recordings were made thirteen years later, after she had been successively a member of the company in Riga, Hamburg, Vienna and Dresden. During that time she sang Tosca, Sieglinde, Desdemona, Norma and Venus, as well as the Queen of the Night, Lucia, Rosina and the Queen in *Hugenotten*. It was mostly arias from her brilliant repertory she chose to record. They substantiate what Hanslick wrote, though we may question whether the Italian school had much to do with her interpretations. Perhaps the most characteristic of them is 'Bel raggio' from *Semiramide*. It is impossible not to be impressed by the astonishingly fleet execution, by the clarity of the passage work, especially in the coda. All the gruppetti and trills are done with comparable skill. The tone is pure and the head register absolutely steady, though she never ventures above a high B and then only in passing; the middle, however, has become wavery and she seems unable to sustain phrases, the last notes being invariably weak and breathy. It seems hard to believe she was only thirty at the time, for the voice has lost all freshness and bloom. She uses a variety of rubato effects with stylistic continence, marking the rhythm securely, but the attack is without real brilliance; there is nothing of Tetrazzini's swagger, nor anything open-throated or spontaneous in the delivery, which is all rather small-scale, at times coming dangerously near to crooning. As an

141 Irene Abendroth

interpretation it hardly exists. Whereas the early gramophone found it difficult to contain the abandoned emotionalism of the versimo singers, whose effects needed the wide spaces of La Scala or the San Carlo, it exaggerated the importance of singers whose artificial vocalism was never accepted outside the German-speaking countries.

When Abendroth retired at the early age of thirty-six, she was succeeded at Dresden by MARGARETHE SIEMS (1879–1952), a pupil of the Hungarian soprano Aglaia von Orgeni. Orgeni, a pupil of Pauline Viardot, had not had a notably successful career herself. At Covent Garden in 1866, Cox commended her acting in *Traviata* but wrote 'she could not sing'. Instead, she taught. She moved to Dresden, a city with a great musical tradition; both Weber and Wagner had been residents and the original *Tannhäuser* was first produced there. In after years, Strauss made it the centre of his activities, preferring it to Vienna or Berlin. The premieres of *Feuersnot, Salome, Elektra, Rosenka-*

142 Margarethe Siems as the Marschallin in
Rosenkavalier

valier, Arabella and *Intermezzo* were all given in
Dresden. The orchestra was internationally renowned, and if the singers were not the greatest,
they were accomplished and thoroughly rehearsed.
In the period before the First World War, the King
of Saxony subsidised the opera to the tune of
£150,000 per annum, a very substantial sum in
those days. It was probably this endowment rather
than the singers which made Dresden so attractive
to composers who were anxious that their new
works should have the right kind of musical
preparation.

Siems, like Abendroth, was not naturally a high
soprano; though she sang Lucia, Gilda, the Queen of
the Night, Frau Fluth and Philine, her repertory
embraced Aida, Mimi and Butterfly, and for Strauss
she created Chrysothemis in *Elektra,* the Marschallin and Zerbinetta in the original version of *Ariadne
auf Naxos.* The centre of her activities was
Dresden but she sang elsewhere in Germany and
occasionally went abroad: to Milan, St Petersburg
and London, where she appeared with the Beecham
company at Covent Garden and Drury Lane, on both

occasions as the Marschallin.

On records, her coloratura is certainly amazing, if
perhaps not quite as fluent as Abendroth's, and the
trill is less perfect—she does not always manage to
sustain the lower note. There is nothing in her
singing in the least spontaneous, the artifice is very
obvious, particularly so in her cautious approach to
top notes. The whole of the head register is stopped
down, only the edges of the cords vibrating. This
makes it difficult for her to manage an easy, flowing
legato, and except through narrow intervals in the
middle and lower part of the voice, when she does
relax the grip, virtually impossible to use portamento. It robs her interpretations of breadth and
grandeur; the voice does not soar aloft, the phrasing
does not cohere; it is singing without eloquence.
There is a bland monotony in the delivery. In the
Queen's aria 'O glücklich land' from *Hugenotten*, this
may seem appropriate, but the spirited cabaletta
reveals the method's limitations, the lack of a
clean and precise attack takes the vitality out of
the rhythm, and the intonation is vague. At the end,
after a long and elaborate cadenza, Siems lands up
in quite a different key from the one she had started
out in and there is a striking discord as the orchestra
re-enters and she squeezes out a thin D in alt, at least
a semi-tone sharp. In a recording of Leonora's
fourth act aria from *Troubadour*, she takes the lid off
the voice, so to speak, and we can hear what it
sounded like when she opened her throat; beneath
the iceberg-like tip of sound, all that the inhibiting
German technique permitted to come forth, there
was a warm and attractive voice fighting to get out.
She was at her best in the operas of Strauss; it was he
alone of all the composers whose music she sang
who actually wrote for this kind of technique.

The eldest of Orgeni's pupils who made records
was ERIKA WEDEKIND (1868–1944), a sister of the
dramatist, Frank Wedekind. For fifteen years, from
her debut as Frau Fluth in Nicolai's *Lustigen Weiber
von Windsor* in 1894, she was a prominent member
of the Dresden ensemble with a repertory that
included Papagena, Urbain, Jemmy in Rossini's
Wilhelm Tell, Angela in Auber's *Schwarze Domino*
and Yum Yum in the *Mikado.* She sang in Moscow,
and at Salzburg in 1901 as Zerlina and Blondchen. In
1903 she came to Covent Garden as Rosina and
Lucia. *The Times* thought her one of the best Rosinas
since Patti:

[Her] voice is a light soprano, and she is what the
Germans call a 'coloratur' singer of rare skill, her
execution of scales being almost as perfect as Mme

Melba's. She sang 'Una voce' with a profusion of ornament which was almost bewildering, and her best feat of vocalisation, the delicate repercussion of high notes was exhibited to great advantage both here and in the lesson scene in which she sang a brilliant song by Taubert, announced as 'Ich muss nun einmal singen'![2]

Unlike Abendroth and Siems, Wedekind had a naturally high soprano voice and her singing was more spontaneous. The technique resembles Abendroth's, but she had not the same extraordinary fluency. By 1906, the year she made her first recordings, though the voice is tired in the middle and lower range and the intonation is not always correct, in 'soubrette' music, Frau Fluth's aria for example, her piquant delivery and dainty charm are appropriate.

HERMINE BOSSETTI (1875–1936) was another pupil of Mme Jager-Wilczek. She made her debut at Wiesbaden in 1898, as Annchen in *Der Freischütz*, and remained there two seasons before going to Vienna for a year. From 1901 and for the rest of her career until 1924, she was a principal with the Munich opera. Her repertory included Marie in *Verkaufte Braut*, Flosshilde, Waldvogel, Rosina, Norina, Eva, Octavian, Zerbinetta and Marie in *Regimentstochter*. She appeared at Covent Garden for the first time in 1905 as Eva, when *The Times* critic thought that 'she sang in the ultra teutonic way that pleases a good many people in Germany and few in England'.[3] She returned in 1907 and 1913. After her retirement, she taught first in Frankfurt and later in Munich.

Recordings confirm a typically German method and a light soprano voice. She sings Zerlina's 'Welches Glück' from Auber's *Fra Diavolo*† (at that time a popular repertory piece in Germany), attractively and with neat coloratura; only the top most notes are squeezed slightly above pitch.

MARIE GUTHEIL-SCHODER (1874–1935) was an altogether more interesting artist than most of her contemporaries, though her singing—her few records suggest—was by no means remarkable. She was born in Weimar and studied at the Arch-ducal Music School there with Virginia Naumann-Gungl.

† This aria, 'Or son sola' in the Italian version, comes from Auber's *Le Serment*. It does not appear in the original French edition of *Fra Diavolo*.

143 Erika Wedekind

144 Hermine Bossetti as Eva in *Die Meistersinger*

She made her debut at the Weimar Opera as the First Lady in *Zauberflöte* in 1891. To begin with she sang only small parts. Then in 1895 she had a great success when she undertook Carmen for the first time. Thereafter she established herself a leading artist in Leipzig, Berlin and in 1900 in Vienna, where she remained a great favourite with critics and public alike until her retirement from opera in 1926. She was especially admired in the contemporary repertory. Bruno Walter in his autobiography writes of her unforgettable portrayal of the leading role in Bittner's *Die rote Gret*. In Vienna she was in the first performances of Strauss's *Elektra* and *Rosenkavalier*. She sang the role of Oktavian in her one appearance at Covent Garden with the Beecham company in 1913. After 1914 she was particularly associated with the works of Arnold Schoenberg. She sang the soprano solo in his second string quartet 'with expressive force'. In the later part of her career she became a stage director in Vienna and Salzburg.

Unquestionably Gutheil-Schoder's personality and musicianship were not the kind that impress

146 Hedwig Francillo-Kauffmann

145 Marie Gutheil-Schoder as Eva

themselves on wax. In duet with the agreeable tenor of Franz Naval (they sing from *Hoffmann* and *Weisse Dame*), we can hear a pretty, light-weight soprano voice. Unfortunately it seems to have hardly any support, tentative and collapsing at the end of rising phrases, which she is obliged to break off abruptly. The manner is charming but the intonation is vague even by the most indulgent standards.

The Orgeni method was somewhat modified in the singing of HEDWIG FRANCILLO-KAUFMANN (1878–1948), which was most likely the result of some later study that she undertook in Italy. Her career was principally in Berlin, Vienna and Hamburg. Hers was a high soprano voice, bigger, more brilliant than Wedekind's. The technique was not as mannered. In Leonore's 'Seid meine wonne' from Flotow's *Alessandro Stradella*, an attractive piece, she shapes the opening phrases with a firm legato and better focussed tone than we can hear in the recordings of some of her contemporaries. There is too, a greater range of colour and dynamics, and though the style is still very German, the singing is more affecting. There is real liveliness in the concluding 'andante con moto', even if the tone, especially at the top, is not very ingratiating.

147 Gertrude Förstel as Eva

As well as Mmes Orgeni and Jager-Wilczek, there were other important teachers active in the German speaking countries—among them Selma Nicklass-Kempner. Two of her finest pupils were from Leipzig: GERTRUDE FORSTEL (1880–1950) and Freida Hempel. Förstel, who later took lessons from Orgeni, had only a brief operatic career. From her debut in 1901 as Amina, for six seasons she was a member of Angelo Neumann's Prague German Opera. Thereafter she sang in Vienna and Bayreuth, but after 1912 confined herself to concert work. At first she specialised in the brilliant repertory, singing Gilda and Lucia, as well as Amina. By the time she made her first series of recordings in 1904, she had relinquished these in favour of Marguerite, Pamina and various lyric roles in Wagner's operas: Woglinde, Waldvogel, the Hirtenknabe and a Blumenmädchen. Among her records are several duets, in one of which, 'Sieh o Norma', Förstel is Adalgisa to Siems's Norma. It is interesting to hear this music for once in its original key (F major) and with two sopranos; it is a great pity that though the voices blend well enough, pitch problems largely vitiate the listener's pleasure. Förstel's first solo recording was of her teacher Orgeni's arrangement of the old Russian song, the Nightingale. It shows off a bright voice with a fluttery vibrato. The slow measures at the beginning are full of expressive nuances and a particularly neat trill; the allegro, however, is a tame affair, the high notes got out only with some effort. It is not difficult to hear why she gave up Lucia and Amina.

Unlike the careers of so many of the German sopranos of this period, FRIEDA HEMPEL's (1885–1955) was by no means a provincial affair: as an opera singer and later a recitalist she enjoyed a wide reputation on both sides of the Atlantic. Her first season was at Breslau, when she sang Violetta, the Queen of the Night and Rosina; for the next three years she was at Schwerin, expanding her repertory to include Gilda, Leonora in *Troubadour* and Woglinde in *Rheingold*. Her Berlin debut took place in 1905, as Frau Fluth; two seasons later she became a regular member of the company, and in the following five years was a great favourite whether as Lucia, the Queen in *Hugenotten* or Marie in *Regimentstochter*. In 1907 she came to Covent Garden; however, Melba, Kurz and Donalda had divided up the Gildas, Lucias and Violettas and so Hempel was left with Bastienne, Gretel, Eva, Elsa and Frau Fluth, all very worthy, but not the stuff calculated to storm citadels. She did not return. Her next visit to London, in 1914, was at Drury Lane, in *Zauberflöte* with the Beecham Company. Though she was not yet thirty (if we believe her own incredible declaration), the highest notes of the Queen's music had already begun to move out of her orbit and she never did have a success equal to that which she enjoyed in the United States. There, for seven seasons at the Met between 1912 and 1919, she sang a wide variety of roles including Gilda, the Queen of the Night, Susanna, Olympia, the Queen in *Ugonotti*, Adina, Marie, Oscar, Lady Harriet in *Marta* and Annetta in *Crispino e la Comare*, into which she interpolated 'a glittering 'Carnevale di Venezia''.[4] She was popular with the critics, though to judge from the relatively small amount of space expended on her, she was never a great public idol as Melba, Tetrazzini and Galli-Curci were at different times. When she sang Rosina in 1915, Aldrich praised 'her brilliant and accomplished singing . . . not for a good while has so pure and vibrant a soprano voice delivered the florid measures with so great ease and certainty'.[5] But Henderson qualified his enthusiasm for her Oscar, sung 'with spirit, personal charm and certain musical excellence'—'it did not rise above the level of easy mediocrity'.[6] Undoubtedly her biggest critical successes were as the Marschallin in the first

148 Frieda Hempel as Susanna in Mozart's *Figaro*

New York performances of Strauss's *Rosenkavalier* and in the 1914 revival of Weber's *Euryanthe*:

Miss Hempel made a remarkably fine Euryanthe, and her impersonation deserves to be put down among the very best she has offered to New York. She alone commanded in sufficient measure not only the dramatic but the florid element in Weber's music, the union of which makes it so difficult. In beauty of voice and in the ingenious and pathetic significance of her acting she was wholly admirable.[7]

One explanation put forward to explain Hempel's

precipitate departure from the Met was that Gatti was determined to secure Galli-Curci's services, and that lady had made it crystal clear that she did not wish to find Hempel there. However it seems at least likely Hempel felt that having given her best to the opera public and made her name, it was time to take advantage of it. She began another career that would occupy her for another twenty years, as a successful recitalist; like Sembrich, choosing what were in those days 'advanced' programmes: songs by Mozart, Schubert, Schumann, Brahms and Wolf. It enabled her to surrender graciously what were by then becoming increasingly unreliable high notes and at the same time commended her to the critics who were becoming increasingly respectful of 'serious' music. When she sang, in a New York concert in 1921, Donna Anna's 'Non mi dir', Aldrich praised her extravagantly:

Here was the true Mozartian style in as near perfection as it is now to be heard; a limpid and translucent delivery of the melody in the most equable tones, in an untroubled legato, in artistic and well-considered phrasing; and in a few measures at the end, in finished coloratura.[8]

Records do not unequivocally corroborate either the perfection of her technique or of her Mozartian style. The voice was a high and naturally brilliant soprano, extending at the beginning of her career at least to the F in alt. Like Förstel's, it had a certain vibrancy, it was freer, more animated, less contrived and artificial-sounding than many of her contemporaries. In the middle register, in 'Ernani involami', the tone is firm and well focussed and there is real breadth in her phrasing; only the chest notes sound rather immature. It is interesting to compare her first recordings made for Odeon in 1906, when she was only twenty-one, with the later series done for HMV and Victor. In the earliest, where most of the titles are in German, the style is very provincial—Rosina's aria from *Barbier*, for example, with its over-elaborate ornamentations— but the top is noticeably more responsive. By 1911 in Adam's variations 'Ah! vous dirai-je, maman', although the passage work is fluent and the staccati make a very dazzling effect, there are frequent imperfections; the head notes, squeezed out very much in the German style, do not always quite hit the mark, and the intonation is sometimes sharp, sometimes flat. In later recordings too, sustained high tones show signs of an incipient wobble—in Constanze's 'Che pur aspro al cuore' ('Martern aller

Arten') and at the end of Baronin Friemann's 'Auf des Lebens raschen Wogen' from Lortzing's *Wildschütz*. Elsewhere too, she is overambitious, climactic high notes turning into anti-climaxes when she is obliged to attenuate them. A small group of electrical recordings made in the late 1920s, mostly vocally un-ambitious music, support her great reputation as a musician far more eloquently. In the brilliant repertory, within its technical limitations her singing is musical and often attractive, but ultimately it lacks that individuality which would have put her alongside the greatest singers of her day: Sembrich, Melba, Tetrazzini, even Galli-Curci. Perhaps she realised it herself which is why, in her recitals, she used to doll herself up as Jenny Lind; it gave the occasions a particular identity, even if it was a spurious one—they had very little in common, not repertory, nationality, even appearance.

The career of SELMA KURZ (1874–1933) was less extensive than Hempel's but her reputation, at least amongst record collectors, is perhaps even greater. She was a big star at the Vienna Opera for thirty years from 1899 to 1929. Born in Silesia, she first went to Vienna to study with Johannes Ress, and later travelled to Paris and took some instruction from Marchesi. It is possible to hear in her singing certain traits of the Marchesi school, but in all salient respects she was a German style singer. Hers was an outstanding voice, like Hempel's with a range to the high F, but with an even finer quality and greater power. In Vienna she sang Gilda, Lakmé, Oscar, the Queen of the Night, Urbain in *Hugenotten*; she was a successful Constanze, Violetta, Mimi and Butterfly and on occasion managed Tosca, Elisabeth and Sieglinde. Her appearances outside Vienna were rare but she came to London in three seasons before the First World War. On the occasion of her debut as Gilda, in 1904, *The Times* critic wrote:

> Her voice is of remarkably sympathetic quality, she possesses an admirable method and vocal skill as made it imperative for her to repeat 'Caro nome'. The second performance of this great song was even better than the first, but it was not alone her voice that won her such a success. Her acting is extraordinarily fine and her facial expression is of itself eloquent.[9]

She followed this with Elisabeth in *Tannhauser*, when her success was 'so emphatic that the loss of the more experienced artist [Ternina] was compensated for in great measure. Not that this new singer is another Ternina, any more than in *Rigoletto*

149 Selma Kurz in the title-role of Delibes's *Lakmé*

she proved to be another Melba'[10]—a view that Melba must have concurred with, for thereafter Kurz sang other Melba roles; in 1905 Marguerite in *Faust* and Juliette and, in 1907, Lucia. In most of these she was admired, but there were reservations. In particular, her habit of singing sharp was first noted in *Tannhäuser* and when she sang Gilda again, in 1907, it was considered by *The Times* to have 'spoilt the end of "Caro nome".'[11] It has been suggested that her failure to secure further engagements at Covent Garden was the direct consequence of Melba's jealousy over her success as Lucia in the summer of 1907, but it seems far more likely that the determining factor was Tetrazzini's sensational debut that autumn. It was not only Kurz who suffered from the comparison; Melba, too, never again ventured Lucia at Covent Garden. Kurz did, however, return in 1924, for some performances of *Bohème* and *Traviata*.

Unlike many high sopranos, Kurz's voice suited the acoustic recording mechanism; comparisons with her electric records suggest that the quality was well caught. The production of the voice is smoother than Hempel's, the high notes specially are free of vibrato. Like most German sopranos the tone is instrumentally pure, almost white in the head register when she fines the sound down to a mere thread. Her florid technique is considerable: staccati and runs are done with much skill and she can sustain the famous trill, as it seems, without end. She is capable of a greater variety of dynamics than Abendroth or Siems and there is not the drastic separation between the head register, which can only be managed in piano, and the rest of the voice. The finish on her technique was especially admired by her contemporaries. Yet it is curiously unaffecting singing with little range of expression; she is not able to differentiate effectively between, say, Bellini's melancholy Elvira and Verdi's spirited Oscar. We only have to compare her 'Saper vorreste' to Tetrazzini's to hear what is lacking: with the Italian diva, we can almost see the mischievous face, the interpretation has such wit and delightful spontaneity; by comparison Kurz is characterless, and technically her legato is not as eloquent nor the rhythm so secure. Altogether her singing is the victim of the German method; it does not sound natural and is not really musical. Indeed, in Vienna, among her fellow musicians, she was known as 'the Singer with no Ear'. As with Hempel, the top of the voice is produced with some caution and she cannot make a brilliant effect with sustained notes. Even her legendary trill is mechanical; unlike Patti's—a thing of beauty and musical in itself—there is too much of Dr Johnson's dog about it. We can sympathise with Mancinelli during a performance of *Ballo* at Covent Garden, when he stopped her in her tracks in that interminable cadenza. She makes a lovely effect when a dreamy manner and pallid tone are appropriate, in 'Caro nome' for example, but even here we may note precisely that sharp intonation the *Times* critic complained of when she sang it at Covent Garden within a year of making this recording.

30. Lilli Lehmann

It was not, however, the high sopranos with their artful vocalism who dominated the stages of the principal German theatres during the final decade of the nineteenth century. This was the age of Wagner, whose works were finally coming into their own, and Wagner having consigned coloratura to the birds—quite literally in *Siegfried*—those whom nature had provided with light and high voices were increasingly pre-occupied with ways of producing weightier, more serious sounding tones. In the realisation of such ambitions none was more successful than LILLI LEHMANN (1848–1929). By dint of study and as a result of a tenacious disposition she was able to overcome the obstacles in her way, not the least of them a voice originally unremarkable in size and quality. With it she advanced steadily through the coloratura and lyric repertory of her youth until she became the greatest Wagnerian of them all. Her career began in Prague in 1869 as the First Boy in *Zauberflöte* (in due course she sang every soprano role in the opera!), progressed through Vielka in Meyerbeer's *Feldlager in Schlesien* (a Jenny Lind role), Philine, Lucia and Gilda to Valentine, Violetta and Carmen, then Sieglinde and finally Brünnhilde and Isolde; at the same time she retained Fidelio, Donna Anna, Constanze and even Norma—had not the Master expressly excluded it from his general strictures on Italian Opera?

Lehmann was by no means the first great Wagnerian soprano. Teresa Vogl, Rosa Sucher, Katerina Klafsky, Thérèse Malten and Amelia Materna were all active in the last two decades of the nineteenth century, but Lehmann's dedication, versatility and stamina—like Tietjens before her, she often sang a different opera every night of the week—eventually outdistanced all her contemporaries. By will-power as much as anything else, a modestly endowed singer, who had spent almost the first twenty years of her career in Germany and Austria—at one stage she even signed a life contract in Berlin—emerged in the later 1880s as the world's leading Wagnerian soprano. So great and so authoritative was her personality that her essentially provincial vocal style she converted into the prevailing mode. It remained the accepted 'Wagner style' well into the twentieth century.

She was in her late fifties and had been before the public for nearly forty years when she made two series of recordings. Her voice is in good condition even if the quality is not always agreeable. She can

150 Lilli Lehmann as Venus in *Tannhäuser*

voice is typically German-sounding, the tone pure and squeezed and with very little vibrato; it is the best part of the voice. The middle is the weakest and evidently much worn, especially at the junction with the chest register, i.e. around the F, F sharp and G above middle C, where the singer finds it frequently difficult to keep the voice together and is often obliged to resort to an ugly coup de glotte, a particularly wearing device. The attack was, by all accounts, the weak link in Lehmann's technical armoury:

> [It] was imperfect throughout her career. Doubtless her artificial method of breathing was at fault. At any rate she aspirated a large percentage of those tones which had to be taken on open vowels.[1]

In the closing measures of her recording of Donna Anna's Vengeance aria, we can hear all too plainly the difficulty she had getting in and out of the chest register; at times the voice sounds on the verge of total collapse. But such is her genius that she even manages to turn this frailty to positive account—we believe in Donna Anna's 'vendetta' the more when, as it seems, her rage almost prevents her spitting out the word! The interpretation is a classic, a permanent rebuttal of the argument that it is impossible to include every appoggiatura and still maintain an urgent sense of drama. No performance of the long recitative is more dramatic; yet every appoggiatura is there, the continuo player correctly waits for the singer to finish each phrase before proceeding and Lehmann makes abundant use of portamento. In this last respect it is perhaps fair to make some objection: not, however, in its application, in which she is, as elsewhere, a model of taste—where, one wonders, came forth that notion that portamento is solely a Victorian affectation, an excess of sentimentality? Nothing could be further from the truth. From the beginning it has been an integral part of singing; we have noted references to it in the writings of Tosi, Burney, Agricola and Quantz, and in connexion with the chant in mediaeval dissertations. It is Lehmann's manner of execution that is questionable. In the classical Italian style the voice, properly supported on the breath, was left to find its own position, to sweep freely through an upward or downward interval. But with Lehmann, the voice is determinedly squeezed out; by so doing she accomplishes more of the interval than is vocally 'natural', and the effect, instead of sounding spontaneous, becomes mannered and obtrusive. Faults or no, Lehmann is one of the very few singers

manage high C, negotiate coloratura with clarity and for the most part accurately (though she has a tendency to sing sharp), and she still has an impressive range of dynamics at her disposal. The registers are more clearly defined than in many German sopranos of this period. Age, which tends to separate them, may have had something to do with it, but it seems reasonable to assume that an artist as concerned with dramatic expression realised better than most the importance of their proper development. The telling chest register recalls Shaw's description of Tietjens. The head

on record equally successful in both of Anna's arias. The coloratura of 'Non mi dir' holds no terrors for her, even if the closing measures are not as effortlessly nor as brilliantly sung as they must once have been. As well as the solo titles, she recorded duets from *Così, Figaro* and *Norma* with her neice Hedwig Helbig. The *Figaro* lacks the charm that distinguishes the Sembrich-Eames version, but the *Norma* is perhaps the only performance on records where the two singers seem actually to be listening to each other, and concerned sister-like to match and blend their tones so as to avoid that familiar war of tremolos (Lehmann, as often in her career, sings the lower part in thirds). Lehmann's technique was not the result of a couple of year's study with one or two teachers, it was the consummation of a life-time's experience. Not surprisingly, it was a very personal thing, even eccentric, and her attempt to codify it into a teaching method for others to follow was not really successful. Her pupils, like those of Jean de Reszké, who also learned mostly from experience, seem to have found that her solutions posed for them even bigger problems.

Lehmann's interpretations were cast in heroic moulds, she was a high priestess of her art, and it was with the tragic and noble roles that she was most completely in tune: Fidelio, Isolde and Norma—Donna Anna she almost raised to their stature. As Violetta, recordings suggest she was less successful in suppressing the authoritarian tone in her voice. There was something absurd about so determined a lady being left to die alone and forgotten in seedy lodgings; incredible too, when she insisted on giving to the poor even her last few louis—her very name in the profession was a by-word for stinginess. Yet she could be generous in her praises, as she was to Bonci; but then he was not a soprano. She could be womanly too; David Bispham found her back-stage once darning Victor Maurel's socks! And she loved animals, she once wrote a letter to the Editor of the *Chicago Tribune*, in quaint English but with characteristic clarity, demanding more space for the monkeys at the zoo. Her records inspire respect, even admiration, but scarcely affection. It is difficult not to hear, as well as Constanze, Norma, Fidelio and Donna Anna, the old termagant with her crushing rejoinders, the one who so massively put down Nordica when she tried to pay her respects in the crowded foyer at Bayreuth—'I'm not taking any pupils this season!'

Her great international reputation was made in the works of Wagner. When she appeared at Covent Garden for the first time in 1884, creating a sensation with her Isolde, 'few people remembered the singer who four years previously had sung at Her Majesty's as Violetta and Philine'.[2] The following year, in her New York debut, she chose Carmen, but it was Brünnhilde, Venus and later Isolde that brought her the widest acclaim. It was only when she was established in these roles that she magnificently condescended to sing Norma for her own benefit, and in so doing created an unrivalled impression of virtuosity. Strangely, she has left us only a brief fragment of her Wagnerian greatness—from *Walküre*, 'Du bist der Lenz'. She sang Sieglinde, but it was never as famous an impersonation as her Brünnhilde or Isolde; why—we may ask—nothing of them?† The likely answer would seem that by the time she came to make recordings she had given up Wagner, whereas, albeit by then in the provinces, she was still singing Constanze, Donna Anna, Violetta, and even Norma. Though she had once claimed all three Brünnhildes were not as difficult as Norma, that was on paper; in actuality, in the big international houses, she had come up against an obstacle that at her age was insurmountable—the orchestra. When she sang Ortrud in her last season at Covent Garden, in 1899, Klein wrote that 'many of its important passages lie in a part of the voice where Mme Lehmann is utterly unable to cope with the sonorous undercurrent of the Wagner orchestra'.[3] Though Wagner had written considerate tessitura, the voice was not offset by the orchestra; rather it was surrounded by it. In the middle register, where so much of the vocal writing lay, to make any effect she was obliged to resort to a strenuous and forceful attack, the deleterious and long-term consequences of which we can hear in her records. That she was still able to get the voice out at all was a testament to her technical expertise, to all those years spent singing coloratura; it still lubricated the voice.

Lehmann was the only one of the first generation of Wagnerian sopranos to survive (or whose voice did) to make records. Sucher and Vogl had retired long before the end of the century, so had Malten; an Englishwoman who heard her a lot in the mid-nineties wrote that 'she didn't sing, she shocked the glottis'.[4] Klafsky died in 1896, at the untimely age of forty-one, while Ternina, fourteen years younger than Lehmann, and perhaps the greatest of them all, was obliged to quit the stage when still a young woman. It was not only the weight of orchestration that had confounded these singers; after all at

†There is a test pressing of Isolde's Liebestod in the Yale University Sound Archive.

Bayreuth the orchestra pit was covered over and in many of the smaller German houses it did not require such an effort to be heard above it. There was the problem of the new Bayreuth style, where the emphasis was placed increasingly on the text, on the self-conscious delivery of every hard consonant even at the expense of the vocal line. By the end of the nineties the 'Sprechgesang' style had come to be the accepted style, although, as we have already noted, it was directly contrary to everything that Wagner himself had said or written on the subject. *The Times* critic, in 1907, after being exposed to a prolonged bout of it from a visiting German troupe, complained that he did not understand what the word meant—there is no precise equivalent in English—what it sounded like to him was barking. A perfect translation.

31. *Sopranos of the Bayreuth School*

In the early years Wagner's music had been sung successfully by singers whose repertory also included works by Verdi, Massenet, even Rossini and Mozart, but by the beginning of this century the tendency to specialise in Wagner had already begun. Apart from the particular demands of voice and stamina which his music called for, this specialisation helped to strengthen the mystique so actively promoted from Bayreuth by Cosima that the Master's works were something apart. As records abundantly testify, many beautiful and essentially lyrical voices were lost in the attempt to sustain Brünnhilde and Isolde in the new Bayreuth style. Of the generation of Wagnerian sopranos who succeeded Lehmann, only one seems to have been truly equal to all demands: that was Anna Bahr-Mildenburg, and even she lost her voice at a relatively early age.

The eldest, SOPHIE SEDLMAIR (1857–1939) started as an operetta singer and appeared as such with success throughout Germany and Austria and even once in New York. It was not until 1893 that she made her operatic debut as Leonora in *Fidelio* at Danzig. She afterwards sang in Breslau, at the Kroll, Berlin, and in Leipzig, and eventually succeeded Materna in Vienna, remaining there until 1907. In 1897 she sang at Covent Garden as the *Siegfried* Brünnhilde opposite Jean de Reszké; her debut role was Isolde. *The Times* wrote:

> The debut of Frau Sedlmair, in the part of Isolde was decidedly successful; that the voice seemed a little small for Covent Garden is only an experience common

to all, or almost all, who sing there for the first time. As with the majority of German singers the sustained passages are less effective than the declamatory passages, but in both her voice is of good quality and in perfect tune ... Her gestures are appropriate and not too conventional and she evidently possesses the precious gift of intelligence. Her singing of the Liebestod was praiseworthy.[1]

Records made about five years later fit in very well with this judgment. The voice does not sound more than a good-sized lyric soprano. In Senta's Ballade the tone lacks a precise focus that would have enabled it to make a really imposing effect over a full Wagner orchestra. The attack is rather rough and forceful; yet it is an attractive instrument, the intonation, for a German singer of that era, generally accurate. The tone—not particularly fresh—is still pure and the high notes tell well; in the middle there are signs of wear and some hoarseness and the chest register is not always clearly defined. The phrasing is short-breathed—what *The Times* critic may have

151 Sophie Sedlmair as Brünnhilde in *Walküre*

meant when he wrote of her being less effective in sustained passages. But it is a fine and thrilling interpretation; we may believe that had Nordica and Ternina not been available the following season she might have been invited to Covent Garden again.

PELAGIE GREEF-ANDRIESSEN (1860–1937) studied with her mother and then, like Sedlmair, became an operetta singer. Her operatic debut at Leipzig as Aida in 1884 came after spending two

years with a touring company organised by Angelo Neumann. She remained there until 1890, afterwards moving to Cologne and then later to Frankfurt. At Bayreuth she sang Brangäne, and made guest appearances in Vienna, Berlin and Salzburg where she took the role of the Countess in *Figaro* in the Mozart centenary celebrations of 1891. The following year she came to Covent Garden as Fricka in *Rheingold*. *The Times* wrote:

> [Mme Andriessen] who succeeds Frau Sucher as 'leading lady' of the German troupe, is a singer of a good deal of force, though neither in quality of voice, nor in intensity of emotional expression can she compare with her predecessor, whose unavoidable departure is a severe blow to the undertaking. In the ungrateful part of Fricka the new soprano is sufficiently convincing.[2]

Apparently neither the public nor the management felt this, for after she was indifferently received as the *Walküre* Brünnhilde, her Covent Garden career came to an end.

Her records were made between 1900 and 1907, by which time her career was largely over. There are a few song titles, also rather curiously Dalila's 'Sieh mein Herz'; otherwise the pieces are from Wagner operas. It seems to have been a big dramatic voice with a clean focus throughout its entire range, but with a rather shallow and monotonously white tone. In Brunnhilde's 'Ewig war ich' she sings with feeling but without a real legato; there is a serviceable trill and she snatches the high C easily enough. Isolde's 'Dein Werk? O tör'ge Magd!' (she gives us Brangäne's reply as well), takes her to the limits—here is the Bayreuth 'Sprechgesang' in full flight with its violent attack and exaggerated vibrato. The climax is thrilling but crude singing.

152 Pelagie Greef-Andriessen as Klytemnestra in Weingartner's *Orestes*

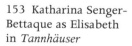

153 Katharina Senger-Bettaque as Elisabeth in *Tannhäuser*

154 Ellen Gulbranson as Brünnhilde in *Siegfried*

155 Thila Plaichinger as Brünnhilde in *Walküre*

She has the usual problems of intonation, here exacerbated by the undernourished accompaniments.

KATHARINA SENGER-BETTAQUE (1862– 19??) was from Berlin. When she had completed her studies she made her debut at the Hofoper in 1879. During the next decade, as a lyric soprano, she sang in Mainz, Leipzig, Rotterdam and Hamburg. In the summer of 1888 she appeared at the Bayreuth Festival as Eva and a Blumenmädchen in *Parsifal*. That autumn she was engaged at the Met; there she sang Selika, Marzelline in *Fidelio*, Elsa, Marguerite, Freia in the American premiere of *Rheingold*, Eva, Sieglinde and Elisabeth in the first performances at the Met of the Paris version of *Tannhäuser*. In 1894 she became principal dramatic soprano at Munich, where she remained for the remainder of her career. She gave New York a sample of her dramatic talent when she returned to the Met in 1904. By this time, unfortunately, both her Brünnhilde in *Walküre* and

Siegfried were thought 'well below the acceptable'[3] and she was not liked as Fidelio.

Senger-Bettaque made very few recordings, but to judge from Elsa's 'Euch luften' it does not sound to have been a dramatic voice. What we hear is a pure lyric soprano, she phrases expressively with some attractive messa di voce effects, the tones still limpid, poised, and for the most part steady on the breath. There is no trace here of the Bayreuth style.

The Norwegian ELLEN GULBRANSON (1863–1946) though officially a pupil of Mathilde Marchesi was in fact taught by her daughter Blanche. Certainly there are few traces of the Marchesi method in Gulbranson's singing. From her first stage appearances at Bayreuth in 1896, for some twenty years, she specialised in the principal roles of the Ring Cycle, Isolde and Kundry. She sang in Vienna, Berlin, Budapest and regularly at Bayreuth until 1914. At Covent Garden she was the Brünnhilde in three different *Rings*, in 1900, 1907 and

1908. Of these, the second was the most successful though even here *The Times* critic did not think she was

> to be counted among the ideal exponents of the role. Musically she was always efficient and sometimes, as in the awakening of Brünnhilde extremely fine; in the great tragic scene of the second act of *Götterdämmerung* too, she worked up to a powerful climax, but in the opening scene she was rather lacking in distinction . . . at the same time we have nothing but admiration for her reading of the closing scene.[4]

Gulbranson's records are exceptionally rare. Brünnhilde's Battle Cry reveals a pure but lyric soprano, very German in style, with only the cleanly attacked high C suggesting anything at all of Marchesi's teaching. From this evidence it hardly seems to have been a voice of heroic dimensions. There is something rather engaging in her choice of Grieg's 'Swan'; she was, according to one critic, of 'unsurpassable ugliness', was this perhaps wishful singing? If so, she got it wrong; Grieg's setting is of Ibsen, not Hans Anderson.

THILA PLAICHINGER (1868–1939) was five years younger than Gulbranson and born in Vienna. She studied with Joseph Gänsbacher, later Luise Dustmann and Mme Mampe-Babbnigg. Her debut was at Hamburg in 1893. The following year she became resident dramatic soprano in Strasbourg (then in Germany), where she remained until 1901. In that year she moved to Berlin, where she was a principal contract artist until the First World War broke out. During that time she made guest appearances in Vienna and Munich and came twice to Covent Garden, in 1904 and with the Beecham company in 1910, on which latter occasion she sang both Elisabeth and Venus in the Dresden version of *Tannhäuser*. Her first season at Covent Garden included Isolde:

> She seemed a little lacking in vocal power at first, no doubt because she has not yet found the part of the auditorium at which the voice should be directed. The quality is decided, rich and fairly sympathetic though she is no exponent of the bel canto . . . Plaichinger has the merit, so rare with German singers of always singing in tune and her mezzo voice is very agreeable. Her phrasing and the accuracy of her rhythm show her to be a true musician and she made a distinct success.[5]

Her records were made about this time and show off a voice naturally more attractive than Andriessen's but a technique with similar faults. The head notes have the same shallow tone and the pitch is frequently sharp. In duets from *Siegfried* and

Tristan with the fine Dutch tenor Jacques Urlus, the middle register is not correctly supported. It would be easier to blame the recording equipment if it were not that Urlus's intonation is never in doubt.

Of these singers, undoubtedly the most talented was ANNA BAHR-MILDENBURG (1872–1947). She was a pupil of Rosa Papier-Paumgartner, herself a Marchesi pupil. Two years after making her debut (in Hamburg, in 1895, as the *Walküre* Brünnhilde) she sang for the first time at Bayreuth, as Kundry. Thereafter, she was the reigning dramatic soprano at Vienna for nearly a decade, and made regular visits to Bayreuth and other major theatres. At her debut at Covent Garden in 1906, as Isolde, *The Times* wrote:

> [She] made a great impression, for she is that rare thing, an actress with the grand manner, and her attitudes and gestures at such symbolical moments as when she holds the cup, when she raises the torch above her head, or when she rises transfigured above Tristan's

156 Anna Bahr-Mildenburg as Isolde

157 Katharine
Fleischer-Edel as Elsa
in *Lohengrin*

1899 she was offered and accepted a contract at Hamburg, it was to be her home for the next twenty years. During that time she sang at Bayreuth: in 1904 Elisabeth and Elsa, in 1906 Brangäne and Sieglinde, and in 1908 Sieglinde and Elsa. She made guest appearances at the Vienna Opera in 1901 and at Covent Garden in 1905 and 1907. Of her debut *The Times* wrote:

> Though a singer who almost deserved the epithet 'great', [she] leaves something to be desired as an actress. Her voice is of telling quality and rang through the theatre in a manner all too rare with newcomers and as Sieglinde she sang ideally especially in the love duet.[7]

body, were really memorable in their dignity and power. She presents quite an unusual type of Isolde, and at many points suggested some picture of Burne-Jones; her facial expression as well as her costumes, made her seem a very twentieth-century version of the legendary princess, but she was none the worse for that. Her voice is remarkably powerful and on the whole is pure in quality; her soft passages do not at present tell as they should, for her mezza voce is far from perfect. A momentary lapse from pure intonation in the great duet from the second act was probably due to want of familiarity with the theatre. It will be interesting to see her in other parts for her success was undeniable, even in spite of such faults as we are obliged to notice.[6]

Unfortunately, Bahr-Mildenburg made only one record, the recitative 'Ozean, du Ungeheuer' from Weber's *Oberon*. It is a striking document, declamation in the grand manner, the attack sure and clean. It is an altogether freer interpretation than we should expect these days, but correct stylistically. The voice is a big and brilliant instrument, as powerful in the chest as it is in the head register. Deprived of the aria itself and cabaletta, we cannot know whether she was equally imposing in legato and coloratura singing. In her artistic commitment there is an echo of Lehmann, though one can scarcely imagine that lady, even in earlier days, as profligate vocally, throwing in the optional B flat at the end to such reckless effect.

KATHARINE FLEISCHER-EDEL (1873–1928) hardly had a voice to compare with Bahr-Mildenburg's, but she was greatly admired in the more lyric roles of the Wagner operas. She was a student of August Iffert at the Dresden Conservatory and made her stage debut at the opera there, as a Brautjungfer in Weber's *Freischütz* in 1894. She remained at Dresden for three years. In

Two years later her acting seemed to have improved while her singing was admired as before. As Elisabeth 'her voice was beautifully fresh all evening'[8] and as Elsa she was praised for 'clearness and purity' and for the way 'she put a great deal of pathos into the character without destroying its simplicity',[9] though here the *Illustrated London News* noted some false intonation. She sang these two roles and the *Siegfried* Brünnhilde when she made her only visit to the United States, to the Met in the autumn of 1906.

In a recording of Sieglinde's 'Du bist der Lenz' we can hear a good-sized lyric soprano voice with some of that 'clearness and purity' the critic referred to above. She phrases sensitively and has a genuinely radiant tone for Elisabeth's Greeting from *Tannhäuser*, but in both pieces she spoils the climax by a hard attack, gripping the note then squeezing it out rather than producing it cleanly. It affects the intonation; the high B is not a true or successful note.

The Polish soprano FELICIE KASCHOWSKA (1872–1951) was another important Wagnerian soprano of this period. She was discovered by the great tenor Tamberlik when she was only fifteen years old. At his prompting she commenced her studies with Troschei in Warsaw; later she went to Vienna to work with Gänsbacher. She made her debut at the Warsaw Opera as Alice in Meyerbeer's *Robert le Diable*. In 1888, at the age of sixteen (if we are to believe her), she appeared at the Met on the opening night of the season as Urbain in *Hugenotten*. She returned the following year and again in 1891 singing Jemmy in *Wilhelm Tell*, Siebel in *Faust*, the Hirtenknabe in *Tannhäuser*, Wellgunde in *Rheingold* and *Götterdämmerung* and Ortlinde in *Walküre* before graduating to Senta, Maria in Nessler's

158 Felicie Kaschowska

was a pupil of Papier-Paumgartner. She made guest appearances at the Paris Opéra, La Scala, in Buenos Aires and at the Met, where she sang the *Walküre* and *Siegfried* Brünnhildes and Elisabeth in *Tannhäuser* though without making much impression.

On records her voice much resembles Bahr-Mildenburg's but is on a smaller scale. Her interpretation of 'Ozean, du Ungeheuer', which continues through the opening measures of the aria 'Noch seh'ich die Wellen toben', is an altogether more modest affair. The declamation, in particular, is less secure and the high B flat pushed sharp.

159 Lucie Weidt as Brünnhilde in *Siegfried*

Trompeter von Säkkingen and Sieglinde. During the next decade she sang extensively in Vienna, Budapest and various German theatres. In her maturity she also sang dramatic roles from the French and Italian repertories. In 1908 she returned to the Met as Brünnhilde in *Walküre* and Leonora in *Trovatore*.

LUCIE WEIDT (1879–1940) succeeded to many of Sedlmair's and Bahr-Mildenburg's roles in Vienna and remained a principal there until 1926. She too,

32. *Gadski and Destinn*

Not every German soprano barked. Two of the most outstanding who didn't, Johanna Gadski and Emmy Destinn, followed in the tradition of Lehmann and Ternina (though their repertoires were not in every respect the same), and both enjoyed considerable international careers. The latter, Czech by birth, from Prague (then in Austro-Hungary), was German by training. The elder, JOHANNA GADSKI (1872–1932), came from Pomerania and studied in Stettin with Mme Schöder-Chaloupka. She also made a precocious debut at the Kroll Theatre, Berlin, at the age of seventeen, as Agathe in *Freischütz*. During the next eight years, she sang successively in Stettin, Mainz, Berlin and Bremen. In 1895, with the Damrosch company, she made her US debut as Elsa; the following year she returned as Hester Prynne in Damrosch's *Scarlet Letter*. In 1899, she sang Eva at Bayreuth following the first of three engagements at Covent Garden. There she joined ranks with Lehmann, Nordica, Litvinne, Brema and Breval, and according to Klein 'at once earned the favour due to an artist of rare vocal and histrionic attainments'.[1] In particular, he rated her 'the finest Eva we have had in London with the single exception of Rosa Sucher'. In 1900, she came to the Met and began a career in New York that was to last without interruption until 1917. As Aldrich wrote later,

> New York may claim to have a special interest in her and her progress as an artist, for here most of it has been achieved and here she has risen to the higher reaches of her art.[2]

It was only the truth. In New York she progressed through a wide variety of parts: Senta, Donna Elvira, Santuzza, Valentine, Amelia, Pamina, Aida, Roschen in Dame Ethel Smyth's *Der Wald*, Eva, Ero in Mancinelli's *Ero e Leandro*, Elsa, Elisabeth, Aida, Sieglinde and the Countess in *Figaro* before embarking on her first Brünnhilde in *Walküre*, and Isolde. In due course, she added the other two Brünnhildes and in spite of competition, mostly from Destinn, still retained much of her Italian repertory. Her singing had its limitations:

> [There is] a certain monotony, resulting from the comparatively slight range of colour and emotional expressiveness with which her voice is infused.[3]

But her virtues outweighed these:

> She is, first of all, a singer in the real sense of the word [with] an uncommonly beautiful voice, in which the evidences of full control and skilful use are rarely lacking . . . She has the dramatic instinct, guided by intelligence and artistic understanding, and she has sincere sentiment and a serious view of the artist's task.[4]

In later years, there were other reservations; in particular it was remarked that her phrasing was often short-breathed, and not infrequently she sang flat. Even so, when her American career came to an abrupt end in 1917, few people would have agreed with Henderson that this was only the consequence of the 'deterioration of Mme Gadski's voice and art'.[5] In fact it was directly attributable to the behaviour of her husband, a German reserve officer, who had made the sinking of the 'Lusitania' an occasion for public celebration. Feelings ran very high and the Met management had little alternative but to dispense with Gadski's services. She did return to the USA briefly with a touring company in 1929 and again in 1930, when she sang Isolde and Martha in d'Albert's *Tiefland*, but by that time 'her voice like her figure was in wretched condition'. She was killed in an automobile accident in Berlin, in 1932.

Her records substantiate much of the criticism above, good and bad. It was a big voice of fine quality. The technique was basically German, but exposure to singers like Nordica and Fremstad seems to have modified some of its more repressive features. Elvira's 'Mi tradi', unfortunately abbreviated so as to fit on to one side of a '78' record, was made soon after she had taken this role in Mahler's famous revival of *Don Giovanni* at the Met in 1908 with Eames, Sembrich, Bonci, Scotti and Chaliapin. It is a distinguished interpretation, having much of Lehmann's authority, but with a warmer and fresher voice. In the recitative the declamation is done in the correct classical style with every appoggiatura in place. In the final phrase 'E quest' ambasce?', there is a delicate glissando from the E flat. The aria makes a great effect with its clean delivery and sweeping portamenti. Do the many subtle rhythmic inflexions come from Mahler? We know that he spent a great deal of time moulding his stars into a constellation, into what Henderson thought was the best integrated *Don Giovanni* ever heard at the Met. It might explain why elsewhere in Mozart she is much less successful, in Pamina's 'Ach, ich fühls' (here 'Ah, lo so'), there is a great deal of contrivance in the exacting tessitura, the voice teetering up to the high B flats, and her 'Porgi amor' is a victim of short-breathedness. She made a large number of Wagner records, some of which are particularly successful; 'Ho-jo-to-ho!' has a brilliant high C and easy trill, and in Brünnhilde's pleading 'War es so schmälich' from the last act, the lovely tone and her eloquent delivery make a very poignant effect. As the Brünnhilde of *Götterdämmerung* her shortcomings are more in evidence; here she did not quite have the grand sweep of a Nordica, Leider or Flagstad.

Few singers have been more greatly admired than EMMY DESTINN (1878–1930). In Berlin, in London and New York, she was adored by the public, admired by the critics and respected by her colleagues. As a child she had wanted to be a violinist, and did in fact make her first public appearance as such at the age of eight. By the time she was fourteen, however, and having developed a remarkable voice, she decided to become an opera singer. In Prague, where she was born Emmy Kittl, she studied with Marie Loewe-Destinn. Out of gratitude to her teacher, when she came to make her debut in Dresden in 1897 as Santuzza, she changed her name to Destinn. A year after she sang the same role in Berlin at the Kroll Theatre; her talent was recognised at once and she remained a member of the company for ten years. She travelled to Bayreuth in 1901 to sing Senta in *Fliegende Holländer*; later she was a guest in Vienna, Prague and Paris. In 1904 she was engaged at Covent Garden, making her first appearance as Donna Anna, afterwards adding Elsa, Santuzza and Nedda (on one occasion in both roles on the same evening) and finally Aida. In this part she enjoyed some of her greatest triumphs. Klein wrote:

> The power that she displayed when she rose to the climax of the Nile Scene I shall never forget.[6]

Earlier that same season the Italian soprano Giannina Russ had made her Covent Garden debut as Aida; in other circumstances, she might have fared better, but she could not compare with Destinn and was never invited again. Destinn returned to Covent Garden every season until 1914. In that period she sang Carmen, Valentine, Madama Butterfly, Tatiana, Senta, Maddalena, Gioconda, Elisabeth, Armide, the title-role in d'Erlanger's *Tess*, Tosca, Minnie, and Amelia. Her Met debut took place in 1908, as Aida:

> She has a voice of great power, body and vibrant quality, dramatic in expression, flexible and wholly

160 Johanna Gadski as Aida

subservient to her intentions, which are those of a singer with keen musical feeling and intelligence. It is a voice possessing tones of great beauty, especially in the upper ranges. She showed the possession of strong dramatic gifts. She too was fired with the prevailing spirit and let the audience hear the utmost sonorities of which she was capable.[7]

Her Aida was a classic impersonation. Florence Easton, who thought her without question the most wonderful female singer of her time, wrote rapturously of Destinn's singing of 'O Patria mia'—'it took the breath away.'[8] Alda declared: 'No one in my time ever sang Aida to compare with Destinn.'[9]

In New York as in London, Destinn appeared in many different roles. Her amazing musical memory, the result in part of her early training as an instrumentalist, enabled her to learn even the most difficult music with ease and rapidity. To the repertory she had sung in Berlin and London, she added Wally, Marie in *Verkaufte Braut*, Lisa, Ricke in *Germania*, Alice in *Falstaff*, and Eva. After Aida, her greatest triumphs were in *Madama Butterfly*. Alda recalls:

> She was a stout lady and far from looking the part of the little Japanese lady. But her manner of singing was so perfect, her voice so divine—like drops of water— and the pathos she put into the role . . . all unforgettable.[10]

161 Emmy Destinn and friend

An opinion shared by the London critics when she sang the part there:

> The chief weight of the evening was on Miss Destinn's shoulders and hers was the triumph. Puccini might have written the part for her so aptly did it suit her voice, so brilliantly did she deliver it.[11]

Her success as Butterfly was doubtless one reason why Puccini composed his next heroine, Minnie in *Fanciulla del West*, especially for Destinn.

Destinn's art was not of the subtlest sort. As Aldrich noted after a New York concert in 1916, she was at her best in music requiring 'directness and simplicity . . . vehemence and dramatic force'.[12] In Henderson's phrase, 'she was a woman of the people'[13] and perhaps for that reason she felt it easier to identify with Aida, Butterfly, Santuzza and Tosca, rather than the big Wagnerian roles, which she never sang, though they would have fallen easily within her vocal compass. She did appear occasionally as Salome but soon gave it up claiming to find it too exhausting.

As a Czech born in Prague when that city was still in the Austro-Hungarian Empire, throughout her life she was deeply conscious of her nationality and of the accumulated indignities heaped on her own people. When the First World War broke out she returned home and established herself in a castle in Bohemia, using it as a centre for activists in the Czech independence movement. Even there she did not entirely escape from the world of the melodrama. One day a young airman, rather in the fashion of the Polish lady in Shaw's *Misalliance*, baled out into the castle grounds. After being nursed back to health by Destinn, he married her and the misalliance was a reality. What happened to him is not sure, but as soon as the war was over, Destinová, as she now styled herself, quickly returned to the scene of her erstwhile glories. She sang again at Covent Garden and the Met. Though she was only in her early forties, she was already in indifferent health. She had grown very fat and suffered greatly from high blood pressure which eventually forced her into retirement. She was only fifty-one when she died from a stroke.

It must be said at once that her records are disappointing; very few satisfy the expectations aroused by the enormous reputation she enjoyed in her lifetime. On them we hear a large, full-throated dramatic soprano with a brilliant yet rounded upper register. What they have not preserved is the thrill that her voice created in the theatre, that unforgettable power that Klein wrote of. The effect big voices make is the most difficult to preserve on record, not only because they are big—and especially in the early days this created problems for the recording engineer—but also because the gramophone is the great equaliser; on it every voice can be played back to reproduce the same number of decibels of sound—twiddle the knobs and Lily Pons's voice is as loud as Flagstad's. At best, records give only a two-dimensional account of a singer's art; even stereophony is not a true guide to the third, and in the case of Destinn it was the third dimension that was especially remarkable. Not surprisingly, big voices tend to have big faults; but it is perhaps unfair on singers like Nordica and Destinn that the primitive equipment of those days seemed to have no difficulty in keeping an account of those faults for our scrutiny. However, it did not invent what was not there. Destinn's scale is unequal, the chest voice noticeably thinner and duller than the middle and head registers. Perhaps, because of this, the high notes, though brilliant and of such imposing dimensions, are not always properly based; especially in the execution of awkward intervals, and when she puts on the pressure, the tone becomes thin and pinched and the intonation sharp. This sort of thing we can hear very well in a couple of souvenirs from Leoncavallo's German opera *Roland von Berlin*, a work in which Destinn had sung in its first performances at the Berlin Imperial Opera. There is a similar disappointment in the grand duet from *Hugenotten* with Karl Jörn; where we might have expected to have found her at her very best, she is too often strident with much crude attack and forced high notes. On the other hand Liszt's setting of Hugo's 'Oh quand je dors' is a very lovely piece of singing, even if her manner is a little public for the expression of such tender sentiments; the difficult and exposed high-lying phrases are done with admirable suavity and some beautifully floated pianissimi. Generally, however, she was not a refined singer. The Styrienne from *Mignon* is a graceless and leaden affair and in *Butterfly*, in spite of much intensity and deep commitment, there must have been something else in her interpretation that we are missing. Others have made so much more out of 'Un bel dì' (1908), which above all requires imaginative treatment. Even her much vaunted 'D'amor sull'ali rosee' disappoints; the voice moves securely enough and the trills are well turned but, apart from some not quite perfect intonation and rather whining tone, the phrasing is four-square

162 Destinn as Milada in Smetana's *Dalibor*

and there are none of those poetic touches, that subtle use of rubato to give an impression of quasi-improvisation, which other, less well-endowed singers have brought to this music. A duet with Caruso—the only one unfortunately—gives us an opportunity to compare a good musician with a memorable one. The piece, 'Sento una forza', is from *Il Guarany* by Gomes; since the singers never appeared in this opera in the theatre nor undertook concert engagements together, we may assume they learned it for the record. A comparison between the two is instructive. Destinn sings with solid tone and phrases attractively enough, but when Caruso repeats the phrases after her with irresistible charm contrived by the most expressive portamenti and delicate rhythmic effects, we know the limits of Destinn's art. Where she does make a stunning effect is perhaps where she was most at home, in the music of her compatriots. In Milada's aria from Smetana's *Dalibor* she ranges through the wide intervals with great authority and fearless abandon. It is a fact that even today, notwithstanding three quarters of a century's innovations in recording techniques, there are still voices like hers that do not sound themselves on records, and never quite re-create the thrill they can make in the theatre or concert hall.

33. Contraltos

The German contraltos are rather better represented on record than either the French or Italians. First among them, a singer six years older than Lehmann, was MARIANNE BRANDT (1842–1921). She made three recordings for the Pathé company in 1905, when she was sixty-three years old and her voice still in good condition. After a period of study at the Vienna Conservatory she made her debut at Graz in 1867, as Rachel in *Jüdin*. There followed engagements at Olmutz and Hamburg; then in 1868 she arrived in Berlin and had a most emphatic success as Azucena and Fidès. There she was a member of the company for eighteen years and appeared in a wide variety of contralto roles as well as Valentine in *Hugenotten*. In the summer of 1869 she went to Baden-Baden to work with Pauline Viardot. It was Viardot who first appreciated her real potential and encouraged her to 'sing any music you like so long as you do not have to tire and force your voice'.[1]

In 1872 she made her first visit to London, to sing Donna Elvira and the title role in *Fidelio*, hardly contralto parts. As Klein put it, she was a puzzle:

Was she a soprano, as most Fidelios and Donna Elviras are supposed to be? Was she a contralto, that was her official designation at the Hofoper in Berlin? Or was she the mezzo-soprano subsequently identified with the greatest Brangänes and Kundrys of her day? Well, the truth is she could be all three in turn. Her voice had an abnormal range of qualities as well as of compass and power. She had the low notes of a contralto, the high notes of a soprano, and the rich, full medium of a mezzo-soprano.[2]

In her only other London appearances, in 1882 at Drury Lane, she sang Fidelio again; also Brangäne and Ortrud. In Germany, where she was one of the leading singers, she sang the part of Waltraute in the first performance of *Götterdämmerung* at Bayreuth in 1876, and six years later alternated with Materna and Malten as Kundry in *Parsifal*. At the Met, where she was a principal during four seasons from 1884, her repertory ranged from such principal roles as Fidelio, Fidès, Donna Elvira, Amneris, Rachel, Ortrud, Siebel, Eglantine in Weber's *Euryanthe*, Adriano in *Rienzi*, Brangäne and Astaroth in Goldmark's *Königin von Saba* to Maddalena in *Rigoletto*, Wellgunde in *Götterdämmerung*, Magdalene in *Meistersinger* and Gerhilde in *Walküre*, which she would sing as well as Fricka. Her sudden departure from the Met seems to have been for reasons less vocal than political; during a performance of *Fidelio*, Lehmann, who could not endure the success Brandt had had in one of her favourite roles, stationed herself at the back of the stage box and just before the great duet, when Fidelio says 'Nichts, mein Florestan', broke out into loud and raucous laughter, causing Brandt to miss her cue. After this, she preferred to withdraw.

Even on records the voice has still a considerable range. The head register has the clean focus of the German method but is more brilliant, being freer and less contrived, with a fuller enharmonic range. The middle of the voice, like Lehmann's, is the most worn. The chest register, though without much quality, is fully developed. As Henderson noted, after her New York debut:

163 Marianne Brandt as Kundry in *Parsifal*

Her method [is] eclectic, by which we would imply that she has the vigorous enunciation and accent of the German school of song, and no little of the fluencey and taste of the Italian . . .[3]

Her age notwithstanding, the voice seems to be holding together well, without those incipient signs of disintegration we can hear in the recordings of Lehmann and Patti. The disappearance of this type of contralto voice, as we have already noted, is not a change in nature but the result of a change in training. The decline of the contralto from prima donna status in the early nineteenth century to that of a lay-figure, the gradual emergence to eventual supremacy of the dramatic soprano, encouraged teachers and pupils to concentrate on the production of heroic and brilliant high notes and ignore the chest register. Unfortunately, as so many recordings by German sopranos of this and later periods, show, a voice that is not fully developed in all of its registers cannot be fully expressive; it is the chest register that provides the basic colour throughout the entire voice—Rossini said that the contralto voice was the basis of all singing. Abuse of the chest register, as Garcia points out, will produce all kinds of vocal problems, but a lack of it leaves the instrument under-nourished, white in prevailing tone colour, often unsteady—particular features of Wagnerian singing over the last three quarters of a century.

In spite of her age and some tremulousness, Brandt's singing is still smooth and her intonation mostly true. She has the besetting German infirmity, an impure attack, principally the long-term effect of the language's hard consonants; her technique is less mannered than Lehmann's or Schumann-Heink's. In the opening phrases of 'Ah mon fils' (in German), there is much left of a grand legato style; especially effective is the use of downward portamento; done spontaneously, it gives that intensity that in earlier years had caused Finck, otherwise restrained in his enthusiasms, to acclaim her 'the most thrilling Fidès the world has ever seen and heard'.[4] An abridged account of Orsini's Brindisi from *Lucrezia Borgia* presents the problem of a voice no longer responsive in the rapid figurations; she compensates for this by marking the rhythm with splendid gusto. Is it possible to conjecture anything of Viardot from these records? It seems likely that in Fidès's aria there is an echo of the earlier singer's style and interpretation; Viardot created the role.

The greatest of Marianne Brandt's successors was

ERNESTINE SCHUMANN-HEINK (1861–1936). At the age of fifteen, at Graz, she was the soprano soloist in a performance of Beethoven's ninth Symphony. Two years later, in 1878, she made her stage debut as Azucena at Dresden, where she remained for the next four years. In 1882, at Hamburg, she was engaged to deputise for an ailing Marie Goetze, and so great was her success that she was given a long-term contract. There she sang a wide variety of roles, ranging from Amneris, Orpheo, Orsini in *Lucrezia Borgia*, Ulrica and Adriano in *Rienzi* to Bertha in *Barbier von Sevilla*, Quickly in *Falstaff* (in the first Hamburg performances), Mamma Lucia in *Cavalleria Rusticana*, the Third boy in *Die Zauberflöte*, Nancy in *Martha*, Puck in *Oberon*, Martha in *Faust*, Mercedes in *Carmen* and even Katisha in the *Mikado*. Unlike Brandt, save for an occasional Donna Elvira, she never ventured into the soprano repertory. While under contract in Hamburg she made guest appearances in Berlin, and in 1892 Harris invited her to Covent Garden. There she sang in the Ring Cycle under Mahler's direction. Klein recalls her debut as Erda in *Siegfried*:

> Her voice . . . so entrancing in its solemn, mystical beauty, its breadth, firmness and volume, that we would fain have listened to Erda a good deal more. For the full revelation of her unique tone, together with the singer's extraordinary gift of pathetic and touching expression, we had to wait for her Waltraute in *Götterdämmerung*.[5]

Her other roles included Erda and Flosshilde in *Rheingold*, Fricka and Waltraute in *Walküre* and a Norn and Waltraute in *Götterdämmerung*. She also sang Brangäne to Sucher's Isolde; then, in a postscript to the season at Drury Lane, she revealed very considerable gifts as a comedienne in the part of the old Countess in Nessler's *Trompeter von Säkkingen*. In 1896 she sang in the *Ring* at Bayreuth. The following summer and for four seasons thereafter she returned to Covent Garden, in those years adding Magdalena in *Meistersinger*, Ortrud, the Prologue in Mancinelli's *Ero e Leandro* and Magdalena in Kienzl's *Der Evangelimann*. Her first United States engagement was as Ortrud in Chicago in 1898. The following January, in the same role, she made her Met debut. She reappeared regularly for the next three seasons, but only occasionally thereafter. In New York, to her London repertory she added Fidès in *Le Prophète*, Frau Reich in Nicolai's *Lustigen Weiber von Windsor* and Mary in *Fliegende Holländer*. Her final performances in

164 Ernestine Schumann-Heink as Erda in *Rheingold*

separated'.[7] That same year she went further, making a triumphant debut (and also a great deal of money) touring in a musical comedy: *Love's Lottery* by Julian Edwards. This introduced her to a new public, and in the course of the next quarter of a century her name became a household word in the United States; except for Caruso, she was perhaps the best-known opera singer of her day. In later years, through the medium of the radio, she reached out to new audiences. Towards the end of her life when she made her first feature film, the 1935 musical *Here's to Romance* with Nino Martini; it was enough that she played herself.

Hers was a magnificent contralto voice; to judge from recordings made when they were at about the same age, more impressive than Brandt's. The range extends from the D below middle C, in Schubert's 'Der Tod und das Mädchen', to high A—there is even a fleeting B flat in Fidès's 'O Prêtres de Baal'. All three registers are fully equalised in weight and, at least in the early years, the passages between them properly smoothed over. Like Lehmann, but in a different way, her singing is expressive despite the constraints imposed upon it by the German technique; though the head register reminds us rather of the Flying Scotsman coming out of a tunnel, the rest of the voice is sufficiently free for her to manage a good legato, as in Sapho's 'O ma lyre' and the arias of Dalila. She declaims Adriano's 'Gerechter Gott' with great authority, even if the attack is not always square on the note and there is too much hard attack. A fact that Aldrich noted:

> As to the style and finish of her vocalisation, there has often been room for questioning ... her attack is sometimes rough and explosive, as when she slides and gropes for the tone and does not strike it fairly in the middle. She has a tendency to force her lower tones beyond their natural richness and fullness, and in her upper tones she is sometimes unsteady and somewhat off pitch.[8]

opera were at the Met in 1932; though she was over seventy, she was still able to declaim Erda's prophecy, 'with an eloquence that took the breath away'.[6]

Soon after her arrival in the United States, she began to extend her activities away from the opera house. She became a popular concert and recital singer. Following an appearance at Carnegie Hall in 1904, Aldrich wrote that 'she indulges in no excesses of facial play or gesture, nor does she forget the concert stage and opera stage are widely

Her coloratura records, in particular the Brindisi from *Lucrezia Borgia* and a Bolero by Arditi, have always been highly regarded by collectors; and they deserve to be, for they are remarkable. She delivers herself of a whole armoury of effects: there is a fine trill, she contrasts the registers with great skill and the ornaments are nimbly and cleanly executed. Yet in spite of what sounds today like an astonishing facility, closer examination reveals that it is not all quite as accurate as it seems to be on first hearing. We should not expect to hear anything suggestive of that great glory of the old Italian School which Chorley extolled in Viardot's rendering of Orphée's 'Amour viens rendre à mon âme', the canto di bravura, no rushing divisions from the chest; it is all rather artfully managed in a light medium or head voice. Nevertheless, from a great Ortrud and Brangäne, it remains a feat.

Schumann-Heink was a large and homely body and many are the stories told of her prodigious appetite; yet she was so warm and real a personality that there was even something engaging about her gluttony. A friend who came across her one evening in her hotel dining alone, in front of her the most colossal steak, could not help smiling. 'Surely,' he enquired incredulously, 'you're not going to eat all that alone?' 'No, not alone,' was the reply, 'I think I'll have some potatoes with it, then apple pie and cheese!' It was compensation for those early years when she had not known where the next meal was coming from. Life had been hard then and not made any easier by three unfortunate matrimonial essays, from which she had accumulated seven children. During the First World War, she had sons fighting on both sides; in the United States, where many loyalties were divided, it helped to make her popular with everyone! Her image as an earth mother (how appropriate Erda should have been one of her great roles) could not fail to appeal in the land where Motherhood was a far more sacred vocation than music-making. She came to occupy a place there rather like that of Dame Clara Butt in England. At her first New York recitals she had offered the songs of Schubert, Schumann, Loewe, Franz and Richard Strauss; later on she preferred Nevin, Chadwick, Jacobs-Bond, Ganz, Rasbach and O'Hara—a compliment to her audiences? If so it was not one that the critics greatly appreciated, but even they could not deny—

> the generous warmth and fervour of her delivery, her dramatic articulation of certain phrases, the breadth and intensity with which she enters upon a work . . . and, in whatever else she is lacking, it is not in the whole-souled devotion to the task she has in hand.[9]

If Schumann-Heink was the greatest contralto of her day, an exception in any age, many of her contemporaries were by no means inconsiderable. ROSA OLITZKA (1873–1949), born in Berlin but from a Polish family, enjoyed wide successes internationally. She was a pupil of Desirée Artôt de Padilla, a famous soprano who had studied at various times with Viardot and Lamperti and whose

other German pupils included Goetze, Irene von Chavanne and Max Dawison. Olitzka's first stage appearance was at Brunn in 1892. The following summer she made her Covent Garden debut as Erda in *Siegfried*, she returned every year until 1897 and again in 1899, 1900, 1901, 1905 and in the German season of 1907. At the Met she appeared during four seasons between 1895 and 1901. Her repertory included many of Schumann-Heink's roles: Brangänc, Ortrud, Fricka, Erda, Magdalena, the Hirtenknabe in *Tannhäuser* and assorted *Valkyries*. To these she added: Carmen, Ulrica, Siebel, Stephano in *Roméo et Juliette*, Frederic in *Mignon*, Amneris and Urbain. She made guest appearances in Berlin, St Petersburg and Paris, where she was the first Waltraute in *Le Crépuscule des dieux*, given under the direction of Cortot. Later in her career she sang with the Chicago and Boston companies. By that time, as Parker put it, 'her method was not one that it behoves the nurslings of the opera house to copy'.[10]

Her technique seems to have been less completely

165 Rosa Olitzka as Carmen

166 Edyth Walker as Brünnhilde in *Walküre*

German than Schumann-Heink's. By the time she made records, though she was only in her early thirties, the voice often sounds worn. She makes the best impression in part of the fourth act duet from Aida for Radames and Amneris, here reduced to a solo and sung in German. She phrases with the right kind of tragic grandeur and there is much intensity in her delivery. In 'Say yes, Mignon', a salon number by that indefatigable purveyor of trifles Mme Guy d'Hardelot, she cuts no ice at all. And from a later series Sapho's 'O ma lyre' reveals a quavery tone and uncertain top notes.

EDYTH WALKER (1870–1950), from Hopewell, N.Y., was a pupil of Aglaia von Orgeni. In 1894, at the age of twenty-four, she made an auspicious debut as Fidès in *Prophet* at the Berlin Imperial Opera. The following year she was engaged at Vienna, where she remained until 1903. By all accounts these were her best years; at this time she

confined herself mostly to the contralto repertory, but later on, when she attempted soprano roles that were beyond her reach, her voice inevitably suffered. On her first visit to London, to Covent Garden in 1900, in a company that included Schumann-Heink, Olitzka and Homer, she appeared as Amneris, Urbain, Waltraute in *Götterdämmerung,* Ortrud, Erda in *Rheingold* and *Siegfried,* and Fricka in *Walküre*. But when she came again in 1908, she had moved up to Brünnhilde in *Walküre* and Isolde, in which, according to one critic 'she found the top B a matter of some difficulty, and the high C was distinctly a shriek'.[11] In Salzburg, in 1901, she sang Donna Elvira. Two years later she made her Met debut as Amneris. Krehbiel appraised her thus:

> Miss Walker is . . . the possessor of a voice of lovely quality, though not of great volume. There is a decided charm in her singing, the most marked artistic grace of which is the perfect evenness of its quality up to the point where the pitch puts a strain upon her.[12]

During three seasons she appeared in a variety of roles, as well as those she had sung in her first London season: Brangäne, Siebel, La Cieca, Orsini, Orlofsky in *Fledermaus*, Nancy in *Marta*, Leonora in *Favorita*, the title-role in Goldmark's *Königin von Saba* and Brünnhilde in *Walküre*. But she failed to make any lasting headway against the established Met favourites, in particular Fremstad and Homer. She returned to Europe, first to Berlin and Hamburg and later Munich, where she remained until 1917, the year the United States entered the First World War. In 1910 she paid two further visits to Covent Garden singing Isolde, Elisabeth, Thirza in Dame Ethel Smyth's *Wreckers* and she was London's first Elektra; like the opera's, her notices were equivocal. The *Observer* wrote:

> Incredible as it may seem to those who know the score, it was possible for Mme Walker, never a hair's breadth from the centre of the note, to vocalise perfectly the most trying and strenuous passages.[13]

Incredible indeed; one cannot help wondering just how well the critic really did know the score, for all available records—though there are none from *Elektra*—suggest that Edyth Walker's soprano excursions found her vocalisation very far from the note. There can be few records made by a singer of undoubted talent that fall quite as disagreeably on the ear as her renderings of Ortrud's Curse or Brünnhilde's Battle Cry; not only is the intonation

167 Margarete Matzenauer as Ortrud in *Lohengrin*

revealed to advantage. She is so much more at home in the contralto range; Erda's Prophecy is only slightly less impressive than Schumann-Heink's, and there is charm and personality, in an unfamiliar piece, Magdalena's 'O schöne Jugendtage' from Kienzl's *Evangelimann*; she had created the part of Magdalena in its first Vienna performances.

Like Edyth Walker, MARGARETE MAT-ZENAUER (1881–1963) was German by training but not birth; she was born in Temeszvar in Hungary. Her father was a bandmaster and her mother a singer. She studied first in Graz, later in Berlin with Antonia Meilke and Franz Emmerich and in Munich with Preuses, whom she married in 1902. Her official debut took place at Strasbourg as Puck in Weber's *Oberon*. Between 1904 and 1911 she was a principal at the Munich Opera, where she built up a great reputation for her splendid voice and remarkable virtuosity; she sang Brünnhilde in *Walküre* and Donna Anna as well as Erda and Fricka. In Paris and London she made guest appearances as Isolde, Kundry and Ortrud and was acclaimed for her musicianship and picturesque looks. In 1911 she went to the United States and began a career at the Met that was to continue through nineteen seasons until 1930. In her first season she appeared in fifteen different roles in twelve operas; like Brandt, her repertory knew no vocal frontiers. After her debut as Amneris, Henderson wrote of her 'superb, rich and very flexible' voice and of 'genuine vocal art'.[14] Afterwards came Brangäne, Waltraute and Flosshilde in *Götterdämmerung*, Ortrud, Hate in *Armide*, Orfeo, Erda in *Siegfried*, the Nurse in Dukas's *Ariane et Barbe Bleue*, Fricka in *Rheingold*, Fricka and Waltraute in *Walküre* and La Cieca. Her most remarkable achievement was Kundry, done at the last minute in lieu of an ailing Fremstad with only one piano rehearsal; it was also the first time she had ever sung the part. Aldrich hailed it as a tour de force:

> Although Mme Matzenauer is so much a contralto, she has in her voice the higher notes that enable her to sing the music of Kundry without obvious effort, even in the passages in the second act that are sometimes a trial. Her voice had power and significant and changing color of dramatic expression.[15]

Prompted by this success in the soprano range, she ventured on Brünnhilde in *Walküre*, but here her 'singing was thought laboured and ineffective'.[16] Over the years she continued to give demonstrations of her versatility as Ulrica, the

vague but the effort involved in squeezing out the voice is almost painful to listen to—it was, literally, in the grip of an ambition that took it far above itself. Hers was a light contralto voice, the style and technique similar to that of Orgeni's soprano pupils but with a more fully developed chest register. She could accomplish an occasional top note but could not move in the high tessitura with ease or effectively. Of her soprano records, perhaps the most successful is of Elisabeth's Prayer from *Tannhäuser*, where the fine quality of the voice is

Brünnhilde of *Siegfried*, Dalila, Leonora in *Fidelio*, Marina in *Boris*, and the Countess in *Figaro*—though in this part Aldrich thought:

> Her voice is not fitted for the music, which is high for the range that nature gave her, and seemed so even though she sang some of it transposed to a lower pitch.[17]

Later came Fidès, Isolde, Azucena, Eboli, the Sexton's Widow in *Jenufa* and the High Priestess in *Vestale*. After leaving the Met, she continued to make occasional appearances: she sang Dalila at the Lewisohn Stadium in 1934 and appeared in recital as late as 1938.

As a concert and recital singer she was equally well regarded by the critics. Two days after the Armistice in 1918, she was the soloist with the Philadelphia Orchestra under Stokowski. The programme included Chausson's *Poème de l'amour et de la mer*, three songs by Tchaikovsky (orchestrated by the Maestro), the Immolation from *Götterdämmerung*, as well as the National Anthem (another Stokowski arrangement). Aldrich wrote:

> Margarete Matzenauer was magnificent. The sense of magnificence, of opulence, of a nature endowed with all the musical and dramatic gifts is felt when she comes before her audience. Add to this, personal beauty, the type we call oriental, and described in the Song of Songs. Such a combination would be positively oppressive in any woman who had not the directing artistic intelligence of Mme Matzenauer. She is thinner than last year, but her voice is nothing if not richer. It was poured out with heartfelt passion controlled by her beautiful art. Just now, in a period of squalling or moaning with the mouth full of mush, the singing of this woman carried us back to the glorious days of Lilli Lehmann and Milka Ternina.[18]

Matzenauer's recordings range from Gioconda's 'Suicidio' and Brünnhilde's Battle Cry to Orfeo's Lament and Siebel's Flower Song. Like Destinn's, few of them are really satisfying: we notice—far less than the opulent voice and majestic style which so impressed her contemporaries—a prevailing insecurity. The tone is spread, the intonation is rarely exact and there seems to be much contrivance involved in manipulating the voice, especially in the soprano range. She is at her best in slow and shapely music, in Selika's Slumber Song from Meyerbeer's *Afrikanerin*, where her soft-grained tone and soporific manner are appropriate dramatically. The coloratura is not as tidy as that of

Schumann-Heink, the trills and roulades not quite perfect. Altogether we must believe that there was another dimension to her art which records quite failed to notice.

34. Heldentenors

The challenge of Wagner was quite as great for tenors—every tenor fancies himself a superman—as it was for the sopranos. Even a singer as feted as Jean de Reszké, who might well have contented himself with what he did so well (the heroes of Meyerbeer, Gounod and Massenet with an occasional Italian Lohengrin thrown in), eventually found the pressure of critical opinion irresistible and learned German so that he might undertake Siegfried and Tristan in the original language. Not surprisingly his success, though it was a costly one bringing his career to a premature end, was an inspiration for a whole generation of tenors who followed after him, of whom few had the artistry or the physical resources to cope at all eloquently with the demands of the Wagnerian music drama.

The oldest Wagnerian tenor to make records, HERMANN WINKELMANN (1849–1912), was in fact older than de Reszké and the only creator of a Wagner tenor role whose art we can recall. His style ante-dates the Bayreuth barkers. There is something Italian in the soulful delivery and rather sweet tone; also in the technique and use of portamento. Winkelmann was a student of Koch in Hanover and made his debut as Manrico at Sonderhausen in 1875. Three years later he became a principal with the Hamburg company, where he was Loge in the local premiere of *Rheingold* in 1878, Siegfried in *Götterdämmerung* in 1880 and Tristan in 1882; there too he created the title-role of Nero in Rubinstein's opera. In the spring of 1882, with the Hamburg company he appeared in London at Drury Lane Theatre, where he sang Lohengrin and Tannhäuser and was London's first Tristan and Walther. Later that same year, at Bayreuth, he created the title-role of *Parsifal*. From 1883 until 1906 he was a leading member of the Vienna Imperial Opera, where he sang all the major Wagnerian roles and 'for close on twenty years was the only thinkable Siegfried'. His repertory also included Renaud in *Armida*, Florestan, Masaniello in *Stumme von Portici*, Jean in *Prophet*, Robert in *Robert der Teufel*, Pollione in *Norma*, the title roles in Massenet's *Le Cid*, *Otello* and Goldmark's *Merlin*.

In the Prison aria of Dalibor from Smetana's opera, sung in German, which Winkelmann recorded at the age of fifty-six, the voice has retained much of its quality though it is no longer very responsive and the breath does not always last out to the end of a phrase. The timbre is characteristic and affecting and, unlike so many of the later Bayreuth singers, there is an attempt at graceful and expressive phrasing. It does not sound as big or heroic a voice as Tamagno's was at the same age, but it has a brilliant spin on the tone that would have made it tell even in a big theatre over a Wagnerian orchestra.

Towards the end of his career in Vienna many of Winkelmann's principal roles were taken over by ERIK SCHMEDES (1868–1931). Schmedes was born in Copenhagen and came from a musical family. His brother was Haakon Schmedes, a well-known violinist. As a boy, Erik had studied the piano, but on Pauline Viardot's suggestion, at the age of twenty-four, he decided to become a singer instead. He went to Berlin to study with Nikolaus Rothmuhl and later in Vienna took further instruction from

168 Hermann Winkelmann in the title-role of Smetana's *Dalibor*

169 Erik Schmedes as Lohengrin

Johannes Ress, both of whom advised him to become a baritone. He made his debut at Wiesbaden in 1891 as Valentin in *Faust*. During the next three years he was a principal baritone at the Nuremberg Opera; at the end of that time, however, on the advice of Bernhard Pollini, the Director of the Hamburg Opera, he renewed his studies, this time with August Iffert in Dresden, and after only a short period, re-emerged as a heroic tenor. In 1898, he enjoyed a great success as Siegfried, at the Vienna Imperial Opera, where he was to remain a member of the company for twenty-five years. There he sang all the principal Wagnerian roles; also Florestan, Otello, Canio, Don José and Pollione. In later years he was Vienna's first Cavaradossi and first Herod in *Salome*. The year following his Vienna debut, he was invited to Bayreuth as Siegfried and Parsifal; he was greatly admired and returned every summer until 1907. In 1908 he was engaged at the Met but his voice was deemed too small for the theatre;[1] he was rated an indifferent Parsifal and made no impression as Pedro in *Tiefland*, Siegfried or Tristan.

Schmedes's large recorded output includes titles from Kienzl's *Evangelimann*, Pfitzner's *Rose vom Liebesgarten* and Marschner's *Templer und Jüdin*, as well as pieces from the *Ring, Tristan, Lohengrin, Meistersinger, Otello* and *Prophet*. His is a typically German-style voice, showing all too obviously the effect of the Bayreuth Sprechgesang. Each note is hurled out, as one American critic put it, like bits of Dutch cheese fired from a cannon. The head register is powerful and brilliant, but the tone is overloaded and spread. It is this kind of pressure on the voice that is responsible for that slow wobble which, later on, became such a feature of Wagnerian singing. There is nothing persuasive in his interpretations, no legato in the singing, little eloquence in the phrasing.

One of the most celebrated singers of his day and a noted exponent of the Bayreuth style was the Belgian tenor, ERNEST VAN DYCK (1861–1923). Originally he studied in Paris with St Ives Bax. He made his stage debut at Antwerp in 1884. Three years later, he sang the title-role in the first performances of *Lohengrin* in Paris. Later, in 1892, he was the first Siegmund there, in 1895 the first Tannhäuser at the Opéra since the debacle of 1861, and in 1908 the first Siegfried in *Le Crépuscule des dieux*. In Vienna, in 1892, he created the title-role in the world premiere of Massenet's *Werther*, and later on sang in the local premieres of Mascagni's *Rantzau* and Puccini's *Bohème*. His career at Bayreuth began in 1888, in the title-role of *Parsifal*; he returned on many occasions thereafter, singing Lohengrin in 1894, and in 1912, appearing for the last time as Parsifal. On his first visit to Covent Garden in 1891 he sang des Grieux in Massenet's *Manon* and *Faust*. The following summer he added Lohengrin, and in later years Tannhäuser, Siegmund, Loge and Tristan, his last appearances being in the spring of 1907. His Met debut in 1908 was as Tannhäuser; during four seasons he also sang Loge, Lohengrin, Siegmund, Tristan and des Grieux in *Manon*.

Van Dyck was probably Julius Kniese's most

170 Ernst van Dyck as Parsifal

celebrated pupil, and he believed, as W. J. Henderson tells us, that in order to

convey the illusion of a musical dialogue in the declamatory voice parts of the Wagner dramas, the legato must be abandoned, the pure, fluent, round musical tone set aside and the consonants delivered with the fullest possible insistence on their value, and the vowel sounds are treated with regard only for their conversational characteristics, and with none of their availability as tone producers.[2]

Henderson goes on to describe the effect of this on

his singing:

> He was wont to deliver the operatic text of Wagner in a
> hard and brittle staccato, in a dry tone without
> resonance and almost wholly devoid of singing
> quality.[3]

Henderson was not alone in this opinion; by 1904,
though he was only forty-three, it was generally
agreed that van Dyck's voice was gone. Thereafter,
his engagements were the result of his considerable
histrionic skill; in particular, his Loge was thought
to be without equal.

His few recordings are hardly a pleasure to listen
to. In Werther's Song of Ossian he carefully
measures each word in a rather prosaic reading—
not much poetry in the singing anyway. There is
little beauty or suavity of tone and the phrasing is
not helped by some ugly slurs and a couple of hard-
driven A sharps.

By the turn of the century, the enormous
popularity of Wagner's operas was no longer
confined to Germany: it was an international
phenomenon. So great was the demand that the
world's major opera houses were obliged to press
into the service of his works singers who were
hardly equipped for duty. In the period following
the departure of Jean de Reszké, in particular at the
Met and Covent Garden, many were called but few
chosen. One of the most remarkable—if not in voice,
certainly in versatility—was Andreas Dippel
(1866–1935) from Cassel. After studying in Berlin,
Milan and Vienna, he made his debut as Lionel in
Flotow's *Martha* at Bremen in 1887. He remained
there until 1892, and then spent a year in Breslau
before securing an engagement in Vienna. His Met
career began in 1890, where he returned for twelve
seasons until his final appearances in 1908. At the
end of that time for two years he shared the
management of the theatre with Giulio Gatti-
Casazza. In 1910, following some internal dissen-
sion, he moved to Chicago. In America he was not
regarded as a front-rank singer, but his astonishing
capacity for learning roles at the last minute helped
the management out of many a difficult predicament
and in his portrayals his intelligence made up
for a lack of fine vocal art. Some idea of his
remarkable versatility may be had from reading
through the list of roles he sang during the Met's
1904–5 season: Alfredo, Tannhäuser, Ernesto, Loge,
Almaviva, Tristan, Edgardo, Siegfried, Turiddu,
Eisenstein, Rodolfo, Walther, Cavaradossi, Parsifal,
Rodolfo, and Don José!

Georg Anthes and Alois Pennarini, principal

tenors at Dresden and Hamburg, both had brief
international careers. The former sang at Covent
Garden in 1903 and again in 1906, appearing as
Lohengrin, Siegmund, Tannhäuser and Walther. He
was not liked. In New York, he attracted most
attention in a performance of *Lohengrin*:

> When [he] stepped into the swan boat to take his
> departure from his too inquisitive bride, he leaned
> back too far and his weight capsized the fragile craft.
> Thus the unusual spectacle of the sudden disap-
> pearance of Lohengrin in the River Scheldt was
> presented.[4]

Only ten days after this, he was the victim of
another mishap; in the first act of *Siegfried*, before
he had time to strike the anvil once, it split apart.
Pennarini appeared at Covent Garden in the 1902
season, as Lohengrin, Walther, Tannhäuser, Siegmund and Heinrich in Dame Ethel Smyth's *Der
Wald*, showing off a 'powerful hard German voice'.[5]
It was his only London season.

As with Dippel and Anthes, we have only a few
cylinder records of Alois Burgstaller. He seems to
have been, at any rate briefly, a more important
artist. A graduate of the Bayreuth school, he was a
student of Hermann Levi and Julius Kniese, before
making his debut at the Festspielhaus in 1894. Three
years later, he enjoyed a considerable success as
Siegfried and thereafter for some time remained a
popular favourite. In those years he sang in Paris,
Brussels and various German cities, but it was after
his first visit to the Met in 1903 that he enjoyed the
widest acclaim. He was one of the first of the
Bayreuth singers to appear in New York, displaying
a fresh young voice and a good lithe figure but,
according to Henderson, 'as innocent of the art of
tone production as a child'.[6] In seven seasons he
undertook all the principal Wagnerian tenor roles
and was the first Parsifal at the Met, as a result of
which he incurred Cosima's wrath and never again
sang at Bayreuth. According to Krehbiel it was an
admirable impersonation, though:

> His voice is not an heroic one, and there are moments
> in which it is wanting both in sympathy and volume,
> but at every truly great moment confronting him he
> rose to its obligations . . .[7]

He returned for only one season with Gatti by
which time (1908) 'his voice was not in good
condition.'[8]

Unlike Burgstaller, Ernst Kraus had an especially
powerful voice and has left us a considerable

number of records. He took up a career as a singer on the advice of Heinrich Vogl, an early Wagnerian tenor. The first three years of his career were spent at Mannheim. Then in 1898 he was engaged at the Berlin Imperial Opera, where he remained until 1924. He appeared regularly at Bayreuth between 1899 and 1909, as Siegmund, Siegfried, Erik and Walther and during that time, like Burgstaller, was particularly identified with the Sprechgesang style. He sang in London for the first time in 1900 and returned often during the next ten years. In New York he sang in only one season, 1903–4. His repertory included Siegmund, both Siegfrieds, Tannhäuser, Lohengrin, Tristan, Max in *Freischütz*, Walther and Florestan.

A recording of Siegfried's Anvil Song reveals a powerful voice, especially at the top. The words are

171 Heinrich Knöte as Walther in *Meistersinger*

all declaimed forcefully but the attack is not always clean and the execution is approximate; not an attractive singer.

The successful German tenors outside Germany in the years immediately before the First World War were HEINRICH KNOTE (1870–1953) and Karl Burrian. Knote was born in Munich and trained there with Emmanuel Kirschner. He made his debut in 1892 as Georg in Lortzing's *Der Waffenschmied* and during the next eight years at Munich sang principally in the lyric and buffo repertory as Pedrillo, David, Tamino, Stradella and Lionel in *Martha*. By degrees he began to undertake heavier roles including Manrico. Then, in 1900, following the death of Vogl, he appeared as Siegfried for the first time. Thereafter he dedicated himself to the Wagner repertory but still occasionally sang Italian roles. During his first Covent Garden season in 1901 he was not especially successful, but in later years as Walter, Tannhäuser and Tristan his interpretations were greatly admired. In New York, where he appeared for the first time at the Met in 1904, Henderson described him 'as the best lyric tenor we have yet received from Germany'.[9] Other critics too wrote of 'temperament . . . elegance . . . warmth'.[10] During these seasons he sang Lohengrin, Tannhäuser, Erik, both Siegfrieds, Walther, Tristan, Assad in Goldmark's *Königin von Saba*, and when Caruso declined to sing Manrico— he claimed it was all shouting—Knote had a very real success with his 'pleasing lyric quality'[11] in 'Ah, si ben mio' and bold delivery of 'Di quella pira', even though this was transposed. His career at Hamburg continued until 1931, when he was still able to make an effect as Siegfried. His final appearances in the United States were with a company organised by Hurok in 1923 and 1924, singing Rienzi and Walther.

Knote's recording career began in 1906 and he made his last visit to the studios in 1930. There are a large number of Wagnerian excerpts in which he is predictably impressive through with many of the usual unattractive features of the German style. Surprisingly, one of his best records is from Verdi's *Troubadour*—'Ah, si ben mio' ('Dass nur für mich')—where he shows a splendidly resonant voice and a good legato only hampered by the attack; a nasty way of grazing on to the high notes. Altogether, in spite of a rapid and sometimes too strong vibrato, this is more expressive singing than from so many of his contemporaries who fell under the direct influence of the Bayreuth school: in fact Knote never sang at Bayreuth.

172 Karl Burrian as Herod in *Salome*

Karel or KARL BURRIAN (1870–1924) was a Czech. He studied in Prague and Munich with Wallenstein, Piwoda and von Kraus. During his debut season at Brunn he sang Manrico and Jenik in *Verkaufte Braut*. In the course of the next ten years he was successively a principal in Reval, Aachen, Cologne, Hanover, Hamburg, Budapest and Dresden, where he succeeded Anthes in the Wagnerian repertory. There, in 1905, he created the role of Herod in the world premiere of Strauss' *Salome*. In 1904 he came to Covent Garden for the first time as

Tristan and Tannhäuser and returned in 1905, 1910 and 1914. He sang in Paris, Prague, and Vienna, but his greatest triumphs were reserved for New York, at the Met, where he appeared every season between 1906 and 1913. In those years his roles included Tannhäuser, Lohengrin, Herod, Tristan, Loge, Siegfried, Siegmund, Parsifal and Florestan. As Herod, Aldrich found it 'an extraordinary portrayal of the most difficult character. His personality full of apt and characteristic traits. His declamation expressive and enunciation clear cut.'[12]

In New York his Tristan, which he sang with Fremstad while Mahler conducted, was also enthusiastically received by the critics and public. An orchestra player recalls that he was 'an intelligent artist though his voice was not remarkable for natural beauty. Nevertheless his stagecraft was especially imposing.'[13] There is a fragment of this interpretation on record, from Act Two, 'Wohin nun Tristan scheidet'; alas, nothing survives of Fremstad's response or of Mahler's conducting, and of the orchestra there is only an insubstantial echo. Like Knote, Burrian on records has a strong, evenly-produced voice, retaining some aspects of a legato style. Apparently he liked to make records lying on a couch, apt for Tristan, even if the beer bottle in his hand was not. A big, imposing figure on stage, he had matching appetites; as well as eating and drinking on an appropriate scale, he fancied himself a ladies' man. It was the consequences of an amorous escapade that pretty well finished off his career. A jealous husband replaced the beer with bleach; the effect on his voice may be imagined.

Two rare recordings of the tenor ALFRED VON BARY (1873–1926) suggest that a singer with a fine voice found it easier to accommodate the Bayreuth style. Von Bary was nearly thirty when his voice was discovered by Nikisch, and he began his studies with Richard Müller. He made his first appearance on stage as Lohengrin at Dresden. He sang there very often and also in Munich, but his greatest successes were at Bayreuth, where he was engaged each summer from 1904 to 1914. His roles included Siegmund, Siegfried, Lohengrin, Tristan and Parsifal. We can hear something of the strength and fine quality of his voice in 'Siegmund heiss ich' from the first act of *Walküre*; here the clean declamation is appropriate as well as effective and contrived without destroying the shape of the piece.

Six days after Burrian's Covent Garden debut in 1904, the Danish tenor VILHELM HEROLD (1865–1937) made his first appearance there. While Burrian was singing Tristan and Tannhäuser,

Herold was portraying Walther and Lohengrin. The following year he added Roméo and Faust, and was compared to Jean de Reszké with 'his elegant and beautifully controlled voice, fine musicianship, style and inspiring presence'.[14] In spite of these successes, he preferred to remain in Germany and Scandinavia, where he was a great favourite. After 1922 for two seasons he was Director of the Copenhagen Opera.

Though Herold mostly sang the German repertory, he was French-trained. The voice itself was rather hard and guttural-sounding, but he was a resourceful artist, as we can hear in his recording of the Romance from *Fra Diavolo*, a vigorous and well characterised interpretation, with some very adept falsetto singing which rises smoothly out of the rest of the voice.

More perhaps than any of the singers above, the Dutch tenor JACQUES URLUS (1867–1935) had in abundance those qualities necessary to make the proper effect in the big heroic roles. He was already twenty-seven when he made his debut in the unlikely part of Beppe in *Pagliacci*, in Amsterdam in 1894. During the next five years he sang Raoul, Manrico, Joseph in Méhul's *Joseph*, Faust and Samson. In 1900 he became a principal tenor at

173 Alfred von Bary as Siegmund in *Walküre*

174 Vilhelm Herold as Don José in *Carmen*

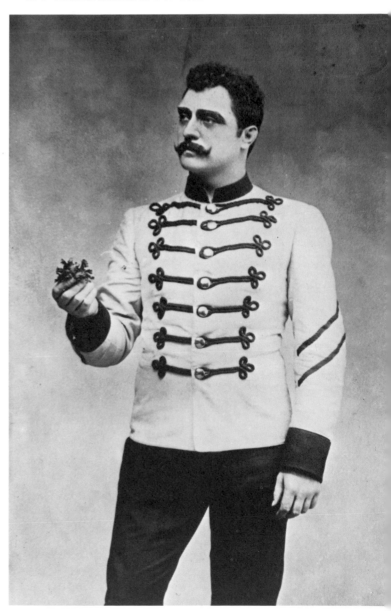

175 Jacques Urlus as Lohengrin

Florestan, and showing in them, as Henderson put it 'rather more legato than teutonic singers usually possess'.[15] He returned to Covent Garden in 1924, still singing 'with some beauty of tone'. He sang Tristan for the last time in Amsterdam in 1932. He was also a noted concert artist, particularly as soloist in Mengelberg's annual performances of the *Matthäuspassion* and also in Mahler's *Das Lied von der Erde*.

Urlus's voice was a powerful, fully developed dramatic tenor. The dark, almost baritonal, quality of the lower range was well-suited to the music of Wagner and enabled him to declaim with the right intensity yet without sacrificing a good legato style. Only the highest notes on records are rather tight and lack the heroic ring that made Melchior unique. Outstanding is Rienzi's Address to Rome, delivered in a grand and monumental manner. That he was an accomplished technician we can hear in Adolar's 'Mandelbaum' aria from Weber's *Euryanthe*, where he negotiates the awkward, high tessitura smoothly. Here the high notes are artfully balanced between the chest and head register.

Of these non-German, though German-style, tenors, the most highly regarded and the most acclaimed was LEO SLEZAK (1873–1946). Slezak was a pupil of Adolf Robinson, a noted baritone who had sung in Damrosch's German seasons at the Met in the 1880s; he was himself a pupil of Lamperti and later he taught Rudolph Berger and Joseph Schwarz. Slezak made his debut at Brunn in 1896 as Lohengrin. After a season in Berlin and Breslau, in 1900 he was invited to Covent Garden. He sang the title-roles in *Siegfried* and *Lohengrin*. At this stage of his career it was his remarkable voice and striking physique—he stood more than six-foot-two—that excited the most admiration; he was still by all accounts a clumsy and inept actor. His London debut had the misfortune to clash with news of the relief of Mafeking and he failed to receive the attention he deserved. The following year he was engaged by Mahler for the Vienna Imperial Opera, where he reigned as the supreme tenor of his day, his position equal to that of Caruso at the Met. He sang a vast repertory from Siegfried to Belmonte, embracing Raoul, Canio, Radames, Hermann, Jean in *Prophet*, Assad in *Königin von Saba*, Lohengrin, Rodolfo, Walther, Tannhäuser, Manrico, Faust, des Grieux, Otello, the title role in Flotow's *Alessandro Stradella* and Manrico. He remained a member of the company for thirty-three years, during that time making triumphant guest appearances in Germany,

Leipzig where he was a member of the company until 1914. In this period he appeared at Covent Garden with the Beecham Company, in 1910 and again in the German Season of 1914, as Tannhäuser, Tristan, Walther and Parsifal. The following year at Bayreuth he sang Siegmund. In 1912, he was invited to the Met and remained a member of the company for five seasons. In that time his repertory included Tristan, Siegmund, Lohengrin, Walther, Tann-häuser, both Siegfrieds, Parsifal, Tamino and

abundant outpouring of tone and with admirable declamation and diction'.[19] For most New York critics and opera-goers it was the finest since Jean de Reszké's. He continued to earn golden opinions through four seasons, adding such diverse roles as Tamino, Faust and Lohengrin, but in spite of his great successes he did not return after 1913. From that year he confined himself almost entirely to the German-speaking countries.

Slezak was a highly successful concert and lieder singer. After a recital in 1909, Aldrich wrote:

> The remarkable beauty and power of his voice have often been enjoyed in the lyric drama, in which he is one of the distinctions of the Opera House ... Mr Slezak has an unusual power of giving apt and significant expression to a variety of moods, expression that is gained by subtle means in the molding of a phrase, the color of the voice, the suggestion of a dramatic or emotional motive; and his singing of Lieder is vitalised thereby in a fascinating way. In most things his phrasing is admirable and his enunciation is of unusual excellence and clearness.[20]

In later years he also appeared in operetta—he played the title-role in a revival of Offenbach's *Barbe-bleue* in Berlin in 1929—and finally as a character actor in films. He wrote four books of memoirs, all of them full of entertaining anecdotes.

Slezak recorded extensively from 1901 through into the early electric period. His recordings provide abundant testimony as to the size and fine quality of his voice. It was a large lyric tenor, and though he did sing Siegmund and the young Siegfried on occasion, generally he confined himself to the early Wagner roles, in particular Tannhäuser and Lohengrin. He shows a remarkable command of mezza voce and—when the voice is not extended— an eloquent and characteristic style; for better, for worse, it is hard to confuse Slezak's voice with any other tenor. He was a master in the handling of the head register through various gradations of dynamics, as in Assad's 'Magische Töne' for example, fining it down to a perfect falsetto high C. Unfortunately in full voice the high notes are often pinched and forced, like Schmedes's; this constriction eventually produced that slow wobble which is such an unattractive feature in so many of his recordings. He is at his best in music that requires style and technique as much as voice; Belmonte's 'Wenn der Freude Tränen' is sung with more character than we are accustomed to, and yet the coloratura is clean and there is even a good trill. No doubt, as with Destinn, in the spaces of a big theatre the overloaded and powerful top notes would have

176 Leo Slezak in the title-role of *Siegfried*

Holland, Scandinavia and Russia. In 1905 he sang Tannhäuser at La Scala with Giannina Russ and Sammarco. His Met debut took place in 1909, as Otello: 'an impersonation not soon to be forgotten.'[16] There followed Manrico, Radames—'the most impressive in . . . years',[17] Tannhäuser with 'splendour of voice, skill in tone production and clear enunciation',[18] Stradella, Hermann in *Pique Dame* and finally Walther which, according to Aldrich, 'he sang with chivalrous ardor and

made a considerable effect; in the confined circumstances of the recording studio they are disagreeable.

Like Slezak, KARL JÖRN (1873–1947) divided his
attention between the Wagnerian and Italian
repertory. Born in Latvia, he studied singing first in
Riga and then in Berlin with Johannes Ress. He
made his debut at Freiburg in 1896, as Lionel in
Martha. After engagements in Zurich and Hamburg,
in 1902 he joined the Berlin Imperial Opera as a
principal lyric tenor and stayed there for six years.
In 1906 he was invited to Covent Garden, where he
sang the Vagabond in Poldini's *Vagabund und die
Prinzessin* and Nureddin in Cornelius's *Barbier von
Bagdad*; also two performances of Loge in *Rheingold*.
In the German season in 1907 he sang Loge again,
and added Fenton in Nicolai's *Lustigen Weiber von
Windsor*, Erik and Walther. In six seasons at the Met
after 1908–9, his repertory included Walther,
Tannhäuser, Jenik in *Verkaufte Braut*, the King's
Son in Humperdinck's *Königskinder*, Froh in
Rheingold, des Grieux, Max in *Freischütz*, Parsifal,
Lohengrin, Siegmund, Canio, Faust, Tamino,
Hoffmann, Loge, Turiddu and the Italian Singer in
Rosenkavalier. He settled in the United States, and
made his last appearances with a German company
organised by Gadski in 1928, when he was still
apparently in fine vocal fettle.

Records reveal a lyric voice of good size with
rather a tight and typically German production. The
tone is occasionally reminiscent of Slezak, though
neither as characterful nor as attractive. There is,
too, something of the same facility in mezza voce.
The high notes, though powerful—the high D flat in
the Grand Duet from *Hugenotten*, for example—are

179 Felix Senius in the title-role of Pfitzner's *Palestrina*

produced in a rather disconcerting fashion, with a
constricted attack in falsetto before reinforcing the
tone. He could be an expressive artist, as we hear
him in company with Knüpfer in the duet 'Solo,
profugo' ('Ja, seit frühester Kindheit') from *Martha*,
singing with some charm and pleasant tone.

Mention must be made of two of Germany's
outstanding concert and lieder singers: the tenors
GUSTAV WALTER (1834–1910) and Felix Senius.
Walter, born in 1834, is the oldest German singer on
record. For the first thirty years, from his debut at
Brunn in 1855 as Edgardo, he had a distinguished
career as a principal lyric tenor at the Vienna Imperial
Opera. After his retirement in 1887 he devoted
himself to Lieder singing. He was one of the first
important German singers to give only song recitals.
His performances of Schubert, Schumann and
Brahms were considered without equal.

He was seventy-one when he made three records.
There are two songs and one operatic aria; a
souvenir of one of his famous impersonations,

177 Karl Jörn   178 Gustav Walter

Wilhelm Meister in Thomas's *Mignon*. The voice is
still in good condition and reminds us with its sweet
quality of Winkelmann. In Schubert's 'Am Meer'
the tone is pure and forward and free from the
mannerisms of the latter German style. It is an
intense performance, yet managed without exaggerated emphasis of the text and conceived entirely
in vocal terms, sung with exemplary line. It is a
record of great historic importance.

FELIX SENIUS (1868–1913) was often referred to
as the successor of Walter. He was from East
Prussia, but his career began in Russia in 1895. He
gave his first lieder recital in 1900. As a concert artist
he was a renowned interpreter of the tenor music in
Handel's *Messiah* and Mendelssohn's *Elijah*. He sang
in London on several occasions and Sir Henry Wood
writes appreciatively of his 'beautiful tenor voice'
and 'artistic delivery' in Debussy's *L'Enfant Prodigue* and Elgar's *Dream of Gerontius*. He died from
ptomaine poisoning after a banquet given in his
honour at Königsberg in 1913.

In the aria 'Un' aura amorosa' from *Così* he shows
off a lyric tenor of fine quality and executes the
high-lying tessitura smoothly and cleanly. It is an
affectionate rendering with many a hold and ritard
and a wide variety of nuance and gradation of
dynamics. Only the rather open mixture of registers
in the upper range is exceptionable, signs of that
pinched and strident tone that disfigures so much
German singing of this period.

35. Baritones and Basses

Unlike their French and Italian confrères, the
German baritones still sang in the same range as the
singers of Handel's and Mozart's day; although
Wagner's baritone roles call for occasional high Fs,
even Gs, the tessitura, as we have noted before, is
predominately in the middle of the voice and not
like that of Verdi, Gounod and Massenet cast
relentlessly in the top fifth. In general German
baritones tend to have darker, lower-pitched voices
than the French or Italians.

One of the oldest and most important was KARL
SCHEIDEMANTEL (1859–1923), a pupil of Julius
Stockhausen, himself a pupil of Garcia. Scheidemantel made his debut in 1878 at Weimar and
remained a principal there for eight years before
moving to Dresden. His career there lasted for more

180 Karl Scheidemantel as Kurwenal in *Tristan*

than thirty years. He sang at Covent Garden in 1884
Telramund, Kurwenal, Pizarro, an 'excellent'[1]
Wolfram and Rucello in Stanford's *Savonarola*. He
returned in 1899 as Hans Sachs. After 1886 he
appeared regularly at Bayreuth, in *Tristan, Meistersinger, Tannhäuser* and *Parsifal* (alternating between Amfortas and Klingsor). In 1890 he sang
Wolfram at Vienna and two years later the same role
at La Scala. In Dresden he took the part of Kunrat in
the world premiere of Strauss's *Feuersnot* in 1901,

and in 1911, Faninal in *Rosenkavalier*. He also
sang in *Hugenotten, Wilhelm Tell, Lucrezia Borgia,
Rigoletto, Troubadour, Tosca, Trompeter von Säkkingen* and *Hans Heiling*. He translated into German
Mozart's *Così fan tutte* and *Don Giovanni* and
two textbooks on singing.

At forty-eight the voice is already old and grey-
sounding; years of repertory singing have very
obviously taken their toll. It has lost not only
quality but also elasticity and the breath support
seems far from certain. Yet the manner is still that of
an important singer. In Wolfram's 'Als du in
kuhnem Sange' the style is noble, the phrasing
shapely and there survives—at least in intention—
in the passage 'War's Zauber, war es reine Macht'
something of a real legato, an echo from that earlier
era when the Master himself still reigned.

Stockhausen's other pupils included the tenor
Anthes, whose voice can be heard only on a few of
Mapleson's noisy fragments and the baritones
Cornelius Bronsgeest and BAPTIST HOFFMANN

181 Baptist Hoffmann in the title-role of Rossini's *Barber*

(1864–1937). Hoffmann was seven years younger
than Scheidemantel and made his debut at Graz in
1888 as the Hunter in Kreutzer's *Nachtlager von
Granada*. The same year he secured an engagement
at the Cologne Opera where he remained until 1894.
There followed a three-year contract at Hamburg,
after which he moved to the Berlin Imperial Opera,
and was a member of the company there for the next
twenty-two years.

The voice and technique on records reminds us of
Scheidemantel; although the instrument itself is
more responsive and the tone fresher, he has similar
problems at the top of the voice. In the Love Duet
from Leoncavallo's *Bajazzo*, he sings with some
warmth and charm but his intonation and that of his
partner Emilie Herzog is by no means precise.

The greatest of Stockhausen's pupils was the
Dutch baritone ANTON VAN ROOY (1870–1932), a
commanding-looking man with a noble voice.
Originally he was a recital and concert artist, and it
was not until he was twenty-seven that he made his
operatic debut. This was at the direct instigation of
Cosima Wagner; at the Bayreuth Festival of 1897 he
sang Wotan in the *Ring* cycle and created a furore.
He soon established himself as one of the greatest
artists of his day and returned to Bayreuth regularly
as Sachs, Kurwenal, Amfortas and the Dutchman.
From 1898 he appeared at Covent Garden and the
Met. Aldrich described his Amfortas, which he sang
at the Met on Christmas Day 1903, as—

> noble, heart-rending in its pathos, deeply moving in its
> utterance of the agony of the soul which he bears,
> sometimes denoting a greater robustness of body than
> the posture of circumstances would seem to warrant,
> yet perhaps thereby only increasing the poignancy of
> the pain under which he suffers.[2]

This was in fact the first performance of *Parsifal*
given outside Bayreuth. Until that time the work
had been the sole prerogative of the Festspielhaus, it
was given at the Met in defiance of Cosima's explicit
diktat. By making himself a party to this heresy, van
Rooy brought his Bayreuth career to a premature
ending. He continued to appear in New York until
1908, and returned to Covent Garden for the last
time in 1913, but by that time, though he was only
forty-three, his voice was worn out. During his first
Covent Garden season he had appeared in recital at
the St James's Hall and confirmed his original
reputation as a great interpreter of songs, in
particular of Schumann's *Dichterliebe*.

Van Rooy's records were made between 1902 and

182 Anton Van Rooy as Wotan

breaking up the line. It is said his voice failed as a result of the forceful manner he acquired from Julius Kniese; if this so it is odd that there should be so little sign of it on his records. Wotan's 'Abendlich strahlt' from *Rheingold* is done with majestic authority yet suavely phrased. In the Farewell from *Walküre* we can endorse Aldrich's judgment—in spite of the ludicrously thin accompaniment—an interpretation 'magnificent in its breadth and accent of sorrow'.

The German baritone THEODOR BERTRAM (1869–1907) also had only a short career but one scarcely as glorious as Van Rooy's. He made his debut at Ulm in 1889, thereafter appearing with success in Hamburg, Berlin and Munich. In 1899 he was engaged at the Met and returned in the following season. In 1900 he appeared at Covent Garden and again in 1903 and in the spring of 1907. His repertory included Wotan, Wolfram, Telramund, the Dutchman, Pizarro and Pogner. In-

183 Theodor Bertram as Hans Sachs in *Meistersinger*

1908. They show us a voice, though seemingly of ample proportions, rather lighter in timbre than we might have expected from a great and authoritative Wotan. The high notes are its chief glory, the lower octave is by comparison weak; the first D below middle C is a poor note and there seems to be nothing at all below the B flat. The upper range is of a singularly beautiful quality with clear vowels and silvery tone; a rapid but narrow vibrato, more apparent in his later recordings, is never disturbing. The declamation is eloquent and contrived without

itially he seems to have been well liked, but later, especially in his last season at Covent Garden, the voice was no longer considered agreeable.

The influence of Bayreuth, where he sang regularly between 1901 and 1907, is obvious. By comparison with Van Rooy in Wotan's 'Abendlich strahlt', there is little sign of any legato and none of that noble phrasing. The voice, a good instrument, is produced smoothly enough, but it is not pre-eminently steady and the top notes are rather tight. He sounds more at home in a rumbustious piece from Lortzing's *Der Waffenschmied* than in the commanding heights of Valhalla.

Strictly speaking the American baritone LEON RAINS (1870–1954) could as easily have been classified among the French singers; his method has the typical smoothness of that school, but since he spent the greater part of his career in Germany, as a principal bass baritone at the Dresden Opera from 1899 to 1917 (when the United States entry into the First World War obliged him to withdraw to his own country), it seems more appropriate to count him among the Germans. In Paris he was a student of Jacques Bouhy. He made his debut in the United States with the Damrosch-Ellis company. In 1904 he sang Hagen at the Bayreuth Festival, and at Covent

Garden in the same year Heinrich in *Lohengrin*, the Landgrave in *Tannhauser* and Pogner. In neither theatre does he seem to have made much impression. Equally uneventful was his one season at the Met, in 1908–9, when he sang just two performances: as Hagen and Méphistophélès. In the later part of his career, in the United States, he sang mostly in recitals.

Rains's voice on record is warm and soft-grained with a wide range and even production enabling him to encompass bass and baritone roles. It does not seem to have been especially large, nor is there any great variety of dynamics. Given the generally low standard of technical accomplishment in Germany, his execution of Marcel's 'Piff, paff, pouff' (in German)—neat and clean—no doubt made a good impression in Dresden, but set against the standards of Plançon and de Reszké it did not amount to much in London or New York. He was a good and decent singer with a firm voice and limpid legato style which in spite of a pronounced vibrato is attractive to listen to. As a duettist he had the fine manners of that period, accommodating Minnie Nast (the first Sophie in *Rosenkavalier*) in the Swallow Duet from *Mignon*, and managing the music of Marcello in the fourth act duet from *Bohème*, with

184 Leon Rains as Méphistophélès in *Faust*

185 Leopold Demuth as Don Giovanni

Hermann Jadlowker, fluently and with some grace, notwithstanding the German translation.

Like Rains, LEOPOLD DEMUTH (1861–1910) had a wide ranging voice, from the bass F to the high A. Born in Brunn, he went to Vienna to study under Josef Gänsbacher. He made his debut at Halle in 1889 in the title role of Marschner's *Hans Heiling*. During the next eight years he was a principal in Leipzig and Hanover. In 1897 he was engaged at the Vienna Imperial Opera. There he remained until his early death in 1910.

Demuth was a prolific recording artist. There are titles from Weber's *Drei Pintos*, Goldmark's *Heimchen am Herd*, Bizet's *Djamileh*, Liszt's *Heilige Elisabeth*, Nessler's *Trompeter von Säkkingen* and Maillart-Abt's *Glockchen des Eremiten*, as well as from the more familiar repertory. We can hear him in company with another of the stars of the Vienna Opera, the bass Hesch, in the Ford/Falstaff duet from *Lustigen Weiber von Windsor*, a wonderfully unctuous performance where their dark voices blend splendidly.

WILHELM HESCH (1860–1908) was from Bohemia. He made his debut at Prague as Plunkett in *Martha*. During the next ten years he sang in Hamburg before arriving in Vienna. His repertory included Sarastro, the Cardinal in *Jüdin*, Leporello, Gremin in *Eugen Onegin*, Kaspar in *Freischütz*, Figaro, Osmin, Don Alfonso, Sachs, Wotan, Falstaff and principal roles in the operas of Lortzing and Nicolai.

Like Demuth he made guest appearances in most of the leading German theatres, but Vienna remained the centre of his activities throughout his career.

Like Demuth too, Hesch made a great number of records. None is finer than 'O wie will ich triumphieren' from *Entführung*. Here is a bass voice as easy at the top as it is at the bottom and even across a wide range, the execution clean and accurate: a voice of first class quality.

The position of PAUL KNÜPFER (1865–1920) in Berlin was like Hesch's in Vienna. Born in Halle, his debut took place at Sondershausen in 1887. For the next ten seasons he sang in Leipzig; then in 1898 he was invited to Berlin, where he spent the rest of his career. He was a regular visitor to Bayreuth; there he sang Gurnemanz, Hunding, Pogner and Daland. At Covent Garden in 1904 he shared the roles of the Landgrave, Heinrich and Pogner with Rains and he also sang König Marke. He returned in 1906 adding Daland, Hunding and the title-role in Cornelius's *Barbier von Bagdad*. In 1907 he sang Falstaff in Nicolai's *Lustigen Weiber von Windsor* and in 1913 was London's first Ochs, an interpretation which was greeted rapturously.

186 Wilhelm Hesch as Méphistophélès in *Faust*

187 Paul Knüpfer as Falstaff in Nicolai's *Lustigen Weiber von Windso*

PART V

Singers of Imperial Russia

36. Sopranos and Contraltos

For most of the nineteenth century the Italian vocal style prevailed in Imperial Russia. The Russian aristocracy, one of the richest in the world, had for long been lavish patrons of the Italian opera. Most of the great virtuosi from the days of Giuditta Pasta had appeared regularly in St Petersburg and Moscow earning the largest fees—more in one short season that they could expect in a whole year in Italy—and at the same time receiving the most extravagant plaudits from the court and fashionable world, even from the critics: when Viardot came to Russia for the first time, the composer Serov acclaimed her in pages of adulatory prose. The Tsar distributed decorations to the gentlemen and jewellery to the ladies. While the great charmed in the big cities, in the far-flung outposts of empire the visit of a troupe of Italian singers was a social event of the first magnitude. Tolstoy, in *Anna Karenina*, has left us a vivid account of the manners of Russian society at the opera. The indigenous opera was late in developing, and when it did, inevitably, it adopted the Italian style for its model. The father of Russian opera, Glinka, on his first visit to La Scala was so deeply affected by the music of Bellini and the bewitching art of La Malibran that he composed a brilliant divertissement on themes from *Sonnambula* for piano quartet, taking Malibran's variations as a point of departure for his own. Even in the works of Moussorgsky and Rimsky-Korsakov, in spite of the high proportion of declamatory music, there are still arias—the Fare-well of Boris, for example—which call for the suave and lyrical line of the Italians. Russian singers profited from the examples so often in front of them, with the result that when the tenor Ivanov went to Italy he created a sensation and Donizetti added another aria for Gennaro in *Lucrezia Borgia* especially for him.

The Russian vocal style was provincial but retained many of the older Italian traditions—indeed long after these had been modified, even rejected, by the Italians themselves. The older Russian singers indirectly provide important evidence of the pre-verismo style in Italy. Many of them had studied in Italy or had Italian teachers and enjoyed an advantage denied to almost all the Germans of singing alongside the greatest singers of their day. By the last decade of the nineteenth century many leading Italian artists, Francesco Tamagno and Mattia Battistini among them, spent a large part of each season in Russia, returning year after year. Others, like Olimpia Boronat and Medea Mei, for whom Tchaikovsky wrote Lisa in the *Queen of Spades*, settled in Russia; the former married a nobleman, the latter the tenor Nicolai Figner.

Perhaps the most remarkable Russian dramatic soprano of this period was NATALIA YERMOLENKO-YUZHINA (1881–19??). She studied first in Kiev with Zotova and later in Paris with Paul Vidal. After making an impressive debut in St Petersburg in 1901, she secured a contract with the Marinsky Theatre. She was a member of the company for the next five years and again between 1915 and 1920. In 1905 she moved to the Bolshoi where she remained until 1915, except for a two-year period

188 Natalia Yermolenko-Yuzhina as Judith in Serov's opera

59 Antonina Nezhdanova as Volkhova in Rimsky-Korsakov's *Sadko*

spent with Zimin's Private Opera. Her roles included Brünnhilde, Valentine, Gutrune, Violetta, Margherita in *Mefistofele*, Norma, Marina, Jaroslavna, Lisa, Tamara in *The Demon*, Masha in *Doubrovsky* and the title-role of Judith in Serov's opera. In Paris in 1908 when she appeared with the Diaghilev company as Marina in *Boris*, the French critics praised her glorious voice and imperious manner. Oda Slobodskaya in conversation with Vivian Liff recalled hearing her as Norma and being greatly impressed by her voice, especially in the dramatic moments of the score, but had reservations concerning her florid technique which she felt was not really equal to all the demands of the role.

After her marriage to the tenor David Yuzhin, she sang under his name. In about 1924 she left the Soviet Union and settled in Paris. Thereafter we find no trace of her.

Records reveal a full dramatic soprano voice, the registers strongly contrasted but properly equalised, extending easily from the bottom A to high C. The tone is rather vibrant and the singing lacks a really eloquent or expansive legato. The evidence does not suggest a refined or sensitive artist. 'O Patria Mia' leads up to a strong and brilliant high C and in Sapho's 'O ma lyre' we can hear the strength and quality of the lower range. Yet neither interpretation is really expressive. There is no real piano singing and she has a habit of breathing in odd places; perhaps the Russian translations are to blame. She is at her best in an appallingly difficult dramatic piece from Serov's *Judith*; according to Slobodskaya the role was one of her finest, a more compelling impersonation than Litvinne's. She despatches the wide-ranging and cruel tessitura, though not exactly effortlessly, certainly to great effect.

If Yermolenko-Yuzhina was the outstanding Russian dramatic soprano, then ANTONINA NEZHDANOVA (1873–1950) was the greatest lyric coloratura. She studied with Sophia Rubinstein, sister of the pianists Anton and Nicholas, and then with Masetti at the Moscow Conservatory. Her debut took place in 1902 in Moscow, when she sang the role of Antonida in Glinka's *A Life for the Tsar*. She was immediately given a contract by the Bolshoi and so began a career in that theatre which was to last more than thirty years. Her repertory was enormous. She sang Juliette, Gilda, Rosina, Lakmé, Tatiana, Lisa, Desdemona, Elsa, Tosca, Frau Fluth, Leila, the Queen of the Night, the Queen in *Les Huguenots*, Ophélie, Zerlina in *Fra Diavolo*, Tamara in *The Demon*, the title-roles in Rimsky-Korsakov's *Snow Maiden* and *The Tsar's Bride*. At the Bolshoi alone she sang thirty-seven different roles. Though she sang in other Russian theatres, she appeared outside Russia in only one season, in 1912, at Monte Carlo and in Paris, where she was Gilda in *Rigoletto* with Caruso and Ruffo. She was also a celebrated recitalist and introduced many new songs by Arensky, Rimsky-Korsakov, Glazounov, Scriabin and Rachmaninov, who dedicated his Vocalise to her.

It was a lyric soprano of fine quality extending to the F in alt. In coloratura, particularly staccato passages, the ornamentation is easy and brilliant, and if not accomplished by the highest standards—the triplet passages in the Queen of the Night's second aria are not really triplets—it is quite without the contrived mechanics of the German school. She is, however, at her most affecting in lyrical music. She makes a charming effect in the Cradle song from Napravnik's *Harold* duetting with the violin obbligato, her tone as sweet and true. The Russian language does not disturb the eloquent flow of Leila's 'Comme autrefois' from *Les Pêcheurs de perles* (though here we may note an occasional hard attack) and in the same opera, in duet with Leonid Sobinov, the leisurely rubato and expansive style are most attractive. Her recording of the Hymn to the Sun from *The Golden Cockerel*, made within a few years of the opera's premiere, is notable for its vocal poise and lovely quality even in the highest reaches; also for the clean and precise execution of the ornaments.

MARIE MICHAILOVA (1864–19??) was a prodigious recording artist. Her career, however, was unexceptional. She was born in Kharkov and commenced her studies there before moving to St Petersburg; later she went to Paris and Milan. She made her debut at the Marinsky Theatre in 1892 as the Queen in *Les Huguenots*. In the same year she took a small part in the premiere of Tchaikovsky's *Iolanthe*. She remained there for the rest of her career, in spite of the blandishments of various impresarios, including Oscar Hammerstein. Only once did she sing outside Russia and that was in a concert tour of Japan. She retired from the stage in 1912, after a farewell performance as Antonida in *A Life for the Tsar*.

Her singing of part of the first-act aria for Antonida suggests a sweet, light-weight voice and singing full of melancholy charm and grace. It should be remembered that in pre-war Russia a beautiful voice in the drawing-room was almost as important as a big one in the theatre; private engagements were extremely lucrative and through the success of her many gramophone records Michailova was one of the most sought-after salon singers.

The Finnish soprano ALMA FOHSTROM (1856–1936), born in Helsingfors when Finland was under the suzerainty of the Tsars, spent the major part of her career in Russia. She was from a musical family; her brother was a cellist and conductor and her sister was also a soprano and sang under the name of Elina Vardar. Fohström studied singing in St Petersburg with Nissen-Saloman and later in Milan with the elder Lamperti. Her debut took place in Helsingfors in 1878, as Marguerite. The same year she was engaged at the Kroll Theatre, Berlin and thereafter sang widely in Germany, Scandinavia and Italy. In 1885, for Mapleson at Covent Garden,

190 Marie Michailova as Lakmé

she stepped into the breach as Lucia when Patti became indisposed. The *Illustrated London News* while reserving final judgement was not much impressed, 'her voice was of pure soprano quality, but injudiciously trained . . .. We may say at once that there would be no difficulty in finding half-a-dozen English sopranos better qualified to fill the part of Lucia'. In the United States, also with Mapleson, she appeared as Zerlina in *Fra Diavolo*, the New York *Evening Post* reported that 'she acted her part with much grace and dainty naïvete'. Afterwards she sang Lucia, Amina and Dinorah, satisfactorily but without, according to Mapleson, being able to draw large audiences. In 1888, in one of Damrosch's German seasons at the Met, she undertook Marguerite, Bertha in *Prophet*, Eudoxia in *Jüdin* and Mathilde in *Wilhelm Tell*. In 1890 she joined the Imperial Opera in Moscow, where she appeared regularly during the next fourteen years. From 1909 until the Revolution she was a Professor at the St Petersburg Conservatory, later she taught in Berlin and Helsinki.

Her recordings are of the utmost rarity. In Alabiev's 'Nightingale', a fuller version than the more familiar arrangement by Orgeni, although she was at the end of her career, the voice has a certain quality and the singing charm and taste. On this evidence, and notwithstanding the *Illustrated London News*, there are signs of good schooling; even though the breath support is no longer secure, the graces are managed neatly and skilfully.

The contralto NINA FRIEDE (1859–19??) was born in St Petersburg where she took her first lessons at the Conservatory under Iretskaya. In 1880 she went to Vienna to study with Mathilde Marchesi. Two years later she was heard by the impresario Galletti at one of the annual recitals Marchesi organised to show off her advanced students; Friede was engaged for a season at the Teatro Nicolini in Florence. She made her debut as Pierotto in Donizetti's *Linda di Chamounix*. Later

192 Nina Friede

191 Alma Fohström as Violetta

that year she appeared at the Liceo, Barcelona as La Cieca and Urbain. The following season she made concert appearances in Moscow and St Petersburg. Between 1884 and 1891 she was a principal at the Marinsky Theatre. Her repertory included Amneris, Lyubova in Tchaikovsky's *Mazeppa*, Olga and the Nurse in *Eugen Onegin*, Spring in Rimsky-Korsakov's *Snow Maiden*, Pauline in *The Queen of Spades*, Khontchakovna in *Prince Igor*, Laura, Siebel, Stephano in *Roméo et Juliette*, Charlotte, Marguerite in Berlioz's *Faust*, Rogneda in Serov's opera of that name, Dalila, Parseida in Massenet's *Esclarmonde* and many small roles. Her operatic career continued into the early years of this century, in Warsaw, St Petersburg, Moscow, Odessa, Monte Carlo and Paris. She was also a popular concert and recital artist.

She made her few recordings in 1903. In a performance of Stephano's 'Que fais-tu blanche?' the voice still has a sweet and appealing timbre, though the lower range is hoarse and the breath

193 Eugenia Zbrujeva

be the centre of her activities for the rest of her career. Her repertory included Carmen, Siebel, Hansel, Lehl in *The Snow Maiden*, Ratmir in *Russlan and Ludmilla*, Khontchakovna, Avra in Serov's *Judith*, Svoyatchenitsa in Rimsky-Korsakov's *May Night*, Anne Boleyn in Saint-Saëns's *Henry VIII* and Martha in *Khovanshchina*, in which she appeared with Chaliapin in its premiere at the Marinsky. Between 1907 and 1912 she made various concert tours abroad with Taneyev, Siloti, Chaliapin, Rachmaninov and Glazounov, singing in Paris, Berlin and other Western European cities, though she does not appear to have sung in London. From 1915 she was Professor of Singing at the Petrograd Conservatory and then from 1921 in Moscow.

In one of Vanya's aria from Glinka's *A Life for the Tsar*, which does not appear in some editions of the score, we can hear a dark, powerful, vibrant voice, very Russian, ranging easily across the wide and difficult intervals, particularly impressive at the top. The recitative she declaims cleanly and to

194 Anastasia Vialtseva

support very uncertain. In spite of a tentative manner—understandable in the circumstances—the singing has distinction, the phrasing is full of charming and delicate inflexions and she uses rubato most expressively. The comparatively early decline of her voice, like that of Mantelli's, followed inevitably from attempting to sustain a repertory that was too dramatic for it.

Perhaps the finest Russian contralto voice of this period belonged to EUGENIA ZBRUJEVA (1869–1936). She was the daughter of a composer. She studied singing at the Moscow Conservatory in the class of Lavrovskaya. In 1894 she made her debut at the Moscow Imperial Opera—the Bolshoi, as Vanya in Glinka's *A Life for the Tsar*. She remained a member of the company until 1905. In that year she moved to the Marinsky, which was to

considerable dramatic effect, in the aria she sings with some warmth of tone and a limpid legato, even if the voice is not remarkable for its variety of colour or expression.

Though ANASTASIA VIALTSEVA (1871–1913) was principally an operetta and gypsy singer—the only operatic roles she sang at all often were Carmen and Dalila—she deserves a mention here for she was one of the great charmeuses of the day. Her voice was not an instrument of imposing dimensions, but in a little, typically Russian song 'Oh what a glorious night' the tone is warm and brilliant, the singing so lovely with its tremolando effects that she communicates a real pleasure without our needing to understand a word of the text. She died by her own hand at the height of her fame after being rejected by her lover, circumstances that to us today seem about as remote from reality as the scenarios of the operettas she sang in and the sheltered world of riches and privilege she amused and adorned.

37. Tenors, Baritones and Basses

Among all the Russian singers of that era the most admired and feted was the tenor NICOLAI FIGNER (1856–1919). After studying in St Petersburg he went to Italy where he made his stage debut at the San Carlo in 1882. For the next few years he sang throughout Italy, appearing at the Reggio, Turin, in 1887, when he took the principal tenor role in Catalani's *Edmea* (positively the last Italian opera with a mad heroine). It was also the occasion of another notable Scala debut, that of a young conductor—Arturo Toscanini. After visiting Madrid and Bucharest, Figner appeared in the Golden Jubilee Season at Covent Garden in 1887 (altogether a memorable year for opera in London, what with Harris's season at Drury Lane). He sang Arnold in *Tell*, Fernando in *Favorita* with Medea Mei (the Italian soprano who was soon to become his wife), the Duke, Elvino and Carlo in *Linda di Chamounix*. In Russia, where he spent the rest of his career, he was admired as much for his charm of manner and graceful acting as for his voice. With his wife he sang in the world premieres of Tchaikovsky's *Queen of Spades*, *Iolanthe*, Napravnik's *Doubrovsky* and *Francesca da Rimini*.

It is unfair to judge his records too harshly, for they were made at the end of his career and by that time the voice was sadly frayed and uncertain. In the songs, however, there survives something of his

charm and elegant style.

The gramophone has preserved for us the voice of IVAN ERSCHOV (1867–1943) when he was still in his prime. He was a student at the St Petersburg Conservatory between 1888 and 1893. At the end of that time he made his debut at the Marinsky Theatre, later to be the scene of many of his greatest triumphs. Immediately afterwards he went to Milan for further study with Rossi, a well-known teacher of that time. While in Italy he sang in Turin and Reggio Emilia. After returning to Russia in 1894, he spent a season in Kharkov. The following year he

195 Nicolai Figner as Enzo in *Gioconda*

rejoined the Marinsky, where he remained a principal of the company for thirty-four years. Erschov's popularity in Russia was enormous and he was thought by many to rival Tamagno in the heroic repertory. He sang Otello, Tristan, Lohengrin, Tannhäuser, Siegfried and Florestan, as well as Sobinin in *A Life for the Tsar*, Berendy in *The Snow Maiden*, Finn in *Russlan and Ludmilla*, Sadko, the title-role in *Doubrovsky*, Tucha in *The Maid of Pskov* and Grushka Kuterma in Rimsky-Korsakov's *Legend of the Invisible City of Kitezh*.

Erschov's voice has a resplendent quality entirely of its own; though characteristically Russian it is without the pallid tone and effete manner that is so monotonous and unpleasing in many of his contemporaries. The tone is unusually limpid and brilliant, and he has a complete control over the whole instrument at virtually any dynamic level through a range that extends from bottom C to the D above high C. It would be hard to find a tenor with a better integrated voice, in which the registers are more properly equalised and

196 Ivan Erschov as Raoul in *Les Huguenots*

197 Erschov in the title-role of *Sadko*

blended. His singing style is rooted in the messa di voce, and with this as the basis of his effects he has a seemingly inexhaustible range and variety of nuances at his disposal. Erschov is one of the few singers on record whose vibrato sounds a genuinely affecting device, something to be used at will and not the consequence of technical frailty. He is notably successful in the music of Meyerbeer, where precision of detail is of the essence of the style. In the Pastorale from *Le Prophète*, the beautifully drawn portamenti, the subtle gradations of dynamics and the marcato effects are quite masterly. He cannot (no one could) outsing Tamagno in the grand manner, but there is more expression in his performance, more flexibility in the rhythm too. The Brindisi goes with a splendid swing and at the end the cadenza is done with the flair of Battistini. He makes a real love song out of Raoul's 'Plus blanche' (in Russian, as are the selections above), singing in a lovely poised mezza voce, the elegant phrasing sweeping on through the climax, punctuated ardently but wholly without those strenuous accents that do nothing to inform this music. Undoubtedly one of the greatest tenors.

Among the lyric tenors Figner was succeeded by LEONID SOBINOV (1872–1934). At first he had trained to be a lawyer, and he did in fact finish these studies before he finally decided on a career in the opera. From 1892 he was a student of singing at the Moscow Conservatory. After various successes and some interruptions he graduated with a Gold Medal for Singing. By this time he had already appeared on stage with a touring Italian company, as Beppe in *Pagliacci* and the Steersman in *The Flying Dutchman*. He made his official debut at the Bolshoi as Sinodal in Rubinstein's *Demon*. Thereafter he sang the role of Bayan in *Russlan and Ludmilla*, Vladimir in *Prince Igor*, Faust, Alfredo, the Duke and Lensky, in which part he was thought to surpass his great predecessor Figner. Sobinov belonged to the same generation as Chaliapin and was much influenced by the new style of the Moscow Arts Theatre, then directed by the dramatist Nemirovitch-Danchenko and Stanislavsky. His singing was more Russian

198 Leonid Sobinov as the Prince in Dargomizhsky's *Russalka*

than Figner's, and though it retained the basic aspects of the old Italian school, in particular a smooth and elegant legato, it lacked the individuality of style that we can hear in the singing of Erschov. After seven years at the Imperial Opera, Sobinov joined the company of Savva Mamontov. Mamontov was a remarkable character. After making a fortune building railways he spent it all on promoting the paintings of the school of Golovin and Serov and the music of the modern Russians, in particular of the so-called 'Five'. In 1904 Sobinov went abroad for the first time, to La Scala, and in spite of the traditional Italian dislike of foreign tenors he enjoyed a very real success as Ernesto in *Don Pasquale*. In later years he sang there on a number of occasions, as Fra Diavolo, Alfredo, the Duke, Fenton, Faust in *Mefistofele*, des Grieux in Massenet's *Manon* and Roméo in Gounod's opera. He was equally well received in Monte Carlo as Almaviva and Ernesto. After 1907 he divided his time between the Bolshoi and the Marinsky; his repertory had come to include Gerald in *Lakmé*, the Prince in *Russalka*, Dmitri in *Boris*, Nadir, Berendy in *The Snow Maiden* and Werther. Later he appeared in Gluck's *Orphée, Bohème, Mignon, Lohengrin* and Napravnik's *Doubrovsky*. When the revolution came, Sobinov, a man of humble origins himself, preferred to stay in Russia. He continued to appear on stage and in the concert hall both in Russia, where for a time he was Director of the Bolshoi, and abroad on visits to Warsaw, Helsinki, Berlin and Paris. His farewell performance took place at the Bolshoi in 1933. In the later part of his life he joined the teaching staff of Stanislavsky's Opera Studio.

Sobinov's records have always been greatly admired by collectors and lovers of fine singing. It is a good-sized lyric tenor, evenly produced and with an especially lovely, though slightly throaty, quality—it may have been this that prevented the voice rising easily above the top B flat. His singing is notable for its smooth legato and elegant style. His interpretations of Russian music are the most important, but Ernesto's 'Cercherò lontana terra' from *Don Pasquale*, though sung in Russian and with a plangent Russian horn providing a throbbing obbligato, is beautifully expressive, touching yet not lachrymose. We can hear the same clean execution and shapely phrasing in Lohengrin's Address to the Swan. In Levko's Serenade from Rimsky-Korsakov's *May Night* there are some delicate morendo effects and piano singing. Yet for all its obvious virtues his singing soon becomes monotonous; there is a sameness in the delivery, insufficient variety of colour and expression, a want of the kind of purely vocal imagination that makes Erschov so fascinating. But it would be unfair to exaggerate this; next to some of his Italian and French contemporaries (and most of the Germans), he remains a sensitive artist and beautiful singer.

Three at least of Sobinov's contemporaries deserve some mention here. The eldest was ANDREI LABINSKY (1871–1941). His career began in the chorus of the Marinsky, but after attracting the attention of the management he became a pupil of Gabel at the St Petersburg Conservatory. In 1897 he was raised to the status of a principal. He stayed at the Marinsky until 1911, and then moved to the Bolshoi, where he remained for the rest of his career.

In 1920 he was appointed Professor of Singing at the Moscow Conservatory. Labinsky's repertory included Lensky, Sinodal in Rubinstein's *Demon*, Berendy, Sobinin, the Prince in *Russalka*, Dante in Napravnik's *Francesca da Rimini*, Roméo, Lohengrin, Don José, Radames and Faust.

On records it sounds a typical Russian tenor voice, with an attractive and plaintive timbre and a rapid but narrow vibrato which is not disturbing. It would seem to have been a darker yet more brilliant voice than Sobinov's. In the aria of the hapless Prince Sinodal from Rubinstein's *Demon* (which leaves little doubt where Rimsky got some of his oriental notions from) the tone is limpid and the manner appropriately melancholy. But here and in the Song of the Indian Guest—not a very poetic

199 Andrei Labinsky as Lensky in *Eugen Onegin*

200 Alexander Davidov and Alexander Davidov!

interpretation—the high notes have a tendency to slip below pitch.

ALEXANDER DAVIDOV (1872–1944) made his debut with the Tiflis Opera in 1893. Thereafter he sang with the Odessa opera and in 1896 joined Mamontov's company in Moscow. The following year he created the title-role in the world premiere of Rimsky's *Sadko*. From 1900 until 1912 he was with the Imperial Opera in St Petersburg. During those years he made various guest appearances and sang in Paris with great success. His career was brought to an untimely conclusion through deafness.

Davidov's recording of Eleazar's 'Rachel, quand du Seigneur' takes us back to a tradition that antedates Caruso in this music. He sings in a passionate yet restrained fashion. Throughout the drama is conveyed in the sorrowful tone, in the long cantilena with its purely vocal inflexions. Though it was not a particularly fine voice and the style, in 'Je crois entendre encore', is rather provincial, the singing exerts its own fascination. In the duet 'Un dì felice' (like all the selections, in Russian) he nicely balances vocal grace and ardour; by comparison Michailova's Violetta, neatly sung, sounds pretty indifferent. In one of those 'Troika' songs he shows off an effect he managed so well, the glissando.

The third of this trio had the most successful career, IVAN ALTCHEVSKY (1876–1917). He began his vocal studies with his brother, afterwards taking lessons from Palecek; later, in Paris, he went for further instruction to Félia Litvinne. His debut was at the Marinsky where he remained for four years. His roles included Sobinin, Don Juan in Dargomizhsky's *Stone Guest*, Sadko, Raoul, Faust and Don José. At the end of that time he appeared at the Monnaie, Brussels for one season, where he sang the Danish Knight in a revival of Gluck's *Armide*. In 1906 he was engaged at Covent Garden as Roméo, Faust and Lensky and in the local premiere of *Eugène Onegin* with Destinn and Battistini. The following year at the Manhattan he sang Corentin to Tetrazzini's Dinorah. Between 1908 and 1911 he appeared on various occasions in Monte Carlo and Paris, where he made a great impression as the elderly Prince Shuisky when Diaghilev introduced *Boris Godounov*, in a cast that included Yuzhina, Smirnov and Kastorsky as well as Chaliapin. The critic Henri de Curzon wrote:

One could hardly wait then to see him as Romeo. However, he portrayed this role of grace and youth with a rare brio . . . though his clarion voice with its

prodigious high Cs, is less at home here than in *Les Huguenots* for example, in which M. Altchevsky has just triumphed with éclat. At least, he knows when it is necessary to vary the vocal colouring.[1]

Altchevsky continued to appear regularly in Russia. In 1907 at the Bolshoi he created the role of the Astrologer in Rimsky-Korsakov's *Golden Cockerel*. He was a principal of the company until 1917 when he suffered a mental breakdown from which he never recovered.

His records are extremely rare. In the inevitable Song of the Indian Guest from *Sadko*, the voice is dry, of no particular quality, and it does not sit steadily on the breath, the ends of phrases having a tendency to collapse. It is an unimaginative

201 Ivan Altchevsky

202 Enzo di Leliva

performance and the 'oriental' roulades are not clearly articulated.

The Polish tenor TADEUSZ LELIVA (1867–1929), or Enzo di Leliva as he liked to call himself in his Italian incarnation, was in fact born and brought up in the Ukraine and the natural timbre of his voice is very Russian. After spending some while studying medicine in Kiev, he began his vocal studies under Mme Masini in Warsaw. In due course he went to Paris to work with Jean de Reszké. After some performances in Saratov and Kiev, he made his debut in Warsaw in 1902 as Radames. In the course of the next two years he sang the Duke, Jontek in *Halka*, Alfredo, Hermann in *The Queen of Spades*, Canio, Enzo, Fernand in *La Favorite* and the title-role in Orefice's *Chopin*, which became his favourite part. He was a good-looking man with a fine stage presence. The Warsaw critics seem to have been impressed by his singing too:

> A strong voice of beautiful timbre, skill in sforzandos, great beauty in mezza voce and sensitive use of dynamics.[3]

In 1904 he began his Italian career appearing at the Lirico, Milan as Dufresne in *Zazà*. Thereafter he divided his time equally between Poland, Russia and Italy. In 1909 he sang Pinkerton and Canio at Covent Garden, but in a company that included Anselmi, Affre, Slezak, Dalmores and Zenatello there was no shortage of strong or beautiful voices and he did not secure a return engagement. Later on he made guest appearances in Spain, Portugal and South America. As a result of increasing deafness he was obliged to retire at the end of the 1919 season.

It was a characteristic voice with an attractive and plaintive quality. In spite of his identification with the Italian repertory his Eastern European origin is very obvious. The dramatic music of Radames takes him to the limits; he only gets

203 Joachim Tartakov as Figaro in *Barbiere*

through it with the aid of a liberal helping of aspirates. He is far more at home in lyrical music, delivering a little barcarolle of Leoncavallo's with charm and some grace.

The baritone JOACHIM TARTAKOV (1860–1923) studied at the St Petersburg Conservatory with Camille Everard. After making his debut in 1882, he travelled to Italy where he sang for two seasons. Upon his return he was engaged at the Marinsky. There he soon established himself a leading baritone. His roles included Rigoletto, Tonio, Germont, Eugen Onegin, the title-role in Rubinstein's *Demon* and many others. From 1900 he

204 Nicholai Shevelev as Vindex in Rubinstein's *Nero*

205 Waclaw Brzezinski
as Marcello in *Bohème*

was the Director of the Marinsky Theatre, a position he continued to hold through the February and October revolutions until his death. Tartakov was a popular concert artist, especially in the music of Tchaikovsky.

The voice sounds a little uncomfortable in the lower reaches of the Demon's 'Accursed world' but it is still grand and imposing at the top, if obviously past its best. He sings in a suitably doleful manner, but was not on this evidence a suave singer or a subtle artist.

NICHOLAI SHEVELEV (1874–1929) was a pupil of the famous Italian tenor Leopoldo Signoretti. He sang with the Mamontov company from 1896 until 1903, and then for two years between 1906 and 1908 with Gvidy's Opera in St Petersburg. At the end of that time he moved back to Moscow and joined Zimin's Private Opera. He remained with it for the rest of his career except for an interlude between 1914 and 1921, when he appeared with several provincial companies including the Tiflis Opera. After his retirement he was appointed Professor of Singing at the Tiflis Conservatory.

Shevelev had an agreeable baritone voice which was lighter than Tartakov's. He phrases sensitively but sounds strained by the exacting tessitura in Henri VIII's 'Qui donc commande?' from Saint-Saëns's opera and at the top has a tendency to sing flat. In the Demon's 'Don't weep my child' there is some affection in his delivery, but the line is not really smooth and the voice has too much vibrato. There is the same flaw in the 'Epitalamio' from Rubinstein's *Nero*—a kind of drinking song and once a very popular piece with baritones—and the rhythm needs to be more strongly and incisively marked. He was a pleasant but hardly first-class singer.

The Polish baritone WACLAW BRZEZINSKI (1878–1955) went to Italy to study singing and made his debut at the Teatro del Corso in Florence, in Flotow's *Marta*. In 1906 he joined the Lemberg Opera; his first appearance was as Silvio in *Pagliacci*. He stayed there for the rest of his career. Though he undertook all the principal baritone roles from Figaro and Rigoletto to the operas of the Polish composers, in particular those of Moniuszko, he was basically a lyric baritone and sang the earlier repertory of Donizetti and Verdi with special effect—it is said that his remarkable range enabled him to take the tenor high C with ease. In 1911 and 1912 he made guest appearances in Italy; there he was nicknamed the 'Polish Battistini'. After his retirement he taught singing in Warsaw and later at Lodz.

In a recording of Hamlet's Brindisi (sung in Polish),

we hear a high, brilliant and good-sized baritone voice, the tone precisely focused. It is a performance of some character with an incisive and thrusting rhythm. There is a splendidly accurate cadenza before the reprise. Although the voice resembles Battistini's in range—he interpolates an easy high A flat into 'O sommo Carlo' from *Ernani*, in this piece he lacks his predecessor's smooth legato style and eloquent phrasing.

Traditionally it has always been the Russian bass voice that has been the most highly admired. There are few on record more remarkable than that of LEV SIBIRIAKOV (1869–1942). Another pupil of Rossi, he made some appearances in Italy before returning to Russia. During the next few seasons he progressed through various provincial centres, Tiflis, Kharkov, Kiev and Baku, before reaching the Marinsky. There he was prominent in the major roles of the German and Italian as well as the French and Russian repertories. In 1910 he went to the United States to appear under Henry Russell's direction at Boston, as Mefistofele, Méphistophélès and Don Basilio, all of which he sang in Russian. A critic wrote:

> Sibiriakov has impressive but not ponderous bulk, and orders his poses and movements skilfully. His voice is a rich, smooth, flexible bass, skilfully directed, capable of emotional and characterising significance. . . . His tones give sensuous pleasure and he knows how to sing. And yet he has not much finesse, and he is no subtle penetrator of operatic character and operatic music.[2]

It was not a particularly successful debut, perhaps because the public found him, as has been suggested, a crude actor, or more likely because, as was rumoured at the time, he was impolitic enough to make a pass at Mrs Russell. At any rate he never sang in America again. In the summer of 1911 he appeared at Covent Garden, as Marcel in *Ugonotti* (which he sang in Russian), in a cast that included Tetrazzini, Destinn and Sammarco; the critics spent a word or two commending his impressive voice, but that was all. He remained a favourite in Russia until the Revolution. In later years he moved to Brussels, where he was active as a teacher and continued to appear from time to time in the opera, the last time as Boris at the Monnaie in 1938 when he was in his seventieth year.

Sibiriakov's voice has that dark quality we associate with bass soloists in Russian choirs, the low notes wonderfully rich and weighty. The top however is equally impressive, rising easily and securely to the F sharp above middle C. These upper notes are precisely focussed with the right proportion of head resonance. The production is firm and smooth, though he does not, like Kastorsky and Chaliapin, have a really expressive legato style. His interpretations are disappointing; there is a want of nuance, of shading, no mezza voce. In the Demon's arias the singing is stentorian but without subtlety or depth of characterisation. A recording of Marcel's 'Piff, paff, pouff' is secure technically but lacking finesse, the delivery is monotonous and the style is provincial. It is not surprising he failed to make much impression in this role on a Covent Garden audience which had only recently heard Journet and could still remember Edouard de Reszké and Plançon.

206 Lev Sibiriakov as Don Basilio in *Barbiere*

207 Vladimir Kastorsky in the title-role of Borodin's *Prince Igor*

VLADIMIR KASTORSKY (1871–1949) was only briefly a student at the St Petersburg Conservatory. In 1894 he joined a travelling operatic troupe which appeared in various towns throughout Russia. It was not until 1898 that he became a principal at the Marinsky Theatre, making his debut as Tzertza in Serov's *Rogneda*. He remained a member of the company for the rest of his career. His roles included the Miller in *Russalka*, Gudal in *The Demon*, Dosifey in *Khovanshchina*, Gremin, Tomsky, Nilakantha, Hagen, the Count in *Figaro* and Sobakin in *The Tsar's Bride*, which he created in 1907. In Paris he sang Pimen to Chaliapin's Boris. In later life he returned to the provinces, singing with his own operatic quartet. After the revolution he was appointed Professor of Singing at the Leningrad Conservatory.

The voice is not as deep nor as powerful as Sibiriakov's but, as we hear it in Nilakantha's 'Stances' from Lakmé, it has its own individual quality. The high notes are especially beautiful with a lovely 'heady' quality. A rapid but attractive vibrato does not disturb a suave and affecting legato. He phrases expressively with limpid por-tamenti and a wide range of dynamics. The Miller's aria from the first act of *Russalka* goes with a nice jaunty lilt and he makes some attractive rubato effects.

38. Chaliapin

At any other time Sibiriakov and Kastorsky might have come to enjoy wider acclaim than they did, but unfortunately for them they were put in the shade by their contemporary FEODOR CHALIAPIN (1873–1938). Chaliapin ranks with Caruso and Maria Callas as one of the three greatest singers and most potent and influential operatic artists of the twentieth century. In one respect his achievement was even more remarkable than theirs. The naturally affecting quality of high voices had given the soprano and tenor the ascendancy in opera for more than a century and a half; even the most renowned basses from Galli and Lablache to Edouard de Reszké and Plançon had been reduced to playing subordinate roles. Chaliapin changed all that, not by trying to outmatch them where he never could

208 Feodor Chaliapin as Holofernes in Serov's *Judith*

have—in the production of clarion high notes or brilliant fioritura—but by transforming the bass from a character and supporting player into the protagonist. In his great days he never played comprimario roles. No company could have afforded to waste him on them, for he was also the first bass to demand, and receive, fees as high if not higher than any prima donna or primo tenore; in the 1920s in the United States with the Hurok company he received $3,500 a performance, a record that stood unbroken for thirty years, until—

appropriately enough—the arrival of Callas. He accomplished this supremacy by means of the Russian opera, until his time something provincial and obscure. From its beginnings in the works of Verstovsky and Glinka the bass had played important parts, but it was not until Moussorgsky's *Boris Godounov* that the Russian histrionic and vocal genius found an opportunity for full expression. It was Boris that made Chaliapin and which he popularised, first in Russia and then throughout the world. He stamped his personality indelibly on the part, creating a performing tradition that is still extant. Equally he transformed and expanded traditional conceptions of non-Russian roles, particularly Mephistopheles in the operas of Gounod and Boito. Chaliapin was the quintessential Russian. Born of peasant stock in the first generation after the freeing of the serfs when a whole people were becoming aware for the first time of their own identity, he was himself an expression of that awareness and his art of a nation's deep-rooted and all-embracing culture. From his childhood he was familiar with the music of the people: real folk music, not the boozey balalaika numbers that he used to sing in later years for fun—and money. The folk music of Russia a hundred years ago was rich and varied, especially the unaccompanied songs for groups of different voices with their simple but affecting harmonies. From this experience Chaliapin acquired that unerring ear which enabled him to make such an effect in his early recording of 'They won't let Masha walk by the brook', a tour de force 'in which the line of the melody is sheer perfection and the story is graphically told by subtle graduations of colour and an almost insolently masterful use of dynamic variations'.[1] Like Caruso, as a boy Chaliapin sang in a church choir, and though he was never a devout man, all of his life Russian liturgical music evoked a deep response in him and one which he communicates fervently in so many records, in particular in Gretchaninov's Twofold Litany 'Glory to the Thee, O Lord', one of the greatest pieces of declamation on record.

But formative though the influence of folk and church music was and important as it remained to him for the rest of his life, it was through the theatre that his art was to find complete expression. By his own account he was twelve years old when he was taken to see one of the many travelling companies that trouped back and forth across old Russia. It was love at first sight, and from that time he does not seem to have seriously entertained any other ambition than a career on the stage. His first theatrical experiences date from 1889 when he was only fifteen; in the following year he undertook his first major operatic role that of Stolnik in Moniuszko's *Halka*. At first he appeared in plays as well as opera, but as his voice developed his inclination towards the lyric theatre grew. Then in 1892 he had the first of those lucky breaks which are such a feature of the careers of the greatest artists: he met Dmitri Uzatov, a retired tenor who was then teaching in Tiflis. Uzatov realised the young man's potential and

offered to give him lessons, apparently for nothing. He was a formative influence on Chaliapin, not so much for the reason usually given—that it was he who introduced Chaliapin to the works of Moussorgsky and Rimsky-Korsakov (he would have found them anyway)—but for the technique he gave him. Thirty-five years separate Chaliapin's first recording session for the G & T company in Moscow in 1901 from the last in Japan in 1936. Even then when he was sixty-three and in failing health—he died two years later—his singing is still richly expressive, his voice in fine condition; only the greatest technical skill as well as sheer physical strength could have sustained him through such a career so that at the end he was still singing with virtually unimpaired mastery. This skill he acquired from Uzatov. We are not surprised to discover that Uzatov's teacher, Camille Everard, was a pupil of Garcia.

Chaliapin's histrionic genius has never been seriously questioned, and happily we still have some record of it in the Pabst film *Don Quixote* (the French version with Dorville as Sancho Panza is superior to an English adaptation); the death scene alone would put him alongside Garrick, Kean and Salvini. Yet the idea of him, so often repeated, as actor first and only a singer afterwards is flatly contradicted by his records. They provide incontrovertible evidence that his singing was profoundly musical, that all the many expressive devices he used, as with Battistini, were not extra-musical, grafted on or interpolated, but arose out of a vocal line informed by a legato that was securely poised on the breath. The infinite variety of nuances, the range of vocal colouring, his peculiar management of ornaments and cadenzas—though stylistically at odds with tradition—were, all of them, rooted in a classical vocal technique. It is only a seeming paradox that he who inveighed so strongly against the self-regarding virtuosity of his day should unwittingly have exemplified the ideals of the great singing masters of the seventeenth and eighteenth centuries. For them singing was a complete form of expression. A mastery of vocal art, of its graces and refinements, was an essential part of the musical idiom of the day. But they took as much account of the words and were equally concerned with conveying dramatic truth. It may well be that if Tosi could have heard Chaliapin and Plançon, he would have thought the Russian, not the Frenchman, the paragon of bel canto. For all his undoubted mastery, there is a certain contrivance in Plançon's technique, a self-conscious gentlemanly style. His singing lacks the spontaneity and intensity that were so much prized by the classical masters, and which are such remarkable features in Chaliapin's recordings. Artifice is wearing; whereas Chaliapin's voice, to the top F, remained fresh and responsive long after he had turned fifty, at the same age Plançon's high notes, as recordings attest, were noticeably thin and unreliable. Of the countless singers on records Chaliapin was probably the most completely integrated artist, his genius most perfectly fusing drama and music:

> He never seemed technically or consciously to sing. I mean that he did not need to make any obvious effort or laryngeal adjustment to modulate from his everyday way of speaking to the act of singing. There were magical moments when Chaliapin would suddenly modulate from histrionics to the purest vocalism and achieve the most perfect legato of any Italian.[2]

It may seem odd to compare him with Patti; yet what Verdi wrote of her could equally well apply to him; '. . . perfectly organised. Perfect equilibrium between singer and (actor), a born artist in every sense of the word.'[3]

In 1894 he left Tiflis and went to St Petersburg, where he secured an engagement with the Panayev company, one of the many private companies which were such a feature of operatic life in pre-revolutionary Russia. In the autumn of that year he moved to the Marinsky Theatre, making his debut as Méphistophélès in Gounod's *Faust*. Thereafter he sang Zuniga in *Carmen*, Count Robinson in Cimarosa's *Matrimonio Segreto*, Russlan, Doubrovsky in Napravnik's opera, and what was to become one of his favourite roles, the Miller in Dargomizhsky's *Russalka*. Though he made a considerable impression, his success was by no means complete. His acting style in particular was thought crude, undisciplined, not properly formed and obviously provincial. In 1896 he left the Marinsky to join Mamontov's company, first in Nizhni-Novgorod and later in Moscow. The two years he spent with Mamontov were crucial. At last he had the opportunity to develop his talent in a conducive artistic environment and to undertake for the first time those roles that were to bring him lasting fame, as well as making his fortune. For Mamontov he sang Susannin in Glinka's *A Life for the Tsar*, Ivan the Terrible in Rimsky-Korsakov's *Maid of Pskov*, Dosifey in Moussorgsky's *Khovanshchina*, Holofernes in Serov's *Judith*, Salieri in Rimsky's *Mozart and Salieri*—which he created—and, above all, the

title-role in Moussorgsky's *Boris Godounov*. He returned to the Imperial Opera in 1899, first to the Bolshoi and then to the Marinsky. By this time he was the mature artist we hear in his recordings. Until the Revolution he sang regularly at both theatres.

In 1901 he made his first visit outside Russia when he sang the title-role in Boito's *Mefistofele* at La Scala, in a cast that included Emma Carelli and Enrico Caruso; Toscanini conducted. Although the opera had been given on a number of occasions in previous seasons, Chaliapin's sensational interpretation completely outclassed his predecessors'; even Boito was impressed: 'Only now do I realise that I never had, up to this time, any but poor devils.'[4] 'Not only a splendid singer but a superlative actor. And in addition to this, he possesses a positively Dantesque pronunciation.'[5] He returned to La Scala on various occasions during the next thirty years. From this time Boito's *Mefistofele* became one of his favourite parts. He sang it with Philip II, Don Basilio, Holofernes, Ivan the Terrible and Colline during his many visits to Monte Carlo. In 1907 he made his Met debut in the role, but there for the first time he suffered a set back. New York society was scandalised when—

> he casts off a cloak resembling Papageno's parrotlike habiliments and bares himself to the rump. It is stupendously picturesque, of course . . . but calls to mind, more than anything else, the vulgarity of conduct which his countryman Gorki presents with such disgusting frankness in his pictures of Russian low life . . . Mr Chaliapin is undoubtedly an artist, even if his ideals are not praiseworthy. His physical appearance ought not to create greater admiration than his splendidly rotund voice and his eloquent declamation. . . .[6]

Amid all the critical cerebration over his stage-craft, only Henry Finck recognised his real genius; even the usually perceptive Henderson rated it 'cheap claptrap'. Chaliapin dissolved into what Geraldine Farrar called a 'huge pout',[7] and vowed never to return to New York. When he did in 1921, the Russia he knew and loved had been swept away, and the world too had lived through a holocaust without parallel in the history of mankind. What the sheltered pre-war society had thought 'vulgarity' and 'disgusting frankness' experience had shown to be real. He reappeared as Boris and this time swept all before him, but that is another story. . . .

209 Chaliapin and Rosina Storchio as Méphistophélès and Marguerite in Gounod's *Faust*

Glossary

Note: Terms are here defined as they are used in connection with vocal music. Bracketed numbers refer to the Bibliography.

Acciaccatura. Here refers to an ornament related to the appoggiatura (q.v.): a short, crushed note produced on the beat, immediately before an essential note of a melody.

Appoggiatura. A 'leaning' or supporting note, which prepares and delays the main note. A basic ornament of the Baroque and Classical periods which remained popular into the early Romantic age. In Italian opera, particularly in recitatives (q.v.), it enables the singer to mark the stress on the penultimate syllable without disturbing the vocal line. In all vocal music it helps to preserve a smooth legato, to give a stylish and elegant finish to a melodic or harmonic progression. Since it was not regarded as an intrinsic part of the harmony, it was rarely notated until the time of Vincenzo Bellini (1801–35); nevertheless, unless the score contains an explicit directive to the contrary—*senza appoggiatura*—the singer is expected to provide it.

Arpeggio. Where the singer sounds the notes of a chord successively in the fashion of a harpist.

Aspirate. A common technical frailty, where a note instead of being attacked cleanly is preceded by an audible exhalation of breath. In rapid coloratura (q.v.) intrusive h's make it impossible for the singer to execute all the notes accurately and smoothly.

Bel canto. Literally, beautiful singing. A term of comparatively modern origin, first generally used in the later part of the nineteenth century to describe the art of those singers—in particular Adelina Patti—which remained unaffected by the verismo style (q.v.) and still exemplified the classical virtues set out by Tosi, Mancini and the other great singing teachers of the eighteenth century. See

text p. 8. Nowadays, through misuse, it has come to mean pretty well anything the writer likes.

Cabaletta. Used principally in connection with nineteenth-century opera to describe the concluding and frequently most brilliant part of an extended scena or duet, often with a marked rhythm, and generally, but not always, to be sung faster than the preceding aria or cavatina (q.v.).

Cadenza. A brilliant, usually unaccompanied passage introduced at the fermata (q.v.) preceding the cadence proper. In the seventeenth and eighteenth centuries it was of the singer's own invention, designed to show off virtuosity and skill in composition, within the particular character and style of the music. From the middle of the nineteenth century composers have taken to writing out cadenzas in full. Those of many famous singers and singing teachers of the past survive in the common lore and are still in general use, e.g. those for the Mad Scene from *Lucia* by Fanny Persiani (the first Lucia) and Mathilde Marchesi. Certain composers wrote cadenzas for particular singers; Rossini composed a number for Patti, to sing in *Barbiere* and *Semiramide*, and for operas by Bellini and Donizetti.

Cantilena. A smooth and flowing melody.

Canto di agilità. A brilliant style showing the singer's fluency and accuracy in the rapid execution of ornaments and graces of all kinds. See Garcia (37) p. 68.

Canto di bravura. Similar to the canto di agilità but grander and bolder, in particular requiring skill in the use of the chest register (q.v.): of all the florid styles, the most dramatic. See text p. 9 and Garcia (37) p. 69.

Canto fiorito. The florid style, under which general heading Garcia lists the canto di agilità (q.v.), the canto di bravura (q.v.) and the canto di maniera (q.v.). See Garcia (37) p. 68.

Canto di maniera. This style, which Garcia further sub-divides into the canto di grazia and the canto di portamento, eschews the more brilliant effects of the canto di agilità (q.v.) and the canto di bravura (q.v.), requiring instead delicacy and finesse in the execution of ornaments and graces and a mastery of mcssa di voce (q.v.). See Garcia (37) p. 68.

Cavatina. Originally an entrance aria, but the term is nowadays interchangeable with aria.

Coloratura. Literally, coloured. Refers not, as modern usage has it, to a type of high soprano voice but to those passages of ornamentation—divisions, cadenzas, embellishments and so forth—which, as it were, colour the vocal line.

Continuo. Refers to a practice in baroque and classical opera, where the simple chords providing the harmonic bass indicated by the composer in the score were extended by unwritten elaborations ad libitum on various instruments, chiefly the harpsichord.

Corona. See Fermata.

Coup de glotte. A type of vocal attack. The term is discussed fully in the text on p. 20.

Division. Literally the dividing up or breaking down of long notes into figures compounded of shorter connecting notes. A particular feature in baroque music—as in the opera and oratorios of Handel—it was a harmonic as well as melodic amplification.

Embellishments. Term describing ornaments and graces used to decorate a given melody. In the seventeenth and eighteenth centuries embellishments were largely the singers' prerogative. Garcia in the second part of his *L'Art du Chant* gives the most reliable guide to the conventions in the late Classical and early Romantic opera.

Falsetto. See discussion of voice registers in text on pp. 6 and 7.

Fermata or *Corona*. Literally, a pause.

Gruppetto. See Turn.

Glissando. Where the voice is drawn across an interval between one note and another; similar to the portamento, but while that is accomplished smoothly, in the glissando the steps are marked in whole or half tones.

Intonation. Refers to the singer's ability to keep to the correct pitch, i.e. sing in tune.

Legato. A smooth, flowing vocal line. This is only possible where the voice is correctly supported by the breath. See also Portamento.

Messa di voce. The art of swelling and diminishing a note. For a full explanation see text p. 9.

Marcato and *Martellato*. Literally where the notes are marked or hammered out. Although these are non-legato markings, the breath support must remain smooth and continuous. There should not be, in Sir Henry Wood's words, 'shock of diaphragm, nor aspiration'. Undoubtedly two of the most difficult effects to contrive, depending as they do on complete control of the breath supply. See text p. 53.

Mezza voce. In half voice.

Morendo. A favourite vocal effect, where the singer gradually diminishes a note to a mere thread of tone.

Opera buffa. Comic opera.

Opera seria. A term in general use until the time of Rossini's *Semiramide* (1823) and Meyerbeer's *Crociato in Egitto* (1824) to describe operas treating serious subjects as distinct from opera buffa.

Portamento. For a full account of the meaning of this term the reader should turn to the text, p. 8.

Parlando. Where the singing is subordinate to the patterns of speech. An effect used especially in opera buffa, see recitative.

Recitative. Term used to denote the more or less extended passages of singing in baroque, classical and early romantic opera where the story is advanced between the arias and other set pieces. Garcia distinguishes the recitativo parlante, used exclusively in opera buffa, in which note values are determined by the natural rhythm of speech, from the recitativo stromentale, where the manner of delivery reflects the character of the music, as it would in an aria or set-piece.

Register. See text pp. 6 and 7.

Roulade. A brilliant vocal figure.

Sprechgesang. A declamatory style where the quality of speech is introduced into song at the expense of lyricism. It seems to have originated in Bayreuth in the period after Wagner's death. See text pp. 17 and 18.

Staccato. A note that is cut off quickly. Although this is a non-legato marking, the execution should be accomplished smoothly, without exaggeration and without disturbing the flow of breath.

Tessitura. The prevailing range in which an aria or cabaletta is written.

Timbre. The quality or tone of a voice.

Tremolando. A deliberate trembling of the voice, or variation of intensity in the sound, in order to contrive an emotional effect.

Tremolo. See Vibrato.

Trill or *Shake*. The rapid alternation of two notes, sometimes a semi-tone apart, sometimes a whole tone; it is possible to trill even in thirds.

Triplet. A rhythmical unit divided into three equal parts.

Turn. The Italian term is gruppetto. A four-note ornament, using the note above, the note itself, the note below and then concluding on the note itself— or vice versa.

Verismo. From the Italian, meaning truth. An operatic style originating in Italy in the later part of the nineteenth century. Its pre-occupation with 'ordinary' people, naturalistic style and usually contemporary settings (e.g. in *Cavalleria Rusticana*), at the time made it seem the epitome of realism; nowadays much of it seems merely sensational.

Vibrato. A deliberate or uncontrolled vibration of the voice. For a full discussion of the historical use of the terms tremolo and vibrato see pp. 14 and 15.

Vocalise. Refers to the exercising of the voice and to compositions written especially for that purpose. Certain modern composers, Rachmaninov for example, have used it to describe a song without words.

Voce bianca or *voix blanche*. When the voice is not properly supported by the breath and the throat is not fully opened, the tone develops a 'white' colour. As an expressive device, in Lieder singing for example, it has come to be considered a legitimate effect, but since it invariably affects the intonation, it should be used very sparingly.

Notes

The first number throughout refers to the Bibliography, which is numbered; the second to the page.

Introduction: The Record
1. 74: 193
2. 37: II, 82–8

Introduction: The Singing
1. Quoted 60: 53
2. Quoted 43: 25
3. Quoted ibid.: 28–9
4. Quoted 45: 14
5. Quoted ibid.: 37
6. 73: 61
7. Quoted 11: 399
8. Quoted 51: 20
9. 68: 13
10. 81: 16
11. 80: 232
12. 14: 174
13. 68: 18
14. 60: 451
15. 12: 174
16. Quoted 11: 373
17. 28: 119
18. Quoted 43: 28
19. 16: 71
20. 52: 22
21. 37: II, 13
22. 17: 64–5
23. 95: 187
24. 43: 40
25. 95: 176
26. Quoted 102: 99
27. 76: 816–17
28. 90: 395
29. Quoted 44: 169
30. 42: 167
31. 66: 21–2
32. Quoted 44: 258
33. 22: 237
34. 71: 2

PART I The Old School

1. Patti, Albani and Sembrich
1. 52: 37
2. 99: 202
3. 83: 104

4. 94: 49–50
5. 112: XIII, 79
6. 52: 106
7. 42: 251
8. 9: 183
9. 91: 219
10. 52: 135
11. Quoted 57: 83
12. Quoted 112: XVIII, 102

13. Quoted ibid.: VIII, 90
14. 35: 210
15. 18: 193–4

2. Melba and the Marchesi Pupils
1. 32: 51–2
2. 122: COLH 125
3. 44: 420–1
4. Quoted 84: 445
5. 44: 420
6. 84: 227
7. 32: 51
8. ibid.: 54
9. Quoted 84: 239
10. 4: 131–2
11. Quoted 112: VIII, 86
12. 104: 121
13. 118
14. Quoted 119: ML 5836
15. Quoted 89: 97
16. Quoted 84: 285
17. 94: 81
18. 95: 187
19. 93: 133
20. 4: 264–5
21. 93: 136
22. ibid.: 135
23. 115
24. 4: 265

3. Dramatic Sopranos
1. Quoted 84: 330
2. 52: 116
3. 86: 232
4. 35: 232
5. 4: 170
6. Quoted 84: 296
7. Quoted 57: 185
8. 4: 177
9. ibid.: 200
10. Quoted 112: VII, 58
11. 4: 82
12. ibid.: 542
13. Quoted 57: 305
14. 4: 160
15. 44: 248
16. 106: 22.6.97
17. Quoted 84: 254
18. Quoted 89: 68
19. Quoted 112: XVII, 175
20. Quoted ibid.: AVII, 176

4. Three Contraltos
1. Quoted 57: 145
2. 4: 116
3. ibid.: 269
4. Quoted 84: 311
5. 88: 284
6. 104: 77–8
7. Quoted 112: XIX, 107
8. 4: 283
9. 79: 50–1

5. Tenors
1. 65: 37
2. 53: 131
3. 42: 269
4. 53: 305
5. 56: 467–8
6. 42: 269

7. 90: 255
8. 4: 145

6. Baritones and Basses
1. 53: 102
2. 42: 269
3. 90: 61
4. 56: 466
5. 96: 64
6. 104: 91
7. 56: 204
8. 4: 583
9. 56: 468
10. 104: 76–7
11. 56: 468
12. 104: 81–2
13. ibid.: 82
14. 56: 338
15. 4: 291
16. Quoted 84: 308
17. Quoted 57: 218
18. Quoted ibid.: 370
19. 4: 322–3

PART II The French Tradition

7. 'Le Beau Idéal'
1. 105: 31.1.1874
2. ibid.
3. ibid.: 25.7.1874
4. 56: 224
5. Quoted 64: 97
6. ibid.: 108
7. 110: 28.11.1895
8. Quoted 64: 48
9. Quoted ibid.: 97
10. Quoted ibid.: 277
11. Quoted 84: 343
12. 4: 318
13. 31: 19
14. 4: 388
15. ibid.: 430
16. Quoted 57: 246
17. 4: 160–1

8. Lyric Tenors
1. 103: 8–9
2. Quoted 84: 193
3. 4: 315
4. Quoted 112: XIX, 91
5. 38: 126

9. High Cs and Heroic Voices
1. Quoted 112: III, 84
2. 4: 12

10. The Successors of Faure
1. Quoted 84: 199
2. 53: 111
3. Quoted 84: 199
4. 90: 36–7
5. Quoted 89: 52
6. 56: 243–4
7. 17: 103
8. Quoted 57: 115
9. Quoted ibid.: 117
10. Quoted ibid.: 122
11. 4: 201
12. ibid.
13. ibid.
14. ibid.

15. 17: 103
16. 94: 67
17. Quoted 84: 284
18. 56: 449
19. Quoted 57: 182
20. ibid.: 190
21. Quoted 57: 190
22. 23: 125
23. 4: 312

11. Principal Baritones
1. Quoted 57: 134
2. ibid.: 317
3. 106: 14.7.1897
4. 4: 46
5. Quoted 84: 317
6. Quoted 57: 193

12. Plançon, Edouard de Reszké and the Basses
1. Quoted 112: VIII, 151
2. Quoted 89: 60
3. 44: 114
4. Quoted 64: 135
5. Quoted ibid.: 36
6. Quoted ibid.: 137
7. 9: 266
8. Quoted 64: 179
9. ibid.: 235
10. 27: 209
11. Quoted 84: 199–200
12. ibid.: 332

13. Dramatic Sopranos
1. 49: 82
2. 70: 230–1
3. 17: 59–60
4. 44: 219
5. 4: 111
6. 31: 32
7. Quoted 57: 127
8. 106: 12.5.1899
9. ibid.: 23.1.1907
10. Quoted 57: 166
11. 4: 82
12. 106: 21.1.1907
13. 104: 247
14. 117
15. 4: 218–19
16. ibid.: 329–30
17. ibid.: 330
18. 26: 86
19. ibid.: 89
20. ibid.: 93
21. ibid.: 107
22. 38: 145
23. 26: 83

14. Lyric Sopranos
1. Quoted 123: GV 18
2. 4: 152–3

15. Three Contraltos
1. 116
2. Quoted 84: 244
3. 56: 400
4. Quoted 57: 214
5. Quoted 84: 311
6. 109: 14.11.1907
7. 4: 355

PART III The Emergence of Verismo

16. 'La Gloria d'Italia'
1. Quoted 112: VIII, 248
2. Quoted 113: V, 268
3. 122: COLH 116
4. 3: 65
5. 94: 224
6. 67
7. ibid.
8. Quoted 113: IV, 82
9. Quoted 84: 216
10. Quoted ibid.
11. 28: 324
12. Quoted 84: 255
13. 53: 147
14. Quoted 84: 262
15. Quoted 112: XIV, 114
16. 26: 63

17. Scotti, de Luca and Pini-Corsi
1. Quoted 84: 387
2. 56: 456
3. 44: 442
4. Quoted 57: 138
5. Quoted ibid.: 153
6. Quoted ibid.: 155
7. 44: 222
8. 4: 12
9. 67

18. Verismo triumphant
1. Quoted 67
2. Quoted 113: I, 422
3. 57: 169
4. Quoted 67
5. Quoted ibid.
6. Quoted 84: 306
7. Quoted ibid.
8. 4: 243
9. ibid.: 330
10. 120: Cantilena 6201
11. Quoted 112: VI, 126
12. 84: 299–300
13. 4: 371–2
14. ibid.: 374–5
15. Quoted 57: 240
16. Quoted ibid.
17. Quoted ibid.: 303
18. Quoted ibid.: 324
19. Quoted ibid.: 303

19. The Basso
1. Quoted 84: 226
2. 106: 24.11.1905
3. 105: 2.12.1905
4. Quoted 84: 386

20. Tradition and the Italian Tenor
1. Quoted 67
2. Quoted ibid.
3. 91:
4. 106: 22.6.1887
5. ibid.: 24.5.1892
6. 56: 378
7. 110: 30.12.1893
8. Quoted 57: 114

9. 106: 24.7.1900
10. ibid.
11. Quoted 84: 307
12. Quoted ibid.: 309
13. Quoted 57: 208
14. 44: 250
15. ibid.
16. 4: 348

21. Lyric Tenors
1. 4: 162
2. Quoted 4: 163
3. Quoted 112: IX, 151
4. Quoted ibid.
5. Quoted 84: 294
6. Quoted ibid.: 306
7. Quoted ibid.: 342
8. 112: VII, 211
9. 105: 12.10.1905
10. Quoted 84: 333
11. Quoted ibid.: 332

22. Dramatic Tenors
1. 44: 207
2. 2: 108–9
3. Quoted 67
4. Quoted 84: 233
5. 90: 161
6. 44: 207
7. 9: 69
8. 40: 84
9. Quoted 67
10. 19: 88
11. 44: 174
12. Quoted 121: 80
13. Quoted ibid.
14. Quoted 107: 9.1953
15. Quoted 112: XIV, 104–5
16. Quoted ibid.

23. Caruso
1. 44: 40
2. 44: 305

24. Sopranos 'B.C.'
1. 105: 12.6.1886
2. ibid.: 26.6.1886
3. ibid.
4. ibid.: 25.6.1887
5. 106: 14.7.1897

25. Sopranos after Cavalleria
1. Quoted 112: XVI, 199–200
2. Quoted ibid.
3. Quoted ibid.: XVI, 217–8
4. Quoted ibid.: XVI, 214
5. Quoted ibid.: XVI, 201
6. Quoted ibid.: XVI, 201–2
7. 9: 167
8. 106: 21.6.1895
9. Quoted 113: IV, 279
10. 112: XI, 174
11. Quoted 57: 182
12. 106: 19.6.1908
13. 39: 121
14. Quoted 57: 296
15. Quoted 112: XVIII, 79
16. Quoted ibid.: VII, 209

26. Four Dramatic Sopranos
1. 84: 304
2. Quoted 112: XII, 9
3. Quoted ibid.: XII, 10

27. Tetrazzini and some 'Coloraturas'
1. Quoted 23: 145
2. 44: 238
3. Quoted 96: 76
4. 4: 613
5. Quoted 96: 77
6. 106: 3.6.1909
7. 48: 70

28. Italian Contraltos
1. 55: 255
2. 105: 31.10.1891
3. 106: 14.5.1896
4. ibid.: 17.5.1896
5. ibid.: 14.6.1896
6. Quoted 67
7. Quoted 84: 326
8. Quoted 57: 202

PART IV Wagner and the German Style

29. The Instrumental Example
1. Quoted 112: VI, 79
2. 106: 30.5.1903
3. ibid.: 15.1.1907
4. 57: 279
5. 4: 479
6. Quoted 57: 248
7. 4: 446
8. ibid.: 647
9. 106: 18.6.1904
10. ibid.: 15.7.1904
11. ibid.: 18.6.1907

30. Lilli Lehmann
1. 44: 39
2. 84: 210
3. 52: 222
4. 8: 171

31. Sopranos of the Bayreuth School
1. 106: 14.6.1897
2. ibid.: 22.6.1892
3. 57: 171
4. 106: 6.5.1907
5. ibid.: 9.6.1904
6. ibid.: 6.6.1906
7. ibid.: 8.5.1905
8. ibid.: 21.5.1907
9. ibid.: 27.5.1907

32. Gadski and Destinn
1. 56: 450
1a 52: 179
2. 4: 77
3. ibid.
4. ibid.
5. Quoted 57: 269
6. Quoted 84: 303
7. 4: 235
8. Quoted 112: XXI, 236

9. 3: 115
10. ibid.: 129
11. Quoted 84: 310
12. 4: 502
13. Quoted 57: 233

33. Contraltos
1. Quoted 52: 197
2. ibid.: 194–5
3. Quoted 89: 11
4. 35: 213
5. 52: 178
6. Quoted 89: 551
7. 4: 58
8. ibid.: 104
9. ibid.: 220–1
10. 33: 59
11. Quoted 84: 334
12. Quoted 89: 144
13. Quoted 84: 346
14. Quoted 57: 229
15. Quoted 112: XXIII, 11
16. Quoted 57: 229
17. Quoted 89: 307
18. 4: 579

34. Heldentenors
1. 57: 203
2. 44: 179
3. ibid.: 180
4. Quoted 89: 134
5. Quoted 84: 296
6. Quoted 57: 154
7. Quoted 89: 145
8. Quoted ibid.: 185
9. Quoted 57: 170
10. Quoted ibid.
11. Quoted ibid.: 176
12. 4: 178
13. Quoted 112: XVIII, 153
14. 84: 305
15. Quoted 57: 239
16. Quoted 89: 211
17. Quoted 57: 215
18. Quoted ibid.
19. Quoted 89: 212
20. 4: 354

35. Baritones and Basses
1. Quoted 84: 209
2. 4: 50

PART V Singers of Imperial Russia

36. Sopranos and Contraltos
No notes

37. Tenors, Baritones and Basses
1. 114: 12.1908
2. Quoted 123: GV 1

38. Chaliapin
1. 123: GV 10
2. 122: COLH 141
3. 99: 202
4. Quoted 39: 118
5. 111: 15.3.1901
6. Quoted 89: 183–4
7. Quoted 23: 163

Bibliography

The following is a (very) Select Bibliography, including only those works which I consulted most often.

1. AGATE, James. *Ego 6*, London, 1944.
2. ALBANI, Emma. *Forty Years of Song*, London, 1911.
3. ALDA, Frances. *Men, Women and Tenors*, Boston, 1937.
4. ALDRICH, Richard. *Concert Life in New York*, New York, 1941.
5. ARDITI, Luigi (ed. Baroness von Zedlitz). *My Reminiscences*, London, 1869.
6. ARRAL, Blanche (ed. Ira Glackens). *Bravura Passage*, unpublished.
7. BAUER, Roberto. *New Catalogue of Historical Records 1898–1908/9*, London, 1947.
8. BEDDINGTON, Mrs Claude. *All That I Have Met*, London, 1929.
9. BISPHAM, David. *A Quaker Singer's Recollections*, New York, 1921.
10. BLOOMFIELD, Arthur J. *San Francisco Opera, 1923–61*, New York, 1961.
11. BUKOFZER, Manfred. *Music in the Baroque Era*, London, 1948.
12. BURNEY, Charles. *Musical Tours in Europe*, London, 1773.
13. BURNEY, Charles. *The Present State of Music in France and Italy*, London, 1773.
14. BURNEY, Charles. *The Present State of Music in Germany*, London, 1773.
15. CAAMANO, Roberto. *La Historia del Teatro Colon, 1908–1968* (3 vols), Buenos Aires, 1969.
16. CACCINI, Giulio. *Le Nuove Musiche*, Florence, 1602.
17. CALVE, Emma. *My Life*, New York, 1922.
18. CAPELL, Richard. *Schubert's Songs*, London, 1957.
19. CELLETTI, Rodolfo. *Le Grandi Voci*, Rome, 1964.
20. CHALIAPIN, Feodor (ed. and trans. Nina Froud and James Hanley). *An Autobiography as Told to Maxim Gorky*, London, 1968.
21. CHALIAPIN, Feodor. *Man and Mask*, New York, 1932.
22. CHORLEY, Henry F. *Thirty Years' Musical Recollections*, London, 1862.
23. CONE, John Frederick. *Oscar Hammerstein's Manhattan Opera Company*, Norman, Oklahoma, 1966.
24. CUSHING, Mary Watkins. *The Rainbow Bridge*, New York, 1954.
25. DAVIS, Ronald L. *A History of Opera in the American West*, Englewood Cliffs, N.J., 1965.
26. DAVIS, Ronald L. *Opera in Chicago*, New York, 1966.
27. DE HEGERMANN-LINDENCRONE, L. *In the Courts of Memory*, New York, 1912.
28. DE HEGERMANN-LINDENCRONE, L. *The Sunny Side of Diplomatic Life*, New York, 1914.
29. DONINGTON, Robert. *A Performer's Guide to Baroque Music*, London, 1973.
30. DONINGTON, Robert. *The Interpretation of Early Music*, London, 1963.
31. DOWNES, Olin (ed. I. Downes). *Olin Downes on Music*, New York, 1957.
32. EAMES, Emma. *Some Memories and Reflections*, New York, 1927.
33. EATON, Quaintance. *The Boston Opera Company*, New York, 1965.
34. FARRAR, Geraldine. *Such Sweet Compulsion*, New York, 1938.
35. FINCK, Henry T. *My Adventures in the Golden Age of Music*, New York, 1926.
36. GAISBERG, F. W. *The Music Goes Round*, New York, 1942.
37. GARCIA, Manuel. *L'Art du Chant*, Paris, 1847.
38. GARDEN, Mary & Biancolli, Louis. *Mary Garden's Story*, New York, 1951.
39. GATTI-CASAZZA, Giulio. *Memories of the Opera*, New York, 1941.
40. GELATT, Roland, *The Fabulous Phonograph*, London, 1956.
41. GLACKENS, Ira. *Yankee Diva: Lillian Nordica and the Golden Days of Opera*, New York, 1963.
42. HANSLICK, Eduard (ed. and trans. H. Pleasants). *Music Criticisms 1846–99*, London, 1951.
43. HENDERSON, W. J. *Early History of Singing*, New York, 1921.
44. HENDERSON, W. J. *The Art of Singing*, New York, 1938.
45. HERIOT, Angus. *The Castrati in Opera*, London, 1956.
46. HETHERINGTON, John. *Melba*, London, 1967.
47. HOMER, Anne. *Louise Homer and the Golden Age of Opera*, New York, 1974.
48. HURST, P. G. *The Golden Age Recorded*, London, 1963.
49. KELLOGG, Clara Louise. *Memoirs of an American Prima Donna*, New York, 1913.
50. KEY, Pierre. *Enrico Caruso, A Biography*, Boston, 1922.
51. KLEIN, Herman. *An Essay on the Bel Canto*, London, 1923.
52. KLEIN, Herman. *Great Women Singers of My Time*, London, 1931.
53. KLEIN, Herman. *Musicians and Mummers*, London, 1925.
54. KLEIN, Herman. *The Golden Age of Opera*, London, 1933.

55. KLEIN, Herman. *The Reign of Patti*, London, 1920.

56. KLEIN, Herman. *Thirty Years of Musical Life in London: 1870–1900*, London, 1903.

57. KOLODIN, Irving. *The Story of the Metropolitan Opera*, New York, 1966.

58. KUTSCH, K. J. & RIEMENS, Leo (trans. Harry Earl Jones). A *Concise Biographical Dictionary of Singers*, Philadelphia, 1969.

59   KUTSCH, K. J. & RIEMENS, Leo. *Unvergängliche Stimmen: Kleines Sängerlexikon*, Berne, 1975.

60. LANG, Paul H. *Music in Western Civilisation*, London, 1942.

61   LAWTON, Mary. *Schumann-Heink, The Last of the Titans*, New York, 1928.

62. LEHMANN, Lilli. *How to Sing*, New York, 1942.

63. LEHMANN, Lilli. *My Path Through Life*, New York, 1914.

64. LEISER, Clara. *Jean de Reszke*, London, 1933.

65. LEVIEN, John Mewburn. *The Singing of John Braham*, London, 1944.

66. LEVIEN, John Mewburn. *The Garcia Family*, London, 1931/2.

67. LIFF, Vivian. *Singers at La Scala*, unpublished.

68. MANCINI, Giambattista. *Pensieri, e riflessioni pratiche sopra il canto figurato*, Vienna, 1774.

69. MAPLESON, J. H. (ed. H. Rosenthal). *Memoirs*, London, 1966.

70. MARCHESI, Mathilde. *Marchesi and Music*, New York, 1898.

71. MARCHESI, Salvatore. *A Vademecum for Singing-Teachers and Pupils*, New York, 1902.

72. MELBA, Nellie. *Melodies and Memories*, New York, 1926.

73. MICHOTTE, E. *La Visite de R. Wagner a Rossini*, Paris, 1906.

74. MOSES, M. J. *Life of Heinrich Conried*, New York, 1916.

75. MOUNT-EDGCUMBE, Richard. *Musical Reminiscences of an old Amateur*, London, 1823.

76. MOZART, W. A. (ed. and trans. E. Anderson) *Letters* (3 vols), London, 1938.

77. NEWTON, Ivor. *At the Piano*, London, 1966.

78. PLEASANTS, Henry. *The Great Singers*, New York, 1966.

79. PONDER, Winifred. *Clara Butt: Her Life Story*, London, 1928.

80. QUANTZ, Joachim. *Autobiography (1754)*, in Marpurg, *Historischkritische Beytrage*, I, Berlin, 1755.

81. READ, O. & Welch, W. L. *From Tin Foil to Stereo*, New York, 1959.

82. RAMEAU, Jean-Philippe. *Code de Musique Pratique*, Paris, 1760.

83. RONALD, Landon. *Variations on a Personal Theme*, London, 1922.

84. ROSENTHAL, Harold. *Two Centuries of Opera at Covent Garden*, London, 1958.

85. RUFFO, Titta. *La Mia Parabola*, Milan, 1937.

86. RUSSELL, Henry. *The Passing Show*, London, 1926.

87. SAINT-SAENS, Camille (trans. E. G. Rich). *Musical Memories*, London, 1921.

88. SANTLEY, Charles. *Reminiscences of My Life*, London, 1909.

89. SELTSAM, William H. *Metropolitan Opera Annals*, New York, 1947.

90. SHAW, G. B. *London Music in 1888–89*, London, 1937.

91. SHAW, G. B. *Music in London 1890–94* (3 vols), London, 1932.

92. SLEZAK, Leo. *Song of Motley*, London, 1930.

93. SORABJI, Khaikhosru. *Around Music*, London, 1932.

94   SPALDING, Albert. *Rise to Follow*, London, 1946.

95. SPOHR, Louis (ed. and trans. H. Pleasants). *Musical Journeys*, Norman, Oklahoma, 1961.

96. STRONG, L. A. G. *John McCormack*, London, 1949.

97. TETRAZZINI, Luisa. *My Life of Song*, London, 1921.

98. TOSI, Pier Francesco (trans. J. E. Galliard). *Observations on the Florid Song*, London, 1742.

99. VERDI, Giuseppe (ed. and trans. C. Osborne). *Letters*, London, 1971.

100. WALTER, Bruno. *Theme and Variations*, New York, 1946.

101. WEINSTOCK, Herbert. *Rossini*, New York, 1968.

102. WEINSTOCK, Herbert. *Vincenzo Bellini*, London, 1972.

103. WHARTON, Edith. *The Age of Innocence*, London, 1966.

104. WOOD, Henry, J. *My Life of Music*, London, 1938.

NEWSPAPERS AND PERIODICALS

105. *The Illustrated London News*
106. *The London Times*
107. *Musica e dischi*
108. *Music and Musicians*
109. *The New York Sun*
110. *The New York Times*
111. *Novye Vremya*
112. *The Record Collector*
113. *Record News*
114. *Le Théâtre*

MISCELLANEOUS

115. Author's conversations with John Freestone
116. Metropolitan opera intermission interview with Mary Garden conducted by John Guttman
117. Author's conversations with Max de Schauensee
118. *National Encyclopaedia of American Biography*
119. Sleeve notes to American Columbia record
120. Sleeve notes to Rococo record
121. Sleeve notes to Club 99 record
122. Sleeve notes to E.M.I. record
123. Sleeve notes to Rubini record

Index

Numbers in bold refer to extended discussion of a singer in the text.